D1391637

The
Antique
Collectors'
illustrated dictionary

The Antique Collectors'
illustrated dictionary

Compiled by David Mountfield

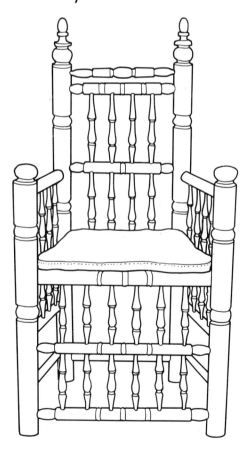

Hamlyn
London · New York · Sydney · Toronto

INTRODUCTION

This book is a dictionary of terms connected with antiques. It aims to provide speedy enlightenment for the ordinary citizen temporarily flummoxed by an unfamiliar or but vaguely comprehended word, whether it is the name of an object (*Épergne, Tyg, What-not*), the description of a style or pattern (*Acanthus, Knorpelwerk, Rococo*), or a relatively technical term (*cire perdue, smalt, tin glaze*). Although it would be silly to pretend that this is a comprehensive compilation of all known terms (such a work belongs, perhaps permanently, to the realm of theory), it is intended to include all, or nearly all, the words that the average collector, as distinct from the connoisseur, in the British Isles or North America, is likely to encounter. Some terms have been omitted for lack of space; no doubt others that ought to be here have been overlooked.

The purpose of *The Antique Collectors' Illustrated Dictionary* is to identify, not to instruct. In that respect it differs from the many books now available with names like *The Shorter Dictionary of English Furniture* or *The Collector's Dictionary of Clocks*, which consist of short essays on a limited number of subjects arranged alphabetically. Splendid works though many of them are, especially those published by Country Life, they ought to be called 'encyclopaedias' rather than 'dictionaries'.

However, it is frequently difficult and often impossible to define terms used in antique-collecting with scholarly precision within the compass of one or two sentences (it is sometimes impossible within any compass), and it has therefore proved necessary in *The Antique Collectors' Illustrated Dictionary* to adopt occasionally a rudely practical approach to certain problems of definition. Thus, the most common usage of a term is recorded whether historically accurate or not, minor exceptions have to be ignored, and there is in general emphasis on what seems typical rather than what is especially distinguished. In short, the definitions given here are not necessarily exclusive and readers are earnestly advised to treat this book as a handy source for quick reference — while hunting in antique shops, during conversations with the Joneses, or while reading other books — not as a dogmatic appraisal of the decorative arts.

Terms are defined as far as possible in simple language; where technical or obscure words occur in definitions, the relevant alphabetical entry may be consulted.

What are Antiques?

An explanation will be found under the alphabetical entry but something more needs to be said here as the meaning of the term used in the title of the book naturally governs what is, and what is not, included within its covers. 'Antiques' is a term that has changed its meaning several times and, ideally, needs to be replaced by two or three new terms.

Unless they happen to be customs officials, people nowadays when they talk about 'antiques' do not usually mean objects more than a hundred years old, or made before 1850, they mean objects that are interesting or valuable enough to be worth collecting and are no longer made — at least in their traditional form. That is, broadly, the definition adopted in this book save that with a few exceptions objects made since about 1900 are excluded and objects made in the 19th century have been subjected to a selective process not operative in earlier periods. Thus, mass-produced articles have been included only when by reason of rarity, desirability, or some other characteristic, they are felt to be of special interest. Collectors of Civil-War barbed wire, early film posters, Nazi insignia and other exotica will not find their fields of interest well covered.

A more flexible rule has been adopted in certain areas (e.g. oriental carpets, precious stones) where any cut-off date seems too arbitrary.

There are many terms that, while important in antiques, do not necessarily describe old or collectable articles, particularly general terms like *carpet, chair, vase*, etc. A few terms of this kind have been excluded on the grounds that everyone knows what they mean, but in the majority of cases, where there is some germane and perhaps generally unconsidered point to make, they are here. The same is true of less common terms whose meaning is superficially obvious, such as *games table, knife case, snuff grater*.

Some words have two or more meanings, often quite unconnected. In general, only meanings applicable to antiques are listed; where space is precious it seems pointless to mention that a dumb waiter may also be a tongueless manservant or a coaster a type of cargoship. A few exceptions occur in the case of certain technical terms that have several allied meanings, any one of which would not alone have been grounds for its inclusion.

Cross References

In a book of this kind cross references tend to get out of hand. An effort has been made to keep them to a reasonable minimum, even to the extent of defining similar terms under their separate headings where a cross reference would not save significant space.

A 'see' cross reference means that the required information will be found under the entry cited; a 'see also' reference implies further information either for amplification or comparison. Cross references are generally omitted when the term to which attention should be directed already occurs in the body of the entry. They are also omitted in the case of an alternate spelling adjacent to the preferred spelling.

Dating

This presents awkward problems. The date of certain types of articles or techniques can be precisely determined, sometimes to a year or even a month. Far more often dates are vague, and it is difficult to be certain of even the century of the origin of a certain style in glass or a particular item of furniture.

However, the date of an article is obviously important, possibly the most important thing about it, and some kind of system for dating is clearly necessary. In general, dating in this book approaches no closer than a period of several decades, sometimes a century or more (e.g. *late 17th century, Neo-Classical period, Victorian,* etc.), except when exact dates are known. Even this is often too close for comfort.

Where such dating is assigned to a particular article, style or technique, it signifies the period during which the subject first came into common use. It does not necessarily imply that no examples are known earlier than stated, still less that they disappear after that period. It should be remembered that the Victorians in particular were highly eclectic in their taste: practically every major European style was revived in the 19th century (Victorian reproductions are now antiques themselves and, though of course less desirable than the originals, may well be of more practical interest to the average collector).

Geographical Distribution
This book is primarily intended for the collector in the British Isles and North America, and concentrates chiefly on English terms and terms in other languages that are regularly used, or have no substitutes, in English. When a subject is specifically defined as French, or Italian, or Swedish, the assignation refers to its original and most notable, but not necessarily exclusive, location.

The term 'German' is used in the cultural rather than the political sense, implying all parts of Europe where German is traditionally spoken.

Proper Names
The names of individual people are only included when they are in general use as descriptive terms, e.g. *Beilby* (glass), *Chippendale* (furniture), *Wedgwood* (china). This is a category where it is impossible to draw a clear line; the examples given here are fairly obvious, but there are a great many borderline cases for which subjective judgment is the only guide.

Similarly with places: to name every European town that ever turned out a china pot would clearly be absurd; to exclude names like *Meissen, Sèvres, Worcester* would be equally absurd. An attempt has been made to include all the chief centres of tin-glazed earthenware and porcelain as well as the major glassworks in Europe and North America.

Fine Art
Painting and sculpture are excluded from this dictionary; prints, china figures and certain carvings are included. It is not always easy to draw a line between fine art and what is called 'decorative' art, if indeed there is a line: Della Robbia figures, for instance seem to inhabit both worlds and many techniques, such as woodcarving or weaving bridge the gap.

Aback table, a square table; in particular, one that is not self-supporting but is fixed to a wall by hinges or brackets.

Abacus, an ancient instrument, originally Chinese, for making calculations, in which pierced balls slide on horizontal wires within a wooden frame; also, the flat member between architrave and column in Classical architecture; see **Corinthian**.

Abadeh carpets, Persian carpets from the town in southern Iran, Sehna knot, floral patterns, mainly red, blue and brown.

Abbotsford style, early Victorian furniture in the Tudor or Jacobean style, influenced or perhaps only exemplified by Sir Walter Scott's famous house at Abbotsford.

ABC pottery, also glass, pewter, etc.; dishes, mugs or other items for children, decorated with the letters of the alphabet.

Abrash, slight changes in colour sometimes seen in oriental carpets, evidence that the traditional vegetable dyes were used, not modern chemicals.

Abtsbessingen faience, vases and other ware produced at the German factory in that town in the 18th century.

Acacia, or robinia, a hard, durable wood, yellowish with darker veining, native to America but grown in Europe; used in 18th-century English furniture for bandings, inlays, etc.; seldom used for construction.

Acanthus, a common form of decoration based on the thistle-like acanthus, or bear's breech, leaf; to be seen on Corinthian capitals and 18th-century furniture; see **Corinthian**.

Accordion table, a drop-leaf table in which the supporting leg(s) slide in and out, like a drawer, rather than swinging.

Acid-engraving, the method of etching patterns on glass with hydrofluoric acid after scratching the design through a special varnish; cheap and simple, the method was popular from the late 19th century; can nowadays be done using a photo-sensitive resist and a negative of the design.

Acid-gilding, a process invented in the 19th century for creating low-relief gold patterns in china by etching with hydrofluoric acid and gilding.

Ackermann print, a colour print by Rudolph Ackermann of London, who published, among others, satirical prints after Rowlandson during the first quarter of the 19th century.

Acorn clock, a New England mantel clock roughly resembling an acorn in shape, early 19th century, uncommon. 2

Acorn knop, on the stem of a wine glass, an acorn-shaped knop with the 'cup' of the acorn upward.

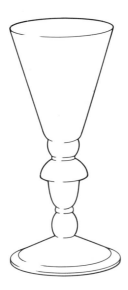

Acorn-turned, a finial or other ornamental pinnacle finished in a form that resembles an acorn or an egg in an egg cup. 2, 64

Acoustic jar, an earthenware jar placed in the wall of medieval buildings, though possibly not for the implied purpose.

Acroter, a small pedestal at the corner and apex of a pediment (e.g. of a cabinet) on which a carved figure or ornament was placed; sometimes describes the figures themselves.

Act of Parliament clock, supposedly one made after the British Act of 1797 (which imposed a tax on timepieces) and mounted in a convenient public place; in practice, any large-dialled mural clock of the 18th or 19th century.

Adam and Eve motif, found on 17th-century dishes of relatively cheap glazed earthenware; that well-known couple were decoratively employed in many media, including glass, fabrics, etc.

Adam furniture, made by or in the style of the Adam family, particularly Robert Adam (1728–92), a cool Neo-Classical style that affected British design in everything from architecture to ceramics. 4, 104

Adams pottery, the product of a numerous dynasty of English potters, who owned various factories in the 18th and 19th centuries; in particular the Greengales pottery and (a different branch) the factory at Hanley, which produced busts of celebrities in parian ware in the late 19th century; see also **Hanley Ware**.

Adder's eggs: see **Druids's eggs**.

Adelaide couch, an open-ended, armless couch with reclining end, suitable for novel-reading Victorian ladies; chiefly French or English, second quarter of the 19th century.

Admiral jug, a Toby jug in the form of an admiral, seated, originally made to commemorate the naval victory of Lord Howe on June 1, 1794.

Adzed wood, a decorative pattern of alternate hollows and ridges on medieval furniture, made with a smoothing tool called an adze, predecessor of the plane.

Aedicule, a Classical frame of pediment and columns or pilasters around doors, windows or niches.

Aeolian harp, a musical device of ancient and obscure origin, consisting of a long, thin wooden soundbox with up to a dozen gut strings which when placed in a draught is 'played' by the breeze vibrating the strings.

Aerograph decoration, colour applied to earthenware by a mechanical method, since the late 19th century.

Aes, a bronze and copper coinage, such as **aes signatum**, an early Roman coin which was large and square with stamped designs.

Affenkapelle, or 'monkey orchestra', porcelain figures of monkeys as musicians, first made at Meissen in the mid 18th century and often copied since.

Afghan carpets, known best by their pattern, a regular arrangement of polygonal shapes; colours tend to be subdued with warm reds, blue and natural prominent; Sehna knot; quality deteriorated after 1900.

African mahogany, a hard wood from West Africa, distinctly red (from pale pink to dark reddish-brown), widely used in cabinetmaking since the 19th century.

African walnut, darkish brown wood from West Africa, used in cabinetmaking since the 19th century.

Afshar rugs, from the Shiraz-Kerman area; bright colours and stylized floral motifs on a basic diamond pattern; Ghiordes knot mainly.

After-cast, a reproduction of a bronze object, cast from a mould of the original.

Agata, a glass in which the characteristic mottled finish was achieved by sprinkling alcohol on the colour, made by the New England Glass Co., late 19th century.

Agate ware, 18th-century pottery with a veined or marbled appearance resembling agate; the veining may be on the surface only but usually extends through the body of the ware; it was achieved by several different processes; also **agate glass**, similarly named for its resemblance to agate.

Agitable lamp, a late 18th-century lamp with removable burner, simple and cheap, sometimes made without a stand to place in a candlestick.

Agra carpets, from the town in India; usually very large, with relatively naturalistic patterns in green, blue and shades of brown.

Agraffe, an ornamental hook-and-loop fastening, frequently gold, as worn to hold together a cleft neckline in medieval women's dress; also a hat badge.

Aigrette, a cluster of diamonds and other precious stones in a flower-like spray, worn in the hair; fashionable in the 18th century.

Air twist, a form of decoration found typically in the stem of English wine glasses from the mid 18th century, in which an air bubble in the glass is given the form of a spiral by drawing out and twisting. **1, 21**

Akce, a Turkish silver coin, first issued in the late 14th century and current for some 300 years.

Alabaster, a white plaster widely used for modelling; also much used for carving, e.g. medieval tombs, which made full use of its almost translucent whiteness; other colours (yellow, red) also found; see also **Gypsum.**

Alabaster ware, porcelain or glass resembling alabaster in appearance.

Alabastron, an Egyptian glass vessel, roughly cylindrical in shape, with two small handles; made by winding molten glass around a clay core.

Alaska diamonds, a popular name for haematite.

Albany couch, a high-ended day bed or reading seat, late 19th century.

Albany slip, made from a fine, dark brown clay found near Albany, New York, on the banks of the Hudson; widely used as a glaze or for the interior of stoneware vessels in the 19th century.

Albarello, strictly a jar of Middle Eastern origin but, more generally, any maiolica jar for drugs, herbs, etc., which curves in toward the centre. **93**

Albata, German silver.

Albertin, an early 17th-century gold coin issued in the Netherlands and bearing the portrait of the Habsburg governor, Archduke Albert, after whom it was named

Alcora ware, maiolica produced at the factory in Alcora, Spain, from the mid 18th century, similar in style to Moustiers (and sharing the same craftsmen).

Alcove, a large recess in a wall (indoors or out), Spanish in origin and meant for a seat; hence **alcove seat, alcove bed,** etc.

Alder, a boldly figured wood that wears to a brownish-pink, strong, and used in 18th-century English country furniture, especially for turnings.

Ale glass, an 18th-century English ► stemmed glass with deep bowl, sometimes engraved with hops and barley motif; strong beer accounted for small capacity (3–4 oz).

Alençon lace, fine needlepoint lace of Alençon, from the late 17th century, especially the intricate narrow lace used for borders on bonnets, for example.

Ale warmer, a copper vessel with ► handle for warming, or mulling, ale in the embers of a fire, some cone-shaped (called 'ass's ear'), others like a foot with a long, pointed toe for pushing horizontally into the coals.

Alexandrite, a rare precious stone found in the Urals and named after the Tsar, fashionable in imperial Russia because it changes from green to red (the imperial colours) between day and night.

Ale-yard: see **Yard-of-ale.**

Alidade, a scientific measuring instrument; on an astrolabe, a rotating arm with sights for calculating altitude.

Allen pepperbox, an early 19th-century American pistol with six revolving barrels, named after a prominent manufacturer, Ethan Allen of Massachusetts.

Allgood japanned ware: see **Usk ware.**

Alligator brooch, an alligator's tooth mounted in silver or gold to form a brooch; also buttons, earrings, etc.; in vogue in the late 19th century.

Allison furniture, made by the New York cabinetmaker Michael Allison in the first quarter of the 19th century and closely resembling the work of Duncan Phyfe.

All-over decoration, chiefly in printing, in which a decorative motif is repeated at regular intervals all over the surface.

Alloy, two or more metals combined, e.g. brass or pewter; also, a precious metal such as silver mixed with a base metal in order either to improve its appearance, wear, workability, etc. or to economize, as in many coins.

Almandine, a dark but lustrous semi-precious stone used in jewellery in the mid 19th century.

Almirah, a word originating in India and used to describe any cupboard or chest of drawers.

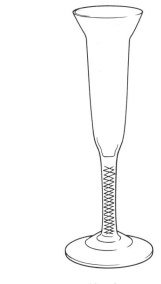
Ale glass

Ale warmer

Almorrata, or almorratxa, a Spanish glass vessel with a number of spouts, often hung from a chain rather than stood on its base, used for sprinkling holy water, from the 16th century. **5**

Alms dish, a broad-rimmed silver dish, not unlike an ordinary, round domestic dish, 16th to 18th centuries, for collecting alms in church; also in other metals or wood.

Altare glass, Renaissance Italian glassware from the city of that name near Genoa; virtually indistinguishable from Venetian glass even to the most expert eye.

Alto relievo: see **High relief.**

Altun, a Turkish gold coin issued in the 15th century.

Amaranth, a deep-violet-coloured wood, sometimes called purple wood, used in marquetry particularly in 18th-century France.

Amazonite, a semi-precious stone of the feldspar family, used in jewellery; brilliant green but opaque, hard, easily cut and polished; favoured in ancient Egypt.

Amber, a fossil resin, reddish-yellow, used chiefly in jewellery since the 18th century but previously in larger objects, such as vases; also, a bracelet made of amber.

Ambergris, a waxy substance obtained from the sperm whale, used in perfumes.

Amberina glass, named for its colour (though some is dark red) achieved by re-heating; produced by many New England glassmakers in the late 19th century.

Amboyna, a wood somewhat like walnut, a rich golden-brown colour, with an intricate pattern of graining; imported to England from the East Indies in the 18th century and used frequently as a veneer.

Ambrosino, a gold or, more commonly, silver coin issued in Milan in the 13th century, bearing an image of St Ambrosius.

Ambry: see **Aumbry.**

Ambulante, any small item of furniture that can be moved easily about the room; in particular, small tables of the Louis XV period.

Amelung glass, made at the Frederick, Maryland, factory of J. F. Amelung in the late 18th century, resembling Stiegel's products; rarity chiefly accounts for its high value (the factory operated for only 10 years).

Amen glass, an 18th-century English wine glass engraved with the word 'amen', in response to an unspoken (because treasonable) toast to the exiled Stewart dynasty; see also **Jacobite glass.**

Americana, objects of interest to collectors that were made in, or have some special connection with, the United States.

1 Three glasses with air-twist stems. English, about 1750–75. On the left an engraved wine glass with trumpet bowl; centre and right two cordial glasses, a dram and a flute glass, the latter for ratafia. (London Museum, London)

2 Acorn clock. American, 19th century. Made by the Forestville Manufacturing Co. of Connecticut. (British Museum, London)

3 Amphora: Attic pottery, 530–520 BC. An example of the black-figure technique. (British Museum, London)

2

3

5 Almorrata. Spanish glass, 18th century. (Hispanic Society of America, New York)

4 Armchair. English, designed about 1770 by Robert Adam for the library of Osterley Park, and made by John Linnell. The frame veneered with rosewood has inlaid decoration and lyre-shaped splat of satinwood; the details, including the Vitruvian scroll motif, are typical of the English Neo-Classical period. (Osterley Park, Middlesex)

American Flint, glassware from the Boston glassworks of that name, highly productive from the mid 19th century; not true flint glass.

American Lowestoft, a notably erroneous term for certain Chinese porcelain imported into North America in the 18th century; the name has stuck and such ware is still called 'Lowestoft'.

American oven, a tin box, cylindrical or oblong, in which food could be baked or roasted at an open fire; late 18th century.

American stove, any of a variety of early American stoves of decorated cast iron; the Franklin stove and the six-plate stove are the best known.

Amesbury pipe, a type of English clay tobacco pipe, made at Amesbury, Wiltshire.

Amethyst, a gem, the best-known of quartz stones, usually a deep and brilliant blue but may be almost burgundy; highly regarded since prehistoric times; its name, from the Greek, implies that it prevents drunkenness.

Amorino or **amoretto**: see **Putto**.

Amphora, a Greek earthenware two-handled vessel, similar to an urn, for holding wine or oil. **3**

Amstel porcelain, white, hard-paste porcelain, similar to Meissen, made on the Amstel near Amsterdam, late 18th century.

Amulet, any device worn on the person to ward off evil, common since prehistoric times and evident since the decline of magic in copper bracelets against rheumatism, etc.

Anamorphosis, a picture that appears distorted except when viewed in an abnormal way; popular curiosities from the 18th century.

Anatolian rugs, a general term for rugs from this region, particularly the so-called Anatolian prayer rugs in loosely woven wool, various patterns.

Anatto, an orange dye made from anatto seeds from Central America; formerly used in wood stains and polish (also in cheese and butter).

Andalusite, a rare gem, brown or green in colour, first found in Spain but more recently coming, in gem-quality, almost exclusively from Brazil.

Andirons, or firedogs, iron supports for burning wood on an open hearth; from the 17th century often decorative and made of silver and bronze as well as iron. **168**

Andradite, the most sought-after gem of the garnet species, occurring in several varieties of which only the black and the green are normally found in jewellery.

Aneling cup, a silver vessel used for anointing in religious ceremonies (also **aneling spoon**); often of particularly fine workmanship.

Ange d'or, a 14th-century gold coin first issued in France under Philip IV showing St Michael and a dragon; subsequently adopted in slightly different forms elsewhere.

Angel, an English 15th-century gold coin worth one third of a pound, minted from the 15th to the 17th century.

Angel bed, a small bed for a child or servant, often without head board, that could be tucked out of the way.

Angle-front cupboard, a standing corner cupboard built on the plan of a square rather than a triangle, the top section usually glazed; late 18th century.

Angled candlestick, a 19th-century device in which a hinge in the column enabled the person lighting the candle to incline it towards him.

Angle lamp, an oil-burning hanging lamp, late 19th century, in which a burner on an arm was set at an angle to the reservoir.

Angler's stool, an X-shaped folding wooden stool with leather or canvas seat.

Angoulême faience, late 18th century, best known for large and rather heavy-looking figures of animals.

Angster: see **Guttrolf**.

An-hua designs, 'secret' designs in some Ming porcelain, of moulded relief under the glaze; they can only be spotted by careful examination.

Animal brasses, horse brasses in the form of animals, horses themselves being most favoured but also dogs, 'sporting' animals (stags, foxes, etc.) as well as more exotic beasts.

Anna, a low-value copper coin ultimately worth one-sixteenth of an Indian rupee; first issued by the British East India Co. and showing its badge.

Annapolis coins, silver shillings, sixpences and threepences struck by I. Chalmers of Annapolis, Maryland, in 1783.

Anodizing, a modern finishing process in certain kinds of metalwork, in which a hard protective coating is applied by electrochemical means.

Ansbach ware, 18th-century faience, especially the large, brilliantly coloured ornamental pieces of the 1730s; also porcelain (late 18th and 19th centuries), including tableware for Frederick the Great.

Antefix, ornamental corners raised above the cornice in case furniture, canopied beds, etc.

Antependium, the decoration of the front of an altar, from early medieval times, generally of embroidered fabric but also wood, metal or other material.

Anthemion, stylized Classical design based on the honeysuckle flower; a favourite decorative motif of the Neo-Classical style; also used structurally as in Hepplewhite anthemion-backed chairs. **90**

Anthracite, a form of coal, very hard, which can be cut and polished for jewellery; carved as curios and souvenirs of the mining industry in the 19th century.

Antimacassar, a protective covering of linen or other fabric to defend upholstered head-rests from the effect of a popular 19th-century hair dressing, macassar oil.

Antimony, a white metal useful as a hardener in alloys; sometimes found in pewter.

Antique, a notoriously ill-defined word; originally applied to the Greek and Roman period; now generally applied to man-made, collectable objects over 100 years old; in practice used less rigidly.

Antiquing, a term that came into use in the second half of the 19th century to describe the process of making an object look older than it is; not originally pejorative, although the practice may lead to confusion, disappointment, and worse.

Antonianus, a Roman coin worth two denarii issued in the 3rd century AD bearing a portrait of the Emperor Caracalla, originally silver but later mainly copper.

Antwerp lace, pillow lace known particularly for its pattern, called 'pot lace' because of its motif of an urn or pot, very popular in the 18th century.

Apostle motif, the twelve apostles found their way on to the handles of silver spoons in the 16th century and have since appeared on other ware, especially Charles Meigh's mid 18th-century 'Apostle' jug, in moulded low relief. **6**

Apothecary jar: see **Drug jar**.

Appalachian dulcimer, an early American musical instrument resembling a zither rather than a dulcimer as it was plucked, not struck.

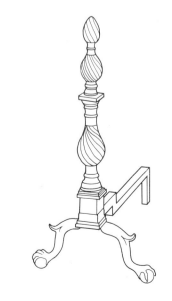

Andiron

Applewood, a hard, pinkish-toned wood, used in the 17th century and later, chiefly for veneers; used structurally in the 18th century in American and English country furniture.

Applied decoration, in furniture any ornamental element (e.g. carved rosettes, mouldings, etc.) made separately and attached to the article; **applied relief** is the term generally used for separately cast or modelled ornamentation in pottery; the French term appliqué is chiefly used for the corresponding technique in metalwork or needlework.

Apprentice piece, a small replica of a piece of furniture made either by an apprentice to display his aptitude or, possibly, as a craftsman's sample; see also **Masterpiece, Samples.**

Aprey faience, made at the French factory established there in the mid 18th century, especially notable for its decoration of birds and flowers.

Apron, in furniture, a downward extension below what would normally be the bottom edge (e.g. the seat of a chair or the frame of a cabinet); purely decorative or, as in a close chair, concealing something unattractive.

Apse, an architectural term for the rounded extension to the choir of a church, applied to similar extensions to the ends of an oblong ornamental box.

Aquamanile, a rare medieval water container, bronze or silver and usually in the form of a lion or other animal, used for pouring water on the hands of diners; more modern examples in various media. **9**

Aquamarine, a clear, pale-blue or green precious stone belonging to the beryl species; jewellers heightened the blue colour by heating; fairly common nowadays.

Aquatint, an 18th-century form of etching, at first monochrome but later colour; the process, used by Goya, employed finely powdered resin to gain graduations of tone and was highly successful when reproducing watercolours.

Aquilino, a northern Italian silver coin, stamped with an eagle, widely current in the 13th century.

Arabesque, a stylized decorative motif linked particularly with Islamic art suggesting floral patterns but ostensibly not based on a living form (owing to the dubious tradition that such representations were forbidden in Islam).

Arcade, a line of ornamental arches, typically in architecture, but found also in relief on furniture (e.g. chair backs) particularly in the Renaissance and Baroque periods; see **Cusp.**

Arcanist, in the 18th century a craftsman who possessed (or claimed to possess) knowledge of closely kept secrets of pottery and porcelain making.

Arcanum, a 'secret', applied to a particular technique in ceramics that had to be protected from possible imitators.

Arched stretcher, characteristic of late 17th-century chairs, in which the stretcher between the front legs is in the form of an arch, usually decoratively carved. **142**

Architect's desk, a table inclined downward toward the user, the angle of slope being adjustable.

Architectural furniture, a term that describes furniture based more or less obviously on architectural designs; also clocks (particularly those surmounted by a Classical pediment), mirrors, etc.; associated mainly with early 18th-century styles.

Architrave, a term borrowed from Classical architecture to describe an ornamental strip, in which the decorative motifs are Classical, surrounding a cupboard door, mirror, etc.; see **Doric.**

Ardebil carpets, from the town in northern Iran, stylized design with central medallion in the old Caucasian manner, red, blue and natural colours, densely woven, Ghiordes knot; not to be confused with the famous 16th-century carpet from the Ardebil mosque in the Victoria and Albert Museum, London.

Ardus faience, 18th-century faience from the French factory in Ardus, notable for decoration of fruit and flowers, plaques and portraits.

Argand lamp, an oil-burning lamp with a circular wick and glass chimney derived from the highly efficient original invented by Aimé Argand of Geneva in the late 18th century; the prototype of most household lamps in the first half of the 19th century.

Argentan lace, needlepoint made at Argentan or Alençon; a hexagonal ground and bold pattern worked in very small stitches distinguishes it from Alençon lace.

Argentella lace, similar to Alençon needlepoint, with an irregular, wide-spaced, dotted mesh.

Argenteus, a large Roman silver coin of the 4th century AD.

Argentine silver, or nickel silver, an alloy of nickel, copper and zinc more durable than the original nickel alloy used for silver-plating in the 19th century; see also **German silver.**

Argyll, or Argyle, a silver gravy warmer resembling a coffee pot with a central tube or surrounding jacket containing hot water; also in earthenware; the term is sometimes used to describe any vessel with an internal warming element; the credit for inventing the piece is given to one of the 18th-century Dukes of Argyll (cr. 1701). **115**

Arita porcelain, Japanese ware at first mainly painted blue and white, imported from the mid 17th century by the Dutch and much imitated in Europe.

Ark, a chest with sloping, roof-like lid and (often) gabled ends for storing grain or flour, made by an arkwright rather than a carpenter which suggests its north-of-England origin; chiefly 16th century.

Armada chest, an iron strongbox, usually of German or Dutch origin, 17th and 18th centuries, usually festooned with bolts, padlocks, keyholes real and false; the predecessor of the safe; no known connection with the Armada.

Armadio, a large Italian cupboard from the Middle Ages, like an armoire or wardrobe, sometimes with low-relief carving; the two-tier type became popular in the 16th century. **7**

Armenian Shirvan carpets, produced in Armenia under Soviet auspices since 1917, betraying a lack of traditional harmonies in design and colour.

Armet, in armour, a close-fitting helmet with hinged visor of the 15th century.

Armillary sphere, a medieval astronomical model consisting of a series of rings for demonstrating the position of the meridian, the equator, etc., with a small globe at the centre representing the earth, the whole often supported by an Atlas figure; see also **Globe. 8**

Arming chair, or armchair, so called from about 1700 to distinguish it from an armless chair which had until then been known as a backstool. **4**

Armitage Sheffield, silver-plated tableware made in Philadelphia about 1800 by the brothers Armitage, immigrants from Sheffield.

Armoire, a large, ornamental cupboard with shelves and hanging space, equivalent to a wardrobe or armadio. **7**

Armorial, decorated with the coat-of-arms of the owner, applied to relevant dinner services, book bindings, etc.; many idiosyncratic examples from China. **21**

Armour, a defensive covering, usually of iron or steel, worn through the ages to protect warriors against offensive weapons. **10**

Arm rail, a characteristic of certain Windsor chairs, sometimes known as New England armchairs, the rail that passes across the back, being pierced by the spindles, continues to form the arms.

Arm rest, the padded section on the arm of a chair; or a wooden stand, like a

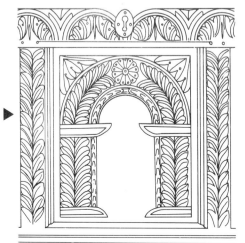

Arcade

6 Covered beaker. German
enamelled glass, 17th century.
The painted decoration shows the
popular Apostle motif.
(Kunstgewerbemuseum, Cologne)

7 Walnut armadio. Italian, 17th
century. The ornate carving in high
relief with figures, lion's masks,
swags of fruit, ribbons and tassels,
is typical of the high Baroque style.
(Castello di Montechiarugolo,
Parma)

8 Armillary sphere. Italian, 16th century. The main band shows the signs of the Zodiac; the bands of the skeleton have Latin inscriptions; the whole is supported by a bronze figure ot Atlas. (Lamberti Collection)

9 Cast bronze aquamanile with engraved decoration. Spanish, 12th century. A zoomorphic vessel of peacock form (crest and tail missing); the combined handle and spout represent the head of a bird of prey. (Pinacoteca, Caligari)

small single-tier cakestand, for resting a weary arm in church.

Arms, weapons used in battle, including spears, swords, firearms, etc.

Arquebus, a term applied to a variety of hand guns from the late 15th century; the early arquebus had a projection that could be hooked over a solid object to prevent recoil; also fired from a tripod.

Arras, originally tapestries from Arras in France, but used generally to describe hanging tapestries of the Gothic period, like that behind which Polonius unwisely hid from Hamlet.

Arras lace, French pillow lace like that of Lille, but less fine and with characteristic scalloped edge.

Arrow-back chair, a type of Windsor chair, in which the spindles are in the form of arrows; fairly common after about 1850.

Art Deco, the decorative style of the 1920s and 1930s inspired by abstract painting and streamlined Bauhaus design and often incorporating exotic motifs drawn from Aztec and Egyptian art; including mass-produced objects in plastic and chrome. **11**

Art Decoration, also **art furniture**, **art wallpaper**, etc., terms that came into use in the mid Victorian period to distinguish between articles made by craftsmen and standardized articles; not everyone would prefer the former, which was sometimes self-consciously 'artistic'.

Art glass, fancy glass of North America embodying new techniques and materials of the late 19th century, including Amberina, Peachblow, Pomona etc. as well as less successful varieties.

Arthur cans, the earliest American tin cans, made of tin-proofed wrought iron in two pieces, the lid being sealed on with wax; named after their inventor.

Artifact, an artificial product; a term generally used to describe very old man-made objects discovered on archaeological sites.

Artificial porcelain: see Soft-paste porcelain.

Artisan, a craftsman, in particular one who is a master of his craft and not, as the word is sometimes used, an unskilled workman.

Art Nouveau, the highly distinctive decorative style of the late 19th and early 20th centuries, characterized by a flowing, erotic line based on plant forms, and influenced by Japanese art. **84, 105, 210, 270**

Arts and Crafts Movement, a Victorian movement led by such figures as John Ruskin and William Morris who reacted against industrialism and standardization and were determined to raise the status of the individual artist and craftsman (between whom they drew no firm dividing line); many arts and crafts societies spawned. **152, 185**

Art Union, a 19th-century society for the encouragement of the arts, or a particular art; it made awards to artists and sometimes organized lotteries with works of art as prizes.

Aryballo, a small round-bottomed flask with strong handles at the neck through which a cord, hanging from the wrist, could be threaded; made in Classical times for oil, perfume, etc.

As, an early bronze Roman coin, showing the double-headed Janus and, on the reverse, the prow of a ship; the later, imperial version has the emperor's head.

Ash, a wood very popular with 18th-century furniture makers, being both hard and resilient; pale, almost white in colour, sometimes heavily veined, often used for seats of chairs; also in upholstered furniture; subject to woodworm.

Ashet, in Scotland, an oval, silver meat dish; also used of any large oval or oblong platter in wood, metal or china.

Assay, to test the quality of precious metal (e.g. the proportion of alloy in a gold or silver object) by chemical or other means.

Assay cup, a shallow, wide-brimmed glass used supposedly to test for poison up to the 17th century; later for less dramatic tasting; see also **Essay**.

Assay groove, a small S-shaped scratch found on concealed surfaces, usually next to the hallmark, of Scottish and European silver before the 18th century, caused by removal of a sample for assay.

Assay mark, a mark stamped on gold and silver objects that indicates the purity of the metal and incidentally also shows the place and approximate date of origin; see also **Hallmark**.

Association copy, a book the contents of which have some special association with a previous owner, especially a copy owned, presented, or annotated by its author.

Astbury ware, Staffordshire pottery of the early 18th century made by John Astbury, his son and others, notable for its red body; John Astbury was possibly also responsible for a whiter-than-white effect achieved by mixing ground flint with white clay.

Astley Cooper chair, named for its inventor (1768–1841), a child's chair with long, straight back and broad rails, with footrest, to encourage the erect posture then considered essential.

Astragal, a small convex moulding cut into the form of a string of beads found around the top and bottom of a column; see also **Beading**.

Astral lamp, a development of the Argand lamp with broad glass dome and ring-shaped reservoir to permit the light to shine directly downward.

Astrolabe, a medieval astronomical instrument of Arab origin, the chief aid to navigation until the 16th century; later examples highly decorated.

Astronomical brasses, one of the earliest types of horse brasses, including suns with rays, crescent moons, stars and, less commonly, the man in the moon.

Astronomical clock, any clock that shows phases of the moon and other astronomical phenomena; many fine 18th-century examples exist.

Athénienne, a late 18th-century three-legged stand or table, for a large ornament; or a candelabrum consisting of an urn on a tripod, Classical in style; or a three-legged ancillary dressing table.

Atlantes, plural of Atlas, carved figures or half figures of a man, functioning as supporting columns particularly in oak sideboards etc. of the 17th century and later; see also **Caryatids**.

Atlantic Neptune prints, sea battles, views, charts and plans of American ports, published about 1780 for the British Admiralty, supposedly useful during the Revolutionary War; complete collections (about 275 prints) rare.

Atlas, a rich Indian fabric woven of silk and cotton imported to England in the 17th century and subsequently imitated; also the figure of Classical mythology who carries the world on his shoulders, a recurring motif in Western art; see also **Atlantes**. **8**

Atterbury dish, a glass dish made by the Atterbury Co. of Pittsburgh in the late 19th century, with the cover in the form of an animal.

Attic, Greek, or more specifically of Athens (capital of Attica), as in Attic pottery, the outstanding pottery of Ancient Greece. **3**

Aubusson carpets, knotted-pile carpets and tapestries made at Aubusson from the 17th century to the present; justly famous though somewhat cheaper than, and inferior to, Beauvais or the Savonnerie. **14**

Audubon prints, from the watercolours of the American ornithologist, John James Audubon, whose famous birds were first published in the 1830s; reproduction still continues.

Augsburg work, a term used to describe the work of Augsburg craftsmen (sometimes also Nuremberg and other southern German centres) in the 16th century, mingling Gothic and Renaissance styles.

Augustalis, a 13th-century gold coin issued by Frederick II of Sicily.

Aumbry, or ambry, originally a compartment in a cupboard for storing arms, but now any large English cupboard of the Gothic period; also a closet.

Aurene glass, made at Steuben glassworks, New York, early 20th century; iridescent and brightly coloured, now rare.

Aureus, the standard Roman gold coin under the Empire, with imperial portrait on obverse.

Auricular decoration, a shell-like ornamental motif, supposedly based on the shape of the ear; first found in silver, Dutch, from the late 16th century; see also **Knorpelwerk**.

Australian blackwood, from one of the acacia family, a dark brown (rather than black) wood, colourfully streaked, which amply rewards polishing.

Autograph mugs, in barbers' shops from the late 19th century, mugs bearing the signature of regular customers.

Automata, decorative objects that move by clockwork, springs, water power, etc. (in other words, elaborate toys); especially figures on clocks, mechanical singing birds, and other moving animals; much favoured by oriental potentates in the 19th century. **12**

Ave Maria lace, the name given to pillow lace made at Dieppe from the 17th to the 19th centuries, with plaited lozenge ground; made in long strips.

Aventurine, a reddish-brown or blue quartz speckled with gold, imitated in glass by mixing crystalline copper with blue glass; a Japanese lacquer also achieves the effect of aventurine, and the term is used to describe the actual (minute) clippings of gold wire in japanning.

Axinite, a rare precious stone, dark brown in colour, which is found in crystals reminiscent of an axe head, hence its name.

Axminster carpets, knotted-pile carpets made at Axminster, England, in the late 18th and early 19th centuries, imitating oriental and European styles; later, cut-pile carpets.

Axson furniture, made by Thomas Axson, of Charleston, South Carolina, in the second half of the 18th century.

Babeury, a painted ornament or toy for a small child.

Babul, the bark of the Indian gum-arabic tree, used for tanning.

Baby cage, or baby-walker, a wooden device of ancient origin for teaching a child to walk, consisting of a frame, which encircles the child and keeps it upright, mounted on wheels or castors.

Baccarat glass, tableware and decorative glass from one of several glassworks in northern France and Belgium, from the late 18th century and highly productive throughout the 19th century; very good quality cut crystal and coloured glass, famous for paperweights. **13**

Bacchus glass, fine 19th-century English pressed glass made by George Bacchus & Sons of Birmingham; especially ornamental dishes, bowls, etc.

Bachelor button, a button backed with a pin, which was pinned on rather than sewn, for quick and easy repairs.

Bachelor's chest, a chest of drawers with a fold-out top to make a writing desk, sometimes with a tier of small drawers on top; English, early 18th century; also a similar American chest with pull-out top.

Bache silhouettes, silhouette portraits, especially 'hollow-cut' (discarding the subject rather than the surround) by English-born William Bache of Philadelphia, about 1800, until he lost an arm and became a successful merchant instead.

Bachman furniture, made by the Bachman family of Lancaster, Pennsylvania, from the late 18th to late 19th century, originally in Chippendale style, later in a variety of contemporary styles.

Backboard, the board covering the back of a piece of furniture; also a wooden board with grooves cut in diamond pattern, for making pastry.

Back drop-leaf, a table with hinged leaf at the back, in particular such a table made by 18th-century Shaker craftsmen, usually maple or cherrywood, with a single long drawer; also found on chests of drawers.

Backgammon board, for playing the very old game of backgammon which in the Middle Ages was called 'tables', perhaps accounting for the modern word 'table'.

Back painting, a print mounted face-down on glass and coloured on the back after most of the paper had been carefully rubbed off; also painting on glass to be viewed from the other side of the glass; see also **Églomisé**.

Backscratcher, a rod about 12 in long ending in a rake-like implement, often in the form of a human hand in ivory; similar implements used for head-scratching in the 18th century by ladies with elaborate hairstyles.

Backstone: see Bake stone.

Backstool, an early name for a single (armless) chair; in fact, a stool with a back on it (single chairs were unknown before the 16th century).

Backsword, a single-edged sword, the non-cutting edge being squared off (like all ceremonial swords today).

Bacon cupboard, a settle with a shallow cupboard forming the back and sometimes an overhanging cupboard above; also, a simple, high kitchen cupboard.

Badekind: see Frozen Charlotte.

Bag lamp, a lard-burning lamp of the mid 19th century in which the lard was held in a bag, one of many peculiar and not very successful lighting inventions of the pioneering American West.

Bagneux shade, a glass dome of the kind popular in Victorian parlours for placing over ornaments, made in Bagneux, France.

Bahut, an ill-defined term sometimes applied to any chest or cabinet in Gothic style; less loosely, a small, easily portable coffer with rounded lid.

Bail, a curved, hanging brass pull for drawers, etc., usually with back plate, commonly used in American furniture during the 18th century; also, a semi-circular, sometimes pivoted, handle on a bucket, basket, etc. **259**

Bain marie, a large, squarish, characteristically copper vessel, containing boiling water, in which are fitted a number of separate, cylindrical containers with lids; for cooking several foods separately at the same time.

Baiocco, a copper coin of the Vatican in the 18th century, bearing the papal arms.

Baize, a woollen material with long nap named for its colour (bay) when first introduced into England in the 16th century, and then identical with bays.

Bakelite, an early synthetic plastic named after its inventor, L. H. Baekeland, in 1913, used for a wide variety of industrial and domestic purposes, generally somewhat brittle and today relatively uncommon.

Baker lamp, an early fluid-burning lamp made by a Cincinnati firm of that name in the first half of the 19th century.

Bake stone, a flat stone shelf at the back of a hearth, used for baking; also backstone.

Bakewell glass, from the famous Pittsburgh Flint Glass Works established soon after 1800, a wide range of wares including presidential tableware, chandeliers, and cameos set in glass as well as cheap pressed glass, bottles, etc.; one of the first American producers of good lead glass.

Bakhmetev glass, from the Moscow glassworks established in the late 18th century and still operating in the early 20th century.

Bakhtiari rugs, woven by nomads of Turkish origin, from southern Iran; red, brown and blue rugs of cotton and wool, often divided into squares with floral motifs; Ghiordes knot.

Balalaika, a Russian stringed instrument of the lute family, triangular with a long neck.

Balance, a device for weighing (scales), consisting of a centrally pivoted beam with two containers of equal weight at either end; made and used since Classical times; also, a device in a watch or clock that regulates the motion; not used on pendulum clocks; see **Balance spring**.

Balance cock: see Watchcock.

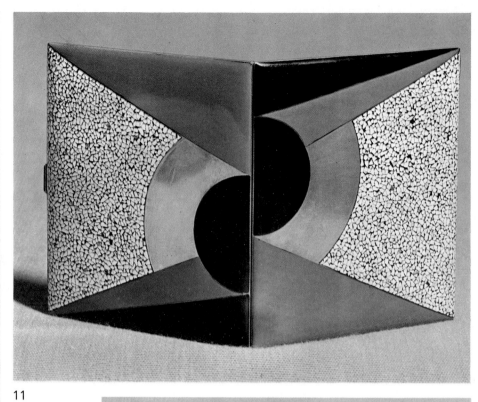

11

10 Suit of armour. Augsburg manufacture, mid 16th century. Said to have been made for Count F. von Teuffenbach. Decorated with etched motifs of grotesques, animals, birds and garlands. (Higgins Armory, Worcester, Massachusetts)

11 Art Deco cigarette case. By Raymond Templier, 1930. The design is in silver, lacquer and eggshell. (Private Collection)

12 Venetian clock with automata. Mid 17th century. On the lower half of the face the movement of the moon is shown. (Lamberti Collection)

12

13 Baccarat glass paperweight. French, second half of the 19th century. Canes of coloured glass burst into a millefiori bouquet. (Musée des Arts Décoratifs, Paris)

14 Aubusson carpet. French, 19th century. The design of flowers and leaves is typical of the period. (Private Collection, Milan)

Balance spring, in clockwork, first used in the 17th century to control the oscillations of a watch balance (and thus vastly improving its timekeeping).

Baldachin, baldacchino, or baldaquin etc., a kind of canopy over a bed, throne or altar, from medieval times, and sometimes supported by cords from the ceiling; also silk and gold fabric. **104**

Baleen, whalebone, used for buttons and carved into ornaments by sailors.

Bale handle: see **Bail.**

Ball and claw, originally oriental, a dragon's or eagle's claw clasping a ball, widely used for terminating the legs of all kinds of furniture during the first half of the 18th century; less common later. **269**

Ball clock, a clock in which the function of the balance spring is performed by a small steel ball that runs to and fro across an inclined groove, or down a spiral and up a spring-loaded tube; or a clock in which the actual drive is provided by heavy metal balls, a method with severe disadvantages; such clocks are very rare; see also **Falling ball clock.**

Ball cushion, a small, round cushion made from the late 18th century, probably as a pin cushion.

Ball foot, spherical termination of the legs of chairs, tables, etc., characteristic of the 17th century but also found earlier and later.

Ball fringe, in upholstery, a fringe that is worked in small balls at regularly spaced intervals.

Ball joint, in an articulated member a joint consisting of a sphere in an enclosing cup (often with screw tightener), allowing movement in any direction.

Ball knop, on wine glasses, especially Silesian stems, a knop that is semicircular in section.

Balloon back, a chairback shaped like a balloon, i.e. rounded and tapering toward the seat; originally French, popular in the early 19th century.

Balloon clock, a mantel clock with a case shaped like a balloon, curving inward below the dial and outward to its base, late 18th or early 19th century.

Balloon seat: see **Bell seat.**

Ball stopper, a bottle stopper consisting of a ball resting on the neck which, when the bottle is tilted, falls out into a retaining bell-shaped cage that guides it back into place when the bottle is stood upright.

Ball urn, vase, etc., a ball-shaped vessel.

Balsamarium, an ancient vessel of glass or earthenware for holding balsam or aromatic oils, sometimes internally divided to contain two separate liquids.

Baltimore glass, products of any one of several glassworks in Baltimore, Maryland, including Amelung glass and Baltimore flint glass; also pressed glass with a fig-shaped pattern.

Baltimore pottery: see **Maryland pottery.**

Baltimore silver, hallmarked and dated silver made in Baltimore in the early 19th century; also silver threepenny coins stamped with the name of the city, late 18th century.

Baluchistan, or Balughistan: see **Beluchistan rugs.**

Baluster, a short pillar, as in a balustrade; a turned, vertical, supporting member in chairs, tables and other furniture; of variable shape but (typically) swelling out like a vase towards the bottom; a half baluster (vertically split) was used decoratively on furniture of the 17th century.

Baluster back, a chair in which the half-baluster form is used in the back.

Baluster stem, a wine glass with a stem shaped like a baluster or an inverted baluster; sometimes called Portuguese swell.

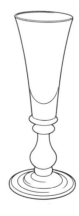

Balustroid, an early 18th-century English style of wine glass in which the old, heavy baluster stem is lighter and slimmer; associated with the advent of the Silesian stem.

Balzarine, a light-weight cloth of mixed cotton and worsted used for women's clothing in the 19th century, usually in narrow stripes of different colours.

Bamboo, a giant grass, with a hard, articulated stem, creamy coloured, which comes from the Far East.

Bamboo furniture, made of bamboo or of other wood, particularly beech, turned and painted to look like bamboo; popular from the mid 18th century to the late

19th, when it became almost cultish for a time.

Bamboo ware, stoneware in the form and colour of bamboo made by Josiah Wedgwood in the late 18th century.

Banana dish, the name given to glass or ceramic dishes on stands with opposite edges turned up like a bushman's hat, found in the American South.

Band, a metal loop binding together adjacent members (e.g. barrel and stock of a gun), a ridge across the back of a leather-bound book, a lattice-like pattern in pressed glass, etc.; see also **Banding.**

Bandana, printed calico of bright spots on a darker ground, typically white on red as in a bandana kerchief.

Bandbox, a light-weight oval or round box, originally of wood for keeping collar bands, etc., now usually of cardboard for keeping hats, for example.

Banding, a flat ornamental or veneered border around a door, panel, drawer, table rim, etc. **240**

Bandolier, a shoulder strap worn by soldiers since the 16th century, originally for carrying a number of powder charges in small wooden containers.

Banister, the same as baluster, but used particularly of the vertical rails in a staircase.

Banister-back, a chair with a split-baluster back, a popular form in 18th- and early 19th-century America, usually maple but more sophisticated examples in mahogany.

Banjo barometer, in which the case is shaped like a banjo, an early 19th-century design. **16**

Banjo clock, a popular shape for American pendulum clocks from the late 18th to mid 19th century (and still made); numerous varieties including some very fine and rare clocks, resulting in many fakes.

Bank, from the French *banc*, the medieval term for a long seat or bench, sometimes covered with a banker; also, a money box made in many forms and materials (china pigs a traditional

favourite), particularly a 19th-century mechanical money box in which insertion of a coin sets off some kind of movement.

Banker, a loose covering or cushion for a seat (bank) usually richly ornamented, from medieval times.

Banner screen, a firescreen on a tripod base in which the screen is unframed tapestry, usually with a tassel at the bottom; early 19th century.

Banquette, a day bed.

Bantam work, caskets, trays, screens, etc. decorated with carved lacquer in the manner of objects originally imported by the Dutch East India Co. from Java in the 17th century.

Bar-back, a chair or sofa with a back of vertical bars, as in certain of the shield-backed chairs associated with Hepplewhite.

Barber's bowl, a circular bowl, usually with a section cut out to fit under the chin; also, a bleeding bowl, for collecting the patient's blood, hard to distinguish from contemporary bowls made for less gruesome purposes; see also **Bleeding bowl.**

Barber's chair, any chair specially made for the barber's clients, generally wooden armchairs; 18th-century types include a simple, high-backed armchair with a semicircle cut out for the neck, a corner chair. with fixed, raised headrest; adjustable chairs date from the mid 19th century.

Barber's pole, a red and white spiralled pole advertising a barber's shop, symbolizing the blood and bandages associated with the old barber-surgeons; formerly topped by a brass basin; also, a motif reminiscent of a barber's pole on the borders of some oriental carpets.

Barbizet-Palissy, imitations of the 16th-century pottery of Bernard Palissy made at Barbizet, Paris, in the late 19th century.

Barbotine method, in late 19th-century French pottery, a technique of painting in coloured slips pioneered by the artist-potter, Ernest Chaplet.

Barbute, in armour, a tall helmet used in 15th-century Italy, without visor but curving round to protect all but the eyes, nose and mouth, closely resembling helmets of Classical Greece.

Barcelona chair, designed in 1929 by the architect, Mies van der Rohe, two square leather-covered cushions on a slim and elegant, curving steel frame; now manufactured by Knoll Associates Inc. **15**

Barcheston tapestry, from one of the earliest tapestry works in England, established in the late 16th century by William Sheldon with (at first) primarily Flemish weavers, making sets of *The Seasons* and similarly popular subjects.

Barège, a worsted or silk and worsted cloth, somewhat like gauze, used in women's clothes, named after the Pyrenean town from which it first came.

Bargello work, in embroidery, a series of similar figures in changing shades of the same colour, Italian in origin and worked in silk.

Barilette, a small cask.

Barilla, ash containing soda from a glasswort plant, growing chiefly in Spanish saline marshes, used in glassworks all over Europe in the 16th century. Also the plant itself.

Barker pottery, made at the Don pottery, Yorkshire, when under the ownership of Samuel Barker, mid 19th century.

Barley-sugar twist, turning in a spiral to give the effect of a twisted column (like a stick of barley sugar); common in late 17th-century furniture, especially chairs.

Barm pot, earthenware vessel for holding barm (the froth that forms on fermenting malt liquor, used in baking).

Barnes porcelain, made at Liverpool by Zachariah Barnes, mid 18th century; soft-paste porcelain generally printed in dark blue.

Barnum buckle, a shoe buckle to which was attached a strap passing under the instep, patented by the circus showman, P. T. Barnum (1810–91).

Barograph, an instrument that records changes in atmospheric pressure, usually as a graph on a revolving drum; made from the late 18th century, though early examples are rare.

Barometer, a scientific instrument for measuring atmospheric pressure, thus determining weather changes; many models ranging from the early cistern types to the aneroid and wheel barometers of later times. **16**

Baroque pearl, a term applied to any pearl of irregular shape. **17, 153**

Baroque style, broadly defined, the predominant style in the arts and design from the late 16th to the early 18th century, abandoning Renaissance Classical disciplines for greater vigour and movement, and eventually merging into the ultra-ornamental Rococo; in England the Baroque style was restrained, in America it hardly existed. **7, 163**

Barrel brass, a popular design for horse brasses, sometimes made as one piece, sometimes with the barrel pendant within a circular ring.

Barrel chair, a late 18th-century chair with high, solid back, roughly in the form of a barrel, often upholstered in leather.

Barrel decanter, shaped like a barrel and often cut in a pattern suggesting hoops and staves, popular in the late 18th century, especially in Irish glassworks.

Barrel organ, a street organ, a mechanical organ, portable or on wheels, deriving its name from the large revolving cylinder with pegs set into it which open the valves.

Bartizan, a small turret projecting beyond and above the corner of a gateway or building; hence, a similar, ornamental feature on furniture.

Basaltes, in ceramics originally Egyptian unglazed, black stoneware; also 'black porcelain' by Josiah Wedgwood, stoneware with hard, brilliant finish and many uses; in modern reproductions spelled basalt.

Bascinet, a helmet of the type common in 14th-century Europe, subject to many variations but commonly with pivoted, snout-like visor and chain-mail curtain to protect the neck.

Bas d'armoire, a lowboy.

Base, the lowest horizontal member in case furniture; the bottom element of a column (plinth), etc.

Base dogs, andirons mounted on a three-sided frame that fitted around the hearth; from the mid 19th century.

Basenet: see **Bascinet.**

Basin, or bason, a circular vessel with sloping sides, wider across the top than from top to bottom, for holding liquids.

Basin stand, an 18th- or 19th-century bedroom piece with a hole for a basin and, sometimes underneath, a space for a ewer; many varieties, some with mirrors and/or drawers, some triangular, some round, etc.

Basket, a wickerwork container with bail handle, or a similar object in silver, porcelain, etc.; also a sword hilt introduced in the late 17th century in the form of a curved cage, giving better protection to the hand than a simple cross-guard. **222, 259**

Basket chair, an armchair of basket or wickerwork, made since ancient times and particularly fashionable, with a loose cushion on the seat, in the 19th century.

Basket stand, a 19th-century worktable usually on tripod feet with circular, galleried trays.

Basket top, a clock with a metal, dome-shaped case top; also, a wooden case of the same shape.

Basketwork, baskets or other objects made by weaving reeds or similar material, used for chair seats since medieval times; also, a pattern resembling basketwork in pottery, for instance.

Bason: see **Basin.**

Bas-relief, or basso-relievo, ornamental carving or moulding in 'low relief', the figures projecting only slightly from the surface, in any material; see also **High relief.**

Bassano pottery, pottery from the Bassano workshops near Venice founded in the 15th century; later famous for their porcelain in the Chinese manner.

15

16

17

15 Barcelona chair. Steel with
leather-covered upholstery.
Designed in 1929 by Ludwig Mies
van der Rohe for the German
pavilion at the Barcelona Exhibition.
(Musée des Arts Décoratifs, Paris)

16 Mahogany banjo barometer.
Signed J. Russell, clockmaker to the
Prince Regent. English, about 1800.
(Victoria and Albert Museum,
London)

17 Brooch in the form of a cock.
South German, about 1600.
Made from a Baroque pearl,
precious stones and enamelled gold.
(Museo degli Argenti, Florence)

19 Enamelled glass beaker. German, dated 1696. The charming painted figures probably represented real people. (Kunstgewerbemuseum, Cologne)

18 *Country Amusements: The Drinking Pool.* Beauvais tapestry, 1773–79. One of a series of pastoral subjects in Rococo taste. (Mobilier National, Paris)

Basses, or bases, the lower valances of a bed, especially when very rich draperies are involved.

Basset table, a small table presumably used for playing basset, a card game of Italian origin and popular in France in the late 17th century.

Bassinet, a cradle for a baby in the form of a wicker basket with a hood or covering over one end.

Basso-relievo: see **Bas-relief**.

Basswood, from a tree of the linden family, a fine-grained softwood that can be woven in thin strips for chair seats, etc.; sometimes applied to tulipwood; see also **Limewood**.

Bat, in Chinese designs, a common motif symbolizing happiness and longevity; also, an oiled sheet involved in a technique similar to transfer-printing; or a lump of potter's clay.

Batavian ware, imported from the Dutch port of Batavia, Java, in the 18th century, and similar English ware; light-brown background with highly coloured panels.

Batch, in glassmaking, the mixture of raw materials before it is melted to produce glass.

Bateman silver, bearing the mark of Hester Bateman, the 18th-century English silversmith who, however, was not unique in her craft, as once was thought, and also seems merely to have carried on her husband's business, not designed or made silverware.

Bath brick, unbaked silicaceous material in the form of a brick used for polishing silver and other metals.

Bath metal, an alloy of copper and zinc in proportions of 32 to 39, made in the late 17th century and reputed to bear a close resemblance to gold.

Batik, a type of dyed cloth in which wax is used to resist certain colours and so produce the design; from the East Indies.

Batik design, ornamental inlay inspired by Indonesian designs, found in Art Nouveau Dutch furniture.

Batiste, or cambric, a very fine fabric, originally linen, later cotton also.

Batten, any narrow strip of wood used in cabinetmaking, in particular as a strengthening agent (*cf* 'batten down the hatches') or to conceal a joint; also a narrow floorboard or lath.

Battersea enamel, mid 18th-century curios, snuffboxes, plates, ornaments, etc. from the Battersea enamel works, London, where the technique of transfer-printing was first developed.

Battery metal, or latten, the earliest kind of English brass, made in the 16th century by the Mineral & Battery Works of London.

Batwing, a motif of Chinese origin adopted for brass backplates of drawer handles in the first half of the 18th century.

Baudekin: see **Baldachin**.

Bauhaus, the highly influential German school of design in the 1920s, founded by Walter Gropius, emphasizing functionalism, industrial techniques and experimentation, producing e.g. the first tubular steel furniture.

Bawbee, a Scottish coin of the 16th century with royal portrait on the obverse and the crown and thistle on the reverse, worth about one penny.

Baxter prints, 19th-century prints by George Baxter, English pioneer of colour printing, in which as many as 20 wood blocks were used to print the colours on a steel engraving.

Bayreuth, faience and porcelain from the highly productive factory at Bayreuth, Germany, in the first half of the 18th century, especially notable for the quality of its painting, equal to Meissen (the best by an ex-Meissen hand, in fact).

Bays, a rough woollen cloth originating in the Low Countries, imported to England in the 16th century, used for furnishings; see also **Baize**.

Baywood, Honduras mahogany, lighter and less closely grained than the West Indian varieties, first imported to England in the late 18th century.

Bead and reel, a Classical moulding of alternating beads and reels.

Bead curtain, a curtain consisting of vertical cords on which glass and wooden beads are threaded, originating in India and popular in the second half of the 19th century.

Beading, a decorative strip looking more or less like a string of beads, a common moulding on 18th-century furniture; also, a similar pattern in silver, glassware, pottery, etc.; see also **Astragal**.

Beadwork, a decoration found on small mirrors or other articles, a pattern or border of coloured beads, popular from the 17th century; also, baskets, ornaments, 'souvenirs', of traditional crafts in Africa particularly.

Beaker, a large stemless drinking glass, without handle or cover and usually in the shape of a tapering cylinder in silver, glass, earthenware, etc. **19**

Bear-baiting, a popular subject in ceramics in 18th- and early 19th-century England; see also **Bear jug**.

Bear jug, an English stoneware jug, first made in the 18th century, in the shape of a bear, from Staffordshire, Derby and elsewhere.

Beau Brummel, a gentleman's dressing table, elaborate, with fitted mirrors, mainly American, and made from the early 18th century (i.e. predating George Brummel).

Beau livre, a book with original illustrations in the actual medium used by the artist (engravings, etchings, lithographs, etc.) and thus limited to a very small (though variable according to the medium) edition.

Beauvais pottery, earthenware from Beauvais, from the late 14th century onward, from ordinary tableware to religious objects and statues, typically in a fine, light clay; later, stoneware from the same district.

Beauvais tapestry, from the works founded in the early 17th century, supplier to Louis XIV; with Gobelins, the best of 18th-century French tapestries, designed by artists such as Boucher; also carpets for a short period in the late 18th century. **18**

Beaver, or bevor, the front part of a helmet which could be raised (or lowered), as in *Hamlet* Act I scene ii.

Becket, a metal eye at the end of a rope, or a hook on which rope was stored; also, a straight-bladed spade for cutting turf.

Bed, the soft furnishings (nowadays, mattress, sheets and blankets) contained in a bedstead, which is the actual structure.

Bed chair, a chair for use in bed, i.e. having seat, back and arms but no legs, from the 18th century; also, a chair convertible into a bed.

Bedroom chair, a general term for lightweight chairs, often with rush seats, of plain wood enamelled, stencilled, etc., particularly in the first half of the 19th century.

Bedstaff, an implement the use of which is now mysterious, defined in the 18th century (by Samuel Johnson) as a stick once used to place in the side of a bed to prevent the clothes slipping off.

Bedstead: see **Bed**.

Bed steps, a flight of two or three light steps, useful in the 18th and 19th centuries when beds were rather high.

Bed table, for use in bed, either a tray with short fold-out legs, with a curved section cut out on one side and the other sides railed or galleried; or a folding table on an adjustable stand.

Bed valance, a pelmet or curtain suspended from the canopy of a four-poster bed, usually made in sets; often canvas in the 16th century, later wool, silk, etc.

Bed wagon, an open, wooden frame containing a charcoal-burning pan, used for airing beds.

Bed warmer: see **Warming pan**.

Beechwood, a pale brown wood widely used from the 17th century in country furniture, often in imitation of the more sophisticated walnut, and in upholstered furniture where it is invisible; like walnut, a favourite of the woodworm.

Batwing

Beefsteak dish, a covered entrée dish, in particular a dish with a detachable handle on the lid, which could be used as two dishes.

Beehive chair, a 19th-century cane or rushwork armchair with cylindrical base and round seat.

Beehive clock, a mid 19th-century mantel clock made in New England, in shape resembling a beehive or flat iron, hence also flat-iron clock.

Beer wagon, a coaster especially for beer, with dished circles for a large jug and beakers.

Beetham silhouette, painted on glass or ivory or cut in black paper, by Mrs Isabelle Beetham of Fleet Street, London, in the late 18th century.

Beilby glass, painted by the Beilby family of Newcastle, England, foremost English practitioners of enamelling in glass in the 18th century, especially armorial designs and Rococo decoration. **21**

Beilby layer, the infinitesimally thin layer of melted glass formed on the surface of certain gems when rubbed with polishing powder, making the surface highly reflective; named after its discoverer in the early 20th century.

Beinglas, German and Bohemian glass of the late 18th century which included bone ash to create its characteristic milky appearance.

Bekerschroef, a cup-shaped silver stand for a wine glass; Dutch, 17th century.

Bellarmine, an early 17th-century stoneware bottle, originally German, with mask of bearded man (supposedly the unloved Cardinal Bellarmino, 1542–1621) on the neck and sometimes associated with witchcraft; still made in the 19th century and often known as Greybeards.

Bell Beaker, a bell-shaped earthenware beaker made by the neolithic 'Beaker' people (England), seldom to be seen outside museums; in glassware, a wide-mouthed vessel curving inward near the foot.

Bell brasses, horse brasses either in the shape of a bell or having a swinging bell set in an ornamental disc; a very popular form in the late 18th and early 19th centuries.

Belleek porcelain, originally, Irish porcelain made at Belleek, County Fermanagh, late 19th century; highly iridescent parian ware hardly thicker than paper, successfully imitated by factories in Trenton, New Jersey, and elsewhere.

Bellevue faience, from the French factory at Meurthe at Moselle, in the late 18th century; also, **Belle Vue pottery** from Hull, England, 19th-century tableware; see also **Hull pottery.**

Bell-flower, a stylized rudimentary carving or inlay of a three-petalled bud on the legs of chairs and tables in the late 18th century; see also **Husk. 97**

Bell metal, an alloy of copper and bronze which produces a good ringing sound making it suitable, in particular, for bells.

Bellows, a fireside implement of wood and leather with metalwork fittings and various kinds of ornament, for creating a draught; their characteristic shape sometimes copied in flasks, bottles, etc., in the 19th century.

Bell pull, the knob, lever or handle attached to a bell cord (predecessor of the bell push); made in every conceivable medium, with various motifs from Greek to grotesque, 18th century onward.

Bell seat, or balloon seat, a chair with rounded, bell-shaped seat as seen in some 18th- and 19th-century American chairs.

Bell sundial, a form of sundial, invented in 18th-century France, in which the sun at noon burned through a thread and sounded a gong; silent on rainy days, however.

Bell top, of a mantel clock, the top of whose case resembles a bell; when the bottom portion has a concave curve it is an 'inverted' bell top.

Bell ware, a wide range of pottery manufactured by J. & M. P. Bell of Glasgow in the second half of the 19th century; also, fine-grained red stoneware by Samuel Bell of Newcastle-under-Lyme, mid 18th century.

Belper ware, stoneware from the 19th-century English firm of Bourne & Co., who had several potteries in Derbyshire, the first of them at Belper.

Belter furniture, made by John H. Belter of New York in the mid 19th century; rather heavy, Louis XV style, heavily carved, in great demand by French émigrés.

Beluchistan rugs, originally nomadic (prayer rugs, horse covers, etc.), size adapted for export in the 19th century; chiefly dark red and shades of brown with polygonal motifs; Sehna knot; wool with goat and camel hair.

Belvedere, an open building on top of the main structure, or a summerhouse or folly, commanding a view.

Bema, a stage in ancient Greece, hence any raised platform, e.g. for a lectern in a church.

Bench, a long wooden seat generally but not invariably without a back, freestanding or attached to a wall, the standard form of seating in the Middle Ages and earlier; also, a cabinetmaker's worktable.

Bench cloth, a cover, often a rug, for a bench, adding a touch of luxury to an essentially spartan piece.

Bench ends, the ends of a bench or church pew, usually carved and often with gabled top or surmounted by a finial.

Bended-back: see **Spoon back.**

Benedict stove, cast-iron ten-plate stove made by Philip Benedict of Lancaster, Pennsylvania, early 19th century.

Benin, an ancient Nigerian kingdom which produced magnificent art, especially bronzes and ivories, during the 16th century. **23**

Bénitier, for holding holy water, sometimes applied to a small earthenware vessel, sometimes to the actual font.

Benitoite, an extremely rare American stone, blue with a brilliance rivalling diamonds, found only in San Benito county, California.

Bennet prints, a much sought-after series of aquatints of American cities engraved by William J. Bennet (1787–1844) and published in New York, 1836–8; also, aquatints of *The Seasons* and a few other subjects.

Bennington ware, perhaps the best known of all American potteries, beginning with red earthenware and stoneware in the early 19th century; later

Bennington parian (similar to English parian), Rockingham, and numerous other wares, many utilitarian and unmarked; the term also describes similar ware made in other places.

Bentwood, early mass-produced furniture, cheap wood such as beech being bent into the required shape after heating with steam; invented by Michael Thonet of Vienna in the mid 19th century.

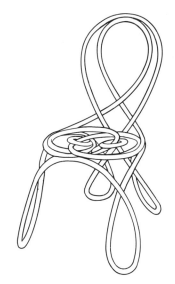

Bérain style, in French faience, a delicate Rococo design of blue and white (later other colours) plates and dishes usually with a central scene elaborately framed, originating at Versailles and associated particularly with Moustiers. **24**

Bergama, or Bergamo, rugs from the town near Pergamum in Turkey, sometimes prayer rugs; rather bright colours and clean geometric patterns, Ghiordes knot; of the type featured by Holbein.

20 Bergère chair. Designed by
Claude Chevigny, 1780—90.
Chevigny was a leading Paris
cabinetmaker during the reign of
Louis XVI. (Musée Nissim de
Camondo, Paris)

21 Two glass goblets by William
Beilby of Newcastle on Tyne. About
1760—80. The goblets have
engraved and enamelled armorial
decoration and air-twist stems.
(Corning Museum of Glass,
Corning, New York)

▲22

23

22 Blue and white ware bowl. Chinese, Ming dynasty, Hsüan-te period, 1426—35. White porcelain with blue underglaze decoration of lotus flowers. (Musée Guimet, Paris)

23 Benin pectoral mask. Ivory, iron, copper, stone, $9\frac{1}{2}$ in high, 16th century. From Bini, Benin, Nigeria, part of the treasury of King Ovonramwe. (Museum of Primitive Art, New York)

24 Moustiers faience tray. French, 18th century. The tray is decorated in the delicate Bérain style which is associated particularly with Moustiers. (Musée des Arts Décoratifs, Paris)

Bergère, an upholstered armchair, 18th-century French; deeper, wider and generally more comfortable than the usual armchair of the period; later, a caned chair of the same type. **20**

Berlin faience, from three 18th-century factories in Berlin and Potsdam, much of it with reddish body and resembling Dutch delftware; also, unusually shaped jars and vases with bold decoration in vivid blue.

Berlin ironwork, cast-iron jewellery inscribed *Gold gab ich für Eisen* ('I gave gold for iron') given to patriotic Prussian women who surrendered their jewellery to pay for the campaign against Napoleon.

Berlin porcelain, first produced about 1750, profited from decline of Meissen and royal takeover (by Frederick the Great); mainly tableware but some unsurpassed figures by former Meissen artists.

Berlin tapestry, from the works founded by a Huguenot émigré from Aubusson and supplied to various European courts in the first half of the 18th century.

Berlin tinware, the product of Berlin, Connecticut, where the first American tinsmiths settled in the mid 18th century, producing japanned tin-plate household wares.

Berlin transparencies: see **Lithophane**.

Berlin work, the dominant fashion in mid 19th-century canvas work embroidery, worked mainly in cross-stitch or tent stitch on canvas in brightly coloured wools from long-haired Berlin sheep.

Berretino, a greyish-blue glaze used for the background in some Renaissance Italian maiolica.

Beryl, the family of precious stones that includes emerald and aquamarine, extremely hard and durable.

Beryllonite, a semiprecious stone looking like clear glass and without outstanding qualities except for its rarity.

Berry pin, a decorative 19th-century pin with a head in the form of a berry.

Besagew, in late medieval armour, a small circular plate set below the shoulder to protect the vulnerable armpit joint.

Beshir carpets, mainly rather large carpets, dark red and blue and sometimes distinguished by a strong yellow line, rather tight-packed design; Sehna knot.

Besom, a broom made of birch twigs, broom, or similar material bound to a stick, in use for centuries and traditionally painted red.

Bessarabian carpets, oriental carpets from the region on the borders of Russia and Romania, with naturalistic designs.

Bestiary, a book about animals, real or mythological, popular in medieval and Renaissance times, usually illustrated.

Betty lamp, the commonest grease-burning lamp in colonial America, consisting basically of a wick, fuel box, and vertical handle from which it could hang, usually wrought iron but sometimes copper, brass, etc.

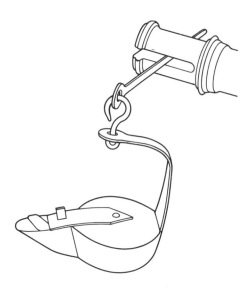

Bevelled edge, sloping away from a flat surface, like a table, but most commonly the angled edge of mirrors and plate glass; in old glass the bevel is generally less pronounced.

Bevor: see **Beaver**.

Beyer prints, lithographs of drawings by Edward Beyer (1820–65) of views of old Virginia, printed in Germany and published in Richmond, Virginia.

Bezant, a Byzantine gold coin or a European coin in imitation of it.

Bezel, a retaining rim, e.g. around the inside of a vessel so that the lid fits tightly, or framing the jewel in a ring, the glass in a watch, etc.

Bezoar stone, balls of animal matter sometimes found in the stomachs of cows and other animals having accumulated around a foreign body (like a pearl in an oyster).

Bianco-sopra-bianco, i.e. white on white, white decoration on an almost-white (pale blue or grey) ground, developed in 16th-century Italian maiolica and found on some English delftware.

Bible-back, a drop-leaf table having as its central section merely a cylindrical member so that the leaves, when up, meet at the centre; with leaves down, it resembles a closed book; early 19th century.

Bible box, possibly for holding the family bible, a carved wooden (usually oak) box or chest, sometimes with inclined lid, 17th century; see also **Book box**.

Bibliopegy, the art of book-binding.

Bibliothèque, a bookcase, sometimes with glazed or grill front.

Bicker, a small, wooden bowl with staves and hoops.

Biddery, metal wares from India in an alloy of copper, lead and tin, imported during the 19th century.

Bideford pottery, from Bideford and other Devonshire potteries, notable for its sgraffito ornament scratched through white to the red body, much exported to the American colonies.

Bidet, a violin-shaped basin, metal or earthenware, sometimes set in a wooden stool; a common convenience in French bathrooms since the 18th century.

Biedermeier style, the German (particularly Viennese) style in furniture in the first half of the 19th century, a bourgeois development of the Baroque, satirically named after comically uncultured characters in a magazine, yet sometimes regarded as the last truly original style before Art Nouveau.

Biggin, a small silver coffee pot cylindrical in shape with strainer and sometimes a stand plus spirit-lamp; also a child's cap or nightcap, whence the coffee pot perhaps took its name.

Biggonet, or biggon, a cap with pieces to cover the ears.

Bijar carpets, from northern Iran (Kurdistan), cotton, wool and camel hair, often very closely woven; patterns of stylized floral, animal and bird motifs.

Bijouterie, trinkets, particularly jewelled items such as small boxes, fans, paperweights, badges, music boxes, toys, puzzles and other curios.

Bilbao, a wall mirror framed in pink or other coloured marble, probably originating in Bilbao, Spain, but found chiefly in America; similar objects such as picture frames; also spelled Bilboa.

Bill, a 16th-century foot-soldier's weapon consisting of a short, broad, curved blade like a billhook mounted on a shortish pole.

Billie and Charley, a forgery, either one made by William Smith or Charles Eaton who deceived the British Museum in the mid 19th century with their 'ancient' coins and other articles, or colloquially any forgery.

Billingsley porcelain, painted or made by William Billingsley (1758–1828) who evolved a new technique of flower painting at Derby and later worked for several well-known firms; Billingsley was less successful as a manufacturer at Nantgarw.

Billon, a metal alloy sometimes used for coins consisting of a large quantity of copper, tin or other base metal and a very small quantity of gold or silver.

Billy Waters, a popular English 19th-century ceramic figure, a black fiddler with a wooden leg, based on a well-known London character.

Bilsted, wood of the sweet- or sugar-gum tree, not unlike mahogany in appearance and used in some colonial American furniture.

Bilston enamel, from south Staffordshire factories producing painted enamel on copper in the second half of the 18th century; best known for plaques, caskets, snuffboxes, door knobs, etc., though larger items were also made.

Binding, of books, the covers and spine of the book; also, the process of applying the binding; in upholstery, strengthening elements applied to seams and edges. **25**

Bin label, a metal or ceramic label attached to a wine bin and describing its contents; possibly the origin of the bottle tag.

Binnacle, a ship's compass housed in a box with a lamp and viewing window for reading it at night.

Binnacle clock, made for a ship, showing nautical watches and striking from one to eight.

Birch broom: see **Besom**.

Birch prints, engravings of paintings by William Birch (1755–1834) and his son Thomas of Philadelphia; in particular, views of Philadelphia and other American scenes published about 1800.

Birchwood, used in 18th-century chairs and sometimes as a veneer (substituting for satinwood); rather pale wood with reddish shadings, difficult to work and not very popular with cabinetmakers.

Bird-back, any 18th-century chair with vase-shaped splat that suggests a pair of birds facing each other, the splat representing the space between them.

Bird brasses, various horse brasses with bird motifs, swans, eagles, peacocks and occasionally the pelican engaged in its popular but mythological practice of feeding its young with its own blood.

Birdcage, an 18th-century device in tip-up tripod tables, resembling a cage with vertical, baluster 'bars', which allows the table to revolve as well as tip; also late 18th-century wirework items intended as decorative covers or as actual birdcages.

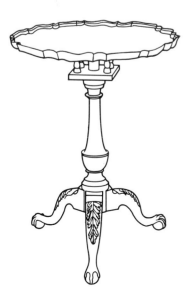

Birdcage clock, an 18th-century fashion, a birdcage (usually gilded and ornamented) with mechanical singing bird and clock in the base, sometimes under the base if the cage was to be hung from the ceiling; also, the rectangular iron frame containing the striking movement in old turret clocks.

Bird's eye, a pattern of dots, like birds' eyes, in some maplewood; also, a pattern in woven fabrics.

Biredchend carpets: see **Khorassan carpets**.

Birjair: see **Bergère**.

Birmingham silver, silver of all kinds from Birmingham, England, which before 1773 was hallmarked at London or Chester.

Birthstone, a precious stone related to a particular month of the year (e.g. diamond for April, emerald for May), an invention of fairly recent date (probably 18th century).

Biscuit ware, unglazed porcelain, first made in France in the mid 18th century and subsequently popular (though expensive) in England and elsewhere, notably for Derby figures; also, any unglazed porcelain or earthenware. **29**

Bishop bowl, a faience bowl in the form of a bishop's mitre, for a punch called Bishop, made chiefly in northern Germany and Scandinavia.

Bismuth, a reddish-white metal with a variety of uses, in particular as a hardening agent in pewter and other alloys.

Bisque: see **Biscuit ware**.

Biwa, an ancient Japanese stringed instrument, like a short lute.

Black bean, the wood of the Australian Moreton Bay chestnut, a fine-grained wood resembling walnut and used in cabinetmaking as, though said not to be durable, it takes polish well.

Black Egyptian ware: see **Basaltes**.

Black-figure, the technique invented by Greek potters in the 7th century BC, the figures being silhouettes on light ground, with detail engraved through the pigment before firing. **3**

Black Forest clock, mid 17th-century clocks of Gothic design made of wood by country craftsmen in the Black Forest,

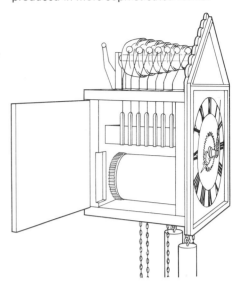

imitating contemporary clocks; often reproduced in more sophisticated forms.

Black glaze, a brilliant glaze, usually very dark brown rather than black, used on English red earthenware in the 18th century.

Blackjack, a plain or tooled leather flask or tankard, often with silver rim and sometimes with mounted silver ornament, from the 17th century or earlier.

Black letter, in printing, type with heavy characters, as used in the first English printed books.

Black line, the usual method of engraving in woodcut, in which the non-printing areas are cut away.

Black oak: see **Bog oak**.

Black walnut, a warm-toned wood with interesting dark markings, extensively used by American cabinetmakers in the early 19th century; see **Virginia walnut**.

Blackwork, in embroidery, black silk worked on linen in backstitch, very popular for many purposes in 16th-century England (where, according to tradition, it was introduced from Spain by Catherine of Aragon).

Bladed knop, on a wine glass stem, a knop with a concave outward curve culminating in a thin edge.

Blade sight, the front sight of a gun consisting of a thin, vertical leaf.

Blanc de chine, 'white china', fine, white, Chinese porcelain, undecorated, notably from Fukien; imitated by several European porcelain factories. **27**

Blanc fixe, in tin-glazed earthenware, decoration in white on a tinted glaze.

Blanket chest, 17th- to 18th-century chest for storing bedding, usually with two drawers (and sometimes two dummy drawers above them) surmounted by a chest.

Blanket crane, a moveable arm attached to the wall near a stove, used for drying bedding or clothes when extended.

Blaze, a word used in the 18th century (rather appropriately) to describe a chandelier, especially one with many branches.

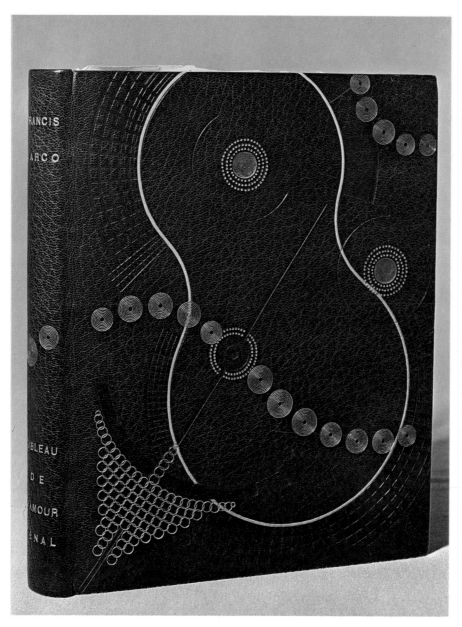

25 Book binding for Francis
Carco's *Tableau de l'amour venal*.
Designed by Pierre Legrain, 1928.
Black morocco leather with an
abstract design in gold, and blind
blocking. (Pierre Bérès Collection,
Paris © by ADAGP, Paris, 1967)

26 Bohemian cut-glass goblet and
cover. 18th century.
(Kunstgewerbemuseum, Cologne)

27 White porcelain figurine of
Kuan Yin, goddess of mercy.
Chinese, Ming dynasty, 17th
century. A fine example of blanc de
chine from Tehwa in Fukien.
(Musée Guimet, Paris)

28 Boiseries in Madame Adelaide's
music room, Versailles. Designed by
Jacques Verberckt in the 1750s.
(Palace of Versailles)

Bleeding bowl, a silver or other metal bowl with single short handle, supposedly for use by barber-surgeons when bleeding patients, called a porringer in America; see also **Barber's bowl.**

Blind, of a structural element in cabinet-making, one that is concealed from view; also, a false drawer, lid, door, etc.

Blind blocking, an impression (e.g. the title or author's name) stamped on a book binding but without the usual gold or colouring, so that the impression remains merely incised (reverse relief). 25

Blinking-eye clock, a clock containing the representation of a face (human or animal) the eyes of which were linked to the movement and blinked as the clock ticked; originally 16th-century German, also made in America and elsewhere in the 18th and 19th centuries.

Blister, a marking suggestive of a blister sometimes found in maple, cedar, and other woods.

Block book, in which each page was printed from a single block, a method rendered obsolete by the invention of movable type though occasionally employed thereafter.

Block foot, in furniture with legs of rectangular section, feet of similar shape but proportionately larger than the legs.

Block front, found chiefly in 18th-century American furniture, typically Newport chests of drawers, the front being shaped from very thick boards that permit a recessed central section and (sometimes) projecting outer sections.

Block printing, in textiles, a coloured pattern printed on the fabric by wooden blocks; see also **Block book.**

Bloodstone, a quartz stone used in jewellery, dark green with crimson streaks said to have been made by Christ's blood at the crucifixion.

Bloomers, a 19th-century female undergarment of long loose-fitting pants, advocated by American women's liberationist Amelia Bloomer (1818–94).

Blow hole, a small hole for ventilation and, in particular, to allow expanding air to escape when heated, e.g. in the handle of a coffee pot.

Blowing tube, narrow tube of iron or other metal with a mouthpiece for blowing through in order to create a draught before bellows came into general use.

Blown-moulded glass, used particularly for wine bottles and other vessels demanding cheap and quick production, molten glass on the end of a tube being placed in the mould which separates into halves after the glass has been blown into shape; several vessels could be made simultaneously by this method.

Blow pipe, the long metal tube used in glass-blowing.

Bludgeon gun, a mid 19th-century American weapon looking superficially like a small metal club but concealing a short-barrelled pistol for emergencies.

Blue and white ware, originally Chinese porcelain developed under the Ming dynasty, in which the decoration was painted in cobalt blue on a white ground; exported to the West on a large scale under the Ch'ing dynasty; extensively reproduced in a wide range of designs by European workshops. 22, 77

Blue-dash charger, the name given to a large tin-glazed earthenware plate or plaque, of various designs, but having a rim diagonally marked with broad blue streaks; originally a Dutch design but common in late 17th-century England and imitated in the American colonies.

Blued steel, steel or iron coloured dark blue or black by heating (or by chemical means), as (probably) in the armour of the Black Prince.

Blue glass, popular with Renaissance Venetian glassmakers and in 18th-century Bristol among other places; colour obtained by adding cobalt.

Blue John, or Derbyshire spar, a purplish stone with light markings used from the mid 18th century for making urns and other chiefly decorative objects, jewellery, etc.

Blue-printed ware, Staffordshire pottery transfer-printed in blue, very popular in the late 18th and early 19th centuries; see also **Historical blue.**

Blue white, the purest kind of white, as found in diamonds.

Blunderbuss, a large-bore gun with flared muzzle, a 'scatter gun' designed to do maximum damage at short range, against boarding parties at sea, etc., in use from the 17th to the 19th centuries.

Blunt instruments, barometers, compasses, measuring devices, etc., made by the American firm of Edward and George Blunt.

Board, a length of wood up to about an inch thick; a table (hence 'board of directors' etc.); stiff cover of a book; **board chest** etc., an unpretentious piece made cheaply from boards, without joining.

Boater, an oval, flat-topped and flat-brimmed gentleman's straw hat; popular from the late Victorian period especially for genteel recreational wear; still *de rigueur* in traditionally inclined English boys' schools.

Bob, in a pendulum clock, the weight at the end of the pendulum rod.

Bobbinet, English lace made by machine (i.e. on bobbins) rather than by hand.

Bobbin turning, turned members (chair stretchers, etc.) that resemble a row of bobbins, or large spheres, from the 17th century.

Bocage, Rococo decoration found chiefly in porcelain figures of the 18th century in which a tree trunk with accompanying foliage and flowers acts as a support for the figures, usually finished quite roughly by comparison with the figures; also in Staffordshire earthenware, etc. 33, 145

Boccaro ware, a term sometimes applied to unglazed red and brown Chinese (Yi-hsing) stoneware, frequently imitated in Prussia in the late 17th and early 18th centuries.

Body, in pottery, the name describing the mixture of materials in potter's clay before it is fired, used chiefly of earthenware and stoneware; see also **Paste.**

Bog oak, black wood of oak retrieved from peat bogs and used for decorative inlays from the 16th century; also from trunks deliberately immersed for a long period; also known as black oak.

Bohemian glass, ornamental glass from one of the chief European glassmaking regions (thanks to its natural resources), best known for the ruby glass first produced in the late 17th century; many other colours, and engraving of the highest quality for 400 years. 26, 114

Bois de rose: see **Tulipwood.**

Bois de Ste Lucie, rosewood.

Bois durci, 'hardened wood', a plastic material of sawdust and animal gelatins used for mouldings in the late 19th century.

Boiserie, carved wood panelling. See also **Chute, Trophy.** 28

Bois noirci: see **Ebonized wood.**

Bokhara carpets, woven by nomadic tribes and sold in Bokhara, wool and jute, Sehna knot, predominant pattern octagonal; associated particularly with a deep red, 'bull's blood' or 'Turcoman red'; the name covers a wide area. 30

Bokhara work, in quilts, coverlets, etc. from the region of Bokhara, characterized by stylized floral patterns embroidered in bright colours; 18th and 19th centuries.

Bolection, a moulding that covers the joint of two surfaces set at different levels, as on a recessed panel, etc.

Bologna pottery, notably large, solid basins, jugs and vases with moulded decoration, from the Renaissance to the 18th century; later, creamware in the English fashion.

Bolognino, a silver coin of many slightly different forms in medieval Italy, the original having been issued in Bologna.

Bolster, a long stuffed pillow, originally cylindrical; hence **bolster arm,** an arm of cylindrical shape on an upholstered chair.

Bombast, or bombace, originally cotton, subsequently any soft fibrous material used as stuffing or padding.

Bombazine, or bombazette, silk or cotton, in particular a black, silk and worsted twill used for mourning clothes.

Bombé, in furniture, particularly a chest or cabinet that swells out (like a bomb) and narrows toward the bottom; predominantly a French style, early 18th century; also in silver and ceramics. **40**

Bonanza, a rich silver- or gold-bearing ore; hence, colloquially, a rewarding discovery, usually as the outcome of deliberate search.

Bonaparte bird prints, coloured engravings by Audubon among others from Prince Lucien Bonaparte's volumes on American birds, about 1830; also lithographs from a later, French work.

Bonbonnière, or comfit box, a small box for sweets in silver, ceramic or japanned ware, sometimes of whimsical form, e.g. shaped and painted like a bird.

Bone ash, calcined animal bones, used as a flux in making glass and particularly porcelain.

Bone china, standard English porcelain first produced by Josiah Spode at Stoke-on-Trent about 1790, a mixture of china clay and stone whitened and strengthened by bone ash, between hard and soft-paste porcelain; **bone porcelain** usually refers to a strengthened variety of soft-paste porcelain.

Bone glass, glass made with bone ash added.

Bonegraces, or bonne grace, narrow curtains at the heads of beds to prevent a draught where the standard wide curtains came together; see also **Cantonnière.**

Bone lace, English pillow lace, so called because in the 16th century the bobbins were made from the bones of animals, and the pins of fishbones.

Bonheur du jour, a lady's desk, made in France from the mid 18th century, with fitted cabinet surmounting desk top often with pull-out extension, delicate painting or marquetry, slim lines; much reproduced in the 19th century. **31**

Bonnet piece, a gold coin issued in the reign of James V, King of Scots, and so named because the king, on the obverse, is wearing a Scottish bonnet.

Bonnet top, or hooded top, in case furniture a curved pediment (including broken pediments) that extends over the whole top, front-to-back.

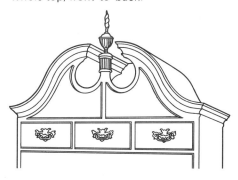

Bonnin & Morris porcelain, from a Philadelphia factory making porcelain, about 1770, in the manner of Bow (whence one proprietor probably came); the business lasted only three years, hence the rarity of its wares.

Boodh, a Buddha figure.

Booge, a term describing the curved part of a pewter plate between the rim and the bottom.

Book binding: see **Binding.**

Book box, a 17th-century carved-oak box probably for books and papers, often having a slanted top and thus serving as a desk; see also **Bible box.**

Book desk: see **Lectern.**

Book hinge, a metalwork (especially silver) hinge in a visible position, e.g. lid of a coffee pot, looking like the spine of a book.

Book mirror, a small mirror with folding cover, like a book, and often in leather; also in hinged wooden case, metal, ivory, etc.

Book rest, a rectangular wooden frame on a stand and held at an angle by a strut at the back, for propping up large books, from the early 18th century.

Book stand, a four-legged stand of more or less square shelves for holding books, sometimes with a drawer below the top.

Book stops, or book ends, heavy ornamental props for a shelf of books, sometimes fashioned of two metalwork half-figures that, placed together, make a whole; mid 19th century onward.

Bootjacks, cast iron, brass or wood implements with horseshoe-shaped element for levering off tight-fitting boots, mainly 18th century; including some humorous and mildly obscene forms.

Bootlegger's pistol, a percussion cap pistol with hammer below the barrel, as used by New England smugglers.

Boot tree, a wooden instrument for keeping the leg of a boot uncreased, consisting of a longitudinally split cylinder into which a wedge was driven.

Booz bottle, made by Whitney Glass Works for Edmund G. Booz, a Philadelphia whiskey merchant.

Borachio, an Italian or Spanish leather bottle of pig, sheep or goat skin, for wine.

Bordeaux, faience and porcelain from two or three factories in Bordeaux from the 18th century; faience characterized by designs associated with Mediterranean centres.

Bordesley tapestry: see **Barcheston tapestry.**

Bordshali-Kazak rugs, densely woven Caucasian carpets, mainly red and blue but with many other colours also, geometrical pattern with medallions or octagons and stylized flowers and animals.

Borlou carpets, Turkish carpets of slightly inferior quality, red or blue ground, stylized patterns, rather soft.

Bosom bottle, a minute bottle of glass or silver containing perfume, hung between the breasts in the 18th century, an age of low necklines.

Boss, a circular raised ornament, specifically the raised, cone-like centre of a shield; also the round relief carving at the junction of ribs in a Gothic vault, etc.; also, a plasterer's hod, a hassock; see also **Embossed.**

Boston chair, or New England chair, rather vague terms for cheap 18th-century American chairs; more particularly, leather-upholstered single chairs with broad splat and bended back in the Chinese style.

Boston glass, the products of a number of Boston (or Cambridge) glassworks in the 19th century, including the Boston Porcelain & Glass Co., early manufacturers of good-quality pressed glass, and the American Flint Glass Works; also silvered (mercury) glass.

Boston rocker, most famous of all American rocking chairs, related to the Windsor chair, characterized by rolled seat and stencilled decoration on a painted surface; produced in large quantities from the early 19th century.

Botdrager, 'pot wearer', a Flemish silver coin of the 14th century with, on the obverse, a lion wearing a helmet or 'pot'.

Boteh motif, in oriental carpets a design like a stylized pear, also known by a variety of other names; the motif found on Paisley shawls.

Botijo: see **Drug jar.**

Böttger porcelain, the earliest product of Meissen, under the supervision of J. F. Böttger, with a slightly yellow body, small bubbles in the glaze, low-relief decoration, about 1710–20; Böttger also made red stoneware in this period.

29 *Pygmalion and Galatea.* By E. M. Falconet, 1763. Sèvres biscuit ware. Falconet was director of the Sèvres factory 1757–66. (Musée des Arts Décoratifs, Paris)

30 Bokhara carpet. Turkestan, 19th century. The classic type, with recurring gul motif, from which all other Turkoman designs are derived. (Private Collection, Milan)

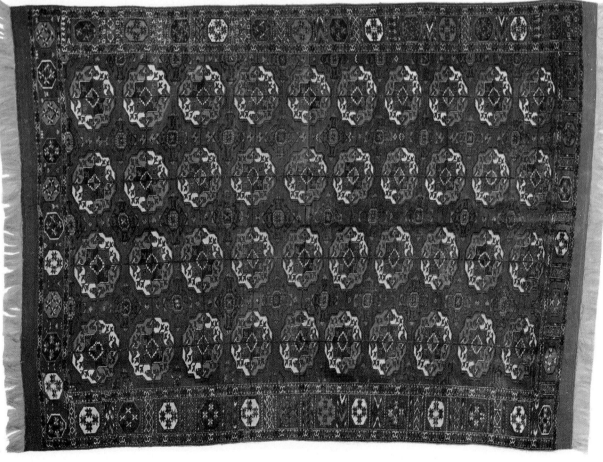

31 Louis XV bonheur du jour.
Designed by C. Topino, second half
of the 18th century. Mahogany with
brass mounts and inlay work.
(Musée des Arts Décoratifs, Paris)

32 Cabinet by André-Charles
Boulle (1642–1732) veneered in
ebony and inlaid. (Musée du
Louvre, Paris)

Bottle glass, cheap glass made of impure materials, which imparted the characteristic green or brown tone.

Bottle jack, a clockwork device in a bottle-shaped container for turning roast meat over a fire; see also **Clock jack.**

Bottle stopper: see **Jug head.**

Bottle tag, or ticket, a silver or enamelled label on a chain, engraved 'rum', 'madeira', etc., for hanging round the necks of bottles or decanters; from the early 18th century.

Bouclé, a pattern in relief on brocade or other heavy fabrics, attained by the incorporation of small metal loops or, later, by loops in the yarn itself.

Boulle furniture, sometimes spelt Buhl, from the workshop of the French craftsman, André-Charles Boulle (1642–1732), who supplied the palace at Versailles; in particular, a type of marquetry combining metal and tortoiseshell inlay; see also **Contre-partie. 32**

Bouquet table, a name sometimes given to a small, circular Victorian occasional table with tripod feet, on which a vase of flowers might stand.

Bourg-la-Reine, 18th-century French porcelain and faience which were made at this factory by Jullien and Jacques between 1774 and 1806. **189**

Bourne pottery, mainly stoneware, made by Bourne & Son of Denby, 19th century; a great variety of mainly utilitarian objects, heavy, hard-wearing and inexpensive.

Bourrelet, a roll of felt inside a woman's skirt to make it stand out in a manner similar to a farthingale, fashionable in 16th- and 17th-century France.

Bouzouki, a type of lute played in Greece and the Balkans, having a small, round-backed body and a long neck.

Bow, one of the most famous English porcelain factories of the 18th century, similar to a farthingale, fashionable in

bone ash introduced about 1750; perhaps best known for bright and graceful enamelled figures; some Bow porcelain is marked New Canton. **33**

Bow-back, a type of Windsor chair; see **Hoop-back.**

Bowenite, or californite, a green stone very similar in appearance and hardness to jade and often used as a substitute for it.

Bow-front, any piece of furniture, particularly an 18th-century cabinet or sideboard, the front of which forms a continuous, convex curve. **275**

Bowie knife, a heavy sheath knife with wide, curved blade up to 15 in long, favoured by James Bowie (1799–1836) and other Texas pioneers.

Bow tongs, sugar tongs made in one piece with spring imparted by the bow of the silver, like fire tongs and as distinct from scissors-type sugar tongs; from the early 18th century.

Box castor, a castor with a box- or cup-like receptacle for squared or rounded legs of furniture, usually brass; from the late 18th century.

Box end, a squared-off end on a bench or pew.

Box form, any piece of furniture in the general form of a box, including silver inkstands.

Box on frame, a predecessor of the chest in colonial America, consisting of a simple box mounted on a separately made frame.

Box pleat, a pleat sewn in square section.

Box toilet mirror, a mirror mounted on a box-like frame containing small drawers.

Boxwood, yellow or light brown wood, very hard and close-grained, used particularly in marquetry.

Brace, in carpentry and cabinetmaking, a member acting as a support or strengthener for other members, e.g. stretchers of a chair; in particular, a strut across a corner.

Bracelet, an ornamental band worn around the arm; in armour, a piece protecting the forearm; in furniture, a band or ring around a turned member such as a chair leg.

Bracket, a short, ornamental shelf, usually detachable, for china figures, busts, clocks, etc.; made in a variety of designs and media from the early 18th century.

Bracket clock, originally a wall clock with its own bracket support, now generally applied to any mantel or table clock.

Bracket foot, in case furniture, a supporting foot at the corner that projects slightly to the front (or back) and side of

the piece and is often curved in cabriole or ogee form.

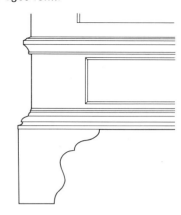

Bracteate, various silver coins circulating mainly in Germany in the Middle Ages, stamped on the reverse to make a type in relief on the obverse; also, any gold or silver ornament made in that way.

Bradford pewter, made by Cornelius Bradford of Philadelphia in the second half of the 18th century; a great variety of wares in the English style.

Bradwell Woodware, red stoneware mugs, teapots, beakers, etc., in imitation of contemporary Chinese imports, from the Bradwell Wood pottery, Staffordshire, late 17th century.

Braganza foot: see **Spanish foot.**

Braiding, a scrolled pattern in embroidery made with twisted thread; also, a similar pattern stamped on fabric.

Bramah lock, a late 18th-century predecessor of the Yale lock, a barrel lock turned by a small key.

Brameld pottery, brown, lightweight earthenware and cane-coloured stoneware made at the Rockingham, Yorkshire, pottery in the early 19th century when it was acquired by the Brameld family; also bone china of very fine quality with gorgeous enamelling and much gilt.

Brampton stoneware, from various potteries near Chesterfield, late 17th to late 19th century, brown stoneware mainly, sometimes with internal green glaze.

Brandenburg coat, a knee-length overcoat with broad, turned-down collar and loose sleeves, late 17th century.

Brandewijkom, an oval silver bowl with handles, for brandy and raisins; Dutch, late 17th century.

Brandishing, or brattishing, carved openwork in wood or stone, as in a frieze or crest.

Brandrith, a fence around a well; hence, an iron support, usually in tripod form, for a pot or kettle.

Brandy bowl, a wide, shallow silver bowl with two handles, used for serving heated brandy; 17th century.

Brandy saucepan, often applied to almost any small saucepan dating from about 1750 or earlier, some with hinged covers, some with lips, some straight-sided, some curved, etc.

Brandy tumbler, a drinking glass for brandy in 17th-century England which appears to have been a very wide, squat beaker with straight sides.

Brank, an instrument for punishing gossips and scolds, consisting of an iron frame fitting over the head with a protruding spike that entered the mouth and prevented speech.

Bras de cheminée, branched candle-holders for wall mounting (sconces) made in France from the 17th century in various media, including silver and bronze, but more often wood.

Brass, an alloy of copper and zinc in varying quantity according to period and place, sometimes with small amounts of other metals added; in use since ancient times; also, any small object (e.g. horse brasses) made of brass. **156**

Brass foot, any termination of furniture legs made of brass, sometimes in ornamental form; common in 18th-century furniture.

Brass rubbing, an impression of an ecclesiastical monumental brass made by placing paper over the brass and rubbing with a type of black chalk; a popular hobby in recent years.

Bratina, a kind of loving cup made in Russia, usually silver, sometimes gold, and richly decorated with enamelling and jewels.

Brazier, a brass or other metal container for burning charcoal etc., usually a shallow pan on footed stand, sometimes accompanied by tongs for applying

embers to a tobacco pipe; also applied to virtually any container for burning coals, from ash cans and portable stoves to chafing dishes and incense burners; also, a worker in brass and copper; hence, brasiery (brassware).

Brazilianite, a semi-precious stone first discovered in Brazil in the mid 20th century, yellow or yellowish-green in colour but too soft and brittle for jewellery.

Brazilwood, dark, reddish wood with dark brown markings, somewhat like mahogany, known since medieval times and frequently used in early 19th-century furniture.

Break, in furniture, any element in the design which breaks up the line of a piece, e.g. breakfront, broken pediment, etc.

Breakfast table, a small rectangular table with short hinged flaps supported on brackets with a drawer, mid 18th century.

Breakfront, any piece of furniture, typically 18th-century bookcases and cabinets, divided vertically into three sections with the central section projecting beyond the others; on large pieces, more than three sections may be involved.

Brewer busts, busts in parian ware of American celebrities produced by the Etruria pottery of Trenton, New Jersey, of which John H. Brewer was co-proprietor, in the second half of the 19th century.

Brewster chair, named after William Brewster of Plymouth colony who had one, an armchair with turned posts and spindles, maple or ash, a more ornamental version of the Carver.

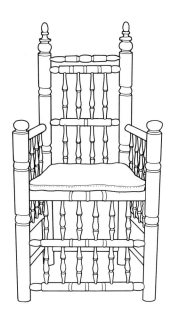

Brianchon, the smooth, nacreous lustre invented by J. J. H. Brianchon and associated particularly with parian ware in nautical forms made at Belleek.

Bric-à-brac, antique odds and ends, bits and pieces; probably applied to china oddments originally, now any miscellaneous lot, usually implying little value.

Bridal crown, a silver headdress, much ornamented, traditionally worn by the bride at weddings in Norway.

Bridgeport Knockdown, a piece of furniture made by the Furniture Manu-facturing Co. of Bridgeport, Connecticut, easily assembled or disassembled; 19th century.

Brigandine, a predecessor of the bullet-proof vest, consisting of a fabric and leather jacket lined with small over-lapping metal plates or densely studded; in use from the 15th century. **36**

Bright-cut, a form of engraving in silver in which an ornamental design is created by a succession of bevelled cuts, leaving facets that reflect light with extra bright-ness; see also **Brilliant cut.**

Brilliant cut, the method, invented in the 18th century, of cutting diamonds to make the most of their brilliance, also used for other stones in slightly varying forms.

Brin, the part of the blade of a fan nearest the hand.

Brisé fan, a type dating from the late 17th century, with very fine and flexible blades in ivory, horn or tortoiseshell, unmounted, and joined by a coloured silk ribbon; also a fan with a scene in oils painted on the blades on each side; made of various materials (including scented wood) in the 18th and early 19th centuries.

Brislington ware, delftware from Bris-lington, near Bristol, mid 17th to mid 18th century, usually classed with Bristol pottery.

Bristol diamonds, a generic term for English sham diamonds made by adding lead to flint glass, a method invented in the 18th century.

Bristol glass, usually describes any 18th-century English coloured glass, par-ticularly blue, though Bristol factories also made clear glass, and coloured glass was produced in other centres too.

Bristol porcelain, continued tradition of hard-paste porcelain begun at Ply-mouth in the second half of the 18th century; also soft-paste porcelain similar to early Worcester, and unglazed biscuit porcelain with applied decoration.

Bristol pottery, delftware from several potteries in Bristol in the 17th and 18th centuries, including puzzle jugs, figures,

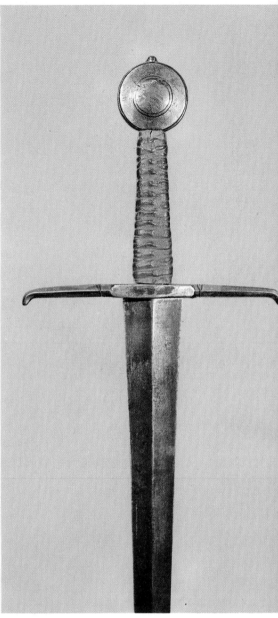

33 Pair of Bow candlesticks.
About 1760. The figures represent
two of the seasons, a popular
subject in the 18th century.
(London Museum, London)

34 Italian broadsword. 14th century.
A classic example, with a round
pommel and leather-covered hilt.
(Malacuda Collection, Milan)

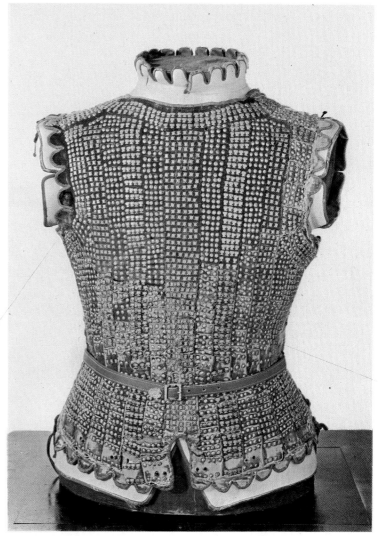

▲ 35

36

35 Chinese bronze wine vessel. Early Chou dynasty. Lei type with T'ao-t'ieh decoration. (Nezu Art Museum, Tokyo)

36 Brigandine. Mid 16th century. Brocade lined with leather and covered with ornate protective studs. (Instituto de Valencia de Don Juan, Madrid)

37 *Dying gladiator*. By Giovan Francesco Susini, Florentine, 16th century. This small Renaissance bronze is a copy of a Greek original. (Museo Nazionale del Bargello, Florence)

plaques, punchbowls, etc.; *bianco-sopra-bianco* decoration on greyish blue glaze is a Bristol characteristic.

Bristol shoes, in delftware with floral decoration, made at Bristol in the early 18th century in imitation of Dutch delft; also glass shoes.

Britannia metal, an alloy of tin and copper with antimony, sometimes including a little zinc; resembling silver fairly closely and taking polish better than most pewter; first used towards the end of the 18th century.

Britannia standard, in English silver, the higher standard (958·3 parts per 1000) introduced in 1697 to prevent plunder of the national coinage by silversmiths, the figure of Britannia being the standard mark. Not compulsory after 1720 when the two standards, sterling and Britannia were in use.

British plate, the name given to a nickel alloy used in Britain for a short period before about 1860, resembling silver and with marks deliberately similar to silver hallmarks.

Broadcloth, originally a cloth of double the normal width (i.e. two yards rather than one), a fine-quality, woven cloth used for men's clothes as well as furnishings.

Broad glass, sheet glass for windows, mirrors, etc., made from a blown hollow cylinder of glass, heated until it flattened out; a process not superseded until the 18th century.

Broadsheet, or broadside, a large sheet of paper printed on one side only, usually as advertisement, propaganda or plain news; from the 17th century.

Broadsword, a straight sword with a double-edged blade, some for two-handed use, lighter types worn by 17th-century cavalry. **34**

Brocade, a decorative fabric in which the pattern is woven with supplementary wefted threads; for garments and upholstery from the 17th century.

Brocaded Imari, Japanese porcelain in red, blue and gold, in a style imitated in much English porcelain in the late 18th century (e.g. Derby brocaded).

Brocatelle, cloth imitating brocade and used for similar purposes; sometimes applied to furniture upholstered with this material.

Broched, ornamentally embroidered material, e.g. brocade.

Broderie anglaise, needlework in which holes are pricked in the material and oversewn around the edges, used chiefly for trimmings.

Broken arch, particularly in mantel clocks, an arched top the diameter of which is less than the width of the clock, so that it terminates in horizontal extensions; see also **Broken pediment.**

Broken cabriole, a term sometimes applied to an early cabriole form in which the outward curve is more pronounced and almost makes an angle.

Broken front: see **Breakfront.**

Broken pediment, case furniture with a triangular or arched pediment which 'breaks off' short of the apex to leave a central space, usually containing an ornament of some kind. **64**

Bronze, an alloy of copper and tin (usually with small amounts of other metals) which, unlike brass, can be easily cast and has been chiefly used for that purpose; at first golden-yellow but darkens with time, acquires bright green deposit if unprotected, vulnerable to air pollution; also, any small figure, ornament, etc. in bronze. **35, 37, 57**

Bronze argent: see **German silver.**

Bronze doré, 'gilt bronze', the French term for what in English is usually called ormolu.

Bronze powder, a metallic powder (not usually bronze) in many colours, some natural, some achieved chemically, used for decorative purposes in the 19th century, e.g. for designs on papier-mâché, oriental scenes being especially popular.

Bronzite, a stone occurring in crystalline form in igneous rocks with a lustre like bronze.

Brooch, an ornament, often decorated with jewels, worn fastened to a dress with a clasp or other fastening device.

Brooklyn glass, products of several factories in Brooklyn, New York, in the 18th and 19th centuries, including Brooklyn Flint Glass Co. (good cut glass) which moved to Corning about 1870.

Broseley pipes, clay tobacco pipes made at Brosely, Staffordshire, from the early 17th century.

Brownfield pottery, from the Albion Works at Cobridge, by William Brownfield, mid 19th century; many types of earthenware including figures in enamelled bone china, early examples of 'basketwork' decoration, dinner service designed by the caricaturist, Phiz, etc.

Brown gold, a method of gilding ceramics, current in the mid 19th century, with a thin paste containing gold chloride which, after burnishing, produced brilliant and lasting gilding.

Brownhills, a Staffordshire pottery making, among other ware, transfer-printed salt-glazed plates, about 1760.

Brunstrom pewter, made in Philadelphia in the late 18th century, probably by at least two pewterers of that name.

Brunswick faience, from two factories in 18th-century Brunswick (Braunschweig), including blue and white ware after Delft and Rudolph Chely's Rococo figures and dishes.

Brussels carpets, a generic name for moquette carpets woven with heavy wool and linen, based on contemporary French designs, from the 16th century.

Brussels lace, famous for quantity and quality since the Middle Ages, including needlepoint and pillow lace, with many characteristic designs.

Brussels tapestry, made since the 16th century, in general slightly inferior to the contemporary French tapestries that it resembled.

Buckler, a small, round shield, usually leather, useful for warding off blows from different angles; also, a wooden shutter over the hawser (cable) holes in ships.

Buckram, a thin, fine-quality cotton and linen fabric; also, a coarse cloth or canvas stiffened with gum or paste and used for linings, etc.

Buddha spoon, a silver spoon made at one or two places in the south of England in the late 17th century (reproduced later) with a finial in the form of an oriental figure.

Bude lamp, one of the many variations on the Argand lamp, with several concentric wicks for brighter illumination.

Buen Retiro porcelain, from the factory established near Madrid in 1760 to supply the Spanish court, early work marked with fleur-de-lis; notable Rococo figures by Giuseppe Gricci and, a famous feat, an entire porcelain-furnished room in the Aranjuez Palace. **39**

Buffalo willow-pattern, willow-pattern plates made in America in a variation that depicts a child riding a buffalo.

Buff coat, either a full-skirted coat of buff-coloured leather, stout enough to resist a sword thrust, or a tight-fitting leather waistcoat laced over the chest.

Buffet, an alcove, perhaps in a corner, with shelves above and (usually) a cupboard beneath; before the 18th century, the word may have meant a sideboard and it is often used in that sense today.

Buffet chair, an upholstered chair; a low stool with central S-shaped cut for lifting is sometimes called a buffet stool.

Bufford prints, by the 19th-century American lithographer, John H. Bufford, chiefly prints of railroad locomotives, less commonly marine subjects.

Buggin bowls, early English lead-glass bowls named after Butler Buggin, whose arms are engraved on the only known examples of these late 17th-century vessels.

Bugle horn, a drinking vessel made of horn and shaped like a huntsman's bugle.

Bugle work, 19th-century ornamentation incorporating elongated beads (bugles).

Buhl work, marquetry in the manner of Boulle; see **Boulle furniture**.

Bukhara carpets: see **Bokhara carpets**.

Bulb, in a turned member, a thick, rounded, giant knop of roughly melon shape, the resemblance to the fruit often heightened by gadrooning; found on chair legs and stretchers of the late 16th and 17th centuries. **68**

Bulla, an Etruscan gold pendant, probably used for holding scent, sometimes in the shape of a head (man or lion).

Bull's eye, a small mirror with curved surface, surrounded by an ornate frame, popular in the early 19th century; also, a central drop in a pane of glass.

Bulto, carved wooden (commonly cottonwood roots) figure covered with gesso and painted, a religious image of the type called *santo*, from New Mexico, mostly late 18th or early 19th century; recent imitations common.

Bumper, originally a firing glass with heavy stem and foot to withstand approbatory thumping; the term is sometimes used to mean any extra-large drinking vessel.

Bumroll: see **Bourrelet**.

Buncombe silhouettes, painted silhouettes by J. Buncombe from the Isle of Wight, showing colourful naval uniforms with faces in silhouette.

Bun foot, a ball foot slightly flattened, found on furniture from the second half of the 17th century, often brass.

Bun foot

Bunting, thin woollen material from which flags, etc. were made.

Bureau, a desk with lid sloping at an angle of about 45° that folds out as a writing table, with drawers beneath; made from the late 17th century; the word is loosely defined and includes various pieces that may be described by other names (e.g. escritoire, secretaire); sometimes called a bureau desk. **91**

Bureau bed, a bed hinged in three sections that folded up into a chest shaped like a bureau, the entire front lifting from the base to release the bed; made in the 18th century but (not surprisingly) never popular.

Bureau bookcase, a bureau surmounted by a bookcase, usually glazed; from the mid 18th century, a common combination.

Bureau dressing table, several 18th-century designs including a small bureau with only two drawers on cabriole legs and surmounted by a mirror; later and better-known types of the Chippendale period were not basically different from the desks.

Burgomaster's chair: see **Roundabout chair**.

Burgonet, a helmet favoured by 17th-century cavalry with crested crown, short peak and hinged chin piece.

Burin, a sharp-pointed tool used in engraving a copper-plate.

Burlingtonian, an adjective derived from Lord Burlington, advocate and practitioner of the Palladian style in English architecture and decoration, a rather formal version of Palladian Classicism.

Burmese glass, coloured glass, yellow to pink, made by the Mount Washington Glass Co. in New Bedford, Massa-chusetts, late 19th century, decorative and utilitarian; an English version made under licence is known as 'Queen's Burmese'.

Burnishing, polishing, chiefly metal; in particular, polishing marks off silver with steel or stone.

Burnt ware, i.e. ware that has been fired (e.g. pottery) distinguished from ware that has not (e.g. wood).

Burr, the rough edge left when metal is engraved; in certain techniques, the burr forms part of the decoration.

Burr wood, cut from a protuberance on the tree (frequently walnut, elm or yew), caused by disease or malformation, and interestingly figured; used as veneer or for other decorative purposes since the 16th century.

Bursa rugs, prayer rugs from northern Turkey in blue, red and cream, silk and cotton, short pile and rather inferior quality, being inclined to lose their gloss quickly.

Burslem, the pottery-making district in Staffordshire (and home of the Wedgwoods) in the 17th century, where many techniques were pioneered.

Bussa, a large earthenware pot for salted fish.

Bussu, a coarse, strong fabric made from the spathes of the South American bussu palm.

Bust, a sculpture of head and shoulders.

Bustle, in Victorian dress, a horseshoe-shaped frame of hoops like a cage, worn under the skirt, allowing the fabric to fall in folds like a curtain behind the wearer.

Busybody, an arrangement of mirrors that, placed in an upstairs window, permitted a view of anyone standing at the front door; used in the 18th century and also known under various other names.

Butler's tray, a wooden, silver or other metal tray that rested on a collapsible X-shaped support; 18th century.

Butter boat, a small silver vessel, vaguely boat-shaped, probably intended for holding melted butter; 18th century.

Butter cooler, a two-handled china dish with pierced cover and compartment for iced water below the tray on which the butter was placed.

Butterfly table, a drop-leaf table associated with colonial America in which the solid supports, rather remotely suggesting a butterfly's wings, swing from a pivot in the bottom stretcher and a hinge in the top board; canted legs.

38 Faience bowl in the shape of a cabbage. Strasbourg, 18th century. (Musée des Arts Décoratifs, Paris)

39 Buen Retiro porcelain clock. 18th century. Attributed to Carlo Shepers, director of the factory, 1770–83. (Museo Arqueologico Nacional, Madrid)

40 Three tea caddies. Left to right: Rococo style with shell and scroll motifs, 1778; square with hinged lid, 1769; and bombé shaped with Chinoiserie figures and Rococo scrolls, 1765. (Private Collection)

39

40

41 Cake basket by Paul de Lamerie, 1731. Latticed sides decorated with flowers and rope patterned handles. (Ashmolean Museum, Oxford)

42 Cafaggiolo maiolica plate with fight scenes, 1515–20. The design includes medallions in the border and scenes of heroes and centaurs fighting. (Fitzwilliam Museum, Cambridge)

Butternut, an American tree of the walnut family. **64**

Butter tester, an 18th-century device, a silver rod semicircular at the end for dipping into butter in order to extract a sample from the centre.

Buttery, a room or cellar, sometimes just a large cupboard, in which wine was stored.

Button, in furniture, a simple door fastener, rectangular and pivoting from the centre to allow the door to be opened or closed; usually metal; also discs or knobs on clothing normally serving as fastenings.

Buttoning, in 19th-century upholstered furniture, a regular pattern of large buttons, covered in the same material as the rest, gathering the fabric into folds and concealing the stitching that fastens it to the back of the piece.

Buttonwood, from the American plane, a hard, reddish wood not easy to work and not very durable, though used in chair-making since the 17th century.

Buttress pillars, imitations of the buttress in Gothic architecture, appearing (for instance) on early Gothic clocks.

Buzuk, an Arabian lute similar to the Greek bouzouki.

Bygones, a somewhat whimsical term describing a limitless variety of historical objects, particularly household articles, which having no artistic pretensions are considered unworthy of the name 'antiques'; their value, however, tends to increase just as rapidly.

Byssus, or byssinel, a fine-quality cloth, either silk or having the appearance of silk, worn in ancient times.

Byzantine, the style of art and architecture developed in Byzantium, the Eastern Roman Empire, during the 5th and 6th centuries AD; attributively also the style derived from, or influenced by, the Byzantine. **120**

Cabaret, a tea set, consisting of matching teapot, milk jug, sugar basin, cups and saucers (sometimes only one) and tray; usually porcelain.

Cabas, or caba, originally a large, flat, rushwork basket for figs, and hence a woman's flat workbasket or reticule.

Cabbage cutter, an implement for making cole slaw, consisting of a narrow, rimmed board (about the width of a cabbage) with a blade set in it to slice up the cabbage as it was drawn back and forth.

Cabbage ware, Worcester china with relief decoration of cabbage leaves; an illusionistic style also popular in Europe; see also **Cauliflower ware.**

Cabinet, a relatively small piece of case furniture fitted with small drawers, shelves and cupboards, which was first made widely in Europe in the late 17th century and was particularly suitable for demonstrating the finer points of the cabinet-

maker's craft; later cabinets often much larger.

Cabinet hardware, i.e. hinges, handles, locks, etc. of chests and case furniture, of wrought iron or brass ('brasses') which, when original, are a guide to the age of the piece concerned.

Cabinetmaker, a maker of fine-quality furniture, i.e. a craftsman superior to a carpenter or a joiner; the term came into use in the late 17th century with the adoption of veneering; corresponding to the French *ébéniste.*

Cabinet-on-stand, an early 17th-century cabinet with glazed or panelled doors set on cabriole legs; later examples heavy and ornate.

Cabinet pedestal table, a small table with three feet and cupboard below.

Cabinet piece, a term of approval, meaning a good-quality piece; also **cabinet wood,** wood fit for cabinet-making.

Cabinet writing table, a cabinet on four legs with pull-out board.

Cable moulding, convex moulding in the shape of a twisted rope, seen in architecture and on furniture, particularly after the Battle of Trafalgar (1805).

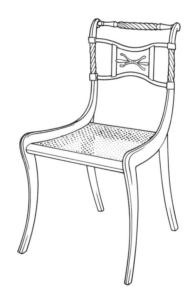

Cabochon, an old style (though still current) of cutting precious stones in domed shape; also, moulding of a similar pattern, in particular a raised oval surrounded by a rim.

Cabriole, a word implying a certain shape (see Cabriole leg), including a small armchair, a two-wheeled carriage or cabriolet.

Cabriole leg, the most common distinguishing feature in chairs, etc. from the late 17th to the late 18th century (and often revived since); a leg that curves outward forming a knee, then curves inward, tapering, to the foot, something like the hind leg of a goat; originally from China (and there over 2,000 years old). **56**

Cabriolet fan, a late 18th-century fan with silk bands, showing a cabriolet (two-wheeled carriage), owned by the owner of the fan.

Cachmere: see **Cashmere.**

Cachemire, a style of decoration in pottery associated with large Delft vases, a rather dense floral pattern in rich colours, based on oriental models.

Cache pot: see **Jardinière.**

Cachet, a seal on a letter (*lettre de cachet*); also, the silver cylinder in which the seal was kept.

Caddy, or catty, a small container for tea, silver, tortoiseshell, porcelain and, most commonly, wood, lined with lead and usually having two compartments (or two matching caddies) for two kinds of tea and a cut-glass bowl for blending them. **40**

Caddy spoon, a silver spoon for removing tea from a caddy, short-handled (to go inside the caddy) and bowl almost invariably of fanciful design (leaves, shells, caps, wings, etc.); not found before the late 18th century.

Cadogan teapot, an earthenware teapot with no lid, imitating the Chinese 'peach' wine jug, English, late 18th century, allegedly commissioned (or imported) by Mrs Cadogan; filled through the bottom via a tube which ended just short of the top and thus unspillable.

Cafaggiolo maiolica, Florentine Renaissance maiolica from the variously spelled Medici pottery, sometimes bearing Medici arms, and influenced by Botticelli, Donatello, and others, with notably vigorous painting in the early 16th century; subsequently less distinguished. **42**

Caffoy, or caffaws, a plush fabric used in 18th-century upholstery; see also **Flock-printed cloth.**

Cage cup, a glass drinking vessel decorated with a cage-like pattern, found in Roman glass; an effect probably achieved by grinding away the superfluous glass.

Caillouté, a pebbled gold effect on blue ground as seen in certain French soft-paste porcelain of the mid 18th century.

Cabriole leg

Cairngorm, a smoky quartz stone, yellowish brown, found in the Scottish Highlands; see also **Citrine.**

Cake basket, usually silver, or silver-gilt, dating from the second half of the 16th century; later examples (early 18th century) oval, with pierced bodies and swing handles; also used for bread, fruit or dessert. 41

Cake table, two sloping-sided tin pans soldered together at the bottom to create a waisted stand useful for manoeuvring a cake when icing it.

Calabash, a large oval gourd used as a vessel for liquids in the 17th century, and hence an earthenware vessel of that shape, originating and still used in Africa.

Calamander: see **Coromandel.**

Calash, a small carriage, or the hood of a carriage.

Calcedonio, or schmelzglas, marbling effect in glass suggesting precious stones, particularly aventurine.

Caldron: see **Cauldron.**

Caleche: see **Calash.**

Calendar clock, a clock that records the day, month and year as well as the hour and minute; rare types have a wheel with four-year revolution, never needing adjustment.

Calender, a machine in which cloth (or paper) is pressed between rollers to achieve a smooth or glossy surface; see also **Watered cloth.**

Calico, or calicut, an oriental, white cotton cloth imported from Calcutta before about 1800; subsequently, similar European cloth; used especially for printing, from the 17th century.

Californite, an ornamental green stone found in California.

Caliver, an early musket, fired from the shoulder without a rest, presumably of a fixed calibre (hence its name), mentioned by Shakespeare.

Calligraphy, the art of handwriting or fine penmanship, used decoratively by oriental artists (especially in China and Persia) in brushwork decoration on pottery, for example.

Calliope, a pipe organ played from a keyboard and operated by steam, once a feature of circuses, etc., and named (presumably) after the epic muse.

Callot figure, a figure in metal or earthenware after the grotesque figures in the etchings of the French artist, Jacques Callot (1592–1635); also in glass.

Calorifere, a stove, in particular a portable stove or one used for heating greenhouses.

Calotype: see **Talbotype.**

Caltrop, or caltrap, an iron ball armed with four metal spikes so arranged that however it falls one spike is always

sticking up; a medieval weapon against cavalry.

Calumet, the peace pipe of the North American Indians, usually a long stem of reed and clay bowl, variously ornamented.

Cama de bilros, a type of bed popular in 17th-century Spain and Portugal, characterized by elaborate and inventive turning and carving.

Camaïeu, painting *en camaïeu* is in various tones of one basic colour, a phrase frequently occurring with reference to the decoration of pottery.

Camail, in armour, a chain-mail curtain attached to the helmet to protect the neck.

Cambrian pottery, from the Swansea pottery where William Billingsley produced his porcelain for a short time in the early 19th century (but less attractively than at Nantgarw); also, a variety of other wares under different proprietors.

Cambric, originally linen of very good quality (good enough for King Henry VIII's shirts) from the Flemish town of Cambrai, but subsequently applied to inferior imitations and to fine cotton cloth.

Cambridge glass, very early American pressed glass, as well as cut, from Cambridge, near Boston, in the early 19th century; overshadowed after Deming Jarves left to found the Boston & Sandwich Glassworks.

Camel-back, a term sometimes applied to certain Chippendale-style chairs or sofas in which the top rail is curved at each end with a larger, upward curve in the centre; rails with a central depression between two upward curves (or 'humps') are also sometimes called camel-backs.

Cameo, a precious stone or shell with design cut in relief, often in another colour or another stone; also, a similar technique in other materials. **197**

Cameo glass, glassware made of layers of glass in which the outer layer is cut away so that the background shows through in the differently coloured under-layer; a rare and difficult technique, practised by the Romans but subse-

quently almost unknown until the 19th century; see also **Crystallo-ceramie.**

Cameo parian, porcelain with two-colour cameo effect in which, initially (mid 19th century), a rich blue was imparted to the background, setting off the (unglazed) white relief decoration; later other colours were introduced.

Camera lucida, an early 19th-century instrument that projected an image through a four-sided prism so that, to an eye placed exactly at the edge of the prism, an image that could be traced appeared on an adjacent sheet of paper; various types, resulting from modifications, were made before the advent of the camera.

Camera obscura, a device for projecting an image through a lens on to a blank surface, known in principle by Aristotle but not converted into a practical, box-like instrument until the late 17th century.

Camis, or chemise, a woman's shift or under-garment; hence, a thin cotton or linen cloth.

Camisarde, a shirt worn over armour or uniform to identify friend from foe.

Camlet, or chamblet, originally an expensive cloth, made of wool, goat's hair, silk or cotton and imported to England from the East in the 15th century; subsequently made in England and used for bed hangings.

Campaign button, a cheap stick pin worn by partisans during American political campaigns, a fairly recent development but already including some 'collector's items'.

Campaign furniture, or camp furniture, chests and lightweight, portable furniture made for armies on the march, particularly from the Napoleonic period.

Campaign handkerchief, forerunner of the campaign button, made in America since the mid 19th century.

Campeachy wood, Caribbean logwood, for dyes.

Camp furniture, made by William Camp of Baltimore in the early 19th century; also, light, folding chairs and tables; see **Camp stool; Campaign furniture.**

Camphene lamp, any lamp, particularly so-called 'safety lamps', made for burning camphene, a fuel consisting basically of alcohol and turpentine, bright-burning but dangerous, mid 19th century.

Camphor glass, mainly American pressed glass, white, and semi-opaque; also, blown-moulded glass of similar appearance.

Camp stool, a light, X-shaped folding stool with leather or canvas seat.

Camwood, from a West African redwood tree, providing a dye used in woollens.

Can, or cann, a flat-bottomed, cylindrical, metal mug with handles.

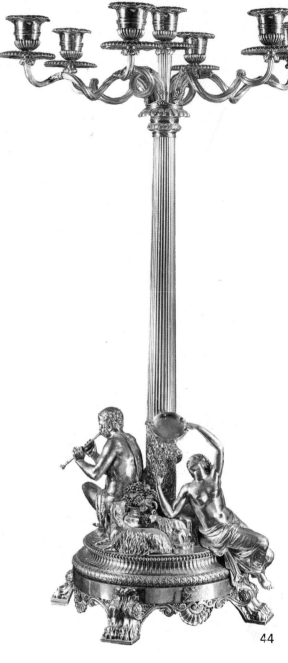

43

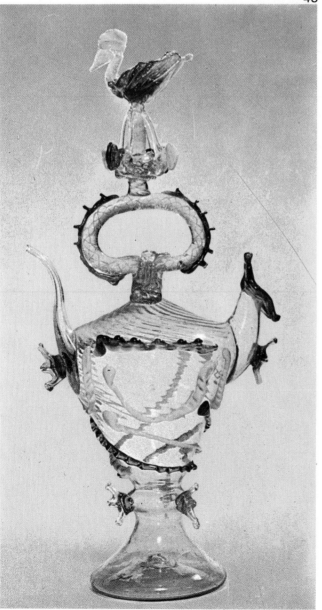

44

43 Louis XVI canapé by George Jacob, with the high back and loose cushions typical of these early settees. (Château de Fontainebleau)

44 Silver-gilt candelabrum designed by the Regency silversmith, Paul Storr, in 1814. One of a pair, height 37 in. At the base of the fluted column is a pastoral scene with Pan playing the pipes, and a nymph with a tambourine and goats. (The Worshipful Company of Goldsmiths, London)

45 Blown-glass cantaro. Catalonian, 18th century. A highly decorated example of a normally mundane vessel. (Corning Museum of Glass, Corning, New York)

46 Detail of a jewellery cabinet designed by Jean-Ferdinand Schwerdfeger for Marie Antoinette. Mahogany with gilt bronze caryatids, mother of pearl, and porcelain plaques. (Palace of Versailles)

47 Cassone of painted and gilded wood. Florentine, 15th century. The painting shows the architecture and costume of Renaissance Florence; carved cupids lounge in niches between pilasters at each corner; lion's-paw feet. (Victoria and Albert Museum, London)

Canadian birch, reddish-brown wood with well-marked, undulating grain, sometimes used for cabinetmaking.

Canalboat furniture, generally small-scale and sturdy, often brightly painted articles including cabinets and chests of drawers made for canal boats from the early 19th century; also, more elaborate fittings for the big paddle-steamers.

Canal horn, a brass horn used by boatmen to signal their approach, probably not made especially for this purpose, but for stage coaches, hunting, etc.

Canapé, a French sofa or settee of the Louis XV period (and later) with high, unbroken back, often with auxiliary cushions and closed ends (*canapé à confidante*). **43**

Canary resist, early 19th-century English pottery made with the resist lustre process in which the ground was a bright canary yellow.

Canary wood, a rather vague term applied to various straight-grained woods, including a type of mahogany.

Candelabrum, a candlestick with two or more branches; usually in pairs or sets, often silver or brass, but also of many other materials, made since the Middle Ages, but largely functional and plain until the 18th century. **44, 111**

Candlebeam, a form of chandelier, having two wooden boards in X-shape with candles on the ends.

Candlebox, a plain wooden or metal box, square or cylindrical, for storing household candles and hung by the fireplace.

Candle case, a cylindrical glass shade with metal fitting to adjust to any candlestick, for preserving candle flame from draught.

Candle mould, for making candles (from tallow) in the home, in various shapes and sizes for making from one to fifty candles at a time, usually tin-plate but also other metal.

Candlescreen, a small, adjustable screen to be placed on a writing table so that the candlelight shining on the paper is not reflected in the writer's eyes.

Candle snuffer, a metal instrument for trimming wicks, looking like a pair of scissors with (usually) a small box for the trimmed wick; also, a cone-shaped extinguisher with handle, or candle thimble; sometimes silver or brass sets of such an instrument with a tray or stand; see also **Douter. 273**

Candlestick, a candle-holder usually (and before about 1750 exclusively) in columnar form; though common since the 18th century, rather rare earlier; silver, brass, porcelain, etc. **33, 80**

Candle trumpet, a candlestick in the form of an inverted trumpet ('mouthpiece' at the top) with handle.

Candlewick, thick cotton cord, like the wick of a candle, used in embroidering bedspreads; also, the linen or cotton cloth on which candlewicking was done.

Candlewood, wood (in colonial America usually pine) that is rich in resin and, split up into narrow pieces, burns brightly; a substitute for candles.

Cane furniture, chairs with seats and/ or backs made from woven rattan cane imported to Europe from Malaya; occasionally used for stands and table tops as well; sometimes applied to bamboo furniture; first popular in the late 17th century.

Canes, the drawn-out coloured rods which make up the pattern in millefiori glass. **13, 182**

Canette, a straight-sided jug for serving hot toddy, often with hunting scenes, in Chesterfield and similar ware, late 19th century.

Cane ware, Josiah Wedgwood's name for one of his fine stonewares, referring to the colour, which varied from cream to light brown, resembling pastry and therefore used for pie-crust ware; also sometimes brightly decorated; ironstone cane ware, developed in the mid 19th century, was one of the earliest oven-proof wares; see also **Bamboo ware**.

Can hook: see **Cant hook**.

Canions, ornamental rolls like sausages around the ends of the legs of breeches, i.e. just below the knee.

Canister, a small silver box or receptacle; also, a basket for flowers, etc; see **Caddy**.

Cannel, a type of coal, very hard, which could be polished and was sometimes carved into ornaments, from the 17th century.

Cannon stove, a large cylinder stove of a type made as early as the 15th century in the Netherlands and particularly associated with colonial Pennsylvania, usually rather large, for heating assembly rooms, churches, etc.

Canoe cruet, a cruet having a silver stand shaped like a canoe, i.e. relatively long and narrow and rising at the ends.

Canopy, over a bed, a tester. **104**

Cantagalli maiolica, from the factory founded by Ulysse Cantagalli in Florence in the late 19th century, producing high-quality ware in the Italian Renaissance tradition as well as oriental styles and rather restrained Art Nouveau vases.

Cantaro, or cantir, a glass vessel for drinking-water, made in Mediterranean countries in the 18th century (and probably centuries earlier), with two spouts, a large one for filling and a small one for pouring. **45**

Canted, meaning the same as bevelled (i.e. inclined at an angle) but generally used of a larger plane (e.g. 'bevelled edge' but 'canted roof').

Canteen, a portable water container for travellers; or a large urn of silver, pewter, etc. with tap for dispensing liquid refreshment; or a set of silver tableware in a case.

Canterbury, a stand on four legs, with rounded back, containing partitions for plates and cutlery which stood by the supper table; also, a music stand with divisions for papers, journals, etc.; according to Sheraton, named for a late 18th-century archbishop who ordered such a piece; many designs.

Cantering horse, apparently a 19th-century advance on the rocking horse, mounted on wheels and propelled by the up-and-down motion of its rider; also called a **velocipede horse**.

Cant hook, or can hook, a long-handled lever with an iron catch at the end for manipulating logs; also (can hook), a flat iron hook that, attached to a rope, was (and is) used for shifting large barrels.

Cantilever, a projecting support, like a bracket.

Cantir: see **Cantaro**.

Canton china, a general term for the Chinese porcelain imported in the 18th century after the reopening of the port of Canton, in particular the blue and white ware that was the chief item of trade in the early years; see also **Nankin china, Blue and white ware**.

Canton enamel, enamelled copper ware in *famille rose* style, imported from Canton from the 18th century.

Cantonnière, a narrow curtain at the corners of the valances at the foot of a bed; see also **Bonegraces.**

Cantoon, a thick, twilled cloth.

Canvas, cloth originally made (probably) from hemp, but also from flax, jute, cotton, etc., and often of double warp in order to withstand hard use, notably as sails of ships, chair seats, etc.; lighter varieties used for embroidery and oil-painting.

Canvas work, a type of embroidery in which the stitches (mainly cross stitch and tent stitch) make a dense pattern on a canvas ground; see also **Berlin work. 264**

Caoutchouc, a vegetable gum that is the main constituent of rubber; a hard, white solid at freezing point, but becoming soft and translucent on a hot day.

Capacity mug, stoneware or earthenware mug or beaker used for measuring a specific quantity of beer, etc., from the 17th century.

Cape Cod glass, in particular the pressed and cut glass in many forms produced by the Cape Cod Glass Co. in the second half of the 19th century.

Capital, the decorative head of a column.

Capodimonte porcelain, from the factory established in Naples in the mid 18th century, in particular creamy soft-paste porcelain figures modelled by Giuseppe Gricci; also a porcelain room for the wife of the King of Naples, a feat repeated at Buen Retiro, where the Capodimonte factory was moved. **39**

Cappadocian pottery, hand-made vessels of heavy, fired clay with painted decoration, from the region of Cappadocia, Anatolia, about 2000 BC.

Capstan, a familiar quayside object for winding on ships' ropes, consisting of a revolving drum with horizontal poles, shaped like a drum with inward curving sides; hence, such a shape in pottery, silver, turnery, etc.

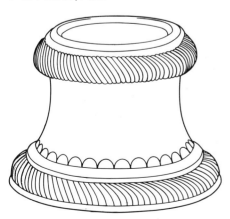

Capstan table, or compass table, a round, pedestal table with drawers; see also **Drum table.**

Captain's chair, the name sometimes given to a variety of low-backed Windsor chair, with heavy, semicircular top rail, the central raised portion of which is made separately.

Capuchine, a stoneware drinking vessel first made at Nottingham about 1700 which, when turned upside down, resembled the sharp-pointed capuche, or hood, worn by Franciscan friars.

Caput, a head, hence 'caput bottle', etc.

Caqueteuse, or caquetoise, a French conversation chair, with a seat wide at the front and narrower at the back, with high back and arms curved outward, apparently designed to accommodate bulky skirts.

Carafe, an open-topped glass vessel, for water or wine, shaped like a bottle, an inverted cone, or an oval, popular on 18th-century tables and then usually engraved; subsequently relegated to the bedroom.

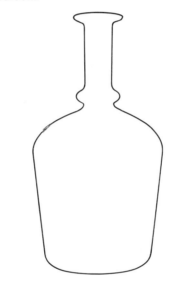

Carat, a unit of measurement determining the value of precious stones and metals; in diamonds a weight, in gold a unit representing one twenty-fourth (thus 24-carat gold is pure gold).

Carbine, a small firearm fired from the shoulder, suitable for cavalry; a rifle.

Carbon oil lamp, an early (mid 19th century) lamp for burning kerosene (paraffin in England), sometimes called carbon oil at that time.

Carboy, a large glass vessel often with a protective wickerwork frame, especially for acids, etc.

Carbuncle, an almandine garnet, deep, bluish red, cut as a hollow cabochon, often displaying a cat's-eye effect.

Carcase, in furniture, the basic structure without the final surface or veneer.

Carcel lamp, first made about 1800, an oil lamp that overcame the problem of supplying fuel to the wick by pumping it up from the reservoir by clockwork; made in brass and other metal.

Card case, a flat box the size of a man's pocketbook with a hinged lid at one end, in silver or other material, for visiting cards, from the late 18th century.

Card table, or gaming table, generally any small table, usually cloth-covered, suitable for playing cards; also, tables made especially for the purpose, including medieval boards marked up for chess and backgammon and the profusion of 18th-century tables, often folding, or including cavities for chips, etc.

Cark, a 16th-century (or earlier) term for a cartload, of three or four hundredweight; also, a cart.

Carlino, various gold or silver coins issued in the late 13th century by Charles II of Naples.

Carlton House desk, strictly, a late 18th-century writing table in mahogany or satinwood of the type commissioned for the Prince of Wales's residence, with a D-shaped superstructure of small drawers and pigeonholes at the back and sides and, usually, a brass gallery.

Carolean, or Caroline, terms sometimes used to describe the English style of furniture and design in the reigns of the Stewart Kings Charles I and (more particularly) Charles II.

Carousel, a tourney in which horsemen executed spectacular movements, also a merry-go-round; hence, the moving figures that appear on some Renaissance (and later) turret clocks, set in motion every hour, half-hour, etc.; or, the wooden horses, swans, etc., beloved by restaurant decorators, that once served on a merry-go-round.

Carpet, usually, a strong, woven fabric (generally with a cotton or linen warp and a woollen weft and pile) laid on the floor; but also the same fabric used for other purposes; floor carpets were not used in England before the 16th century and rare then, and the word originally meant hangings or drapes; sometimes made in cross-stitch.

Carpetbag, a soft 19th-century travelling bag made of carpet fabric.

Carpet bowls, earthenware balls, somewhat larger than billiard balls, made in a variety of patterns and colours during the 19th century for playing a game of indoor bowls.

Carpet cutter, a term humorously applied in the 19th century to a rocking chair with narrow, edge-on rockers, the drawbacks of which the name graphically implies.

Carrack porcelain, one of the numerous general terms describing Chinese porcelain, in this case the blue and white ware initially imported by the Portuguese in their carracks in the late 16th century.

Carrara, Italian marble; also, 19th-century English parian figures; or modelled stoneware by Doulton.

Carriage carpet, a small oriental rug, padded and used as a cushion in carriages.

Carriage clock, made for travelling by coach, a clock with one of several devices to alleviate the bumps of rough roads and wooden wheels, of which the sim-

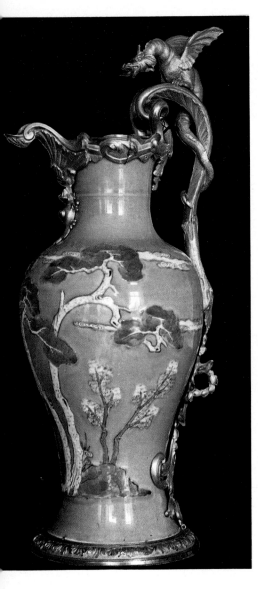

49▲

48 Chinese celadon vase with ormolu mount. A typical example of the 18th-century European urge to 'improve' on oriental art. (Musée du Louvre, Paris)

49 Ribbed ewer and basin. Soft-paste porcelain, Chantilly, about 1750. (Musée des Arts Décoratifs, Paris)

50 Ivory chess board. French, 15th century. The border is carved with courtiers and musicians. (Museo Nazionale del Bargello, Florence)

51 Chelsea porcelain group
depicting one of Aesop's Fables.
(Menstrie Museum, Bath)

52 The Blue Room, Winterthur,
illustrating the American Federal
period. On the right a rare
mahogany New England lowboy
(about 1780–95), and on the left a
cheval mirror (about 1800)
probably from Philadelphia.
(Henry Francis du Pont Winterthur
Museum, Winterthur, Delaware)

plest was a handle set in a universal ball joint; in particular, a small clock with glass panels set in brass and handle on top, often with a leather case, very popular since the 19th century; see also **Coaching clock**.

Carsey, a strong woollen cloth.

Cartel clock, an 18th-century French wall clock, the case of which (perhaps suggesting a shield, as the name suggests) was usually a Rococo design in gilded bronze.

Cartonnier, a lightweight, open-sided box or small cupboard with compartments for storing paper, envelopes, and writing materials.

Carton Pierre, a French invention similar to papier-mâché, of pulped paper mixed with glue and a whitening agent and moulded for decorative work on woodwork or ceilings, in the 19th century.

Cartoon paper, a substitute for ivory in early 18th-century miniatures, consisting of painted primed isinglass that was thickened with pearl white.

Cartouche, a recurring device usually in the form of a curling scroll or shield, sometimes with surrounding floral decoration; in clocks, a small plate or escutcheon on the dial with maker's name engraved. **232**

Cartridge pleat, a cylinder-shaped pleat, invisibly stuffed, used for finishing off tops of curtains, for example.

Carver, a chair, sometimes the armchair provided with a set of dining chairs; in particular, an armchair with straight members and turned spindles similar to, but less elaborate than, the Brewster chair.

Carving, sculpture in wood or other material softer than marble (e.g. alabaster, ivory, soapstone, etc.) for decorative purposes; in furniture, almost exclusively relief and pierced work.

Caryatids, carved female figures, often only head and torso, used in place of a column or pilaster in buildings and furniture, a popular form in the Renaissance, more common than Atlantes, the male equivalents. **46**

Case, of clocks and watches; see **Clock case**.

Cased glass, blown glass in two or more layers, often with white between two coloured layers, which being engraved offers dramatic decorative effects (as in cameo glass); an ancient technique revived in the 19th century; see also **Flashed glass**.

Case furniture, any cupboard, wardrobe, chest, etc., an umbrella term covering furniture used for storage, as distinct from seat furniture (chairs, etc.) and stand furniture (tables, etc.).

Casement cloth, curtain material.

Case of drawers, a term sometimes used for an intermediate piece between a chest and a chest of drawers, consisting of a chest with drawers below.

Cashmere, or cachmere, a soft and expensive woollen fabric once used for shawls and made from the wool of wild goats in Kashmir and Tibet; modern cashmere comes from a less esoteric source.

Cashoes, mahogany.

Casket, a box or chest for jewellery and other valuable items and usually valuable itself; in the 16th century oak, carved and usually inlaid; later, any elaborate chest with various methods of decoration.

Casque, in Renaissance armour, a helmet.

Cassapanca, a large Renaissance Italian chest with added arms and legs which turned it into a seat; a development of the cassone.

Cassel porcelain, from a factory in operation from 1766 till 1788, noted for its blue-painted coffee and tea services and its figures.

Cassolette, a vessel with pierced lid, usually metal but also porcelain, for burning perfume; oval, spherical, cylindrical, etc.

Cassone, an Italian chest from the Middle Ages, later examples being notable for their decoration, painted, carved, gilded, inlaid, etc., often on lion's-paw feet; associated with marriage and often made in pairs. **47**

Casteldurante maiolica, from the pottery near Urbino which flourished in the 16th century and declined later, noted for characteristically pale colours and *en grisaille* painting.

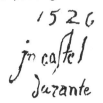

Castellated: see **Crenellated**.

Castelli maiolica, from the Abruzzi, a long-established pottery, which evolved a characteristic style in the Baroque period of fine landscape painting in delicate colours, the work of the Grue family.

Caster, a small vessel, usually cylindrical, with a pierced, domed top, for sprinkling sugar or spices (including pepper); uncommon before the 18th century and usually silver or plate, though occasionally porcelain; also, a castor.

Casting, in pottery, sometimes used instead of moulding for (particularly) stoneware vessels from about 1700, the slip being poured into a plaster mould and, when a 'skin' had been dried out by the plaster, poured out again; in metalware, molten metal poured into a pre-shaped mould.

Casting bottle, predecessor of the caster, a bottle with a perforated top; also, Venetian glass bottles of the 16th century and later for sprinkling perfume, and any later 'lady's toilet' bottles for this purpose.

Cast iron, pig iron, iron with high carbon content, hard but liable to break under stress, less versatile than malleable or wrought iron.

Castleford pottery, various wares from the pottery near Leeds, established in the late 18th century, including creamware, basaltes, tortoiseshell ware and stoneware with bright blue relief.

Castor, a small swivelling brass wheel fitted to the feet of furniture for easy movement, first used in the 18th century though not common until the 19th; also, hats of beaver; also, a caster.

Castor ware, Roman-British pottery, dark surface with slip decoration, hunting scenes, etc., made at Castor, near Peterborough in the 2nd century AD.

Cat, a three-legged wooden or metal stand for holding dishes, so-called because however it fell it would always land on its feet.

Catenary curve, a perfectly regular curve passing through 180°, i.e. half a perfect oval, as formed by a slack rope between two uprights; hence, catenary arch.

Caterpillar rugs, 19th-century patch-work rugs, in which narrow strips were cut from some woollen fabric, tightly gathered and sewn on to the ground fabric; see also **Chenille**.

Cathedral-back, the name given to an uncommon type of loop-back Windsor chair in which the rail is curved slightly inward before the central outward curve.

Cathedral binding, popular in early 19th-century book binding, decorated with Gothic architectural designs.

Catlin prints, from paintings by George Catlin (1796–1872), of North American Indians and other Americana, published in the mid 19th century.

Catoptrick, an 18th-century device utilizing the phenomena of catoptrics in which an apparently meaningless doodle became plain through the agency of mirrors.

Cat's eye, a characteristic of certain cabochon-cut precious stones such as chrysoberyl, a thin, silvery streak of reflected light.

Cattails, the feathery heads of certain rushes used in Roman times and for many centuries afterward for stuffing cushions, bedding, etc., usually with wool mixed in.

Catty: see **Caddy**.

Caucasian carpets, from the region between the Black and Caspian seas, including Baku, Kazak and others, characterized by conformity to geometric patterns with few curves anywhere; Ghiordes (Turkish) knot, antiques rare but modern examples mainly of high quality.

Caudle cup, a two-handled cup with or without cover and saucer, most commonly porcelain but frequently silver, often made in pairs in the 18th century, theoretically for drinking a spiced-wine drink (caudle) but more often formal gifts (like a silver beer mug today).

Caughley pottery, earthenware from the Shropshire factory of that name, established in the mid 18th century and soon afterwards producing porcelain very like Worcester; among Caughley charac-

teristics, the first willow-pattern, peculiarly deep blue underglaze printing, and a strong pink enamel.

Cauldron, a large round pot or kettle, of bronze, iron, copper, etc., often slung from a chain or standing on three short legs; probably the earliest type of cooking utensil.

Cauliflower ware, the name given to the somewhat whimsical yellow- and green-glazed ware first made by Wedgwood and Whieldon in the mid 18th century; teapots, jugs, bowls, etc. moulded and coloured like cauliflowers, cabbages, pineapples, etc.; later imitated elsewhere; see also **Cabbage ware. 38**

Causeuse, a love seat, a small settee for two persons.

Cavetto, concave moulding in the form of a quarter-circle, as seen on the cornices of early 18th-century cabinets.

C curve, a pattern in Rococo design in the shape (approximately) of a C, often combined with an S; see also **C scroll**.

Cedar, a warm reddish-brown wood with a smell pleasant to human beings and unattractive to insects, therefore used for linen and clothes chests from the 17th century and for linings of drawers and cupboards later.

Ceiler, see **Celure**.

Celadon ware, a class of Chinese stoneware with characteristic (though variable) bluish-green colour derived from a feldspathic glaze on a slip containing iron, first made under the Sung dynasty and once reputed to change colour if in contact with poison; see also **Kuan ware. 48**

Celery vase, a tall, usually straight-sided glass vessel curving in to a short stem and broad foot (sometimes square) with engraved decoration, associated particularly with Irish glassworks in the late 18th century; its purpose no mystery.

Cellaret, or cellar, a case on a stand for containing bottles, often with individual lead-lined compartments, fairly common before sideboards came into general use in the 18th century; also, a compartment in a sideboard where bottles can stand upright. **201**

Celluloid, cellulose nitrate and camphor, one of the earliest (mid 19th century) plastics, not very durable.

Celure, or ceiler, a medieval term for a bed canopy; in an effort to distinguish it from tester, it is sometimes defined as a canopy suspended from the ceiling rather than the bedposts, or as the hanging at the head of the bed.

Cemetery rugs: see **Graveyard rugs**.

Censer, a vessel usually of silver designed for the slow burning of incense, as used in churches; suspended or swung by hand; originally round but subsequently more elaborate shapes, e.g. Gothic architectural forms.

Census mug, an American souvenir of 1790, an earthenware mug with the results of the first American census printed on it.

Centaur, a creature half man (the top half) and half horse, from Classical myth, figuring in Renaissance art and ornament. **42**

Centennial, an adjective describing various objects in cloth, metal, pottery, glass, etc. made in connection with the American centenary (1876) and bearing patriotic images of various kinds, from a bewigged Washington to a bald-headed eagle.

Central motif, in oriental carpets, a design based on a central figure such as a medallion, particularly in old Persian carpets.

Centre hinge, a hinge consisting of a pivoting metal loop on the top and bottom of a door, late 17th and early 18th centuries.

Centrepiece: see **Épergne**.

Ceramics, a term embracing all objects of clay that have been hardened by fire, more accurate than 'china' and more comprehensive than 'pottery'.

Cerograph, a wax engraving.

Certosina, Italian inlaid decoration, often in black-and-white patterns of ebony and ivory or bone; found in 15th-century north Italian furniture particularly; also, painted imitation of such inlay.

Cesendello, a glass lampshade, 15th-century Venetian, probably deriving from the mosque lamps of Islam.

Chaffers ware, 18th-century Liverpool delftware and soapstone porcelain by Richard Chaffers who, among other distinctions, is said to have been the first to raise the lip of a jug above the rim.

Chafing dish, a term used rather widely, but in the 17th century a silver or other metal dish or bowl containing burning coals, with a rack or supports on top to keep a plate warm; later, any dish to be placed over charcoal or a lamp to keep food warm.

Chain mail, early European armour, common before the 10th century, consisting of small interlocking iron rings; see also **Mail armour**.

Chair, a seat for one person having a support for the back; with or without arms, originally signifying a seat of special authority or throne; chairs were rare in Europe before the 16th century.

Chair bed, a chair with fold-down back and extendable seat that transforms into a bed, apparently made as early as the 17th century; see also **Day bed**.

53 Tea dish with a hare's fur glaze. Chinese stoneware, Sung dynasty (960–1279) from Fukien. (Musée Guimet, Paris)

54 Chinese carpet. 19th century. Yin-Yang central motif and a recurring cloudband motif around the border. (Private Collection, Milan)

55

56

55 Chocolate pot by Nathaniel Locke. English, 1715. Side handle, swan-neck spout and plain, high-domed cover with an aperture under the finial through which the stirring rod was inserted. (S. J. Phillips Ltd., London)

56 Mahogany ribbon-back chair. Based on a design in Chippendale's *Director* (1754). (Victoria and Albert Museum, London)

57 Chinese bronze vessel inlaid with gold and silver. Chou dynasty. (Freer Gallery of Art, Washington)

Chair table, a rare 17th-century armchair with an extra-large circular or square back which can be lowered to rest on the arms, forming a small table; perhaps ripe for revival in cramped contemporary dwellings.

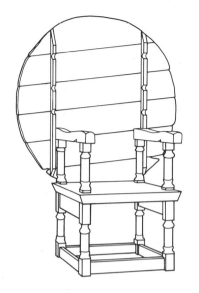

Chaise caquetoire, or 'gossip chair': see **Caqueteuse**.

Chaise d'or, a large cold coin of 14th-century France, showing the king seated on a throne (*chaise*).

Chaise longue, 'long chair', an upholstered armchair with an extended seat for stretching the legs out, introduced in France in the mid 18th century; see also **Day bed**.

Chaise perspective, an upholstered French 18th-century chair decorated with architectural designs in perspective.

Chalcedony, quartz stones of the crypto-crystalline type, which includes agate, jasper, onyx and carnelian.

Chalcography, the art of engraving on copper.

Chalice, a large wine cup, with heavy stem and foot, gold and silver, used at Holy Mass; see also **Communion cup, Paten**.

Chalkware, ornaments made in plaster of Paris in the second half of the 19th century, copying more expensive wares; often 'painted up gaudy' (*Huckleberry Finn*, quoted by Edith Gaines).

Challis, a very fine cloth of silk and wool, or wool alone, with a matt appearance; used in women's clothes.

Chalon, a medieval blanket.

Chamber candlestick, a term describing a candlestick made for frequent moving about, most commonly a short holder in a saucer-like dish with a handle, sometimes in the form of a ring to fit the finger, sometimes with snuffer attached; usually metal, and rare before about 1700.

Chamber clock, a term now used rather widely of almost any domestic clock; originally, the earliest small iron clocks which, unlike previous (turret) clocks, were small enough for an ordinary room.

Chamber horse, an 18th-century device for indoor exercise consisting of a chair with sprung leather seat constructed like a concertina which moved up and down when sat on.

Chamberlain porcelain, Worcester porcelain decorated by Robert Chamberlain in the late 18th century, or made at the Worcester bone-china works founded by his sons about 1800 which eventually (united with Flight & Barr) became the Worcester Royal Porcelain Co. in the second half of the 19th century.

Chamber pot, a round, metal or china pot with rim and handle for night-time use when lavatories were distant or non-existent.

Chamfered, a bevelled or canted surface, forming an intermediate plane on what would otherwise be a right-angled edge or corner; hence, chamfered-top (of a clock case or cabinet); see also **Canted**.

Chamois, exceedingly soft leather from the animal of that name; nowadays, almost invariably an imitation of that material.

Champagne glass, for drinking the sparkling French wine, various types according to place and date; 18th-century English glasses with inward-curving bowl and flared rim, also tall narrow glasses, like ale glasses, are so described; the shallow-bowled type was standard by the mid 19th century.

Chalice | Champagne glass

Champion porcelain, from the Bristol factory of Richard Champion, founded in the late 18th century, which for a short time held a monopoly of hard-paste porcelain in England; some very fine-quality ware with clear, brilliant glaze.

Champlevé, enamelling on metal, especially copper and bronze, in which the design is hollowed out, filled with glass, and ground smooth; in a champlevé dial (of a watch) the dial is ground away around the numerals, leaving them in relief; see also **Cloisonné**. 219

Chanak Kale pottery, earthenware vessels, notably animal-form jugs, from the Turkish pottery of that name; bold and unsophisticated decoration, 18th and 19th centuries.

Chandelier, in effect a candelabrum suspended from the ceiling (rather than stood on a surface), usually glass though also metal, wood, etc.; made in the 17th century and reaching a peak of elaboration with numerous branches, pendants and ornamentation in the late 18th century.

Chandry: see **Candle box**.

Chanfron, the armour plate protecting a horse's head, in use before Crécy (1346).

Changeable silk, woven cloth of different coloured silks which appears to change colour when seen from different angles.

Channelling, carved grooves, or fluting, ornamentation found on medieval and Renaissance furniture.

Chantilly lace, renowned French lace, especially the black silk lace first made in Chantilly in the 17th century and very popular in England two centuries later for shawls.

Chantilly porcelain, no less famous than the lace, produced throughout most of the 18th century, imitations of Japanese porcelain especially notable; the use of tin glaze makes some Chantilly porcelain look like faience. 49

Chantilly sprig, floral decoration on porcelain in the form of a cornflower, sometimes with other flowers, a bee, etc.

Chapbook, a small, inexpensive book on a popular or uplifting subject as sold by travelling pedlars (chapmen) in the 18th and 19th centuries.

Chapin furniture, usually the work of Eliphalet Chapin (1741–?1810) of Connecticut, skilled cabinetmaker influenced by Philadelphia styles, but may refer to several other American cabinetmakers of that name.

Chaplet, a wreath worn on the head, or a string of beads; hence, bead moulding in architecture and furniture.

Chapter ring, on a clock dial the circular band on which the numerals marking the hours appear.

Character jugs, jugs and mugs mainly in earthenware or stoneware, less often porcelain, portraying famous characters, from statesmen and admirals to jockeys and gypsies.

Charger, a large round dish, as used, for instance, for a large roast, sucking pig (or the head of John the Baptist); also, a sideboard dish.

Charka, a small, silver, Russian cup with handle, for drinking vodka.

Charles silhouette, by A. Charles of London, an 18th-century artist who made a speciality of painting on slightly dome-shaped glass.

Charleston iron, the wrought iron for balconies, etc. made in Charleston, South Carolina; similar to the better-known ironwork seen in New Orleans.

Charles X style, of the reign of the French king (1824–30), an interim period difficult to classify, embracing the tag-end of the Empire style and the beginning of Romantic revival.

Charleville musket, a French weapon made in America and used during the later stages of the American Revolution.

Chasing, a method of decorating metal, especially silver, by hammering the metal to produce a design in relief (or incuse), sometimes done in combination with engraving; chased silver was especially popular in the Rococo period. **103**

Chastity belt, a metal girdle with lock allegedly worn by medieval wives during enforced absence of their husbands to prevent unlawful sexual intercourse.

Chasuble, a sleeveless outer garment, particularly such a garment worn by priests.

Chatelaine, a clip with hook attached, in silver or other metal, worn by the mistress of a household on her belt, with keys, purse and other handy objects attached.

Chatironné, a floral pattern on the rims of plates particularly in French faience of the mid 18th century.

Chatoyancy, the cat's-eye effect in certain gems, such as chrysoberyl.

Chayere, an early spelling of 'chair'.

Cheese dish, any dish made especially for cheese, including the familiar china tray with sloping-topped cover; also, silver dishes for toasted cheese, popular in the 18th century, usually rectangular with cover and (sometimes) hot-water compartment.

Cheese knife, having a blade that curves backward at the end and terminates in two prongs; probably not made before the 19th century.

Cheese scoop, a silver spoon of stout form with a wide, scoop-shaped bowl, sometimes with a device for expelling a sticky bit of Stilton from the scoop; also, a cheese knife.

Cheese stand, usually porcelain, sometimes silver, a circular or square plate on a stand; also various other forms perhaps intended for cheese.

Cheese tester, similar to a butter tester.

Cheese wagon, a cheese stand on small wheels, from the mid 18th century.

Cheffonier: see **Chiffonier.**

Chekkers, a medieval keyboard instrument in which the strings were plucked rather than struck.

Chelsea-Derby, porcelain from Chelsea in the style of Derby, after the factory was acquired by William Duesbury of Derby not long before it closed.

Chelsea porcelain, from the factory established in Chelsea, London, in the mid 18th century, one of the best-known (and best) makers of porcelain in Europe despite generally derivative designs; though operating only about 40 years, Chelsea produced many different types, signified more or less by different marks (all frequently faked). **51**

Chelsea pottery, terracotta, biscuit and various glazed wares after Classical and Chinese models, some of fine quality, made at Chelsea Keramic Art Works in Massachusetts in the second half of the 19th century.

Cheminée, a tapestry firescreen. **102**

Chenille, tough velvety cord made of silk thread and sometimes wire; also, patchwork rugs; see **Caterpillar rugs.**

Chequered inlay, a pattern on furniture of alternate squares of light and dark wood.

Cherokee earth, unaker, or china clay.

Cherub, a junior angel, a small nude boy like a putto but with wings, appearing in the art and design of many periods, sometimes as just a head or mask.

Cherrywood, close-grained reddish wood used in French 18th-century furniture and in American furniture (black cherry) in the 19th century when it was ranked with walnut and mahogany; later, it fell from favour.

Chessboard, known from the 17th century, when they were made in exotic woods and ivory; see also **Chessmen. 50**

Chessel, a wooden vat for pressing cheese.

Chessmen, sets of figures for playing the ancient game of chess, fashioned from various materials ranging from wood and bone to silver and porcelain, since the Middle Ages.

Chest, a piece of furniture known since Antiquity, consisting of a large rectangular box with a hinged, flat lid (a rounded lid, strictly, makes it a coffer); superseded as a common item of storage furniture by the chest of drawers about 1700.

Chesterfield, a bulky, upholstered sofa having arms and back of the same height, generally buttoned; also, a type of overcoat popularized by Lord Chesterfield in the late 19th century.

Chesterfield ware, stone caneware, often with sporting scenes, very strong and capable of withstanding considerable oven heat, from the mid 19th century.

Chestnut, a lightish-coloured wood from the sweet and horse chestnut trees, sometimes used in the 18th and 19th centuries as a substitute for satinwood veneer; American chestnut was sometimes dyed to look like mahogany.

Chestnut roaster, a small, pierced, brass box on a long wooden handle, looking like a miniature bed-warmer, for roasting chestnuts.

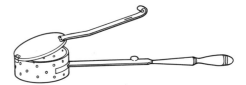

Chestnut server, a metal urn on a broad foot, with domed cover and two handles, used for serving hot chestnuts.

Chest of drawers, in its final form (achieved before 1700), a chest containing four or five drawers, usually fairly plain in design, often with a pull-out board at the top; later examples more ornamental.

Chest-on-chest, the name describing early forms of the tallboy.

Chest-on-frame, an early chest of drawers, on a four-legged stand.

Cheval glass, a large mirror set in a wooden frame, adjustable by some method, most commonly by pivots in the wooden uprights; from the late 18th

59 ▲

58 Cinnabar lacquer vase. Ch'ien Lung dynasty, 18th century. Floral decoration surrounds four deeply carved medallions depicting people and palaces. (Compagnie de la Chine et des Indes, Paris)

59 Coffee pot made by Augustine Courtauld, 1723. English. The tapering sided coffee pot was made throughout the first quarter of the 18th century. (Harvey & Gore, London)

60 Rhenish claw beaker. 7th-9th century. An example of Teutonic glass which was manufactured in all the areas of northern Europe that came under German influence. (Musée des Beaux-Arts, Rouen)

61 Chronometer by Thomas Mudge, 1744. English. The forerunner of all clocks used on large ships. (British Museum, London)

62 Louis XVI clock, probably made by Jean Baptiste Lepaute, of the famous French clockmaking family. Late 18th century. The two dials move, while the tongue of the serpent marks the time; the bronze case set with jewels is in the Neo-Classical style. (Petit Palais, Paris)

century; also, **cheval screen**, a similar piece with a wooden panel replacing the mirror; see also **Horse furniture**. 52

Cheveret, a small, 18th-century writing table, surmounted by small drawers and a detachable file for books and papers.

Chevron, a beam or rafter; hence, an inverted V shape, as in the roof of a house, and, repeated, a zigzag form; an ancient decorative device found on some pre-historic shards, medieval furniture, etc.

Chi, a form in oriental carpets, allegedly the Chinese symbol of immortality, variously described ('sacred sponge', 'like a ribbon', 'spermlike') most commonly as a cloud form in differing shapes. **54**

Chiaroscuro, i.e. 'light and dark', pictures in varying tones of one colour (normally black), thus wood-block prints made with several blocks to create infinitely various tones; in painting, the technique of handling shadow (as exemplified by Rembrandt); also called *claro-obscuro.*

Chicken skin, fine vellum, made from the skin of newborn lambs.

Chien, a Chinese copper coin of almost any date between 500 BC and AD 1900; some have a central square hole.

Chih, a Chinese vessel for tasting wine.

Ch'ien Lung, Chinese porcelain of the 18th century in which technique outweighed aesthetic considerations; imitations of wood, jade, and rhinoceros horn, black lacquered bodies set with mother-of-pearl; some painted with armorial bearings known erroneously as Chinese Lowestoft. **58, 94**

Chienware, stoneware, especially cone-shaped tea bowls, from Fukien during the Sung period, with heavy, dark brown glaze marked with golden streaks like hare's fur. **53**

Chiffonier, or cheffonier, a combination chest and sideboard, having a flat top with drawers and a cupboard (often recessed) below, usually with shelves or mirror above; originally, a late 18th-century French cabinet; a popular decorative piece in 19th-century England.

Ch'i-lin, a motif based on the form of a deer found in Chinese and other oriental carpets.

Chime, in clocks, a sound produced on more than one bell; see also **Strike.**

Chimera, or chimere, a mythical beast with lion's head, goat's body and serpent's tail, or other variations, sometimes appearing in decorations from Ancient Greece to 19th-century Europe; also (chimere), a sleeveless robe, gathered at the back, as worn by Anglican bishops.

Chimney crane, a wrought iron bracket, fixed or hinged, attached to the wall or chimneybreast, on which a pot or kettle could hang.

Chimney glass, a wide rectangular mirror, often of three sheets in a carved or gilded frame, first introduced about 1700, to stand on the mantelpiece.

Chimney piece, an ornamental hood, often of brass, over a fireplace; also, a picture or ornament adorning the chimney breast.

China, the term used originally to distinguish Chinese porcelain from European wares, now used very widely to describe all kinds of porcelain and earthenware, particularly white pottery.

China clay, kaolin, the white clay of granite origin used, together with china stone which provides the glassy appearance, in making hard-paste porcelain.

China doll, a child's doll with head and jointed body of porcelain, made from the 18th century, achieving great popularity in the 19th.

China press, or cabinet, made especially for the display of china, from the mid 18th century, the buffet being originally intended for this purpose.

China stone, feldspathic rock used in making porcelain; also called Cornish stone; see also **China clay.**

Chiné, a silk cloth; also, a type of Doulton stoneware in which the pattern was produced by impressing with suitable cloth.

Chinese back, a term sometimes applied to any of the numerous 18th- and 19th-century chairs with pierced splats reminiscent of Chinese design; see also **Chinese Chippendale.**

Chinese blinds, window blinds painted with scenes in the Chinese manner.

Chinese carpets, known since the Ming period but rare in Europe before about 1900, often naturalistic, showing whole landscapes, and generally small until recent times; frequently silk, sometimes with gold or silver thread and modelled patterns, achieved by cutting the pile to different lengths. **54**

Chinese Chippendale, a type of 18th-century Rococo furniture, often describing anything remotely oriental, but particularly the delicate fretwork imitating Chinese chairs, etc. and associated chiefly with Chippendale. **243**

Chinese export porcelain, made especially for export, often with European designs, from the 16th century and becoming big business in the 18th

century, including 'American Lowestoft', 'Canton china', 'Carrack porcelain', etc.

Chinese lantern, colourfully painted paper or silk on a light, circular bamboo frame that folds flat when not suspended; originally imported from China from the mid 19th century.

Chinese Lowestoft: see **American Lowestoft, Ch'ien-Lung.**

Ch'ing dynasty, or Manchu dynasty, 1644–1912, the period during which most Chinese porcelain was exported to (and made for) Western markets. **95, 129, 236**

Chinoiserie, a term used rather widely, sometimes derogatively, to describe the fashion for furniture and (particularly) decoration in the Chinese manner (but somewhat fantasized) that has periodically seized the West, notably in the late 18th century; not including ·Chinese-made objects or strict copies of Chinese originals, **243, 257**

Chintamani, a motif in oriental carpets consisting of three balls like a 'therefore' sign, the emblem of the Buddha, or, less pacifically, Tamurlane.

Chintz, a cotton fabric, originally from India in the 17th century, which is glazed by one of several methods and printed with floral or other patterns. **185**

Chiopine: see **Chopine.**

Chip carving, ornamental carving of light cuts in the form of geometric designs, found on medieval and later furniture, particularly country-made pieces. **278**

Chippendale, the style of furniture associated with Thomas Chippendale (1718-79), perhaps the most influential of all English cabinetmakers, based on the designs in his famous *Directory,* embracing Rococo, Chinese and Neo-Classical influence. **56, 243**

Chiselling, in metalwork, a form of engraving with chisel and hammer similar to chasing, but particularly the finishing of details in large bronze or other cast pieces to remove faults left by the casting process.

Chitarrone, a large type of theorbo or lute.

Chlamys, in Greek costume a short, man's cloak, worn doubled over the shoulders; hence, a decorative form like the folds of a cloak carved in wood in early Neo-Classical designs; see **Vitruvian scroll.**

Chocolate pot, similar to a coffee pot but with removable cover in the lid for stirring and a lip rather than a spout. **55**

Chopin, a measure of liquid.

Chopine, an overshoe to keep dainty footwear out of the mud; see also **Clog.**

Chotan carpets: see **Khotan carpets.**

Chou, in China the period beginning, traditionally, in the 12th century BC and ending about 250 BC; notable for its bronzes. **35, 57**

Chouval, a carpet bag made by nomadic Turkoman tribes, hanging inside a tent.

Chrism vessel, used in the ritual of anointing with oil and made since ancient times.

Christening cup, also goblet, plate, etc. carrying an inscription relevant to a particular christening or (as with certain English delftware loving cups) a verse appropriate to such an occasion.

Christmas decorations, including coloured glass balls from the mid 19th century, lights for decorating trees that are descended from votive candles, the crèche (miniature tableau of the Nativity with figures of wood, plaster, paper, etc.), mainly 19th century but first made much earlier.

Chromolithograph, a print in which each colour was applied from a separate stone, a lengthy and difficult process that made good examples rare.

Chronograph, a combination watch and stopwatch in which the position of the hands can be altered at will without interfering with the movement, for exact measurement of time; mid 19th century onward.

Chronometer, a watch or clock, in particular a highly accurate timepiece, with compensation devices for changing temperature, as carried by ships for measuring longitude. **61**

Chrysoberyl, several varieties of a precious stone including alexandrite, chrysoberyl cat's eye, and a green or yellow stone without the dramatic effects of the first two, sometimes called chrysolite.

Chrysoprase, a green, translucent quartz stone, a variety of chalcedony, comparable with jade.

Churchwarden, a clay tobacco pipe with a thin stem 15 to 20 in long, so called in the 19th century and possibly earlier.

Churrigueresque, in the style of José Churriguera, the Spanish Baroque architect, highly ornamental.

Chute, a decorative relief panel in wood or metal found in early 18th-century French interiors; see also **Boiserie, Trophy**.

Ciborium, or paten, a large, stemmed silver vessel with cover, the bowl being wide and shallow, on a short stand, containing the bread at Holy Mass; see also **Chalice**; also, the canopy over an altar.

Cider glass, an English drinking glass, from the late 18th century, similar to an ale glass but with apple branches engraved thereon instead of barley motifs.

Cigar case, a flattish, open-ended case, often made of papier-mâché, similar to an eye-glasses case but broader, usually with painted decoration, mainly German or Dutch, from the early 19th century.

Cigarette cards, small cards for collecting, supplied with cigarettes since the 19th century, with pictures of sportsmen, literary characters, railway locomotives, etc., usually building up into sets of fifty.

Cigar-store Indian, a life-size wooden figure of an American Indian (not usually lifelike) carved in the round or (sometimes) cut out of board and painted, which served as a tobacconists' trade sign in 19th-century America (though similar figures occurred in Europe earlier).

Cincinnati furniture, also glass, silver, etc., a general term for the household wares supplied to Western pioneers in the first half of the 19th century, mainly from Cincinnati.

Cinnabar lacquer, the earliest known lacquer pigments (red and black) used in China, the red derived from cinnabar (sulphide of mercury) and conventionally used for lacquering the inside of vessels, with black outside. **58, 187**

Cinnamon stone, a type of garnet, named for its colour.

Cinquecento, the 16th century, frequently so expressed in discussion of Italian Renaissance arts.

Cinquedea, an Italian Renaissance dagger with a blade very wide at the base and tapering to a point, often elaborately decorated and (by all accounts) frequently in use.

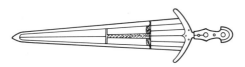

Cinquefoil, a pattern in Gothic architecture and design, consisting of five rounded leaves in a circle, with five inward-pointing cusps.

Circumferentor, an instrument for surveying, from the early 17th century, with degrees marked on a circular brass band around a magnetic needle, with two or four sights, mounted on a tripod; predecessor of the theodolite.

Circus figures: see **Carousel**.

Cire-perdue, 'lost wax', a one-off method of casting bronze or other metal in which a model is made in wax over a core, clay packed around, the wax melted out and molten metal poured into the clay mould; in use since ancient times.

Cist, in ancient religious rites, a small container for sacred objects carried in procession; also, a coffin or sarcophagus of stone slabs.

Cistercian ware, the name given to English black- and brown-glazed earthenware, sometimes with trailed decoration, of the 16th century.

Cistophoros, silver coin current in Asia Minor before (and after) Roman rule showing sacred cists.

Citole, a stringed instrument like a dulcimer.

Citrine, sometimes confusingly called topaz, a crystalline quartz stone, yellow or golden brown but usually achieved in its characteristic colour by heating amethyst; similar to cairngorm.

Citronnier, citronwood, light golden colour, used as a veneer by 18th-century French cabinetmakers.

Cittern, a pear-shaped stringed instrument related to the lute but metal-strung.

Clair de lune, a pale blue glaze on certain Chinese porcelain; also Clair de lune glass, having an opalescent sapphire tint.

Clapboard, a narrow board suitable for staves or wainscots; also, such a board tapered slightly across its breadth and used in construction, each board overlapping the one below.

Claro-obscuro: see **Chiaroscuro**.

Classic, a loosely employed word to describe anything that has achieved universal acknowledgement of its excellence, particularly as the representative of a particular art or style; hence 'modern classic', etc.

Classical, pertaining to Ancient Greece or Rome, or based on the fairly strict rules that governed style in Greek and Roman times; see also **Neo-Classical style**.

Clavel, a word now obsolete that described a mantelpiece or lintel.

Clavichord, a small, stringed instrument with a keyboard, in the form of a shallow box; a Renaissance predecessor of the piano.

Clavicytherium, a variation of the clavichord.

Claw and ball, for practical purposes identical with ball and claw, though sometimes implying such a foot in which the claw is especially dominant. **269**

Claw beaker, a curious (and rare) early medieval German glass beaker decorated with strange hook-shaped prunts like a lobster's claw, possibly deriving from the horn-shaped Saxon beaker. **60**

Claw table, the name given to the many varieties of 18th-century stands or small tables supported by a central column with three curved feet suggesting claws.

Claymore, a Scottish double-edged sword, sometimes applied to any such sword but, strictly, a very large, two-handed weapon of the 16th to 18th centuries, generally with quillons angled towards the point.

63 Mahogany commode made by W. Vile for the Earl of Shaftesbury, 1740–50. (Victoria and Albert Museum, London)

64 American butternut highboy of the Colonial period. Massachusetts, 1725–40. Queen Anne style with broken pediment, acorn turning and flambeau finials. (Henry Francis du Pont Winterthur Museum, Winterthur, Delaware)

65 Figure of Columbine by F. A. Bustelli. Nymphenburg, about 1760. One of the figures from the popular *commedia dell'arte* series. (Victoria and Albert Museum, London)

66 Typical English silver condiment pots of the 1760s. Mustard pot, pepperbox and double salt. (S. J. Phillips Ltd., London)

Clay tray, made of Clay (paper) ware, about 1800.

Clay ware, various household objects, trays especially, made at Henry Clay's Birmingham factory in the late 18th century out of sheets of paper pasted together, japanned and polished; better quality than papier-mâché.

Clear glass: see **Crystal**.

Cleavage, the tendency in diamonds and some other gems to split along a certain line.

Cleft cabriole, a cabriole leg with a pierced cleft in the knee.

Clepsydra, an early water clock, in which water dripped out of (or into) a vessel with the hours marked on the sides, preferable to shadow clocks because independent of the sun; used in Egypt nearly 3,500 years ago.

Clermont-Ferrand faience, rare (because production period was brief) but not especially distinguished mid 18th-century French earthenware, largely imitative of the styles of Moustiers and other centres.

Clews pottery, made at James and Ralph Clews' Staffordshire pottery in the early 19th century largely for export to America and decorated accordingly; also transfer-printed English scenes, literary characters, etc.

Clichy glass, from the works founded in Paris and moved to Clichy-la-Garenne about 1840, specializing in cheap glass for export but producing high-quality coloured and cased glass and engraved glass.

Clinquant, metal foil.

Cloam, or cloamware, clay or earthenware.

Clobbering, white or blue and white porcelain redecorated with various colours, practised in the Netherlands in the late 17th century and later in France and England, with or without intent to deceive.

Cloche, a glass cover, originally bell shaped, nowadays most commonly a protective cover for tender plants, but formerly a display case for wax fruit and other ornaments.

Clock, a device for telling the time visually and/or audibly; strictly, a timepiece driven by clockwork (weights and springs), thus excluding pre-clockwork devices such as water clocks as well as modern electric clocks.

Clock case, the container for a clock movement, whether an elaborate piece of cabinet-work as in a long-case clock, or a simple metal mounting as in a mass-produced alarm clock. **62**

Clock garniture, a clock and matching vases and/or candelabra for the decoration of a mantelpiece. **168**

Clock jack, a device driven by clockwork for turning a roast slowly and evenly on a spit over a fire; see also **Bottle jack**.

Clock lamp: see **Lamp clock**.

Clodion, porcelain, and terracotta, pewter and bronze, modelled or designed by Claude Michel Clodion (1738–1814) who worked for Sèvres among other famous centres; including erotic scenes in the tradition of the Versailles school.

Clog, a wooden shoe worn until recently by the non-affluent in the Netherlands and other countries; also, a slip-on wooden sole to protect finer footwear between doorstep and carriage; see also **Chopine**.

Cloisonné, enamelling on metal in which the divisions in the design are first formed of fine wire soldered to the surface, associated particularly with oriental metalwork though found in medieval Europe; also in lacquer and pottery; see also **Champlevé. 151**

Closed arm, an armchair in which the arm is joined to the seat, usually by a solid section.

Close-helmet, in armour, the close-fitting helmet in general use in the 16th century with visor pivoted at the temples.

Close nailing, in furniture, leather attached to wood by closely adjacent brass-headed nails to create a decorative line.

Close-scale facet, in cut glass or gems, a facet of diamond shape (also six-sided).

Close stool, or toilet chair, in which a chamber pot is set in the seat, made from the 15th century and useful as long as corridors were long and lavatories few and distant; also in box-form.

Closet, a small room or a large built-in cupboard.

Closet bed, a bed built into the corner of a room, with matching panelling, as seen in 17th-century Dutch interiors.

Clothes horse, a simple wooden frame for drying clothes, standing on the floor or attached to the wall; also, clothes bar, crane, or rack for the same purpose.

Clothes press, an armoire or wardrobe.

Cloudband, a motif in oriental carpets, like a twisting ribbon of seaweed, found particularly on Persian carpets of the 16th and 17th centuries, probably deriving from the Chi motif. **54**

Clout, a piece of cloth, bandage or rag ('Ne'er cast a clout, Till May is out'); also, a target in archery.

Club chair, a leather-upholstered armchair appropriate to a men's club.

Club foot, the commonest termination of a cabriole leg, a slightly splayed, rounded form faintly resembling a club; see also **Pad foot**.

Cluster column, a furniture leg formed of several joined columns with a common base and capital, found in medieval furniture (as in medieval architecture) and during the Gothic Revival.

Coach horn, a long (up to 2 ft 6 in) straight copper or brass horn made from the 17th to the 19th century and used by coachmen to warn of their approach.

Coaching clock, a large watch with swivelling handle, for hanging in a carriage; see also **Carriage clock**.

Coach table, a small folding table, used in private coaches.

Coade figures, garden statues of Coade stone, an artificial stone invented in the second half of the 17th century, which could be subtly moulded but remained undamaged by frost and was far cheaper than lead, previously the most favoured material for the purpose.

Coalport porcelain, from Coalbrookdale, Shropshire, founded about 1800 and incorporating Caughley, notable in particular for feldspar porcelain of high translucency, elaborate Rococo forms, fairly successful reproduction of the *rose pompadour* of Sèvres and parian figures.

Coal scuttle, a metal or metal-lined wooden box with open side and often with shovel in a slot at the back, not used before about 1800.

Coal vase, a mid 19th-century replacement for the vulgar scuttle, a vase-like container of japanned metal, usually with lid; many fancy shapes.

Coaster, or slider, a device for shifting dishes and bottles easily along large dining tables, in various shapes and sizes but usually consisting fundamentally of a tray on green baize or on small wheels or castors; apparently an 18th-century invention; see also **Beer waggon**.

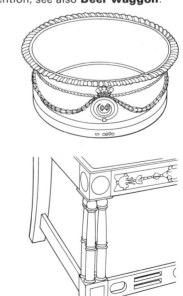

Cluster column

Coa vestis, or Coan robe, an ancient silk robe as woven on the Greek island of Cos (where silk was first woven, according to Aristotle), a clinging, diaphanous garment that 'revealed rather than concealed' the figure.

Cobalt glass, blue glass, made with cobaltous oxide.

Cobb furniture, made by the English 18th-century cabinetmaker John Cobb (died about 1780), who was employed by the King; extremely rare.

Cobirons, simple, undecorated andirons, with a row of metal loops in front for holding spits and sometimes surmounted with enigmatic cages, perhaps for keeping bowls of food warm; also a single iron, against which logs were propped, resembling a pair of shortened andirons stuck end to end.

Cobsa, a traditional stringed instrument of the Balkans belonging to the lute family.

Cochineal, a brilliant red dye derived from a certain insect (females only) found in Central America, used for dyeing cloth and particularly carpets.

Cochrane rifle, an American rifle with a revolving chamber, predating the Colt revolver.

Cockatrice, a mythical creature, part cock and part serpent with barbed tail, capable of killing with a look, like the basilisk; found in heraldry but less common in the arts than in literature.

Cockbeading, a common form on 18th-century furniture, consisting of a string of small semicircles around the edges of drawers, cabinet doors, etc.

Cockfighting chair, a chair with upholstered back and seat and reading table attached at the back; the occupant sat 'back-to-front', leaning on the table; probably no connection with cockfighting; see also **Reading chair**.

Cock metal, a cheap alloy of copper and lead resembling pewter, used for kitchen utensils, etc. in the 19th century, also nefariously by Billie and Charley.

Cock's head hinge, a decorative variation of the H hinge about 1700, in which the four terminals are shaped somewhat like cocks' heads.

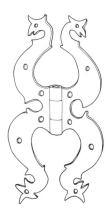

Cockspur, a small silver or other metal spur, scimitar-shaped, attached to the feet of fighting cocks.

Coconut cup, a cup made from a coconut with silver rim, frame, stem and foot.

Cod, a pillow.

Codnor Park pottery, stoneware from the 19th-century Derbyshire pottery later amalgamated with Denby; see **Bourne pottery**.

Codpiece, in Renaissance costume, a pad worn by men over the genitals with close-fitting tights, sometimes lavishly decorated or incorporating a purse.

Coffee can: see **Can**.

Coffee pot, in silver a favourite collector's item, early (late 17th-century) examples being of tapering cylindrical form with conical cover and long spout; many later variations; also other metal and earthenware. **59**

Coffee table, a small occasional table or breakfast table.

Coffer, a portable chest, sometimes covered with studded leather, for keeping valuables, usually distinguished from a chest by the rounded top, though flat-lidded chests were also sometimes called coffers.

Coffer bach, a small coffer, a Welsh bible box, usually oak, sometimes with a pair of drawers below the box.

Coffered, applied to studded leatherwork in chairs, etc., reminiscent of old coffers; also, rounded like the lid of a coffer, or recessed, as in a recessed panel.

Coffin, in furniture used as an adjective to describe various objects of hexagonal plan suggesting a (modern) coffin, e.g. coffin cupboard.

Coffin stool, a joint stool, or any stool for standing a coffin on.

Cogware, a coarse cloth with a nap made of low-quality wool, as worn by the Elizabethan poor.

Coif, a close-fitting embroidered cap or hair net, e.g. the intricate gauze, wire-framed, jewelled and even scented contraptions that held together the elaborate hairstyles of the 15th century.

Coiffeuse, a dressing table; or, a French Rococo upholstered armchair with indented top rail for easy dressing of the hair.

Coiled technique, in earthenware, the vessel being built up with strips of clay by hand, practised in societies where the potter's wheel is unknown, also in glass.

Coin, a small metal disc made since at least the 7th century BC by governments, local authorities and even private individuals for use as money; enormous appeal to collectors thanks to size, general availability and variety; also the French for Corner cupboard.

Coin glass, a coin set in glass, e.g. the bottom of a bottle or the knop of wine glass, a commemorative custom from the late 17th or 18th century, temptingly easy to fake.

Coir, a fibre made from the husk of coconuts, used in ropes, matting, cushion stuffing, etc., from the 17th century.

Colbertine, 17th-century French lace, named after the great patron of French lace and industrial crafts generally, Colbert.

Colcothar: see **Jeweller's rouge**.

Cold gilding, the method in which gold or silver foil is fixed to a metal core by pressure alone, without heat.

Cold painting, the technique of painting in oil or lacquer on glass or prefired or enamelled ware, notably on Venetian glass; the colours tend to come off in time, and sometimes no traces remain.

Colfichet, small two-sided pictures embroidered in silk on paper.

Colichemarde, an 18th-century smallsword, particularly one with a fairly wide blade at the hilt, which narrows suddenly into a rapier-like form.

Collage, the technique of making pictures by sticking odd scraps of material (cloth, wood, paper, feathers, dried leaves, etc.) on to a background; an amateur craft from the 17th century, recently raised to high-art status by Kurt Schwitters and others.

Collapsion cup, a collapsible metal cup, i.e. folding up like a telescope.

Collar, a raised circular band around stems or necks of glass and china vessels, similar decoration on turned members in furniture.

Collector's cabinet, a small chest of small drawers, for storing small objects; see also **Nest of drawers**.

Collector's piece, or item, an object worth collecting, especially an outstandingly fine or unusual example.

Collet, a neckband, including a choker; hence, a metal ring as in a ferrule, the base for the jewel in a ring, and the back of a brilliant-cut diamond.

Collier revolver, a rare predecessor of the Colt and apparently not inferior, but never made in any quantity.

Collinot, a decorative effect in ceramics resembling cloisonné, named after the Collinot pottery in Paris, late 19th century.

Colonnette, a term sometimes applied to columns in furniture too small to share a name with the mighty shafts of (say) the Parthenon.

Colonial furniture, usually meaning American furniture from the early 17th to the late 18th century which, though based on European styles and techniques, rapidly evolved a character of its own. **64**

Colophon, in books, the publisher's imprint or symbol; on older books, the note at the end giving publishing and printing details.

Coloured glass, any glass that is tinted by the addition of a metallic oxide.

67 Fragment of a Coptic textile. Wool on linen, 6th–8th century. Part of a clavus. (Staatliche Museen, Berlin)

68 Oak court cupboard. English, early 17th century. (Victoria and Albert Museum, London)

70 Coromandel lacquer screen.
Chinese, K'ang Hsi period,
17th—18th century. (Compagnie de
la Chine et des Indes, Paris)

69 Louis XVI style console table.
A 19th-century copy of an 18th-
century original. (Musée Condé,
Chantilly)

Colour twist, a spiral of two or more colours in the stem of a wine glass; see also **Air twist**.

Colt revolver, a percussion pistol with an automatically revolving chamber invented by Samuel Colt and produced in large numbers in mid 19th-century America; various types, also rifles, shotguns, etc.

Comb-back chair, the top rail of the back resembling the back of a comb; one of the basic types of Windsor armchair though other chairs (including other types of Windsor) may have comb-backs.

Combing, in pottery, a simple combed or marbled pattern on 17th-century slipware; in glass, decoration with threads that were combed into feathery patterns; see also **Feathering**.

Cometarium, an astronomical instrument for demonstrating the path of a comet in relation to the sun.

Comfit basket, a silver, porcelain, etc. container for comfits, i.e. bonbons, crystallized fruit, sugar-plums, etc.; various fancy designs from the late 18th century; see also **Bonbonnière, Cake basket**.

Commedia dell'arte figures, Harlequin and Columbine, Scaramouche and Pantaloon, and other figures from the Commedia dell'arte tradition in Italian theatre, immensely popular subjects in 18th-century porcelain, notably Meissen. **65**

Commemorative silver, or glass, or china, etc., articles made or decorated to commemorate a particular circumstance, e.g. a wedding. **171**

Commerce table, a small folding table, a card table.

Commode, a highly decorative 18th-century French chest of drawers; a term widely used in that sense in England, but in particular a decorative low cupboard, with or without drawers, usually on short legs and often with rounded or serpentine front. **64**

Communion cup, the silver cup or chalice used for wine in Anglican churches, including a few from before the Reformation; see also **Chalice**.

Compagnie Dessin, Chinese porcelain made to order and imported by the French Compagnie des Indes.

Companion piece, one of two matching articles; also, **companion chair**, a sofa in the form of two or three seats set at angles.

Compass chair, an early 18th-century chair with round seat and narrow spoon back, a shape that was suited to bulky garments and thus reappeared (for instance) in the age of the crinoline.

Compass table: see **Capstan table**.

Compendiario, a style in maiolica in the second half of the 16th century, pioneered at Faenza, in which painted decoration was minimal, colours few, and glaze intensely white.

Compo, or composition, the hard-drying, wood-based plaster used by decorators in the second half of the 18th century (notably Adam) for moulding decorative forms that (when dry) were applied to walls, panels, etc.; see also **Gesso**.

Componé, composed of alternate contrasting colours or shapes, like black and white tiles on a Dutch floor.

Compostiera, matching silver containers, with covers, on a tray, containing two types of food to be mixed according to individual taste.

Compound twist, in a wine glass, an air twist enveloped by further spirals of milk glass.

Concertina: see **Melodeon**.

Concertina table, a folding card table in which the legs pull out on hinged boards like a folding screen or a concertina.

Conch, a horn made from or in the shape of a conch shell; a pattern in the form of shells; also the shell used as a primitive wind instrument.

Condiment pot, a small silver or ceramic pot to hold salt, pepper, mustard etc. for use at table. **66**

Confidante, or tête-à-tête, a settee for two or three people in the form of two joined, upholstered armchairs slightly angled towards each other, popular in the 19th century; see also **Love seat**.

Conge, or apophyge, the concave moulding between two members, e.g. between a column and its capital or base.

Congeries, a haphazard, unsorted collection of articles.

Connecticut sunflower chest, a large chest with one or two layers of drawers, the front of which has three carved panels, separated by split balusters, with sunflowers decorating the central panel.

Connoisseur, a discerning judge of the arts, an expert.

Console, a bracket, often in Rococo scrolled design and sometimes forming a purely decorative element in case furniture; also a console table. **69**

Console table, an immovable side table, supported exclusively on brackets or with two (or three) legs at the front. **69**

Constitution mirror, an American 18th-century rectangular mirror in wooden frame in architectural style, often parcel gilt, with or without an eagle at the top. **79**

Constructivism, the style of the period immediately after the First World War, associated with de Stijl, in part a reaction against the sinuous lines of Art Nouveau; furniture designs based on geometrical, particularly rectangular, shapes, with a preference for primary colours; see also **Art Deco**.

Consulate period, the five years during which Napoleon was consul of France (1799–1804) before he became emperor.

Contador, a 17th-century Portuguese cabinet, usually a small cupboard on a stand with elaborately turned legs, influenced by contemporary Dutch designs.

Contorniate, a bronze coin or token with 'heroic' type of Ancient Rome, apparently a ticket or souvenir of the public games; also contoured.

Contoured, or contourniated, a decorative edge, e.g. of an earthenware dish.

Contre-partie, marquetry or Boulle work, in which the pattern is in tortoiseshell, set in brass, rather than the other way about.

Conversation chair, a single chair with a long seat and padded rail at the back on which a man sits astride; also, conversation sofa, a term applied to various 19th-century 'sociable' sofas; see also **Love seat**.

Conversation piece, any object, especially a picture, which by its particular quaintness or other unusual qualities is likely to provoke inquiry or comment.

Cookes furniture, elaborately carved, 'pictorial' furniture, especially sideboards, by Cookes of Warwick, mid 19th century.

Coopered, fashioned like a barrel, with hooped staves, or a pattern imitating coopering, as in some silver or earthenware bowls.

Cop, in armour, a small plate, basically round though often in ornamental shape, guarding the joints, armpit, elbow or knee.

Copal, a resin used in varnishes.

Copeland china, a variety of wares from the pottery founded by Josiah Spode which eventually came under the control of William Copeland the younger (and still owned by his descendants); many luscious parian Venus figures (about 1850) are particularly noteworthy.

Copenhagen faience, from two potteries, especially Store Kongensgade, founded in the early 18th century, largely blue and white ware, often German-influenced; management problems forced closure.

Copenhagen porcelain, originally (about 1750) soft-paste porcelain, later re-established using kaolin, best known for a service of nearly 2,000 pieces very accurately painted with Danish flowers (Flora Danica); also, biscuit figures, elaborate vases, tableware, etc.; still going strong.

Coperta, a lead glaze over the normal tin glaze of maiolica or delftware to give it added sparkle.

Copper, a versatile metal mined in many countries, in England mainly since the 16th century, the basis of several well-known alloys; changing methods of manufacture between the 17th and 19th centuries made it possible to date copperware by colour, thickness, etc.; also, a large kettle or pot.

Copperbottom, a copper sheet fitted to the bottom of a tin saucepan or (from late 18th century) the bottom of a ship to discourage the teredo worm.

Copper-plate, a copper plate for etching or engraving; a print or an impression made from such a plate.

Coptic art, as produced by the Copts, Egyptian Christians renowned for their textile and other decorative skills. **67**

Coquilla, the nut of a Brazilian palm, resembling hardwood, probably first carved by Portuguese sailors and subsequently fashioned into innumerable objects such as pepper pots, snuff boxes, umbrella handles, etc.

Coquillage, decoration based on shell forms, popular in the mid 18th century.

Coral, the skeletons of small marine animals, hard as rock, usually red or pink but also white, used chiefly in jewellery, also small carved ornaments, comforters for teething infants, etc.

Corbel, in architecture, a supporting projection in a wall, often of bracket-like form; hence, a similar form in furniture, decorative rather than structural, e.g. below the frieze on a Tudor cupboard.

Cordial glass, a drinking glass like a wine glass but with a long, thick stem, heavy foot and small bowl for strong 17th-century drinks; see also **Dram. 1, 294**

Cordovan, or cordwain, Spanish leather, originally of goat's hide, used for shoes in the Middle Ages.

Core-wound glass, a method used by the Egyptians, of making glass vessels, in which a strip of molten glass was wound around a clay core, which could be broken up and removed when the glass cooled.

Corinthian, the third order of Classical architecture characterized by an elaborate capital based on the acanthus; hence, such a form in (particularly) Neo-Classical furniture.

Cork, the bark of the cork tree, used for insulation against (formerly) cold and (now) noise, e.g. cork mats.

Cork glass, from two rather short-lived glassworks in Cork, Ireland, late 18th to early 19th century, including some brilliant (and early) hand-cut flint glass.

Corn dolly, a small doll traditionally made from scraps of straw, wheat, etc. after the harvest.

Cornelian, a brownish-red quartz stone, popular for beads in the 19th century.

Corner cabinet: see **Corner cupboard.**

Corner chair: see **Roundabout chair.**

Corner cupboard, a three-sided cupboard to fit in a corner, sometimes with glazed doors (corner cabinet); at first (late 17th century) hanging, later standing, in two sections or on three legs; the glazed mid 18th-century cabinets were intended for china display.

Cornice, in Classical architecture, the top member of an entablature; hence, the top course of a wall, a decorated band over a window obscuring the curtain rail, cresting on a cabinet, etc.; see **Doric.**

Corning glass, from the glassworks at Corning, New York (also the site of a famous museum of glass), founded in the second half of the 19th century (and formerly in Brooklyn); including contemporary Steuben glass.

Cornish stone: see **China stone.**

Cornucopia, or horn of plenty, associated with the goddess Ceres and frequently used as a decorative motif from the 15th century; also, wall pockets in this form.

Coromandel, a very dark Indian wood from several different trees, used for banding and veneers since the 18th century; the term includes calamander.

Coromandel screen, Chinese screen of carved lacquer in a folding wooden frame, imported via the Coromandel coast (Bengal) in the 17th and 18th centuries. **70**

Coromandel work, oriental carved lacquer work; see also **Coromandel screen.**

Corona, a chandelier, gas light, etc. in circular form.

Coronal, a decorative head-dress, usually jewelled, such as a coronet.

Coronation plate, objects such as plates, goblets, etc., usually of gold, given to royal officials and others for their services in connection with a coronation; rare and valuable, needless to say.

Corpse candle, or corpse light, a thick candle used at funerals until the 17th century.

Corse, an embroidered ribbon serving as a girdle or garter; also a column or shaft.

Corseca, or corseque, a medieval weapon like a combination spear and axe, bearing two hooks. **214**

Corset-back chair, a 19th-century chair with a back nipped in at the seat, suggesting an exaggerated waist.

Corundum, a stone second only to diamond in natural hardness from which sapphires and rubies are derived; used in cutting gems, etc.

Cosmetic box, a small box, usually decorative, for toilet preparations. **187**

Cosmolabe: see **Astrolabe.**

Coster, a general word for (usually) embroidered cloth, wall hangings, curtains, etc. in the Middle Ages.

Costeril, or costrel, a bottle with a sling, as carried by pilgrims, sometimes leather; see also **Canteen.**

Cosy corner, a feature of certain Victorian sitting rooms, a corner, alcove, or inglenook set apart from the rest of the room by wooden screens, latticework, etc., often with fitted furniture.

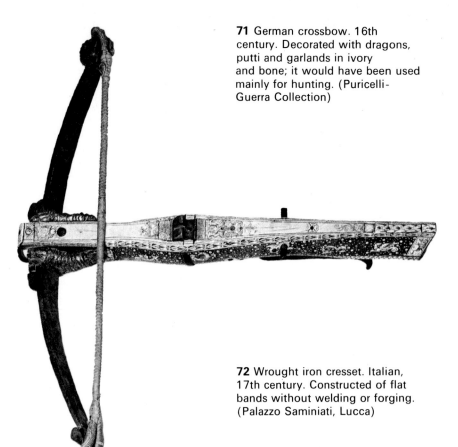

71 German crossbow. 16th century. Decorated with dragons, putti and garlands in ivory and bone; it would have been used mainly for hunting. (Puricelli-Guerra Collection)

72 Wrought iron cresset. Italian, 17th century. Constructed of flat bands without welding or forging. (Palazzo Saminiati, Lucca)

73 Silver cruet. English, made by Anthony Nelme, 1732. Generally known as a Warwick cruet; the largest of the casters was for sugar, the smaller on the right for pepper, and the one on the left which is not pierced was for dry mustard. (S. J. Phillips Ltd., London)

74 Cylinder desk. French, designed by Jean-Henri Riesener (1734–1806). (Musée du Louvre, Paris)

Cot, a swinging cradle for an infant, made in various forms from medieval times, sometimes also referring to non-swinging cradles or to any small bed; see also **Cradle**.

Cothurn, a high shoe, as worn on the 19th-century stage.

Cotswold school, influential school of English furniture design, led by Ernest Gimson, late 19th and early 20th century, traditional craftsmanship and materials in restrained modern design. **152**

Cottage clock, any small 19th-century New England mantel clock in a wooden case.

Cottage furniture, simple mass-produced furniture often of painted wood in 19th-century America; see also **Country furniture**.

Cotterpin hinge, a simple hinge sometimes found on 18th-century chests consisting of two interlocked ring staples.

Cotton, a woven cloth from the fibre of the cotton plant, rare in Europe before the 17th century when Indian cotton began to be imported in quantity, including calico, chintz, etc.

Cotton twist, a pattern in glass of white spirals, as in wine glass stems; see also **Air twist**.

Cottu silhouettes, painted silhouettes by the travelling silhouettist, M. Cottu, who emigrated from France to America about 1800.

Cotyledon, an ancient decorative motif based on leaves sprouting from a bud.

Couch, synonymous in the 18th century with a day bed, gradually becoming more like an ordinary sofa, though generally with a definite head and foot for reclining rather than sitting.

Couching, a method of embroidery involving very heavy thread which is attached to the ground by overstitching.

Counter, a small table, usually with a cupboard, or panels between the legs on at least two sides, incorporating a scale for adding up bills, etc.; also a board so marked.

Counterguard, the guard for the hand on a sword hilt, often of basket-like form. **222**

Countermark, a stamped impression on coins, stamps, etc., authorizing use in some place or time for which it was not originally intended.

Counterpane, a coverlet, often quilted, for a bed, perhaps deriving its name from a common pattern of alternating diamond patches.

Counterprint, a print taken from a print while still wet, rather than from the plate, and thus in reverse (like the plate itself).

Country furniture, a term used to describe furniture made in provincial regions, not by top-class cabinetmakers, lagging in style behind city fashions, and often displaying eclecticism and a talent

for improvization; see also **Cottage furniture**.

Coup perdu clock, 'lost beat' clock, a pendulum clock which registers seconds although the pendulum beats half seconds.

Couronne de feu, a branched iron candlestick.

Court cupboard, not strictly a cupboard, but a buffet or stand for the display of silver, having a shelf above and below a flat top (for serving), usually with heavy turned supports; 16th and 17th centuries, revived in the 19th; see also **Credence**. **68**

Courtesy book, a book of etiquette, 18th century or earlier.

Courthouse chair, a type of low-back Windsor chair with a writing table on the right arm, presumably used by a clerk in a 19th-century American courthouse.

Courting cup: see **Loving cup**.

Courting mirror, apparently as exchanged by young American couples in the late 18th century, a small mirror decorated with coloured glass or pictorial crest.

Courting seat, a tête-à-tête or love seat.

Couter, in armour, a curved plate protecting the elbow joint.

Cove moulding, a simple moulding concave in section.

Coverlet, a counterpane, more strictly a patterned bedspread, designed to be warm as well as decorative, used in many a 19th-century household; some examples signed and dated.

Cow creamer, a small milk or cream jug, silver or porcelain, the mouth being the spout, the curled-over tail the handle, the back detaching as a lid.

Cowlstaff, or colestaff, a strong staff used for carrying heavy loads on the shoulders of two people.

Cowrie, a seashell used as money in certain parts of the world including, formerly, North America.

Crabstock, a form in the shape of an apple tree branch, appearing frequently on the handles and sometimes spouts of 18th-century teapots.

Crabwood, a West Indian wood closely resembling mahogany; also called apple wood.

Crace furniture, Gothic-revival furniture made by the English firm of John Crace & Son, London, founded in the mid 18th century and influential throughout the 19th century; associated with Pugin, apostle of the Gothic style. **285**

Crackle, a decorative effect of fine cracks in glazed ware, a Chinese technique sometimes imitated in 19th-century Europe; see also **Crazing**. **150**

Cracowes, boots with extremely long toes, apparently originating in 14th-century Cracow (Poland).

Cradle, a small bed approximately in the shape of an open box or basket, often with hood, for a baby; often on rockers; made in every conceivable form over the centuries; many old examples survive through achieving heirloom status; see also **Cot**.

Crailsheim faience, from the 18th-century factory at Württemberg, notable for its bright high-temperature colours and floral decoration.

Cran, a three-footed iron stand for a kettle on the hearth.

Crapaud, a low, upholstered armchair introduced in France in the second half of the 19th century.

Craquelure, the hair-line cracks that appear on oil paintings. Sometimes the craquelure may be only in the surface varnish, in which case it can be removed; see also **Crazing**.

Crayon print, engraving of a drawing in chalk, first etched then engraved for greater accuracy, a mixture of stipple, drypoint, and etching techniques.

Crazing, a network of cracks in glazed ware resulting from shrinkage; see also **Crackle**.

Crazy quilt, a patchwork quilt made of differently shaped and coloured patches, like crazy paving.

Cream boat, a silver or porcelain vessel like a small sauce boat, i.e. a long, low jug with wide spout.

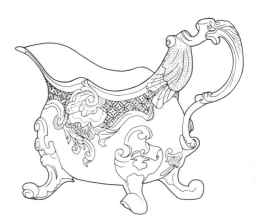

Cream-coloured earthenware: see **Creamware**.

Cream skimmer, a metal scoop, roughly circular and dipping towards the middle, sometimes pierced, with wooden baluster-type handle, for skimming cream off a pail of milk.

Creamware, or faience-fine, a porcelain substitute evolved from the salt-glazed stoneware of Staffordshire mainly by Wedgwood in the mid 18th century, a faintly yellow, lead-glazed earthenware that soon became extremely popular.

Crèche: see **Christmas decorations**.

Credence, a late medieval or Renaissance sideboard, shelf or buffet; credence table may mean the same, or a 16th-century semicircular flap table, or the side table used for bread and wine at Holy Mass; see also **Court cupboard**.

Creel, a wicker basket with lid, rounded in front and flat at the back, with shoulder strap, carried by a fisherman for his catch (if any); formerly, a wickerwork trap for eels or other fish.

Creepers, small fire irons like andirons, for supporting a kettle, etc.

Creil faience, late 18th- and 19th-century ware in the English fashion from the French factory at Creil.

CREIL.

Crenellated, indented like battlements, a pattern found on medieval and Renaissance furniture; also, serrated like a leaf; also castellated.

Crêpe, or crape, a fine gauze-like cloth made from raw silk, usually black and thus associated with mourning dress (e.g. a crêpe hatband); also, any fabric with the crinkly appearance of crêpe; **crêpe de Chine,** white or other colours.

Crescent, an object, e.g. a pendant, of half-moon form.

Cressent furniture, by the great French artist-craftsman Charles Cressent, slender curves and bronze mounts, influencing the development of Rococo in French furniture.

Cresset, an iron frame approximately in the shape of an inverted bell, holding a torch, candle, or oil lamp, usually mounted on a pole. **72**

Crest, originally a badge on a helmet; hence, similar ornamentation on top of a cabinet, mirror, clock, bedstead, etc.

Cresting rail, the top rail of a chairback when in shape or decoration it suggests a crest.

Cretonne, a strong cloth, originally linen, later cotton.

Crewelwork, a form of embroidery in worsted, 16th century or earlier, floral designs, used chiefly in bed hangings, furniture covers, etc.

Crib, a baby's cot, particularly when in the form of a manger, i.e. of stick construction and standing on four legs.

Criblé, a form of wood engraving occurring chiefly in 15th-century France, in which a stippled effect was achieved by making small holes of varying diameter.

Cricket stool, or milking stool, a three-legged stool the legs of which are dowelled into the seat like a cricket table; also used to describe a footstool.

Cricket table, a three-legged table with splayed legs and no stretchers, a very old piece of cottage furniture the name of which has been explained as a variant of crutch, a reference to the insect, and an allusion to the English game.

Crime, or crime piece, a macabre earthenware ornament of the scene of some sensational crime, e.g. 'The Red Barn at Polestead' (Staffordshire).

Crimping, in glass or earthenware, a pattern of small ridges occurring, for instance, at the bottom of a jug handle; in cloth a similar effect, gathering into small folds.

Crinkle-crankle, winding to and fro, or zigzag.

Crinoline, a stiffened cloth originally woven from horsehair, subsequently a hooped skirt with hoops of steel, all the rage in France under the Second Empire and introduced to England by the Empress Eugenie; hence, crinoline (hoop-shaped) stretchers in a chair.

Crinze, a metal drinking cup.

Crizzling: see **Crazing.**

Crochet, lace made with a crochet, or hook, by pulling the thread through loops.

Crockery, more or less synonymous with china, but usually referring to cheap domestic ware.

Crocketed, ornamented with crockets, the small curling-leaf forms seen on spires and pinnacles in Gothic architecture. **285**

Crocodile leg, an extravagance occasionally found in early 19th-century furniture during the brief vogue for Egyptian motifs.

Croft, a small pedestal table with small drawers behind a door.

Cromwellian chair, an appropriately plain single chair of the mid 17th century with leather seat and back and turned legs; also, later, more decorative chairs of the same general type.

Croquet chair, a large wickerwork armchair, usually with cushion back, late 19th century.

Cross-banding, in furniture, a strip of veneer in which the grain of the wood runs across the band, often surrounding drawers or panels in walnut furniture. **275**

Crossbill, a popular name for a glass vessel with two curving necks that cross each other.

Crossbow, a weapon that fires an arrow from the shoulder, operated by a trigger; despite cumbersome cranking-up (and 12th-century papal ban) popular with foot soldiers throughout the Middle Ages. **71**

Cross garnet hinge, a strap hinge of the type seen on stable doors, with a long horizontal piece across the door.

Cross-lyre table, or stand, in which the support is in the form of two lyres, crossing at right angles and providing four points of support.

Cross stitch, or gros point, a type of embroidery stitch in which pairs of stitches make a pattern of crosses on a ground fabric; see also **Canvas work, Berlin work. 264**

Cross stretchers, diagonal stretchers on legs that meet at the centre, forming an X. **163**

Crotch wood, cut from a joint in the tree, where the grain makes an interesting pattern; see also **Burr wood.**

Crouch ware, early English salt-glazed stoneware, first made at Burslem, 'mother of the potteries', in the 17th century.

Crowfoot, a type of ball-and-claw foot.

Crown, an English coin of five shillings value, originally gold but at certain times silver, first issued in the early 16th century, usually with monarch's portrait.

Crown carving, relief decoration found on some English chairs of the second half of the 17th century in celebration, perhaps, of the restoration of the monarchy (1660).

Crown Derby, Derby porcelain, either marked with a crown from the original Derby Porcelain Manufactory, or from the Derby Crown Porcelain Co. established in the late 19th century.

Crown glass, sheet glass made by blowing a large bubble which was transformed into a disc by rotation under heat, distinguishable by the central 'bull's eye'; see also **Broad glass.**

Cruciform, in the shape of a cross, e.g. cruciform bottles, made in early Christian times.

Cruet, a small glass vessel with stopper for holding oil, or for wine in Christian ritual; also, a number of such bottles with olive oil, vinegar, etc. in a frame, for use at table. **73**

Crumhorn, a 16th-century reed instrument with flared upturned end and soft bass tone.

Cruse, a small vessel, metal or earthenware, with a spout, for oil or other liquids; also, a lamp.

Crusie, in Scotland, a lamp like a Betty lamp with no lid; see also **Cruse.**

Crystal, glass that is particularly clear, originally the *cristallo* glass developed in Venice in the mid 15th century, so-called for its resemblance to rock crystal.

Crystallized ware, a 19th-century technique of decorating tin-plate, pictures being painted on coloured varnish.

75 Two daggers. A jambiya from Delhi, 19th century, with precious stones set into the hilt, and a chilanum from Nepal, 18th century, with an ivory hilt. (Wallace Collection, London. Photo: John Webb)

76 Deruta maiolica plate, 1525, with grotesques of candelabra, sphinxes and dragons. (Victoria and Albert Museum, London)

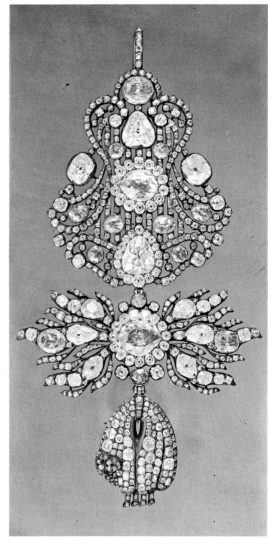

▲77

78

77 Three imitation Chinese vases. Delft, about 1700. Originally destined for an overmantel. (Musée National de Céramique, Sèvres)

78 Order of the Golden Fleece of Maximilian III, Duke of Bavaria, 1765. Rose and white diamonds. (Munich, Schatzkammer)

79 The Duncan Phyfe Room, Winterthur, illustrating the American Directoire style. The mahogany chairs, by Phyfe, are dated 1805; the mirror, from Albany, New York, is of the same date. (Henry Francis du Pont Winterthur Museum, Winterthur, Delaware)

Crystallo-ceramie, the technique developed in 18th-century France for enclosing some kind of ceramic ornament in glass, most frequently in paperweights and plaques containing portraits of the famous.

C scroll, a decorative form chiefly of the late 17th century, found on wooden looking-glass frames, etc.; see also **C curve.**

Cuban mahogany, from the West Indies (not only Cuba), the commonest variety used by English cabinetmakers from the mid 18th century, regarded as slightly inferior to Spanish mahogany, though any difference seems coincidental.

Cucking stool, a ducking stool, on a pivoted beam next to the village pond.

Cuckoo clock, a German hanging clock, most familiar in the recent form of a Swiss châlet, from which a cuckoo appears to announce the hour; first made by the Black Forest clockmakers about 1740.

Cucumber slicer, an adjustable cylinder mounted lengthwise on a pedestal with a blade at one end turned by a handle, found in silver plate in the early 19th century.

Cuenca, a technique in glazing earthenware tiles, etc., used in 16th-century Spain, in which glazes of different colours were held during firing in moulded impressions in the clay; superseded *cuerda seca*; also a carpet-making centre.

Cuerda seca, a technique in glazing earthenware, of medieval Arabic origin, in which the outlines of the design were previously drawn with a metallic grease, which prevented the differently coloured glazes from merging.

Cufic: see **Kufic.**

Cuirass, in armour, a breastplate, or breast- and backplate fastened together.

Cuir bouilli, leather that has been boiled to make it soft and moulded into the desired form before it cools and hardens.

Cuisse, in armour, a piece protecting the thigh.

Cuivre argenté, silver-plated copper.

Cuivre doré, gilded copper, rare, as bronze was usually more suitable.

Culet, in armour, the piece protecting the buttocks, like a miniskirt; in diamonds or other stones, the bottom-most facet.

Cullet, scraps of broken glass remelted and added to a new batch to encourage fusion.

Culverin, originally a hand gun; also, a cannon with an extremely long barrel, highly regarded by King Henry VIII.

Cupboard, one of many rather wide-ranging terms for storage furniture, originally a 'board' for 'cups', then shelves, finally (16th century) shelves enclosed by doors.

Cupboard bed: see **Closet bed.**

Cupboard stool, cupboard table, etc., self-explanatory terms applied to various pieces that include a small auxiliary cupboard.

Cup-hilt, a guard shaped like a bowl or cup on a rapier.

Cupid's bow, an elongated, double-scroll form seen in the cresting of cabinets, chairbacks, etc., of the mid 18th century.

Cupped castor, similar to a box castor but with circular cup for a turned leg.

Cupping-bowl, a small silver bowl with handle, a porringer.

Cup turning, a rounded end on a turned member, e.g. on late 17th-century chairs.

Curfew, couvre-feu, a half-dome cover, sometimes pierced, with central handle, most commonly iron or brass, to keep a fire going overnight.

Curiosity, or curio, a name sometimes applied to an odd, grotesque, or obscene object, e.g. puzzle jugs, boxes without apparent lids, sculpted coal, carved phalluses, etc.

Curricle chair, an upholstered chair with rounded back, early 19th century.

Currier and Ives prints, the best-known, perhaps because most numerous, of American historical prints, 19th-century lithographs of numerous popular scenes and subjects by many artists.

Currule chair, curule chair, a Roman X-shaped stool, revived in the Renaissance and Neo-Classical periods, sometimes with arms and back.

Curtain, a cloth screen hanging from a rod which can be drawn aside to admit light; originally, curtains were found on beds, curtains on windows came later.

Curtain holder, a silver or brass band for holding back a long drawn curtain; also, a cord performing the same function.

Curtal, a Renaissance reed instrument, a predecessor of the bassoon.

Cushion, any piece of cloth stuffed with soft material such as feathers.

Cushion moulding, late 17th-century moulding on cornices, of convex outline, suggesting a cushion.

Cushion stool, a pouffe.

Cusp, a pointed end, as in the tracery of Gothic church windows, found particularly in Gothic-Revival furniture on chairbacks, cabinet crestings, etc.; also, a faceted knop on a wine glass. **117**

Custard glass, creamy or yellowish milk glass.

Cut-card, a technique of relief decoration found commonly on 17th-century silver, in which a separate sheet of silver, pierced or otherwise decorated, is applied to a vessel, often as a border of foliage; occasionally detachable.

Cut glass, glass carved or ground into sparkling facets by revolving wheels with an abrasive, practised by the Romans but subsequently forgotten, revived in 17th-century Bohemia and very popular until the invention of pressed glass; also, imitation of cut-glass decoration on earthenware. **26**

Cutlass, a single-edged sword, often but not necessarily curved, the standard British naval sword in the 18th century.

Cutlass pistol, an uncommon American percussion pistol fitted with a broad, cutting blade underneath the barrel.

Cutlery, strictly, knife blades; less strictly, knives, scissors, etc.; popularly, knives, forks and spoons.

Cutwork, an early form of lace, part of the material being cut away, the edges secured by buttonhole stitches, and the spaces filled with decorative stitching; very elaborate by the 16th century; also the cut-card technique in other media (besides silver).

Cylinder, a hollow circular form of constant diameter; hence, **cylinder desk,** a bureau having a writing compartment with a round top which can be pushed back out of sight, late 18th or 19th century, especially French. **74**

Cylinder dial, a simple, portable form of sundial; see **Shepherd's sundial.**

Cylinder press, a printing press in which a large cylinder is rolled over the paper to make the impression.

Cylix: see **Kylix.**

Cusp

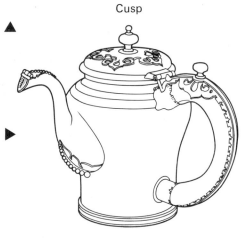

Cut-card

Cyma, an ogee; concave and convex curves as in the profile of a wine bottle or the hip of a woman; traditionally the most beautiful line in art; also, the element so-shaped in cornice or moulding.

Curio: see **Curiosity**.

Cypress, a hard, close-grained, reddish wood, tough and good looking; imported from the Middle East in the 14th century and used for small pieces such as boxes and chests; also, the roots.

Cyst, a small knob or protrusion, e.g. in the bottom of a glass bowl.

Daalder, a silver coin of the Low Countries, similar to a thaler; several designs.

Dado, the broad lower portion of an interior wall when it is different from the rest; a frieze of plasterwork, or merely a strip of different wallpaper just below the picture rail; in architecture, the vertical element in a pedestal between cornice and base.

Dag, a downward point, as in the decorative hem of a garment; also, an early name for a pistol.

Dagger, a short stabbing instrument with blade of various shapes, triangular and usually flat but sometimes three-edged. **75, 225, 253**

Daghestan rugs, Caucasian rugs from the western shores of the Caspian Sea, all wool, Ghiordes knot, red, blue and undyed wool mainly, formal designs including characteristic narrow diagonal stripes.

Dagswain, a coverlet of rough, shaggy material.

Daguerreotype, an early form of photograph, made by the process invented by Louis Daguerre in the 1830s in which mercury vapour condensed on a sensitized silver plate in proportion to the amount of light from the object photographed.

Dais, a raised platform or stage in a room, in particular the site of the high table in a dining hall, or the high table itself.

Dale Hall pottery: see **Edwards stoneware.**

Dalmatic, a loose ceremonial gown worn by Christian priests for certain rituals; also, **dalmatica,** a medieval woman's dress with sleeves in strips and gold borders.

D'Alva bottle: see **Bellarmine.**

Damask, a type of satin weave, or the fabric itself, originally made of silk but later of mixed fibres, in which elaborate figured designs, alternatively matt and glossy, are produced by the weaving technique; luxurious and strong; used for garments, hangings, upholstery and table linen.

Damascening, a technique in metalwork in which the design in gold or silver wire is inlaid in iron or other metal, probably originating in the Near East, but notable in Renaissance Italy.

Damascus rugs, brightly coloured rugs of Angora wool, shipped from Damascus but probably made in Turkey or even Spain and North Africa.

Danburite, a semiprecious stone, usually colourless but also pale pink or yellow, discovered at Danbury, Connecticut, among other places.

Dan Day chair, a Mendlesham chair, said to have been first made by Daniel Day of Suffolk, England, in the early 19th century.

Dandy's stick, a cane used by men-about-town in the 19th century, usually with elaborately carved knob.

Dangle-spit, a spit consisting of a hook hanging from a metal bar and suspended from a rope, relying on free movement to accomplish even roasting.

D'Angoulême ware: see **Angoulême faience.**

Danske, Danish; also, furniture imported from Danzig to England in the late 16th and early 17th centuries, probably including a large range of articles, but particularly chests, etc. of softwood.

Dantesque, a style in furniture of 19th-century Italy imitating early Renaissance design, in particular X-shaped chairs with plush seats.

Danzig chest: see **Danske.**

Danzig cupboard, a heavy, Baroque Polish piece of the late 17th or early 18th century.

Darby and Joan, a homely old couple, assumed to be man and wife; hence, a pair of earthenware figures for cottage mantels; also, a double-seated settee.

Daric, an ancient Persian gold coin showing a king shooting an arrow.

Darning ball, or bell, egg, etc., a small, usually wooden, implement with rounded surface over which cloth is stretched while being stitched, especially useful for darning socks.

Date letter, on English silver, a stamped letter of the alphabet the form of which signifies the date of the hallmark.

Davenport, a small, box-like desk generally consisting of a cupboard or drawers surmounted by a projecting writing compartment with sloping lid, sometimes made to swivel; from the late 18th century; also, a large American sofa. ▶

Davenport ware, earthenware and porcelain from the Longport, Staffordshire, pottery owned by the Davenport family in the late 18th and 19th centuries; mainly fairly cheap tableware.

Day bed, a term often used interchangeably with couch, but distinguished by having a single head in the shape of a chair back, with or without arms and sometimes adjustable; from the late 17th century, though the term is older; see also **Bergère, Duchesse, Chair bed.**

Day lamp, an oil lamp of the Argand type with a reservoir large enough to permit all-day burning without refilling.

Deal, a plain board, or any cheap wood such as pine, used in cabinetmaking for invisible members.

Death-watch beetle, an insect that burrows into old timber, being especially partial to oak, sometimes making a tapping noise which signifies not doom but the procreative urge.

Decal, a transfer.

Decalcomania, a 19th-century technique of decorating (chiefly) furniture by transferring pictures, emblems, etc. from backing paper on to the surface to be decorated; also, a technique in modern printmaking in which ink is applied to paper which is then folded so that some ink transfers to the uninked half of the paper, forming a symmetrical image.

Decanter, a glass vessel for wine, originally (17th century) resembling an ordinary bottle in clear glass but later in a variety of shapes, cut, enamelled, etc., usually with glass stopper; also earthenware. **200**

Deception bed, also **deception table** etc., a piece of furniture the true function of which is disguised from view, e.g. a bed that folds into a cupboard, a table that conceals a cupboard, etc.

Deckle edge, the rough edge of a sheet of hand-made paper, occurring particularly on old books in combination with uncut pages.

Décor à la corne, a mid 18th-century pattern in French faience showing a cornucopia with flowers, birds and insects.

Décor à la guirlande, a pattern of garlands around the rims of plates and dishes, often surrounding a scene from mythology; 18th-century French faience.

Decorative arts, as opposed to the fine arts; the design and decoration of domestic objects e.g. furniture, silver, ceramics, glass, etc.

Davenport

81

80 Pair of mahogany candlesticks in the form of Egyptian water-carriers. French Empire period. Egyptian themes were popular following Napoleon's successes in Egypt. (Praz Collection, Rome)

81 Oak drop-leaf table with turned legs. Spanish, late 17th century. (Museo de Artes Decorativas, Madrid)

82 Doorknocker designed by the French artist, Aristide Maillol, about 1925. Gilt bronze. (Private Collection)

83 Pair of Italian duelling pistols. Mid 19th century. (Private Collection, Milan)

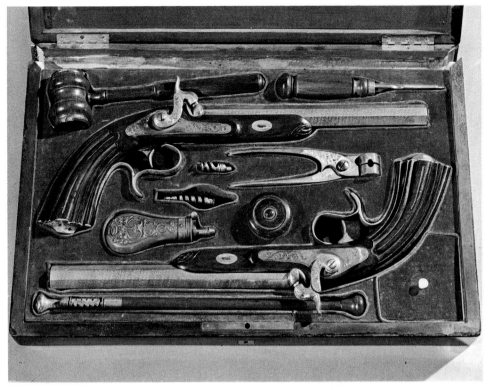

84 Dressing-table in the Art Nouveau style. Designed by C. Plumet. (Kunstgewerbemuseum, Hamburg)

Décor bois, 'wood decoration', found on 18th-century Continental faience and porcelain, decoration resembling the grain of wood that usually forms the background for a landscape scene.

Decoy, a painted wooden model of a duck or other wildfowl used to lure the real thing within range of the hunters' guns, often elaborately made in the 18th century, with glass eyes, etc.

Dedham pottery, formerly Chelsea pottery, American 'art pottery' made at Dedham, Massachusetts, about 1900, associated with the Robertson family and notable, among other wares, for original designs with Chinese high-fired glazes.

Dedication copy, the copy of a book owned, or once owned, by the person to whom it was dedicated and inscribed by the author.

Déjeuner, a fitted tray with tea or coffee pot and cup and saucer for invalids or others breakfasting in bed.

Del., delineat., delin., delt., abbreviations of *delineavit*, meaning he, or she, drew it, following the name of the artist and normally appearing under the left-hand corner of an engraving, etching, or other print.

Delft, the tin-glazed earthenware, often blue-painted, made at Delft, Holland; also **delftware** the name given to all such ware made in England and elsewhere after the spread of the tin-glaze method beyond Holland in the 16th century; see also **Faience, Maiolica**. 77, 161

Della Robbia pottery, English art pottery of many original designs made at the Birkenhead pottery named after the famous family of Florentine Renaissance artists whose maiolica figures have never been surpassed; also, late 19th-century terracotta from other potteries.

Del Vecchio mirror, a looking glass made by a member of the Del Vecchio family in New York, early 19th century; several styles.

Demantoid garnet, a green stone, the most precious of the garnet family, first discovered in the Ural Mountains in the 19th century, used in jewellery.

Demijohn, a large bottle with swelling body and narrow neck, sometimes encased in a wickerwork container.

Demilion, the head of a lion, as used for instance on brass doorknockers.

Demi-lune, 'half-moon', a term applied to certain 18th-century furniture of crescent shape.

Dempsey silhouettes, cut in large quantities by a Liverpool artist of that name in the early 19th century, many of whose customers were emigrants to America.

Denaby pottery, earthenware from the Yorkshire pottery also known as Wilkinson & Wardle which operated for a short time in the second half of the 19th century.

Denarius, the standard Roman silver coin from about 200 BC to about AD 200, usually bearing a portrait of the emperor after the time of Julius Caesar.

Denby pottery: see **Bourne pottery**.

Denga, a silver coin first issued in Russia in the 14th century.

Denier, a silver coin of the Frankish empire imitated throughout western Europe from the 9th century.

Denim, a hard-wearing twill-woven cotton fabric; originally a kind of serge made at Nîmes, hence the name.

Dentils, dentelles, a decorative row of small squares; in Classical architecture dentils occur below the cornice, similarly in 18th-century cabinets, etc.; also, dentelle, a lacy, decorative border, as sometimes stamped on book bindings; see **Doric**.

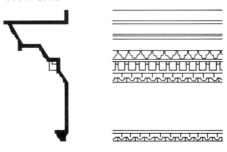

Derbend rugs, from the town in Daghestan on the Caspian Sea; see **Daghestan rugs**.

Derby, porcelain from the famous English factory established in the mid 18th century and associated in its prime with William Duesbury, notable for beautifully painted figures though also producing a wide variety of objects decorative and useful, and responsible for many minor innovations in manufacture and decoration; in decline in the early 19th century; also, other ceramic wares from the Derbyshire potteries.

Derbyshire chair, a 17th-century English oak single chair with a broad, arcaded top rail and no spindles, except (sometimes) two or three ornamental spindles between a central rail and the top.

Derbyshire desk, a small English desk, usually oak, consisting basically of a box with a sloping lid and sometimes a drawer below; from the 17th century.

Derbyshire spar, the stone known as Blue John.

Deringer, a very small handgun of the type invented by Henry Deringer of Philadelphia, about 1825, with large calibre and short barrel, capable of easy concealment.

Deruta maiolica, from the centre at Deruta, Umbria, since the late 15th century, originally similar to Faenza, later distinguished by metallic lustre; including 'petal-back' plates and dishes with profile busts; quality deteriorated after the mid 16th century. 76

Desk, a piece of furniture including a flat or sloping surface for writing, and drawers or cupboard for keeping books and paper. 97

Desk box, a bible box with sloping lid as a writing surface; see also **Derbyshire desk**.

Dessert basket: see **Comfit basket**.

Desserte, a 19th-century French sideboard for the display of various decorative objects.

Dessert stand, a shallow, silver dish on a short central stand, from the 17th century.

De Stijl, a 20th-century Dutch school of artists whose preference for geometric forms and primary colours influenced furniture design in the 1920s and 1930s; see also **Bauhaus, Constructivism**.

Deutsche Blumen, 'German flowers', naturalistic floral decorations on 18th-century porcelain possibly originating with Meissen; imitated in other countries; also known as European flowers.

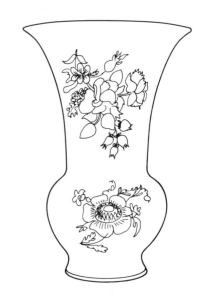

Devotional chair: see **Prie-dieu**.

D front, describing furniture, the front of which is D shaped in plan; also D ended, etc.

Diadem, a gold or jewelled head-dress of Classical times, often revived since; a crown.

Diagonal barometer, made from the late 17th century, with a slanting mercury tube especially sensitive to changes in atmospheric pressure; 18th-century examples often in Classical frame with gilt or brass figures.

Diamond, a rare, valuable stone and the hardest substance in nature, usually a brilliant white but sometimes tinged blue, yellow or brown and occasionally exotically coloured. 78

Diamond-point engraving, the technique of engraving on glass with a diamond-tipped tool, used first in Roman times and common in Renaissance glass; porcelain was sometimes similarly engraved.

Diaper, a cloth with diamond pattern; hence, a similar pattern, or any pattern based on the repetition of a simple geometrical form, carved on furniture, painted on pottery, etc.

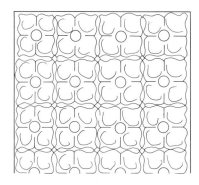

Diatreton: see **Cage cup.**

Dibble, dibber or spud, a pointed, wooden tool for making a hole to plant bulbs.

Die, a metal punch bearing a design from which coins, medals, etc. are struck.

Dilettante, a person interested in the arts but in a casual, non-professional, even frivolous way.

Dillwyn pottery: see **Swansea porcelain.**

Dimity, a strong, double-thread cotton cloth with raised pattern, often in stripes or bars, probably originating in Damietta (Dumiat), Egypt; used for dress and furnishings from the 16th century.

Dinanderie, small brass objects, particularly those made in the Flemish centre of Dinant or thereabouts in the late Middle Ages, including simple household wares and more elaborate ecclesiastical vessels.

Dinar, an early Islamic gold coin bearing an Arabic inscription.

Dinara, a gold coin of northern India, usually with a seated god on the reverse.

Dinner service, a complete set of dishes and plates for serving dinner to six, eight or more people.

Dinner wagon, a moveable stand, or trolley, for conveying food and dishes from kitchen to dining room; also, a coaster.

Diorama, a predecessor of the motion picture, a variably illuminated picture viewed through an aperture; sometimes a long continuous scene which could be made to pass by as though seen from a railway carriage.

Diphros, a simple, square stool on four turned legs used in Ancient Egypt and in Greece.

Dipped seat, the seat of a chair curving up towards the sides; see also **Saddle seat.**

Diptych, a pair of tablets, leaves, paintings, etc. hinged so as to open or close like a book; e.g. a pair of religious paintings for an altar.

Directoire, or Directory, the style in art and design current for roughly a decade after the French Revolution, characterized by a trend toward Classical formality and strong curves, corresponding with early Regency in England; most persistent in North America and associated with Duncan Phyfe among cabinetmakers. **79**

Dirhem, a silver, Islamic coin similar to the dinar.

Dirk, a knife or dagger, in particular the knife carried strapped to the calf in the Scottish Highlands.

Dish, a shallow vessel usually for serving food and thus larger than a plate and often oval or other non-circular shape; see also **Alms dish.**

Dish cover, a dome-like lid, round or oval, sometimes solid silver (more often silver plate), for protecting a dish of food.

Dish cross, an 18th-century device for keeping dishes warm, consisting of a central lamp with adjustable arms capable of holding dishes of varying size over the heater; silver.

Dished, shallow depressions, e.g. in a card table for counters, etc.

Dish ring, a support for a dish consisting of a silver ring, sometimes on three or four feet, which could hold a dish over a lamp; being non-adjustable, superseded by the dish cross.

Dish-top table, an 18th- or 19th-century table, usually round, with the centre hollowed out slightly to make a surrounding rim.

Dispensary jar, a glass or earthenware bottle or jar for medicines, as used by pharmacists; also, bottles for whiskey etc. used by American state liquor-control boards in the 19th century.

Distaff, a forked staff about 3 ft long used for holding wool, flax, etc., during spinning.

Distressed, damaged, when applied to fine furniture; sometimes a dealer's euphemism.

Divan, an upholstered bench, or backless and armless sofa, a piece of European furniture originally expressing nostalgia for the Near East, now characteristic of cheaply furnished bed-sitting rooms.

Dobra, a Portuguese gold coin first struck in the early 18th century, with portrait of the king.

Doccia porcelain, from the factory in Florence founded in the mid 18th century, notable especially for white and painted figures, some with a tin glaze; maiolica also produced.

Document box: see **Bible box.**

Dog cart, a small, open, one-horse carriage with seats set back-to-back, in which originally the rear seat folded up to form a compartment for dogs on the way to a hunt; see also **Dos-à-dos.**

Dog foot, in furniture, a foot in the form of a dog's paw, usually of brass.

Dogwood, hard, yellow or yellowish red wood from the English tree or shrub of that name, occasionally used as inlay in the 16th and 17th centuries.

Dole cupboard, a cupboard found in some churches, usually a hanging cupboard with openwork doors, apparently for gifts of charity, particularly bread, for the poor.

Doll, a children's toy in the form of a human being, made in every conceivable material since prehistoric times.

Dollar, originally the English name for the German thaler and subsequently several other non-English coins, including a large silver American coin; now the standard unit of currency in many countries.

Dolly, a small cart or trolley; also, a wooden implement in the form of a short staff with several extrusions for stirring the clothes in a washtub; see also **Corn dolly.**

Dolly Varden, a dress or large hat with abundant floral decoration, named after the character in Dickens's *Barnaby Rudge.*

Dolphin, a popular decorative device from Classical times and especially during the Renaissance (the fish rather than the mammal), particularly in fountains but also table supports, candlesticks, jugs, etc.

Dome, a rounded roof, hence dome-topped cabinets, etc.; also, a domed canopy on a bed.

Domed foot, on a wine glass, silver cup, etc., a foot of convex section.

Domino, a hood, as worn by certain religious orders; a lady's mask, as worn at masked balls more for titillation than concealment; a rectangular piece of ivory marked with spots, as used in the game of dominoes.

Don pottery, from the highly productive 19th-century Yorkshire pottery, earthenware of almost every kind and some bone china, painted decoration often of fine quality.

Donyatt pottery, slipware, with green-flecked, yellow glaze, from the Somerset pottery flourishing in the 17th century.

Doorframe, a term applied to certain cabinets and bookcases of the early 19th century with façade in the form of a Neo-Classical doorway.

 ▶

Doccia porcelain

85 Louis XV elephant clock. The magnificent bronzework is signed by J. Caffieri, and the clock itself is the work of J. Martinet. (Victoria and Albert Museum, London)

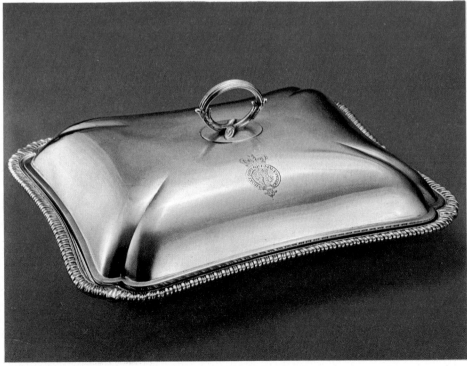

86 Silver entrée dish. English, made by Andrew Fogelburg and Stephen Gilbert, 1792. Gadrooned border and reeded and foliated handle. (S. J. Phillips Ltd., London)

87▲

88

87 Modern engraved glass. Decorated by Paul Tchlitcher-Steuben, 1939. (Victoria and Albert Museum, London)

88 Étagère by the French cabinet-maker, Pierre Hache (1703–76). (Musée Nissim de Camodo, Paris)

89 Silver épergne in Neo-Classical taste. English, by William Pitts, 1790. (Garrard & Co. Ltd., London)

Door furniture, a term to embrace the various metal fittings such as locks, keys, handles, hinges, etc., attached to a door, particularly when the various items are matching.

Doorknocker, made for outside doors since the Renaissance, most commonly brass, in a variety of forms, e.g. lion's head with ring, dolphin, scroll, sometimes grotesque. **82**

Door-stop, or door porter, a heavy object, usually cast iron or bronze, for holding open a door with automatically closing hinge, often with vertical handle, made in a variety of decorative forms from about 1800; see also **Dump.**

Doppelwand: see **Zwischengoldglas.**

Dop stick, a short wooden stick to which a gemstone is attached by wax during cutting.

Doric, the first of the three Greek orders of architecture, simpler than Ionic or Corinthian, characterized by columns having no base and plain capitals.

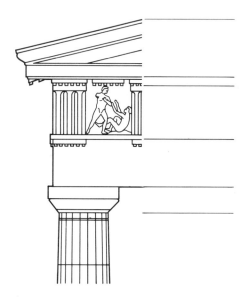

Dorneck, coarse woven Flemish fabric imported from Dorneck (Tournai) and used for coverlets in the 16th century; also manufactured in Norwich, England.

Dorotheenthal faience, from the German factory founded in the early 18th century, with the bright colours and *Laub- und Bandelwerk* decoration characteristic of other Thuringian faience.

Dos-à-dos, 'back-to-back', an expression applied to a double, Janus-like figure in earthenware, to a pair of prayer books bound spine to spine, or to a carriage with two seats sharing a common back; see also **Dog cart.**

Dossal, dosser, or dorcer, etc., an ornamental cloth hung behind or over the back of a chair, in particular the throne of a bishop, or at the back of an altar.

Dosser, a large basket as slung in pairs on a donkey.

Dot Meissen, late 18th-century German porcelain from Meissen, distinguished by a dot between the crossed swords of the Meissen mark; dots also occur on other porcelain marks, e.g. Bow.

Double chair, a settee with back in the form of twin chairbacks.

Double chest, a tallboy or chest-on-chest.

Doublé d'or, gold-plated.

Doubler, a pewter plate or dish like a soup plate with wide rim slanting upward and fairly deep bowl, from the 17th century.

Double-striking clock, a clock that strikes on the hour and again a minute or two later, uncommon but known since the early 17th century.

Doublet, a close-fitting man's jacket or waistcoat, Renaissance and later; also, a jewel consisting of a precious or semi-precious stone, such as a garnet, backed by glass.

Doubloon, a Spanish gold coin first issued well before Columbus but struck in large numbers from the gold of New Spain in the 16th and 17th centuries, usually with arms of Leon and Castile.

Doughty prints, hand-coloured American lithographs of rural and sporting scenes by Thomas Doughty, first issued about 1830.

Doulton ware, earthenware and, more particularly, stoneware made at the Doulton works, Lambeth (London), in the 19th century, best known for decorative household vessels of innumerable kinds in salt-glazed stoneware of fine quality; see also **Carrara, Silicon ware.**

Douter, a candle extinguisher, usually brass, in the form of a pair of scissors with opposed discs at the ends for gripping the wick and dousing the flame; see also **Candle snuffer.**

Dovetail, a common joint in woodwork, favoured for its strength, usually visible in the sides of drawers; wedge-shaped projections are cut in one piece to fit similar excisions in the other.

Dovetail hinge, a type of butterfly hinge, the leaves tapering inwards towards the joint, something like two doves' tails.

Dowel, a wooden peg functioning as a nail in furniture, especially old oak furniture.

Dowlas, a coarse linen cloth used for towels, aprons, etc., and for shirts of a quality regarded by Falstaff as unsatisfactory; also, calico similar to dowlas.

Down hearth, a hearth that is simply a slab of stone, set in the middle of the room below an opening in the roof or, becoming more sophisticated, against the wall with a flue leading outside.

Dowry chest, or dower chest, a wooden chest containing linens and similar articles taken by the bride to her new home.

Drachm, or drachma, a small silver coin of Ancient Greece, much imitated; various types, most common as two-drachm piece.

Dragon, a mythical, serpentine, often fire-breathing beast common in Eastern and Western mythology and occurring in Chinese porcelain, medieval Christian art (symbolizing Satan), etc.

Dragon carpets, in particular, very old Caucasian carpets with heraldic motifs of (perhaps) dragons fighting; found also on other Caucasian and Armenian carpets, sometimes suggesting Chinese influence.

Dragon's blood, a resin from the East Indies used in red varnishes, etc.

Dram, a measure of spirituous liquors; hence, a small glass or silver cup of a dram capacity; also, short for Drammen (timber). **1**

Drammen, Norwegian timber; or, blue-painted Norwegian faience from the late 18th-century works at Drammen.

Drapery, a general word for all kinds of cloth, more particularly cloth used for hangings or 'drapes' (curtains).

Draw-leaf table, or drawing table, an extending table, sections being drawn out on bearers at either end until, at full extension, the centre portion drops to a common level; probably invented in Holland in the late 16th century.

Drawer pull, a drawer handle.

Drawn stem, or drawn bowl, etc., of glass vessels in which the stem is drawn from the bowl in a single operation.

Drawn work, an early form of open-work embroidery, in lace particularly, in which the threads are drawn together to form the basis of the pattern; many varieties.

Drawplate, a block of iron or steel perforated with holes of decreasing size for making gold wire, in use since late Roman times.

Draw runner, or draw slip, terms describing the narrow, pull-out boards (lopers) in a bureau to support the flat writing top when opened; also, drawer runner, the grooved runner for a drawer.

Dredger, a perforated box, often silver, for sprinkling pepper, etc., see also **Caster.**

Dresden china, a popular name for Meissen porcelain.

Dresden faience, early 18th-century faience, especially jars, pots, etc., of large size, from a factory at Dresden, subsequently overshadowed by Meissen porcelain.

$$\frac{D\ H}{2}$$

Dresser, originally a long, narrow side table for displaying silver, etc., subsequently (late 17th century) with tall tiers of shelves above and drawers and cupboards below; also, a dressing table.

Dresser designs, in Victorian silver, highly functional designs for coffee pots, kettles, etc. by Dr Christopher Dresser; drum-shaped bodies, straight handles and clean angles, chiefly electroplate.

Dressing box, or dressing case, a box fitted with small compartments and mirror for women's toilet, a predecessor of the dressing table.

Dressing glass, a mirror attached to a dressing table.

Dressing table, a table designed primarily for women's toilet requirements, with drawers and sometimes an adjustable mirror, made in various forms since the 18th century; also, dressing stand, dressing commode, etc., similarly fitted pieces. **84**

Drilling, or drill, a heavy twill-woven cloth of cotton or linen.

Drinking horn: see **Horn.**

Drinking table, a small social table of indeterminate type; a horseshoe-shaped table, predecessor of the bar.

Drip shield, the flange on a candlestick to catch dripping wax.

Drop front: see **Fall front.**

Drop handle, a handle, as on a drawer, hinged to a back plate so that it hangs vertically but swings up to the horizontal when pulled; common about 1700 and since.

Drop-in seat, the seat of an upholstered chair that rests on diagonal supports across the corners of the frame and can be removed by lifting out.

Drop knop, on the stem of a wine glass, towards the foot, a pear- or cone-shaped knop.

Drop leaf, a hinged flap that hangs down when not in use, hence **drop-leaf table,** any table having one or, more often, two hinged flaps; see also **Gate-leg table.**

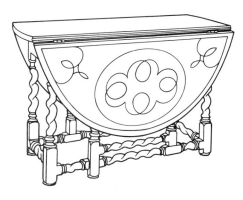

Drugget, a heavy cloth, usually wholly or partly of wool, once used for clothing but since the 18th century chiefly for floor coverings, table cloths, etc.

Drug jar, or pharmaceutical jar, or pot, sometimes with lid and/or spout, for holding the substances used by apothecaries, usually earthenware; the term is seldom used in America where it conjures up images of contemporary decadence; see also **Albarello. 93**

Druid's eggs, glass beads with pattern of stripes, spots, etc., made in Ancient

Egypt and common in the Mediterranean region in Roman times.

Drum brooch, an early Scandinavian gold ornament, roughly drum-shaped with decorative additions.

Drum clock, the earliest portable clock, drum-shaped, which by addition of a ribbon became also the first watch.

Drum table, a circular, Neo-Classical table on a tripod stand, having a deep top often containing drawers; also, a small, low table of cylindrical form.

Drunkard's chair, a name sometimes given to a small settee or love seat.

Dry edge, a phenomenon of some early English porcelain, e.g. Derby figures, in which the glaze receded from a strip around the base leaving a rough surface.

Dry-point, a method of engraving by 'drawing' on the plate with a fine-pointed instrument that leaves a burr of metal, imparting a soft, fuzzy line to the print.

Dscheva, a copper vessel for making Turkish coffee.

Dublin delftware, mid 18th-century tin-glazed earthenware, painted in blue or purple, from the Irish Delft Ware Manufactory, similar to Liverpool delftware.

Ducat, a name applied to medieval European gold coins of many types and countries; in particular a Venetian coin from the 13th century with figure of Christ on the obverse and the doge with St Mark on the reverse.

Duché pottery, made by the Duché family of Philadelphia, Charleston and Savannah in the early 18th century, stoneware and redware, also porcelain.

Duchesne clock, an early 18th-century musical clock made by Claude Duchesne, a French clockmaker settled in England.

Duchesse, a late 18th-century couch of French origin consisting of two identical armchairs linked by a matching stool, or one spacious armchair with stool; see also **Bergère, Day bed.**

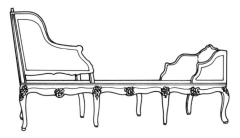

Duckbill joint, one of the innumerable sub-classifications of Windsor chair, describing corners at each end of the top rail that curve out and up in a form suggesting a duck's bill.

Duckfoot, a webbed foot found on some furniture in the early 18th century, and later.

Duck's egg porcelain, the name given to a type of porcelain produced for a brief period at Swansea in the early 19th century, a pale, translucent green.

Dudgeon, hardwood such as boxwood or burr wood used for small turned members such as the handles of knives and daggers in the Renaissance period.

Dudson ware, made by James Dudson of Hanley in the late 19th century, notable for earthenware with inlaid mosaic designs in a variety of colours.

Duelling pistols, a pair of matched pistols, usually kept in their own box, once used by gentlemen in settling private quarrels. **83**

Duesbury porcelain, associated with the prominent artist-entrepreneur, William Duesbury (1725–86) who established a studio for decorating porcelain from various factories and later owned the works at Derby and Chelsea.

Dug-out, a box or chest carved from a solid piece of timber, probably the earliest type of wooden chest.

Dulcimer, an ancestor of both xylophone and piano, in which strings were stretched across a neckless soundbox and struck with hammers.

Dumb stove, a 19th-century American stove with two or three radiating chambers, sometimes in the form of a hollow, cast iron figure, above the fire.

Dumb waiter, a moveable side table consisting of a tier of circular trays revolving on a central column and tripod, for easy access to condiments, cutlery, etc. at the dining table; an 18th-century invention.

Dummy board, a realistically painted human figure, life-size or less, painted on a board and cut out, originating in 17th-century Holland and popular until the 19th century, original purpose questionable but probably for amusement only; also known as fireside figure.

Dump, a glass paperweight or doorstop, popular in Victorian times, roughly dome-shaped with patterns created by air bubbles.

Duncan Phyfe style, a term applied to American furniture of the early 19th century in the Directoire style, associated particularly with Duncan Phyfe (1768–1854), the best-known cabinetmaker of the period.

91 ▲

90 Louis XVI armchair in the
Etruscan style. By Georges Jacob.
The top crossbar has a painted
panel taken from an Etruscan vase,
while the lower bar is decorated
with the anthemion motif. (Musée
Marmottan, Paris)

91 Georgian fall-front bureau.
Walnut, with claw and ball feet.
(Victoria and Albert Museum,
London)

92 Façon de Venise goblet.
Spanish, first half of the 17th
century. (Museo di Capodimonte,
Naples)

92 ▲

93 Maiolica albarello with portrait
of a young man. Faenza, 1470–80.
(Victoria and Albert Museum,
London)

94 Eggshell porcelain plate with
famille rose enamel decoration.
Chinese, Ch'ien Lung period
(1736–95). (Musée Guimet, Paris,
Grandidier Collection)

Du Paquier porcelain, or Vienna porcelain, in the early 18th century the only true European porcelain besides Meissen, producing distinctive chinoiseries and often *Laub- und Bandelwerk* decoration.

Dupondius, a Roman bronze coin similar to the as.

Durlach faience, from the German factory at Durlach, late 18th century, decorated in Chinese style and notable for use of black in outlines etc., and characteristic combination of celadon-green, cobalt-blue and orange.

Dussack, a short (up to 2 ft) straight-bladed medieval single-edged or sword knife.

Dust board, a board inserted in chests of drawers between the bottom of one drawer and the top of the next, often omitted in cheap furniture.

Dust jacket, the paper wrapper around a book.

Dust pan, a flat-bottomed scoop with accompanying brush for removing dirt; old examples in silver, etc., for removing crumbs from the dining table.

Dutch gold, or Dutch metal, a name sometimes applied to imitation gold leaf, made of copper and zinc alloy.

Dutch oven, an open-sided oven for baking in front of an open fire.

Dutch rushes, rough, siliceous rushes of the horsetail type, used in polishing.

Dutch stove, a name applied to several types of stove having a variety of other popular names, standing away from the wall with a flue at the top linking with the chimney; sometimes tiled.

Dutch stroke, in a clock, the repetition of the hourly strike at the half-hour on a smaller bell having a higher note.

Dutch tile, a glazed, painted tile of the kind once used to decorate chimney pieces.

Duty dodger, a name referring to the practice of certain English silversmiths from the early 18th century of removing a hall-marked section from a small or damaged piece and incorporating it in a new large piece, thus avoiding the duty.

Dwarf ale glass, an ale glass with a rudimentary or non-existent stem.

Dwight stoneware: see **Fulham pottery**.

Dyottville glassware, in particular, flasks and bottles from the Philadelphia glassworks owned in the early 19th century by Thomas W. Dyott, depicting masonic and patriotic emblems, busts of famous Americans, etc., in various colours.

Eagle, a common motif in art since Classical times, in various forms, including the German double-headed eagle and the bald-headed eagle of America that decorates anything from chairs and tables to door knobs and can-openers,

79; also, the lectern in a church when carved or cast in the form of an eagle; a gold coin of the United States worth ten dollars.

Ear-back chair, a term sometimes applied to a chair, e.g. comb-back Windsors, in which an outward curve at the ends of the top rail suggests the form of an ear.

Ear dagger, a Renaissance dagger with the hilt terminating in ear-like flanges.

Earthenware, a term that covers all objects made of clay which, after firing, is porous and requires glazing (unlike stoneware) before the objects can be used; see also **Slipware**.

Easel, a wooden frame on which an artist could place his picture while painting.

Easterling, probably the origin of the word sterling, after the eastern European coiners called Easterlings who were brought to England in the 12th century to improve the standard of the coinage.

Eastlake style, American Neo-Gothic furniture of the late 19th century in a cheap, debased version of the style advocated by the English architect, C. L. Eastlake, whose ideas were close to those of William Morris.

East Liverpool pottery, from the 19th-century Ohio pottery, especially notable for its development of Rockingham ware.

Easy chair, at one time an armchair with an adjustable reclining back; subsequently any padded chair designed for comfortable lounging.

Eaton Hall chair, a small 19th-century armchair with round padded seat and a similarly padded form-fitting element, forming back and arms, supported on spindles.

Ébéniste, the French equivalent of the English cabinetmaker, a shortened form of *menuisier en ébène* which distinguished workers in ebony veneer from ordinary joiners (*menuisiers*).

Ébéniste-mécanicien, a cabinetmaker who made furniture incorporating some mechanical ingenuity in moving parts, a German speciality in the 18th century; see also **Mechanical furniture**.

Ebonized wood, or *bois noirci*, furniture stained black to look like ebony, as in many Victorian oriental-style cabinets, etc.

Ebony, very hard, black wood, first imported from the East Indies in the late 16th century, probably the first wood used for veneer, unsuitable for solid construction through brittleness as well as costliness; also found in other colours; 'green ebony', however, may mean ash.

Ecclesiastical plate, gold and silver vessels used in churches, often especially fine and including the chief examples of the art of medieval European smiths, though still rare, especially in England as a result of the Reformation.

Echinus, moulding found in the Greek Doric order, in effect identical with egg and dart moulding.

Eckernförde faience, from the Schleswig-Holstein factory founded in the mid 18th century, vigorous and varied decoration; uncommon, as financial and other difficulties restricted production to a short period.

Écran, a standing screen; see **Fire-screen**.

Écuelle, a shallow, circular bowl with domed cover and, usually, two handles, generally silver but also porcelain, etc., used from the 17th century, probably for soup.

Edkins delftware, or glass, Bristol delftware or glass decorated by Michael Edkins (1734–1811).

Édouart silhouette, cut by Auguste Édouart, who worked in England in the first half of the 19th century, sometimes with painted background.

Edwards and Darly furniture, 18th-century English chinoiserie as advocated in the writings of the designer, Mathias Darly, and his partner, George Edwards.

Edwards bird prints, late 18th-century hand-coloured copper engravings of birds by George Edwards.

Edwards glass, Belfast glass of the late 18th and early 19th centuries manufactured by Benjamin Edwards, father and son, originally of Bristol.

Edwards stoneware, from the Dale Hall pottery established at Burslem, Staffordshire, in the mid 19th century.

Edwin portrait, by David Edwin (1776–1841) of Philadelphia, engravings of notables.

Egg and dart, or egg and tongue, moulding in the form of a row of ovals with dart-like forms in between, sometimes seen on Neo-Classical furniture.

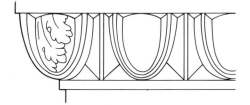

Egg boiler, a late 18th- or early 19th-century device for boiling the breakfast egg, consisting of a small boiler on legs with lamp below and, sometimes, sand-glass egg-timer above.

Eggebrecht faience, produced at the Meissen factory before the successful development of porcelain.

Egg frame, a small silver tray, made from the 18th century in various forms, for holding a number of eggcups and spoons, sometimes with glass salt-cellar and, often, vertical handle.

Eggshell porcelain, associated particularly with Belleek parian, very thin, hard, white porcelain with nacreous glaze; also from various Staffordshire potteries.
94

Églomisé, sheet glass decorated on the underside with silver or gold leaf in which a pattern is engraved, then painted black; also, painting on glass such as mirrors, clock faces, etc.; see also **Back painting**.

Egyptian blackware, Wedgwood's (and others') black stoneware; see **Basaltes**.

Egyptian style, popular in France particularly after Napoleon's campaign in Egypt and in England after the battle of the Nile (both 1798); crocodile motifs, chair arms in sphinx form, etc. **80**

Eidograph, a 19th-century instrument for copying scale drawings.

Eisen, 'iron', hence **Eisenton** ware, the black pottery of late medieval Austria, and **Eisenporzellan,** dark grey stoneware produced at Dresden about 1700.

Elbow chair, the armchair or carver in a set of dining chairs; more generally, a chair in which the arms extend only about halfway from back to front.

Electrogilding, coating with gold by the electroplate method.

Electroplate, coated with silver (or other metal) by means of an electric current, a mid 19th-century invention which virtually killed the traditional Sheffield plate technique.

Electrotype, an actual object, e.g. a leaf, an acorn, a baby's shoe, coated with silver by the electroplate method, or an electroplate object made from a wax model.

Electrum, an alloy of copper, zinc and nickel; also, a natural alloy containing gold and silver, used in early coins.

Elephant clock, a clock in which the case is in the form of an elephant; a whimsical 18th-century idea. **85**

Elers redware, early Staffordshire red stoneware made before 1700 by the Dutch Elers brothers, previously of Fulham, who had an important influence on English stoneware generally.

Elevator, in furniture, a small cup-like receptacle for the legs of furniture, to save carpets from damage.

Elizabethan style, the second half of the 16th century in England, a term (like 'Victorian') owing more to the length of the reign than to any precisely dated style; see also **Gothic style, Tudor style**.

Ell, a measure of length formerly used in the cloth trade, 45 inches in England, 37.2 inches in Scotland, 27 inches in Flanders.

Elliot repeater, a six-barrelled pepper-box pistol made in New York in the Civil War period.

Elliott mirror, a colonial or early Federal American mirror made by John Elliott of Philadelphia, cabinetmaker and part-owner of the Philadelphia Glass Works.

Ellis doll, a Victorian doll with painted wooden head and jointed wooden limbs and body, made by Joel Ellis of Springfield, Vermont.

Ellsworth miniatures, by James S. Ellsworth of Connecticut, mid 19th-century portraits and silhouettes.

Elm, tough, light brown wood, difficult to work and subject to warping; used in chair seats and country furniture from the 18th century, also coffins; see also **Wych elm**.

Elton ware, late 19th- and early 20th-century pottery from Clevedon Court, Somerset, by Sir Edmond Elton.

Email, enamelled.

Email ombrant, a mid 19th-century French technique in pottery, in which a coloured, transparent glaze overlaid a design in varying relief, to create a chiaroscuro effect.

Embattled, crenellated.

Embossed, in silver, relief ornament raised by hammering one side of the metal, as on old coins and medals; or, decorated with applied bosses (e.g. rosettes) in metalwork, furniture, embroidery, etc.; see also **Boss**.

Embroidery, in needlework, the making of patterns in coloured (or silver or gold) thread on a plain cloth ground by one (or several) of innumerable types of stitch, since antiquity.

Embroidery frame, basically a rectangular wooden frame, usually adjustable by some means, for holding taut the cloth ground during embroidery.

Emerald, a precious stone of the beryl family famous for its brilliant green colour and rare in perfect form; a cherished gem since prehistoric times, now capable of synthesis.

Emery stone, a very hard stone, similar to corundum, used in cutting and polishing metals, glass, porcelain, etc., including Roman cameo glass.

Empaistic, embossed or inlaid.

Empire style, covering roughly the French style in the first quarter of the 19th century, though persisting longer in places, predominantly Neo-Classical, more luxurious and ornate than the Directoire, with much gilded ornamentation. **118**

Enamel, a coating, basically coloured glass, applied to metals by firing either as decoration or a basis for decoration; also, such decoration on glass and ceramics; see also **Cloisonné, Champlevé. 119, 196**

Enamelware, enamelled metal, particularly utilitarian iron articles (e.g. saucepans) enamelled for a hard, smooth surface.

En arbelète, a double-S curve like a crossbow (*arbelète*) or the horns of a cow, as seen in some 18th-century commodes.

En cabochon: see **Cabochon**.

En camaïeu: see **Camaïeu**.

Encaustic, coloured decoration fixed by heat in glass, earthenware, etc., in particular the ancient technique of painting in hot wax.

Encoignure, a corner cupboard, specifically a French, marble-topped cupboard of table height, often the bottom half of a two-piece 18th-century cupboard once having shelves above.

En croissant, crescent-shaped.

Encrusted, applied decoration on glassware; also, decorative inlays in stone (e.g. on walls) and metal.

End boards, forming the ends of Gothic chests and benches, usually carved and sometimes gabled.

Endicott prints, 19th-century American lithographs of naval subjects, locomotives, etc. published by a New York firm originally called Endicott & Swett.

Endiron: see **Andiron**.

Endive, a motif based on the characteristically spiky leaves of this plant, found in early English marquetry; also, in 18th-century ornamentation, plaster, etc.

End-of-day glass, small ornaments, pretty, amusing or grotesque, made by glassmakers out of the left-over material at the end of the day's work; also, cheap, mass-produced glass novelties from the late 19th century.

End-on-end drawer, a drawer extending the whole breadth of a drop-leaf table, which can be pulled out from either end.

Endpapers, the sheets of paper, each the size of two pages, which are pasted to the inside of the covers of a book and form the first and last pages of the volume, formerly often marbled, also called fly-leaves.

En face, full face.

Engageants, wide sleeves made of several layers of lace, as worn in the 17th century.

Engaged, linked with or attached to, as in columns attached to a façade.

Enghelskrug, a thin-necked, pot-bellied earthenware jug with pewter stand and lid, German, 16th century.

Engine-turned decoration, a pattern engraved in metalwork turned on a lathe, also adapted to pottery by Wedgwood in the 18th century.

English china: see **Bone china**.

English crystal, good-quality glass (i.e. lead glass).

English Empire style: see **Regency style**.

English oak, a tough and coarse variety, less suitable for furniture than imported European oak and, in any case, often reserved for the navy from the early 16th century; see **Oak**.

English plate, Sheffield plate, that is silver-plated copper rather than white-metal alloy.

96 ▲

95 White porcelain vase with famille verte painted enamel decoration. Chinese, Ch'ing dynasty, K'ang Hsi period (1662–1722). Musée Guimet, Paris, Grandidier Collection)

96 Louis XV *fauteuil de commodité*. Designed by F. Normand (active from about 1746). Also called a *fauteuil de malade*; Voltaire died in this very chair. (Musée Carnavalet, Paris)

97 Mahogany tambour writing desk of the Federal period. Made in Boston by John Seymour & Son about 1800. (Henry Francis du Pont Winterthur Museum, Winterthur, Delaware)

97 ▲

98 Circular fibula in gilt bronze. Danish, 10th century. (Ny Carlsberg Glyptotek, Copenhagen)

99 Modern fibreglass and metal chair by Eero Saarinen. (Produced by Knoll International)

Engobe, light-coloured liquid clay, or slip, used for coating a coarse earthenware body to provide a good surface for glazing and painting.

En gondole: see **Gondole.**

Engraving, in glass, a pattern cut in the surface by small wheels coated with abrasive, such as emery, or diamond-point; also in metal or stone; a print from an engraved copper plate. **87**

En grisaille: see **Grisaille.**

Ennecy carpets, Afghan carpets used as door hangings, made by Christian craftsmen and having patterns based on a cross form.

Ennion glass, ancient Near Eastern glassware marked 'Ennion' in Greek characters, either a signature or a trade-mark.

Enseigne, a brooch worn in the hat in the 15th and 16th centuries.

En suite, of furniture, a matching set.

Entablature, in Classical architecture, the whole arrangement of sections above the capital of a column, including architrave, frieze and cornice; hence, the equivalent part of a cabinet, etc.; see **Doric.**

Entasis, a slight convex curve or swelling in an otherwise straight-sided form; specifically, such a curve in a Doric column, introduced to counteract the optical illusion of concavity created by a straight-sided column.

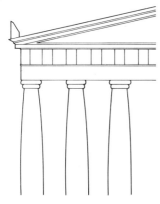

Entrée dish, a silver dish, usually oblong or oval, with separate cover, made in various forms from the mid 18th century, sometimes with stand incorporating a lamp. **86**

Entre fenêtres, 'between windows', a tapestry to hang in that position.

Envelope table, a table with hinged, triangular leaves.

Éolienne, a fine cloth of wool and silk with lustrous effect.

Eolith, a prehistoric flint tool.

E-O table, a games table for 'Even and Odd', popular in 16th-century England, in which dice were tossed into recesses so marked.

Épergne, a centrepiece for a dining table, usually silver, incorporating a number of small dishes around a central bowl; many designs; see also **Centrepiece. 89**

Épinette, or espinette, a spinet.

EPBM, electroplated Britannia metal.

E Pluribus Unum, motto of the United States ('one from many') sometimes found as a decorative device usually on a banner held in the beak of the ubiquitous American eagle.

EPNS, electroplated nickel silver.

Éprouvette, an instrument looking like a foreshortened pistol for testing the efficacy of gunpowder.

Equation clock, a clock showing the equation of time, i.e. both mean time and actual solar time which is seldom exactly 24 hours to the day; from about 1700.

Erect, a term applied to a large, vertical thumbpiece for lifting the lid of a pewter flagon.

Erfurt faience, from the Thuringian factory founded in the early 18th century, including tankards, decorated in high-temperature colours, with pewter lids.

Ersari carpets, Turkoman carpets, mainly dark red and blue, patterned with large basically octagonal shapes (gul motif).

Escalloped: see **Scalloped.**

Escapement, in clockwork, the part of the mechanism that controls the driving power of the spring or weight by alternately checking and releasing it; many different forms, e.g. verge escapement (13th century), dead-beat escapement (18th century), etc.

Escritoire, or scrutoire, a cabinet on a chest of drawers, having a drop-front writing surface supported by metal guys, with small drawers and compartments within; made from the mid 17th century; later topped by a bookcase; the term is used interchangeably with secrétaire.

Escudo, a Spanish gold coin issued in various types and denominations usually with royal arms; also in South American countries.

Escutcheon, a metal plate, in particular the plate around a keyhole protecting the wood, or a small plate, bearing maker's name, on a clock, gun, etc.; also, a shield bearing a coat-of-arms in heraldry; see also **Key plate.**

Escutcheon-lift, a door latch in which the latch is operated by sliding the escutcheon plate upwards, to confound (or confuse) the nefarious.

Eski-Shehir rugs: see **Kirshehir rugs.**

Espagnolette, a bronze or gilt bronze mount, often in the shape of a female bust, or a mask of a faun, on the corners of certain early 18th-century French tables, associated particularly with Charles Crescent.

Esparto grass, a Spanish rush used in making many articles, including paper, shoes, rope, etc.

Essay, a fragment of horn, ostensibly from a unicorn, set in silver, which when dipped into a cup was supposed to reveal the presence of poison.

Étagère, a tier of shelves above a table or cupboard for displaying ornaments, or hanging shelves for the same purpose; see also **What-not. 88**

Etching, a print from a metal plate on which the design, having been scratched through a protective coating of wax, is bitten out by acid; also, a similar technique in glass.

Eternity ring, in jewellery, a finger ring with gems mounted all the way round.

Etoile, a 'star', in particular, an ornament of that form in embroidery.

Etruscan majolica, the name given to certain 19th-century English and American lead-glazed earthenware.

Etruscan style, an 18th-century fashion, encouraged by Robert Adam among others, for decoration in an antique style thought to be Etruscan but in fact mainly Hellenic. **90**

Etui, or etwee, a small, flat case containing various small items like scissors, needles, etc. before the days of ladies' handbags; made in silver or other material since the Middle Ages; also, similar but larger cases for doctors' instruments, etc.

Eulenkrug: see **Owl jug.**

European flowers, painted on porcelain: see **Deutsche Blumen.**

Ewer, a large jug for carrying water, accompanied by a basin, formerly in the dining room, later found on bedroom washstands, generally having a wide spout, narrow neck, ovoloid or vase-shaped body, and round foot; Baroque silver examples often extremely elaborate. **49**

Ewery, a washstand.

Excelsior, the eponymous 'strange device' on the banner in Longfellow's enigmatic poem (1842), appropriated as a tradename by manufacturers of school desks, lamps, glassware, etc.

Exercising chair, a 19th-century mechanical chair which reproduced the movement of horse-riding; see also **Chamber horse.**

Exeter carpets, hand-knotted carpets made at Exeter, England, in the mid 18th century by Claude Passavant, a wool merchant who founded the business with looms and craftsmen from the bankrupt Fulham works.

Exhibition furniture, articles made for or exhibited at an exhibition, especially the Great Exhibition (London, 1851), the Paris exhibitions of 1855, 1867 and 1878, the Philadelphia exposition of 1876, etc.

Ex libris, a phrase appearing frequently on Victorian (and later) bookplates, meaning 'from the library (of)'.

Extending table, a table the area of which can be increased, in particular by pull-out leaves.

Extension lamp, a ceiling-hung oil lamp with pulley and counterweight, which could be easily lowered or raised as required.

Eye picture, a miniature painting of an eye, usually on ivory, a Regency fashion; later 19th-century examples sometimes rather sinister.

Eyrewood: see Harewood.

Fabergé egg, a small jewelled ornament of ovoid form made in the workshops of the great Russian jeweller, Peter Fabergé (1846–1920), who also designed a multitude of other ornaments in gold, silver and precious stones.

Fabric, a cloth made out of fibre, such as wool, linen, cotton, etc.; also any man-made objects requiring a certain skill such as a building, particularly a church; or, the basic material from which an article is made, e.g. the metal from which coins are struck.

Façade, the face or front of a building, hence **façade cupboard** and other pieces of furniture carved in an architectural fashion, with columns, arcading, etc.

Face piece, a horse brass for hanging on the horse's forehead, perhaps originally a brass bearing a portrait of Queen Victoria.

Facet, or 'small face', a small plane, as in a cut diamond or glass, which reflects the light.

Faceted surface, a basically curved ► form cut or carved in facets, e.g. stem of a wine glass.

Façon d'Altare, glass in the style of the Genoese glassmaking centre at Altare, virtually indistinguishable from Venetian.

Façon de Venise, late 16th- and 17th-century European glass in close imitation of the Renaissance Venetian style, often made by ex-Venetian workers, as in the Netherlands, who escaped the strict controls of Venice. **92, 121**

Faenza maiolica, fine, early (late 15th century) tin-glazed earthenware from the Italian centre that gave its name to the French *faience* and German *Fayence*. **93**

Faience, or fayence, tin-glazed earthenware, a name deriving from the Italian town of Faenza, but usually applied to French or German faience as distinguished from the Italian maiolica, English delftware, etc.; see also **Tin-glaze.**

Faience-fine, faience of particularly good quality, in particular cream-coloured earthenware of the English type; see **Creamware.**

Faience parlantes, 'talking faience', ornamental articles in 18th-century French faience, associated particularly with Nevers; inscribed with moral tales, humorous advice, etc.

Faience patriotique, patronymique, etc., French faience bearing revolutionary slogans, birthdate of its owner, etc.

Faille, fine silk material similar to Foulard and used for evening dresses, also trimmings of corded ribbon.

Fairings, small objects in various media sold at fairs, particularly earthenware or

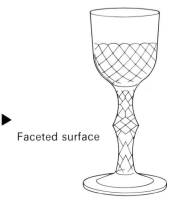

Faceted surface

porcelain boxes, figures and groups, such as the late 19th-century German groups characterized by bawdy seaside-postcard humour.

Fairy lights, small, coloured lamps for outdoor use; also, the night lights, porcelain or coloured glass, for cosy illumination in late 19th-century bedrooms, given the name by their chief manufacturer, Samuel Clarke of London.

Fairy pipe, a small clay tobacco pipe often with bird's-head bowl, for use by women, from about 1700.

Fake, an object of art that is not exactly what it pretends to be, a term sometimes used synonymously with forgery, but usually suggesting an object that has been altered to appear as something more valuable than it is, rather than a complete fabrication.

Falchion, a type of medieval sabre, with short, broad cutting blade.

Falcon, falconet, cannon (large and small).

Falding, a rough woollen cloth with a nap, used for coverings and garments in the 16th century.

Faldstool, an early (12th century) chair, basically X form, with the legs extended upward to arm rests and a back rail, sometimes folding, as the name implies.

Fallals, frothy, frivolous ornamentation.

Fall board, a drop leaf.

Fall front, or drop front, the writing surface of a desk or cabinet, which has to be lowered for use. **91**

Falling ball clock, a clock in global form with hours marked on a moving band around the circumference, suspended from a chain, its weight providing the drive; made in the 16th century; see also **Ball clock.**

Falstaff jug, a Staffordshire toby jug in the form of a figure of Shakespeare's character.

Famille jaune, 'yellow family', a class of Chinese porcelain, basically the same as *famille verte*, but with dominating yellow, or yellow ground.

Famille noire, 'black family', a class of Chinese porcelain, basically the same as *famille verte*, but with black ground, often without glaze.

Famille rose, 'pink family', a class of Chinese porcelain named after the pink colour introduced from Europe in the early 18th century, early examples showing painting of particular delicacy. **94**

Famille verte, 'green family', a major class of Chinese porcelain of the late 17th and early 18th centuries in which the colours are iron-red, yellow, blue, purple and, most characteristically, brilliant green; see also **Famille jaune, Famille noire, Famille rose. 95**

Fan, a device for creating a draught when waved back and forth by the user, made in a vast variety of forms and media since prehistoric times; folding fans, probably invented in China, being

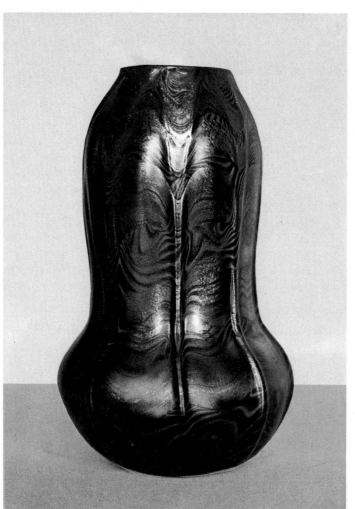

101

100 Favrile vase by L. C. Tiffany, about 1900, in the Art Nouveau style. (Museum of Modern Art, New York)

101 Chinese alarm clock. 17th century. A lighted stick of incense is placed on the dragon; when it has burned down it severs a silk thread releasing two balls; these fall on to a gong giving the alarm signal. (Morpurgo Collection, Amsterdam)

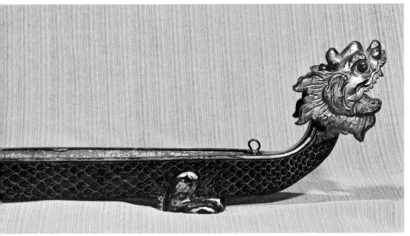

102 Firescreen. French, by
Alexander-Georges Fandinois, about
1855. Black wood frame with
Savonnerie centre. (Château de
Fontainebleu)

103 Silver-gilt flagon. English,
1646. Chased with panels of
dolphins and sea monsters on a
foliate and flower background.
(Temple Newsam, Leeds)

especially fashionable in 18th-century Europe; also, carved decoration on furniture, e.g. chairbacks, similar to scallop form; also a decorative motif in cut glass.

Fanam, one of various small gold coins struck in India and Ceylon (Sri Lanka) up to about 1800.

Fan-back, a carved pattern like a fan on the back of a chair, also occasionally a settee or a bed.

Fancy chair, 19th-century chair japanned, painted with figures and scenes, or even gilded, usually of light construction and with caned or rushwork seat, especially popular in America; see also **Hitchcock chair.**

Fanfare style, a 17th-century fashion in book binding, in which floral motifs are contained in a geometrical pattern formed by interlacing ribbons.

Fantasie Vögel, decoration of exotic birds, found on Meissen porcelain and imitated elsewhere.

Fan top, in furniture, a design in the form of a spread fan occasionally found in 18th-century tables and crestings.

Farmer's watch, a mass-produced 19th-century pocket watch with an agricultural scene on the dial.

Farmhouse furniture: see **Country furniture.**

Farthing, a small English or Scottish coin first issued in silver in the 14th century, in copper in the 17th century.

Farthingale, a woman's skirt of 16th-century Spanish origin in which a series of metal hoops were sewn into the material to hold it out in bell-like form; see also **Bourrelet;** also, a single chair, with upholstered seat and back, from the late 16th century, so called because its wide

seat supposedly accommodated the hooped skirts of the time.

Fastigiated, finished off to a point, like the ridge of a roof (*fastigium*).

Faun, a mythical creature in the form of a man with a goat's horns and legs, usually a symbol of unabashed lechery, appearing frequently in Renaissance and later art.

Fausse-montre, 'false watch', a dummy worn at one end of a watch chain in the 18th century to balance the real watch at the other end.

Fauteuil, an armchair, particularly an upholstered, French chair with open arms often ending in a carved lion's head, bust, etc., from the second half of the 17th century; various types, e.g. *fauteuil à la reine* (flat-backed), *fauteuil en cabriolet* (curved back, later), *fauteuil de commodité* (with gadgets). **96**

Faveur, or favour, a term sometimes used to describe pendants or brooches bearing a portrait, monogram, heraldic or other design of particular significance.

Favrile glass, Tiffany's trade name for iridescent glassware, notably vases, in Art Nouveau style, made by them in the late 19th century, Favrile meaning 'made by hand'; see also **Tiffany glass. 100**

Fazackerley colours, a type of decoration on English delftware, flowers in blue, yellow, violet, green and red, ascribed to mugs ordered by a Mr and Mrs Fazackerley in the 18th century.

Feather banding: see **Herringbone.**

Featherbed, a sack, cushion or mattress stuffed with feathers for sleeping under or on, or (commonly in the Middle Ages) both.

Feather-edge, on late 18th-century (and later) silver spoons and forks, a bright-cut pattern of small lines around the edges.

Feathering, simple decoration in featherlike form, on glass or pottery, attained by combing; also, in cabinet-making, bevelling an edge to a point; see also **Combing.**

Featherwork, pictures or ornaments made from dyed and shaped birds' feathers, e.g. glued on paper, sewn on stiff cloth, set in wax, or forming floral decorations, screens (commonly with peacock feathers), etc.; an ancient craft, very popular in the 19th century.

Fecit, 'he made it', inscribed in conjunction with the craftsman's name on various articles, sometimes engravings, etchings, etc., where the name is to be distinguished from the artist who 'painted' (pinxit) the original picture.

Federal style, the style in American furniture during roughly the last two decades of the 18th and first two decades of the 19th century, essentially Neo-Classical and embracing the Directoire and Empire, or Regency, styles. **52, 79, 97**

Feldspar porcelain, one of the English wares developed about 1800 to fill the gap created by prohibitive duties on imported porcelain, hard, durable white ware similar to bone china except for the addition of feldspar; patented by Josiah Spode II (1754–1827).

Feldspathic glaze, a glaze containing feldspar, or felspar, a group of naturally occurring silicates of alumina, which only fuses at very high temperature.

Fels, a medieval copper coin current throughout the Muslim world.

Felt, stout cloth with a heavy nap made from wool, sometimes with fur and/or hair, under pressure, used for hats and formerly for floor coverings.

Felt table, a felt-covered card table.

Fender, a low guard around the hearth to retain falling ashes and conceal the junction of hearth and floor, generally brass, iron, etc., in use since the late 17th century.

Fender stool, a low bench running the length of the fender, sometimes part of it and upholstered.

Fengite, a type of alabaster, translucent, in the Renaissance sometimes used in windows instead of glass.

Feraghan carpets, from the district in central Iran, including Ibrahimabad, very fine rugs and carpets, generally blue or red ground and herati motif decoration, dense and close-cropped pile, characterized by strong cotton warp visible on the back.

Fergana carpets, from the centre in central Turkestan (Kirghiz), wool, generally red ground, Sehna knot somewhat loosely woven, craftsmanship less than first-rate.

Fernandino style, Spanish furniture of the early 19th century in a style like a heavier version of Directoire.

Fern decoration, found on glass, ceramics, fabrics, etc., in the 19th century, following the fashion for indoor decoration with the fronds of this plant.

Fern glass: see **Verre de fougère.**

Ferrara maiolica, 16th-century Italian maiolica indistinguishable from Faenza.

Ferronière, a band around the forehead with a centrally mounted jewel, fashionable in the 19th century and in much earlier periods.

Ferrybridge pottery, a variety of earthen- and stonewares from the 19th-century Yorkshire pottery first operated by William Tomlinson and Ralph Wedgwood.

Festoon, a decorative motif found most commonly in Baroque and Neo-Classical design, consisting of a garland as though hung from either end and dipping to form a shallow curve (sometimes two or more curves).

Fiat glass: see **Amen glass.**

Fibreglass, or glass fibre, glass spun in threads, thinner than hair, by winding a thread from the end of a rod of glass heated over a flame, a technique employed in pre-Roman times; now either used in the mass or woven into matting. **99**

Fibula, a gold or other metal clasp or pin, as used from the Bronze Age to the medieval era, sometimes ornamented with precious stones, enamel, etc, **98**

Fichtelgebirge glass: see **Ochsenkopf.**

Fiddle-back, in 18th-century chairs, a splat in the form of a violin; also, delicately grained veneer as found on the back of a violin.

Fiddle-head, an ornamental carving on the prow of a ship culminating in an upward scroll like the head of a violin; also, fiddle-pattern spoons and forks.

Fiddle-pattern, a common pattern in 19th-century silver tableware in which the handle broadens out sharply towards the end creating the approximate outline of a violin.

Fiddle-top, an 18th-century table with the top in the approximate shape of a violin.

Fiddlewood, from a West Indian evergreen, so durable as to earn the name *fidèle* (faithful), it is said, corrupted to 'fiddle'.

Field, in a carpet, the whole central area inside the borders; the term is used similarly of a shield in heraldry, the background of a coin, etc.

Fieldbed, a travelling bed for those who travelled in style from the 16th century, the distinguishing feature of which is usually a sloping or arched canopy; in the Middle Ages probably something simpler.

Fielded panel, a raised, chamfered panel, e.g. on a drawer, door of a cabinet, etc.

Fife, a musical pipe, or flute, without keys.

Figure, a human figure carved, moulded, etc., in any medium; also, the natural pattern in wood.

Figure flask, a flask, metal, glass or pottery, in the form of a human figure, notably stoneware spirit flasks of the mid 19th century in the form of various well-known contemporaries, made by Bourne and others.

Figurehead, the carved and painted wooden figure adorning the prow of a ship, most commonly a mythological lady.

Figure-of-eight back, a chair in which the splat is formed of two opposed S-curved members, making a shape like an 8.

Figurine, a small statue. **271**

Filigree, lacy, openwork ornamentation in gold or silver wire, or other metal, porcelain, etc.; in glass, twisted white and coloured threads; also, decoration with narrow strips of coloured paper, rolled up and stuck to a stiff background; see **Quillwork.**

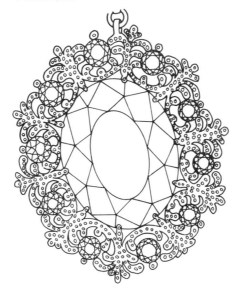

Filler, a paste made of plaster for filling cracks in wood or indentations of the grain before finishing.

Fillet, a narrow band or ribbon, also a flat moulding, a strip between two mouldings, a small bracket strengthening a joint, etc.

Fillet

Fin de siècle, 'end of the century', i.e. the 19th century, often carrying an implication of supposed moral, and even artistic, decadence.

Findighan carpets: see **Shirvan carpets.**

Fine line, in engraved glass, a background pattern of very slight, close-set, parallel incised lines, often at angles, giving a matt effect.

Fine-manner engraving, characteristic of some Renaissance Florentine prints in which the lines of the shading are very fine and close-set.

Finger bowl, a small bowl for water, usually glass, in which the diner dips his fingers when eating something messy, predating forks but still useful when eating asparagus or spare ribs.

Finger vase, a narrow, tin-glazed earthenware vase, a type produced at Delft in the early 18th century.

Finial, a decorative terminal piece, basically of spike-like form but occurring in a variety of shapes, surmounting a pediment, canopy, dish cover, etc. **64**

Finnish carpets: see **Rya carpets.**

Fir, a wood similar to pine but without the dark red streaks; see **Deal.**

Fireback, a cast iron plate for the back of the fireplace, often bearing armorial or other design, including commemorations of contemporary incidents.

Fire board, a board to cover an unused fireplace, usually decorated with embroidery, printed paper, or otherwise; see also **Firescreen.**

Firebox, the part of a stove or boiler containing the fire.

Fire bucket, a water bucket of leather, wood, metal, etc., for fire-fighting, sometimes a presentation piece of fine workmanship with painted insignia or other design.

Fireclay ware, a cheaper version of 19th-century basaltes by Bell of Glasgow, large urns and vases of roughly Classical design and decorated with appropriate scenes on black enamel.

Fire clock, a term covering a multitude of timekeeping devices that depend on burning (including King Alfred's hour-marked candle) or the firing of a cannon; in particular, Chinese clocks of various forms in which a slow-burning fuse burns through a thread at a pre-selected hour, creating some kind of commotion. **101**

Firecracks, found occasionally in early European porcelain, the result of faults in manufacture which caused outward-spreading cracks in the body during cooling.

Firedogs, andirons, the latter name being sometimes preferred for particularly large examples. **168**

Fire gilding, the method of gilding copper or other metal with gold and mercury liquid amalgam by applying heat, whereupon the mercury vaporizes, with deadly effects eventually for the craftsman.

Fire irons, a group of metal implements, with stand, for dealing with the fire, comprising tongs, brush, poker (or fork, in the days when wood was the main fuel) and sometimes a shovel; 18th-century examples sometimes matching fender.

Fire polishing, a technique in glass-making, particularly in finishing pressed glass, which was reheated to add a final polish and remove the seam left by the mould, making it barely distinguishable from cut glass.

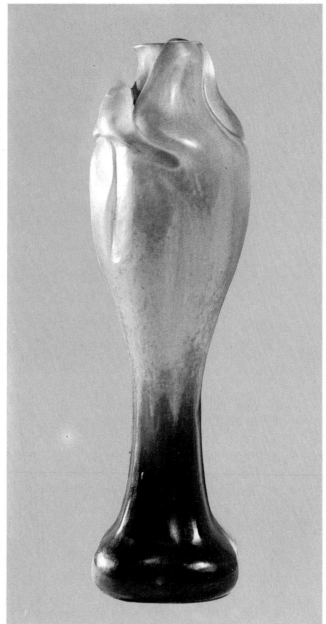

▲104

▲105

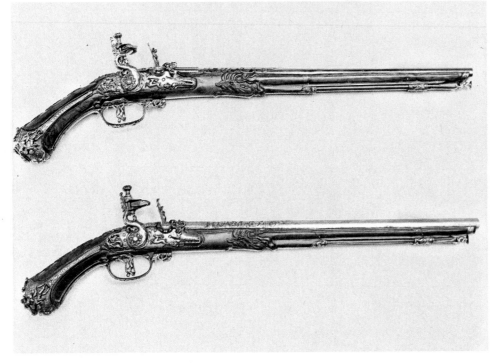

104 Four-poster bed with baldachin. English, designed by Robert Adam, 1776. Painted and gilded wood. (Osterley Park, Middlesex)

105 Vase by French Art Nouveau designer, Emile Gallé. (Kunstgewerbemuseum, Hamburg)

106 Pair of flintlock pistols. Italian, marked Lazar Caminazz, late 17th century. (Museo Poldi Pezzoli, Milan)

107 Ghiordes prayer rug. Turkish, 18th century. The colour green seen in the mihrab is sacred to Muslims and is rarely found in oriental carpets. (Private Collection, Milan)

108 Folding chair of the type found all over Europe in the 15th and 16th centuries. (Museo del Castello Sforzesco, Milan)

Firescreen, or **écran**, a panel, frequently embroidered, mounted and adjustably on a pole with tripod stand, for shielding the face from the heat of an open fire; also, a larger panel on feet for masking the fireplace completely; see also **Fire board**. 102

Fireside figure: see **Dummy board**.

Fire stones, slabs of stone lining a fireplace.

Firing glass, a drinking glass with a short, thick stem and heavy foot, for banging approvingly on the table by way of applause, from the 17th century.

Firkin, a measure of ale (or butter, cheese, etc.) equivalent to one-quarter of a barrel; hence, a small barrel.

Fish-head, modelled porcelain ornament of a fish-head painted in naturalistic colours, English, late 18th and 19th centuries.

Fish-scale embroidery, a pattern, most commonly of flowers, made with the scales of fish sewn on silk, satin or similar material.

Fish slice, a broad-bladed silver knife or flat trowel, usually engraved or pierced, for serving fish, the handle being bone or porcelain, from about 1650.

Fitted furniture, furniture that is built into the room and thus immoveable, such as book shelves, wardrobes, etc.

Fitzhugh, the mystifying name for a pattern commonly found on Nanking porcelain, a broad border of flowers, fruit and butterflies against latticework, usually in underglaze blue.

Fitzroy barometer, a mass-produced Victorian mercury barometer in a rectangular case, named after an English admiral.

Five-poster, a bedstead with an extra upright at the centre of the foot.

Flabellum, a fan, especially one associated with some form of ritual.

Flageolet, a musical pipe similar to the recorder (which superseded it) with six finger-holes, four on top and two below.

Flagon, a drinking vessel similar to a tankard but usually taller, with lid and thumbpiece, pewter or silver, stoneware (notably in Germany), etc. 103

Flagon ring, a matching stand for a silver flagon, like a dish ring.

Flag seat, of a chair, a seat of woven rushes (flags).

Flambeau, in the form of a flame, hence **flambeau finial**. 64

Flambeaux bouillottes, candlesticks on a wide openwork dish with painted parchment shade, seen on early 19th-century card tables.

Flambé glaze, a glowing, deep crimson glaze streaked with other colours, found on some 18th-century Chinese porcelain and later imitated in Europe.

Flamboyant style, in architecture primarily, the final (15th-century) phase of Gothic in France, characterized by sinuous, flame-like forms in tracery.

Flanders chair, a name frequently applied to rather heavy, carved chairs of the Tudor period, probably not all imported from Flanders.

Flanders chest, a carved wooden chest of the 16th or 17th centuries; in particular a chest on which the ornament is applied; not necessarily Flemish.

Flange, a retaining rim or collar, e.g. on a lid to fit into a vessel.

Flap and elbow table: see **Pembroke table**.

Flap table, a drop-leaf table in which the leaves, generally fairly short, are supported on hinged arms.

Flashed glass, similar to cased glass, but with a thinner outer layer, usually coloured, over clear glass.

Flask, a flattened bottle, often lens-shaped, such as a pilgrim bottle, with two lugs for hanging on a strap, frequently pewter in the 15th and 16th centuries; many later varieties.

Flatback, a Staffordshire or other earthenware group, often brightly coloured, left plain and flat on the back, popular for Victorian cottage mantelpieces; also, a term applied to a flat-backed toy tin soldier.

Flat chasing, decoration in low relief on silver achieved by hammering rather than engraving.

Flat-iron clock: see **Beehive clock**.

Flat-jointed table, a drop-leaf table in which the edges of the leaf and the top, which come together when the leaf is raised, are flat surfaces (rather than tongue-and-groove).

Flatware, plates, dishes, etc., as distinct from cups, jugs, etc.

Fleur-de-lis, a motif like a stylized lily, associated with the French monarchy, a common decorative device.

Fleurs des Indes, flower-painting in oriental style on porcelain and earthenware.

Fleurs fines, flower-painting on ceramics in the naturalistic, European style.

Flight & Barr porcelain, Worcester porcelain of the late 18th and early 19th centuries, somewhat yellower and less translucent than the early (Wall) period; bone china introduced also.

Flint, a hard, grey, siliceous stone occurring naturally in rounded forms, used for facing walls, also in certain glass, enamels, and stoneware.

Flint enamel, a 19th-century glaze for earthenware containing calcined flint.

Flint glass, strictly, glass in which the silica was derived from flint, as in 17th-century England, but used generally of English glass whatever the source of the silica.

Flintlock, a firearm of the mid 17th century, or later, in which the firing mechanism involves a piece of shaped flint striking the steel, the dominant form until the mid 19th century. 106

Flip glass, a glass beaker for serving flip, a hot drink containing beer, spirits, sugar and sometimes egg, perhaps not made specifically for this appalling concoction.

Flock, scraps or tufts of wool and other material, used for stuffing a bed, also for making pictures on a board coated with glue.

Flock-printed cloth, the pattern areas printed with an adhesive substance and flock scattered thereon, as with flock pictures on wood (or paper), and in Caffoy.

Floor billiards: see **Carpet bowls**.

Floor cloth, floor covering that imitated tiling (and was in turn imitated by linoleum), consisting of canvas or linen thickly painted to look like marble.

Floral carpets, any carpets with such a design, but particularly Persian carpets of the 16th and 17th centuries, made at centres of the craft (i.e. not by nomads).

Florence maiolica, very early (15th century) Italian tin-glazed earthenware, similar to other early Tuscan maiolica decorated in green (la famiglia verde, 'green family') with brown outlines, later 'relief blue'—very thick dark blue; see also **Della Robbia pottery**.

Florentine green: see **Florence maiolica**.

Florin, originally a 13th-century Florentine gold (also, later, silver) coin; a 14th-century English gold coin worth six shillings; subsequently various European coins including the Dutch guilder and the English two-shilling piece.

Flörsheim ware, late 18th-century German faience from Flörsheim in Hesse, especially notable for attractive painting of flowers ('Strasbourg flowers'), often in high-temperature colours.

Flounce, in needlework, an edging or hem of a garment gathered into pleats or wrinkles.

Flower box, a wooden box, frequently semicircular and painted or inlaid, with circular spaces for glass cups to contain bulbs; from the late 17th century.

Flowered glass, 18th-century glassware engraved with flowers.

Flower-encrusted, in English porcelain, applied decoration of many small flowers, built up petal by petal, on vases, jars, dishes, etc., very popular in the 19th century.

Flower horn: see **Cornucopia.**

Flown blue, early 19th-century English porcelain in which the colour, usually blue, flows into the glaze, specially made to achieve this effect.

Fluorescence, light reflected from an invisible source, a phenomenon observable in certain minerals including precious stones like the ruby, which glows red when exposed to ultraviolet light.

Fluorite, a mineral occurring in a wide variety of colours and having numerous industrial uses; too soft for jewellery but some tougher varieties, e.g. 'Blue John', occasionally used for carving.

Flute glass, a tall, thin and tapering drinking glass popular in the 17th-century Netherlands and usually engraved. **1**

Flutina, a Victorian musical-box containing reeds that made notes resembling a flute.

Fluting, ornamentation of close-set, semicircular, concave grooves, as found on an Ionic column, in which the effect is to emphasize slenderness and lightness. **44, 115, 268**

Fly-leaves: see **End papers.**

Fly leg, the swinging leg of a drop-leaf table.

Foible, the section of the blade of a sword nearest the point, half or more of the total length; see also **Forte.**

Foil, a sheet of gold, silver or other metal, hammered or pressed to extreme thinness; also a light sword with button on the end for fencing; the space formed by cusps in Gothic architecture; see **Trefoil, Quatrefoil,** etc.

Folded foot, in a wine glass, the edge of the foot being folded over to provide double thickness at the vulnerable rim, common in English wine glasses before the mid 18th century.

Folding bed, any of a variety of beds that folded up into a different piece of furniture, from a cupboard to a piano, during daytime; from the 18th century.

Folding chair, a hinged chair which will fold flat for transportation or for storage when not in use. **108**

Folding table, any table with a hinged top allowing its surface area to be extended at will, in particular one in which the hinged leaf folds flat on top of the fixed surface.

Foliation, carved or modelled decoration in leaf form, common during the Middle Ages and the Gothic Revival.

Folio, a book in which four pages are made from one printed sheet, giving a relatively large size, usually at least 13 in high; see also **Octavo, Quarto.**

Follis, a large Roman copper coin similar to the aes, first issued in the late 3rd century AD.

Fondporzellan, a form of decorated porcelain, associated particularly with Meissen and widely copied, in which the painted scene is confined within white panels on a coloured ground.

Fondu, painting on calico or other material in which each colour merges into the next.

Fontainebleau school, the style in the arts in France in the 16th century.

Food cupboard, any cupboard for keeping food; see **Dole cupboard, Hutch.**

Food warmers, devices containing a spirit lamp or candle for keeping food or, more often, a drink warm; in particular, 18th-century earthenware vessels consisting of a covered pot resting on a tall cylindrical base with lamp at the bottom.

Foot, the term for the end of a leg on furniture, many types, all remorselessly classified; also, the base of a wine glass, vase, etc.

Footboard, the board at the foot of a bed.

Footman, a metal stand with four legs to hold a vessel containing hot water or tea; see **Trivet.**

Footpace, a footrest.

Footrest, footplate, etc., a board projecting from the front legs of a chair for resting the feet on; also on tables.

Footring, the projecting ring around the base of a plate, dish, bowl, etc.

Footstool, a low stool, sometimes with matching covering, which was an adjunct of all early armchairs and further emphasized that this was a seat of authority.

Footwarmer, a metal or china container for hot water, for use in unheated rooms, railway carriages, etc.

Forcer, or forser, fosser, fosselet, etc., a chest, particularly a small chest or strongbox, a medieval term that, in the 18th century, also encompassed small cabinets.

Fore-edge painting, a painting on the edges of the pages of a book when slightly fanned out, invisible when the book is closed; found on some 17th-century volumes and at various later dates.

Forest clock: see **Black Forest clock.**

Forest glass: see **Waldglas.**

Forgery, a copy of a work of art made with deliberate intent to deceive, good known forgeries sometimes being quite valuable in themselves; see also **Fake.**

Fork, a silver or other metal implement ending in two, three or four prongs; as tableware, rare in England before about 1700; also, a firefork, a poker ending in two prongs, more suitable for wood than coal, which caused its disappearance.

Form, a bench; also, the essential shape of an object; in printing, a body of type set up for printing.

Form watch, a watch in some decorative unwatchlike form, e.g. a cross, an animal, a lyre, etc., popular in the 17th and 18th centuries.

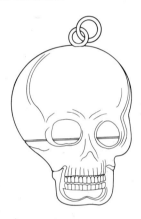

Fornicate, arched or vaulted.

Forte, 'strong', the section of a sword blade nearest the hilt, as distinct from the foible ('feeble') section nearest the point.

Fortin's barometer, an instrument containing a device to overcome error of capacity (occurring through constant change in the mercury level in the cistern) either through a flexible cistern that allows the level to be raised, or by a moving scale that can be brought into line with the cistern's level.

Fosser, fosselet: see **Forcer.**

Foster portraits, early 19th-century profile silhouettes by Edward Foster of Derby, England, commonly in reddish-brown.

Foulard, a light silk or silk and cotton material, originating probably in India, printed in various colours; hence, a handkerchief or scarf of that material.

Four-coloured gold, gold tinted, by varying the alloy, blue, green and white (plus plain gold), a form of decoration popular with late 18th-century watchmakers, especially in France.

Four-poster, the draped and canopied bed, the most important item of furniture and the exclusive form for all who could afford it until the 19th century. **104**

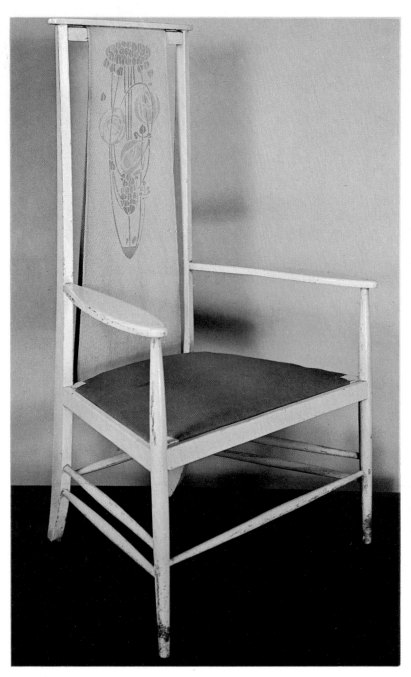

109 Chair by the Scottish Art
Nouveau designer, Charles Rennie
Mackintosh. (University Art
Collection, Glasgow)

110 Silver ginger jar. English, 1663.
With repoussé decoration of
acanthus foliage, swags and masks.
(S.J. Phillips Ltd., London)

111 Louis XIV girandole candelabrum in rock crystal and brass. (Lopez-Willshaw Collection, Paris)

112 Glass pitcher. Roman, 1st century AD. (Museo Civico, Adria)

Fourquette, a long stick forked at one end carried by 17th-century soldiers to support the barrel of their gun.

Foxed, in a book, stained with brownish spots as a result, usually, of being kept too long in a dampish place.

Fox-head, an 18th-century form in ceramics (e.g. a cream jug), glass, silver, etc.; see also **Stirrup cup.**

Frac, an 18th-century gentleman's coat, tight-fitting to the waist and thence flared to below the knee, usually pale green or yellow.

Frame, the surrounds of a picture, door, panel, etc., or the basic structure of a piece of furniture or other manufactured article.

Franc, the basic unit of currency in France since the Revolutionary period, originally struck in silver in the 16th century.

Franche-Comté clock: see **Morez clock.**

Frankenthal porcelain, from the notable Bavarian factory operating in the second half of the 18th century, most esteemed for its symbolic and mythological figures and fine painting.

Frankfurt cupboard, a cupboard on a stand, in architectural form, common in central Germany in the 17th and 18th centuries.

Frankfurt faience, from the pre-eminent German factory established in the second half of the 17th century, originally imitating Delft, with blue-painted Chinese scenes; later more varied.

Franklin clock, a clock with a wooden movement made by Silas Hoadley of Plymouth, Connecticut, in the early 19th century; also, an earlier, simple, brass-faced, weight-driven clock apparently based on a design by Benjamin Franklin.

Franklin stove, a cast iron, open fireplace, standing on short legs and usually with curved sides, originally invented by Benjamin Franklin; many varieties.

Frederican, a term sometimes used for the German (Prussian) Rococo style of the reign of Frederick the Great (1740–86), associated especially with the palace of Sans-Souci.

Free-blown glass, glass vessels blown and shaped free-hand, i.e. with no assistance from a mould.

Freedom box, a silver or gilt box containing a key or document bestowing the freedom of a city.

Free Renaissance style, in architecture and hence furniture, a late 19th-century style strongly, though loosely, influenced by the Italian Renaissance, once described as 'bracket and overmantel style' (Goodhart Rendel); much mass-production.

Fremington pottery, cheap, utilitarian earthenware made at Fremington, Devon, during the second half of the 19th century.

French bed, in England, a bed or couch placed next to the wall, the drapes hung from a bar projecting from the wall, early 19th century.

French chair, a term used occasionally for an elaborate armchair with upholstered back and seat; see **Fauteuil.**

French chalk, a type of steatite, similar to soapstone, used by tailors and dressmakers for marking cloth, or for removing grease marks.

French foot, a bracket foot, on cabinets, etc., with a concave, outward curve; also, a scroll foot on chairs.

French furniture, a colloquial English term sometimes used in the 18th century to describe elaborate Rococo furniture in the French style.

French plate, or *cuivre argenté,* silver-plated copper; a method in which a sheet of very fine silver foil was laid over the copper and made to adhere by gentle heat or burnishing.

French polish, a technique of finishing furniture, first used about 1800 by applying coats of resin dissolved in spirit, which gives a hard glassy surface without obscuring the natural qualities of the wood; still sometimes regarded as inferior to the traditional oil and elbow grease.

French Revival furniture, a term sometimes used of Victorian furniture in the French styles of the 17th and 18th centuries.

French stool, a window seat.

Fresco, a painting, usually but not necessarily on a wall, executed on plaster that is still damp, an ancient technique especially popular in the Renaissance.

Fret, an ornamental openwork design composed of straight vertical and horizontal lines crossing at right angles; also called key pattern.

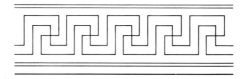

Fretwork, decorative openwork, usually in wood cut with a fret-saw, characteristic of much Chinese-style furniture.

Friendship quilt, a 19th-century quilt also known as Autograph, Bridal, Presentation, etc., made by a group of friends each of whom contributed a piece, for a particular person on a special occasion.

Friesland clock, a common Dutch bracket clock of the 18th century, usually chain-driven, with gilt or brass openwork decoration.

Frieze, in Classical architecture the central member of the entablature, usually ornamented; hence, the corresponding element in case furniture, the section of a wall below the cornice, a horizontal band below a table-top, etc.; also, a woollen cloth somewhat like baize imported from Friesland in the 16th century.

Frigger, a glass object usually of an unlikely kind (rolling pin, walking stick etc.), and sometimes crudely made, produced by glassmakers in idle moments, associated particularly with Nailsea; see also **End-of-day glass.**

Fringe, a decorative border on a garment, carpet, upholstery, etc., consisting of loose threads knotted or otherwise fastened at the base.

Frit, in glassmaking, the mixture of raw materials after they have been mixed and reduced to a glassy substance by moderate heating in a furnace; also in soft-paste porcelain.

Frit porcelain, soft-paste porcelain which, before the discovery of the technique of making true porcelain, was made by a process similar to glassmaking; see **Frit.**

Frog, a leather thong attaching a sword sheath (more recently a bayonet) to the belt.

Frog mug, an earthenware mug with a modelled frog on the bottom or sides, disconcerting to the unsuspecting drinker, late 18th century.

Fromanteel clocks, rare, early English pendulum clocks made by a family of Dutch clockmakers working in London in the 17th century.

Frontispiece, a full-page illustration in a book, appearing before the title page.

Frontlet, a band worn around the forehead.

Frosted silver, a matt surface on silver usually forming the background of a pattern, achieved by dipping in dilute sulphuric acid, common in the early 19th century.

Frounce, or fronce: see **Flounce.**

Frozen Charlotte, a Victorian china doll with immovable head and limbs used as a bath toy, also called Badekind.

Fruit basket, an openwork container, usually of silver, sometimes on a stand, with bail handle, for fruit.

Fruitwood, wood of the apple, cherry, pear, etc., used in furniture making, including veneers, in most periods.

Frying pan candlestick, a common form of brass chamber candlestick, shaped like a frying pan with candle socket in the centre.

Fuddling cup, an earthenware, notably English delftware, drinking vessel consisting of three or more containers joined together with passage for the contents to pass from one to the next, so that to empty one cup it was necessary to empty the lot.

Fulcrum, a headrest, as seen on Roman couches, often in elaborate form.

Fulda faience, fine German (Hessen) faience of the mid 18th century including some of the best German faience figures; production lasted only one generation.

Fulda porcelain, late 18th-century porcelain produced at the former faience factory, figures sometimes based on Frankenthal models, tableware often imitating contemporary Meissen.

Fulham carpets, from the short-lived, mid 18th-century carpet factory at Fulham, London, run by Peter Parisot.

Fulham pottery, early stoneware, as well as earthenware, including ware called 'red porcelain' and salt-glazed, finely modelled figures by the innovating John Dwight; see also **Elers redware**.

Fuller, a blacksmith's tool on which iron was shaped by hammering it into grooves.

Full-moulded, glassware made in a single, hinged mould.

Fumé, smoky or smoked, a term applied for instance to early Catalan glass, which had a smoky appearance.

Fumed oak, a recent (about 1900) finish to oak furniture achieved by exposure to ammonia fumes, which turned the wood a greyish colour.

Funeral hatchment: see **Hatchment**.

Funeral image, a wax model of the dead placed in church as a memorial; few survivors since the Reformation.

Funeral piece, a ring, silver spoon or similar object presented to mourners at a funeral as a memento of the departed; see also **Memento mori**.

Funnel, a silver wine strainer for filling a decanter, used from the mid 18th century; also, a wine glass with straight, tapering bowl.

Furbelow, a decorative hem of a garment, or flounce.

Furniture, a term including all the moveable articles in a room, but generally applied to seats and beds, tables and stands, cupboards and containers (case furniture), made of wood, metal or stone or modern substitutes; also, the adjuncts of an object, e.g. the brass furniture of a chest.

Furniture beetle, the insect whose larvae bore through the wood causing the tiny holes usually ascribed to 'woodworm'.

Furnival ironstone, ironstone china produced in large quantities by T. Furnival & Sons of Cobridge, England, from the mid 19th century, including tableware with relief decoration and attractive painting.

Fürstenberg porcelain, from the German factory founded in the mid 18th century, notable for some fine early figures and for porcelain pictures or plaques.

Fusee, in clockwork, a small drum like a curved-sided cone which compensates for the declining power of the unwinding spring in a spring-driven clock or watch; a 15th-century invention; also, an early name for a friction match.

Fusil, a steel for making fire in a tinderbox; also, a light musket of the late 17th century.

Fustian, tough cloth of twilled cotton, originally imported from Muslim Spain as a mixture of linen and cotton, many varieties, 'much employed for the dress of labouring men' (1882).

Fustic, a yellow dye derived from the wood of two species of tree; also, the wood of those trees, particularly a West Indian variety, used for inlay in the 18th century.

Fusuma, a sliding wall of wooden panels, usually painted or otherwise decorated, in Japanese houses.

Fylfot, or swastika, a geometric design originating probably in India, a cross with L-shaped arms, sometimes seen on friezes but not very popular nowadays.

Gable, in architecture, the section of the wall above the level of the eaves, especially when it extends beyond the lines of the roof; hence, a similar element in furniture, e.g. Gothic chests.

Gad, a metal spike, in particular a tool of that form used in mining; also, any bar of metal; or a rope made from wood fibres, a wooden pole, etc.

Gadnail, an iron nail, a gad.

Gadrooning, or nulling, a decorative pattern on borders and edges, carved, painted, etc., most typically a series of convex curves, or alternating convex and concave curves as frequently seen on the edges of 18th-century tables, silverware etc. **86**

Gaffle, the steel crank on a crossbow; also, a metal spur worn by combatants in cockfights.

Gage, a pot or large drinking mug; also, a glove.

Galena, an ore of silver or lead; also, a rich yellow glaze on early European earthenware, derived from powdered lead sulphide.

Gall, in glassmaking, the scum that forms on melted glass; also, an excrescence on an oak tree, the source of a ferrous dye, dark brown or black, used in oriental carpets.

Gallé furniture, made by Emile Gallé (1846–1904), leading member of the French school of Art Nouveau designers working at Nancy.

Gallé glass, made by or in the workshop of Emile Gallé (1846–1904) who was responsible for many technical innovations and for beautiful cased glass; see also **Moonlight glass. 105**

Gallery, in furniture, a decorative low railing, usually openwork and often metal, around a desk-top, table, etc., popular in the late 18th and early 19th centuries; also, a carpet runner. **269**

Gallipot, gillypot, a small earthenware pot, probably for oil or ointment; see also **Drug jar.**

Galloon, or galon, a strong ribbon or braid, including the gold braid on uniforms, trimming for curtains and dresses, and the decorative tape used to mask the point where upholstery is fastened to wood.

Galosh, or galoche, originally a wooden shoe or clog, later an overshoe or an extra piece of leather protecting the lower part of the shoe.

Galtuk carpets, from the region around Arak, similar to Khamseh carpets.

Galvanized, coated with metal by electrochemical means; in particular, iron or steel coated (not necessarily electrically) with zinc to prevent rust, used for garden furniture, etc. from the late 19th century; see also **Electroplate.**

Galvano-plastic, electrotyping; see **Electrotype**.

Gamba, the base of the viol family of stringed instruments.

Gamboge-yellow, a gum-resin from south-east Asia, whence a bright yellow dye is obtained.

Gambrelled, or hipped, a shape (as in a chair leg) like the hind leg of a horse.

Gambroon, a twilled cotton cloth.

Games table, a small table with a chess or backgammon board inlaid in the top, sometimes containing a drawer for chessmen, etc., from the 18th century (though there was one in Tutankhamun's tomb); see also **Card table.**

Gantry, or gauntry, a wooden frame for holding barrels in a cellar.

114

113 Gravity clock. Made in Madrid by the Italian clockmaker, Francesco Filippini, 1688. The four faces have astronomical markings. (Staatliche Kunstsammlungen, Kassel)

114 Goblet and cover in flashed glass. Bohemian, 19th century. (Corning Museum of Glass, Corning, New York)

115 Silver gravy pot and two sauce tureens. English, made by Carter, Smith & Sharp, 1785. The helmet-shaped gravy pot is called an argyll; all three are half fluted and have gadrooned edges. (Private Collection)

116 Gobelins tapestry *The Hunts of Louis XV*. Designed by J. B. Oudry in 1743. (Palazzo Pitti, Florence)

117 Mahogany armchair in early Gothic Revival style. English, second half of the 18th century. (Victoria and Albert Museum, London)

Garde du vin, a box, sometimes metal-lined, for wine, often made in the 18th century to match a sideboard; see also **Cellaret**.

Garden carpets, from western Iran chiefly, carpets in the design of a garden, including paths, ponds, birds, animals, etc.

Garden furniture, a term encompassing 'rustic' furniture of unplaned timbers, stone and cast iron seats and tables for use out of doors.

Gardner porcelain, from the Russian factory near Moscow established by the Englishman, Francis Gardner in the mid 18th century.

Gargoyle, in medieval architecture, a sculpted stone head, frequently grotesque, on the spout of a gutter, usually on a church roof; examples in bronze from secular buildings also exist.

Garnet, a large family of gem stones, mostly dark red but including several other colours, the green demantoid garnet being the most valuable.

Garnish, a set of pewter, silver, china, etc. tableware; see also **Garniture of vases**.

Garniture of vases, matching sets of vases and/or jars in silver, porcelain, etc., made to decorate the chimneypiece from the late 17th century, often in the Chinese style; see also **Clock garniture. 77**

Gas candle, gas lights in the form of the redundant candle, a frequent form in the early days of gas lighting.

Gasolier, a multiple gas light in the form of a chandelier, with glass shades instead of candles, usually brass, mid 19th century.

Gate-leg table, the most popular form of extending table since the 17th century, in which the rounded, hinged flaps are supported when raised by 'gates' that swing out from the central section; see also **Drop-leaf table**.

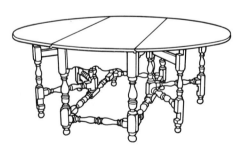

Gate table, a simpler version of the gate-leg (having the leg but not the gate, confusingly) common after the use of mahogany had made stretchers unnecessary; usually larger, heavier and having only four legs (not six).

Gather, in glassmaking, the molten glass that is 'gathered' at the end of the blow-pipe to be shaped and blown into a vessel.

Gatling gun, an early prototype of the machine-gun named after its mid 19th-century inventor.

Gaudy, cheap, bright ornamentation of some kind, usually referring to pottery, e.g. gaudy Welsh or gaudy ironstone; see also **Imari**.

Gaudy Dutch, brightly coloured Staffordshire wares in oriental designs exported in large quantities to America in the early 19th century.

Gauffered: see **Goffered**.

Gauger, a small pewter measuring cup.

Gauntlet, a glove, usually leather, with an extension to protect the wrist, originally, perhaps, from a bow-string as it was released.

Gem, any precious or semiprecious stone that has been cut or polished for decorative effect.

Gemel, a pair of objects joined, as in a gemel ring, gemel jars or flasks having two compartments.

Gendje rugs, Caucasian rugs from the region around that centre, similar to Kazak rugs, decoration frequently linear and colours bright.

Genoa maiolica, made from the late 15th or 16th century, associated especially with wall tiles and panels.

Genovino, a small gold coin issued in Genoa in the 13th century.

Genre, in fine art, anecdotal painting of domestic scenes and the activities of everyday life, as in the Dutch school; also, a type or class, or body of work in a characteristic manner.

Georgian, in Britain, the period covered by the reigns of the first four Georges (1714–1830) but when used of style in the decorative arts usually implying the period up to the Regency, i.e., most of the 18th century.

Gera porcelain, from the late 18th-century Thuringian factory, generally imitative of Meissen and not very successful commercially or artistically.

Gera

German flowers: see **Deutsche Blumen**.

German silver, white metal or *bronze argent*, an alloy of nickel, copper and zinc much used for silver-plating in the 19th century in preference to copper, which showed through more easily; see also **Argentine**.

Gesso, a composition material like plaster, used since the Middle Ages for relief decoration on furniture and elsewhere, usually painted or gilded; see also **Compo**.

Gewgaw, a gaudy trifle, ornament, cheap jewellery, etc.

Ghiordes knot, or Turkish knot, one of the two knots used in oriental carpets, chiefly in Turkey and the Caucasus, in which the yarn is passed over two threads, turned, and the ends brought up between the threads (the original

Ghiordes or Gordian knot was that which posed the problem drastically solved by Alexander the Great).

Ghiordes rugs, from the town in western Turkey, usually of the prayer-rug type, i.e. relatively small; very fine quality, especially older specimens, with rich and intricate designs, close pile and in rare silk rugs as many as 130 knots per square inch. **107**

Ghoum carpets, Persian carpets from the region south of Teheran (Qum), many-coloured formalized patterns often arranged in rows, Sehna knot, sometimes very densely woven.

Gibus, or opera hat, a top-hat that could be compressed like an accordion.

Gien faience, 19th-century French earthenware, imitating the styles of earlier periods, also specializing in printed scenes.

Gig, a light, two-wheeled, one-horse carriage in which the driver sat forward of the wheels; also, a barbed spear for fishing, or the wooden cage in which miners descended the pit.

Gilding, coating with gold by one of several methods, most extremely ancient; on furniture usually on a gesso ground, especially popular in various periods (e.g. late 17th century) since Ancient Egypt; see **Fire gilding**, **Oil gilding**.

Gilet, a richly embroidered waistcoat, as worn by gentlemen in the 18th century.

Gill, a measure of wine or (nowadays) spirits; hence a small silver or glass cup containing that amount.

Gilliland glass, from the Brooklyn Flint Glass Co. (which later moved to Corning), originally owned by John L. Gilliland & Co.

Gillypot: see **Gallipot**.

Gilt: see **Gilding**.

Gilt bronze: see **Ormolu**.

Gilt-edged, books or paper with top and edges (sometimes only top) gilded.

Gimcrack, originally small machinery or intricate workmanship; more recently, clever but worthless, showy but shoddy.

Gimmal, or gimmel, a flat bottle for easy carrying.

Gimp, in embroidery, a narrow, ornamental, usually openwork tape used as a trimming, often based on a strong cord or wire.

Gin bottle, in particular, a stoneware jar and flask the top half of which is modelled as a figure of some contemporary significant figure during the English crisis over parliamentary reform in the early 19th century.

Ginger jar, the name given to tall, lidded silver vessels of the 17th century, richly engraved, and occasionally found in pairs. **110**

Gingham, linen or cotton cloth, originally imported from India, formerly much used for inexpensive dresses and characteristically checked or striped.

Ginori maiolica, from the factory of the Ginori family in Doccia; also, 19th-century Italian earthenware imitating older styles in maiolica.

Giraffe piano, an upright piano that looks like a grand piano set on end, very tall at the bass and curving down towards the treble.

Girandole, a large candelabrum or sconce, usually silver; also used of a variety of other articles, e.g. a jewel with several pendants, a circular, gilded mirror with candleholders, etc. **111**

Girandole clock, an uncommon type of early 19th-century banjo clock, more elaborately ornamental than the traditional banjo clock, with gilt scrolls, eagle, etc.

Girdle: see **Griddle.**

Girdle book, a medieval prayer book with extended binding which could be attached by a button or hook to the girdle.

Girl-in-a-swing porcelain, rather mysterious, early English white porcelain figures, named after a well-known piece, having a high proportion of lead oxide in the body.

Girth, a band of leather or webbed material, as used to strap a pack or saddle on a horse, for example.

Gittern: see **Cittern.**

Giulio, a silver coin of the Vatican, with portrait of the pope, current in the 16th century and named after Pope Julius II.

Giustiniani maiolica, 18th-century maiolica from the Naples factory of the Giustiniani family.

GIUSTINIANI

Glacé, glazed, a term used particularly of cloth with a shiny finish.

Glaive, a cutting and stabbing weapon, such as a lance with a blade at the end; also, a ceremonial lance presented as a prize to the winner of a race; sometimes simply a broadsword.

Glasgow delftware, mid 18th-century tin-glazed earthenware in the Dutch style, and later other wares, from the Glasgow factory founded by Lambeth potters.

Glasgow style, the version of Art Nouveau associated chiefly with the Scottish architect and designer, Charles Rennie Mackintosh. **109**

Glass, an extremely versatile, artificial mineral made basically of silica (sand, flint, etc.) with various additives and fired in a furnace; usually transparent and frequently colourless, very hard though not tough, in use since antiquity but seldom in windows until the Renaissance. **112**

Glass egg: see **Hand cooler.**

Glass-of-lead, Ravenscroft's name for his invention, i.e. lead glass.

Glass paper, sandpaper.

Glass paste, coloured glass, used in cheap jewellery.

Glass picture, a picture made on glass by one of several techniques, including that of engraving in gold leaf on the back of a sheet of glass; see **Back painting, Églomisé. 159**

Glass print, a print made on photographic paper placed under a sheet of glass on the surface of which a design was etched in some kind of non-transparent coating; also, a painted copy of a print, made on glass by the technique known as back-painting.

Glasswork, a general term encompassing various kinds of ornamental work in glass made by an amateur from manufactured glass or fragments of glass.

Glastonbury chair, a Renaissance folding chair with X-form legs, flat back and arms pivoted at the top of the back and front of the seat, all parts being cut boards with no turning; frequently ecclesiastical, like the eponymous piece of the abbot of Glastonbury.

Glaze, in ceramics, a hard, glassy coating, impervious to water and giving a smooth, shiny finish; various types (e.g. tin-enamel) depending partly on the nature of the body.

Glazed quartz fritware, a type of imitation porcelain with a siliceous body (powdered quartz) fused with natron, usually blue or purple.

Glazing bar, a narrow wooden bar in a glass-fronted cabinet, window, etc., which holds the panes of glass in place.

Global clock, any clock of spherical shape; also, an astronomical clock showing paths of the planets, etc., see also **Falling ball clock.**

Globe, a model of the earth, sometimes with paths of heavenly bodies, etc., popular in the Middle Ages; also, primarily decorative representations of the earth, popular in the 18th century, and various articles such as jars, inkwells, teapots, etc. of global form.

Globe writing table, apparently a large globe, the top part of which slid aside to reveal a circular writing surface at about the equator; drawers were also concealed in the southern hemisphere; popularized by William Pitt the Younger, about 1800.

Glockenspiel, 'play of bells', a carillon or chime of bells; also, a musical instrument producing a similar effect by striking bronze bars, played on a keyboard.

Glomi work: see **Églomisé.**

Glove stretcher, an implement like a pair of tongs, made of wood, for stretching gloves into shape after washing.

Gnomon, a rod or pointer, in particular the vertical, shadow-casting element, usually triangular, on a sundial.

Goat-and-bee, a famous jug pattern with a pair of goats lying at the foot and, above, a bee among flowers, originally Chelsea soft-paste porcelain, mid 18th century; also in silver and often reproduced in more recent times.

Gobelins tapestry, from the famous French workshops named after the Gobelins family but under royal patronage from the mid 17th century and perhaps at their peak in the ensuing century, when designs were largely based on oil paintings. **116**

Goblet, a term generally applied to any large drinking cup, or wine glass, with stem and foot, especially if it has a lid. **26, 114**

Go-cart: see **Baby cage.**

Go-chair, a wheelchair.

Goddard furniture, made by one of a family of cabinetmakers in Newport, Rhode Island, in the late 18th or early 19th century, noted particularly for fine block-front cabinets.

Godet, a goblet.

Godwin furniture, designed by Edward Godwin (1833–86), who was greatly influenced by traditional Japanese design, foreshadowing Art Nouveau; also, less distinguished furniture based on Godwin's Anglo-Japanese style.

Goffered, or gauffered, stamped with a raised pattern, often achieved by pressing between blocks or rollers in which the pattern is incised on one and raised on the other.

Goggingen faience, from the Bavarian centre founded in the mid 18th century, floral and Chinese designs, painted in rich, high-temperature colours.

118 Guéridon. French Empire period, mahogany and gilt bronze. The Paris porcelain group of four dancers is late 18th century. (Musée Marmottan, Paris)

119 Enamelled plate with scene representing the month of August, with medallions and grotesques all in grisaille. French, by Pierre Reymond, mid 16th century. (Musée des Arts Décoratifs, Paris)

121 Façon de Venise Guttrolf.
German, 17th century. (Museo di
Capodimonte, Naples)

120 Fragment of a Byzantine
textile woven with a pattern of
gryphons. Silk serge and wool.
(Musée de Valère, Sion)

Gold, the most precious of metals, a splendid colour, non-tarnishing, heavy and so soft that it is usually alloyed with copper or another base metal; having been for a long time too expensive for all but very small objects, its commonest use in the decorative arts is in gilding.

Gold amalgam, a soft alloy of gold and mercury.

Gold-leaf silhouettes, etched in gilded glass, from the late 18th century; see also **Églomisé.**

Gold lustre, made from gold oxides and applied to glazed and unglazed ware, often more red or coppery than gold.

Goldoniana: see **Frac.**

Goldstone, a type of glass giving a golden shimmer as the result of admixture of copper oxide, used in cheap jewellery.

Gombron ware, Persian blue-and-white pottery shipped by the English from Gombron (Bandar 'Abbas) on the Persian Gulf in the 17th and 18th centuries.

Gondola, a boat with high, pointed prow and stem, with cabin midships, propelled by a single oar, as seen in Venice; also the type under an airship, or a type of upholstered chair with curved back; see also **Gondole.**

Gondole, French furniture *en gondole* implies a curved, boat-shaped form, as in a chair back, characteristic of the Louis XVI period.

Gone-with-the-Wind Lamp, an oil-burning lamp with decorative glass shade, late 19th century, popularly named after the contemporary novel.

Gong, a metal disc with wide turned-back rim, usually bronze, suspended and struck with a muffled hammer; in clocks, a spiral of wire on which the hour is struck.

Gooseneck: see **Swan-neck.**

Gorget, originally a piece of armour plate protecting the neck, hence any item of dress in that position, in particular the article of dress, usually lace, covering the neck and breast of women in the 16th century.

Goshenite, a variety of beryl, virtually colourless, sometimes used in jewellery.

Goss china, various wares, including fine Parianware and porcelain inlaid with jewels, from the 19th-century pottery of W. H. Goss, Stoke-on-Trent, which also produced heraldic porcelain souvenirs with coats-of-arms etc. in brilliant enamels.

Gossip chair: see **Caqueteuse.**

Gotha porcelain, from the Thuringian factory established in the mid 18th century, of generally high quality, similar to other contemporary German porcelain.

Gothic clock, the name given to 15th- and early 16th-century iron domestic clocks made chiefly in Germany, usually framed in four iron pillars with an arched canopy for the bell above; also, steeple clocks generally, particularly 19th-century New England clocks with 'Gothic' case.

Gothic Revival, strictly, the 18th-century revival of a somewhat fantasized Gothic style in architecture and furnishings, associated particularly with Horace Walpole's Strawberry Hill in England; also, more generally, the Gothic style of the 19th century, grander, more serious and more widespread. **117, 285**

Gothic style, the prevalent style in western Europe from the 12th century to the Renaissance, in England never entirely superseded; characterized, above all, by the pointed arch, an element which, when found in furniture or decoration, invites the description 'Gothic', as in Gothic clock, Gothic chair, Gothic fire-screen, etc., often referring to 19th-century designs. **117**

Gotzkowsky pattern, a pattern of flowers set in panels, on porcelain, originating at Meissen.

Gouache, painting with colours mixed with gum and, traditionally, honey; similar to watercolour but of denser consistency.

Gouging, simple linear ornamentation on furniture made by gouging out a series of shallow scoops, similar to fluting; see also **Linenfold.**

Gout stool, a curved, upholstered, adjustable footstool on which to rest the afflicted limb.

Grainger Worcester, bone china from the Worcester factory established by Thomas Grainger at the beginning of the 19th century, later noted for leaf-form jugs in parian ware among other innovations.

Graingerized, a book with blank pages for the reader to insert his own illustrations, a practice introduced by the English publisher, James Grainger, in the 18th century.

Graining, the technique of creating in paint the appearance of the grain in wood, sometimes employed to make cheap wood resemble mahogany, walnut, etc.

Grandfather chair, a large, comfortable, upholstered armchair, especially a winged chair.

American 19th-century Gothic clock

Grandfather clock, the popular name for a long-case clock.

Grand feu colours: see **High-temperature colours.**

Grandguard, an armour plate protecting the heart, fixed over the breastplate.

Grandmother clock, the popular name for a relatively small long-case clock, not exceeding about 6 ft 6 in high.

Grand Rapids furniture, late 19th-century furniture in a heavy, vaguely Renaissance style, made in particularly large quantities in Grand Rapids, Michigan; 'bedroom suites characterized by a particularly gloomy grandeur' (Joseph T. Butler).

Grande sonnerie, in clocks, the striking of the hour at every quarter following the tone signalling the quarter, which is struck on a bell of different tone; a system first employed in the late 17th century.

Granite-marbled, earthenware sprayed with a purplish lead glaze creating a marbled effect; an 18th-century Wedgwood technique later adopted by other potteries.

Graniteware, feldspathic earthenware with spotted cream-coloured glaze, sometimes blue-tinted, suggesting the appearance of granite, very strong; several smoother types developed in the 19th century.

Granulation, a decorative technique in metalwork, particularly silver and gold, in which small specks of the metal are soldered on to the surface to create a sparkling effect. **100**

Grapen, a medieval pot on three feet, pottery or bronze.

Grape pattern, a popular decorative motif in ceramics, glass, and in cast-iron seat furniture.

Grapeshot, small iron balls fired from a cannon, more effective against infantry than a single large shot.

Graphite ware, pottery finished with a coating of graphite (black lead), found in several primitive cultures.

Grate, an iron grating; also, the grating on which a fire is laid and, hence, a fireplace; see also **Grille.**

Graveyard rugs, a type of Turkish prayer rug associated with the town of Kula, in which a design based on small buildings and cypress trees apparently suggested (to someone) a graveyard; also known as cemetery rugs.

Gravity clock, an early type of self-driven clock (powered by its own weight), which descended a pillar notched like the teeth of a saw; see also **Falling ball clock, Rack clock. 113**

Gravure, an engraving, in particular one made by photographic means.

Gravy pot, a container for gravy or sauce, the design normally having some form of heat-preserving element, most popular between 1765 and 1800, when they were made in silver, Sheffield plate, porcelain and earthenware; also known as gravy cup; see also **Argyll**. 115

Greaves, in armour, shin plates; hence, high boots.

Grecian, Greek, applied to many articles in the style of the Greek Revival.

Greek key: see **Key pattern**.

Greek leg, on chairs of the early 19th century especially, a leg that narrows steadily towards the foot, usually fluted.

Greek Revival, the fashion for the style of Ancient Greece in architecture, furniture, etc., in the second half of the 18th century, the preparatory phase of the Neo-Classical period.

Greek-slave lamp, a Victorian bronze lamp with figure based on the well-known sculpture by Hiram Powers, which also appeared in Spode china and other forms.

Greek wave pattern: see **Vitruvian scroll**.

Green glass, bottle glass, the natural colour of glass without removal of impurities.

Green-glazed ware, covered with a translucent green glaze developed by Wedgwood in the mid 18th century, used on Wedgwood's cauliflower ware and by many others since. 38

Green pottery, from the Don pottery in the early 19th century, when owned by John Green (and relatives).

Greenwich armour, 16th- or early 17th-century armour made at the royal armoury in Greenwich, near London

Gregorian, a type of 16th-century wig, named after a barber in the Strand, London, who supplied them.

Gregory glass: see **Mary Gregory glass**.

Greiner dolls, 19th-century American dolls the heads of which (and sometimes the bodies too) were made by Ludwig Greiner, German-born resident of Philadelphia.

Grenadillo, a West Indian wood from the same family as the coconut palm, sometimes used for cabinet work.

Grenadine, a light silk or silk-and-wool material, used in ladies' summer dresses.

Grenobie wood, French walnut imported to England in the 17th and 18th centuries, regarded as superior to the native variety for inlay.

Grès de Flandres, salt-glazed stoneware from Flanders and western Germany since late medieval times.

Greybeard: see **Bellarmine**.

Grey hen, a stoneware jar with handle.

Greyhound, a popular ornament in English soft-paste porcelain and earthenware; also, a jug with handle in the form of a greyhound.

Griddle, or girdle, an iron slab or grating for baking oatcakes, etc.

Gridiron, a grating, or grill.

Griffin: see **Gryphon**.

Grille, iron or brass latticework set in a door, as in a prison door; also in cabinets.

Grisaille, painting in grey only, popular on 18th-century porcelain; also on murals, imitating relief. 119

Grisette, grey cloth of cotton or cotton and silk, cheap dress material of the 18th century.

Groat, a small silver coin worth four pence, first struck in England in the 13th century.

Groove-and-tongue moulding, a carved motif of tongue-like forms set in a groove.

Grooved drawers, having a groove in the sides which fitted a runner in the carcase, the usual method until about 1750.

Gros, a silver coin of many types and varying value in European currencies from the 12th century, e.g. the Italian *grosso* and the English groat.

Grosgrain, stiff black silk, used for mourning clothes.

Gros point: see **Cross stitch**.

Grossular, or hessonite, a type of garnet, usually brown or green, used in jewellery.

Groszbreitenbach porcelain, from the Thuringian factory founded in the late 18th century, under the same ownership as the Limbach factory, both imitating Meissen.

Grotesque, an article or decoration in fantastic form, usually including part of a human or animal figure with impossible attributes, e.g. wings turning into leaves, heads springing from branches; such ornaments were made in Roman times and became very popular in the late-Renaissance/Baroque period and in the late 19th century. 76

Ground, the background on which decoration is imposed, in ceramics, embroidery, painting, etc.

Gryphon, or griffin, a mythical beast with head and wings of an eagle and body of a lion, a recurring decorative motif since antiquity. 68, 120

Guadamecil, tooled leather chair seats and backs, originating in Muslim Spain in the 15th century or earlier.

Guard, the relatively narrow band running alongside the main band in the border of a carpet; also, the device in a lock which prevents it turning except with the correct key.

Guard chain, a metal chain carrying keys, etc., worn on the person; see also **Chatelaine**.

Gubbio maiolica, Renaissance maiolica from the centre in Umbria; best known for its gold and ruby lustres, being the work of Giorgio Andreoli who also lustred maiolica from other centres such as Castel Durante.

Guéridon, a round, often marble-topped stand or small table, usually elaborately ornamental, for a vase, candlestick, etc., from the 17th century; particularly such a stand in the form of a human figure. 118

Guernsey, a lidded pewter vessel found in the Channel Islands for serving a standard quantity of liquor.

Guglet, or goglet, a large vessel of unglazed, porous earthenware, for keeping water cool by evaporation.

Guiennois, a gold coin issued in Guienne under English rule in the 14th century.

Guilder, the standard silver coin of the Netherlands since the early 17th century; see also **Florin**.

Guild silver, or pewter, glass, china, etc., articles bearing the insignia of a guild, usually particularly fine examples, used in guild ceremonial.

Guilford chest, a New England chest, 17th or 18th century, carved and sometimes painted; see also **Connecticut sunflower chest**.

Grotesque

Guilloche, a decorative pattern common in Neo-Classical design consisting of a

113

122 Back of a Chinese bronze mirror with characteristic TLV decoration. Han dynasty. (Musée Cernuschi, Paris, Coiffard Collection)

123 Hammered and embossed silver fruit bowl designed by the Danish silversmith, Georg Jensen, 1914. (Musée des Arts Décoratifs, Paris)

125 Detail of a Hamadan carpet.
Persian, 19th century. (Private
Collection, Milan)

124 Diatonic harp. Italian, 1750.
Painted and decorated with flowers
and music-making putti.
(Gemeentemuseum, The Hague)

chain of intertwined spirals, or linked circles; numerous minor variations.

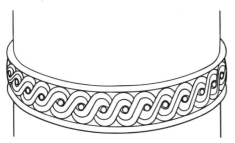

Guimpe, a veil over the hair and neck, in late medieval ladies' dress.

Guinea, a British gold coin worth 21 shillings, issued from the 17th to the 19th century.

Guipure, originally lace embroidery in which a thick cord was used to raise the design in relief, hence any kind of relatively coarse openwork lace embroidery, without ground.

Guisarme, a medieval weapon like a bill or halberd, with a short, curved blade at the end of a long handle.

Gules, in heraldry, a red colour.

Gul motif, in oriental carpets, originally a formalized rose though not recognizable, a basically octagonal shape associated particularly with Bokhara but found in all the main carpet-making regions in one form or another. **30**

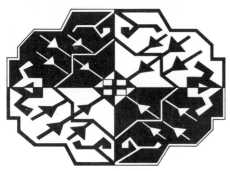

Gumwood, used occasionally for 18th-century American furniture, also barrels and chests.

Gun-metal, an alloy of copper and tin, very strong and durable, hence its use in guns.

Guttae, in Classical architecture, a row of inverted cone-shaped ornamentation.

Gutta foot, on furniture, a square-ended foot, spreading outwards slightly, in which each face of the square is bisected by a vertical groove.

Gutta percha, a substance similar to rubber and derived from a similar source (the sap of a Malayan tree), mouldable when heated but chiefly used for insulating, waterproofing, etc., from the mid 19th century, in the Far East much earlier; also for knife handles, ornaments, etc.

Guttrolf, a German glass vessel with a twisting neck set at an angle for easy pouring, from the Middle Ages. **121**

Gypsum, a mineral (hydrous calcium sulphate) that is the basic constituent of plaster of Paris, also occasionally used for carving, especially in the variety called alabaster.

Gypsy table, a small circular table with bobbin-turned tripod legs that intersect half-way between floor and table top, often covered with a velvet cloth; a type allegedly used by fortune-telling gypsies, late 19th century; a similar construction is sometimes seen in music stools.

Gyron, in heraldry a triangular form on an escutcheon, and hence a similar form in inlay.

Gyroscope, an instrument consisting of a wheel mounted in a ring which, spinning, illustrates the rotation of the earth; an early 19th-century invention.

Haarlem ware, delftware of fine quality, earlier than Delft and probably the first pottery to make the characteristic blue and white Chinese-style ware, though soon overshadowed by Delft.

Habaner faience, from Protestant communities settled in Moravia during the late 16th century; influenced by Italian maiolica and German stoneware and later by Delft, but characterized by religious taboos, e.g. a veto on representation of animals in painted decoration.

Habdalah, a dish of silver or other metal, used in Jewish ceremony.

Habiliment, clothes or trappings, a complete outfit, especially one for warlike purposes, e.g. armour.

Hacienda silver, Spanish-American silver, from Mexico and Peru.

Hadklu rugs, or Hatschlou, rugs woven by several Turkoman tribes of central Asia, rather small, Sehna knot, their characteristic feature being the division of the field into four parts by a form of cross.

Hadley chest, a 17th-century New England chest, associated with Hadley, Massachusetts, usually oak or pine, distinguished from similar pieces by all-over carving of floral patterns and the presence of carved initials.

Hadley ware, from the pottery established by James Hadley in the late 19th century and taken over by the Royal Worcester Co. some years later, including vases in Art Nouveau style.

Haematite, or hematite, an oxide of iron, giving a very dark red colour when used in glassmaking; occasionally cut and polished for jewellery and ornaments since ancient times.

Hafner ware, lead-glazed pottery and stove tiles from central Europe, particularly southern Germany, in various colours and sometimes with designs in relief, made as early as the 13th or 14th century.

Hague porcelain, made during a relatively short period in the late 18th century, no outstanding individual characteristics but a high standard of flower painting, landscapes, etc., sometimes with gilding on a blue ground.

Hagueneau faience, noted for distinguished floral painting in the second half of the 18th century, similar to nearby Strasbourg and under the same management.

Ha-ha, a garden wall, in particular some kind of barrier that does not interrupt the view, e.g. a sunken wall in dead ground.

Haircloth, material woven of horse- or goat-hair, fine varieties sometimes used for clothing, coarser types for upholstery or floor coverings.

Hairwork, a term covering several types of ornamentation using (primarily) human hair, including jewellery in which woven hair, sometimes combined with metalwork or beads, made a pattern, a device that came to be associated with mourning; also, scenes framed in wood, in which the design was 'drawn' in hairs.

Hake, a wooden frame suspended over the hearth, for drying cheeses; also, an arquebus.

Halberd, a type of late medieval spear, about 6 ft long, ending in a spike at the base of which an axehead and a claw projected at either side.

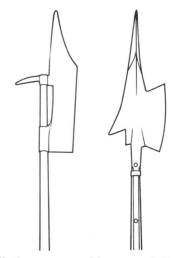

Halb-fayence: see Mezza-maiolica.

Half armour, a light suit of armour protecting the head and trunk but not the limbs.

Half-canopy: see **Half-tester**.

Half-chest, a lowboy.

Half clock: see **Massachusetts clock**.

Half column, a decorative Classical column on furniture, etc., which projects only half-way from the façade; see also **Pilaster**.

Half door, a door made in two parts of which the top may be opened while the lower remains closed, as seen in stables and some cottage kitchens.

Half-headed bedstead, a bed with an elaborate headboard but no tester or draperies.

Half-leg, a drop-leaf table of the gate-leg type in which the outward-swinging legs are, when closed, flush with and apparently part of the fixed legs, so that the table appears to have four legs rather than six.

Half-moon, a term applied to furniture (chairs, tables, etc.) of semicircular shape; see also **Demi-lune**.

Halfpenny, an English coin similar to the penny, originally silver; copper from the late 17th century.

Half-tester, a bed tester or canopy that covers the head of the bed only.

Hall chair, a sturdy, upright, single chair without upholstery (for varied but short-term occupation) in various 18th-century styles; later examples also included iron and studded-leather chairs of vaguely Gothic appearance; see also **Porter's chair**.

Hallifax barometer, an English barometer of the first half of the 18th century made by or after the design of John Hallifax of Barnsley, being a dial barometer with a superficial resemblance to a long-case clock, preceding the better-known banjo type.

Hallmark, on precious metals, a stamped mark that guarantees the quality of the metal, region of manufacture and, usually the date and name of the maker; a system first introduced in England in 1300.

Hall rifle, an early 19th-century breech-loading flintlock invented by John Hall of Maine, with interchangeable parts, used by the U.S. army; other guns were also made by Hall.

Hall seat, a bench, sometimes with a back, placed against the wall in the hall or antechamber; see also **Hall chair**.

Hall stand: see **Hatstand**.

Hamadan carpets, rugs and carpets from the region around Hamadan in western Iran, cotton and wool, Ghiordes knot, often with a central medallion; not usually the finest Persian craftsmanship. **125**

Hambergite, a rare form of beryl, colourless, occasionally cut for jewellery.

Hamburg faience, mainly 17th-century ware, especially jugs, often showing Portuguese influence, with inscriptions or coats-of-arms connecting them with the German city, though the workshop (probably the first of its kind in Germany) is unrecorded.

Hames, a type of horse brass, curved pieces like a tooth attached to the sides of the horse's collar.

Hamilton silver, among others, the work of a 19th-century firm of British silversmiths in Calcutta, catering to imperial officials, etc.

Hammering, 'the most original, artistic and difficult technique' (Libuše Urešova) in working silver and gold, in which articles are shaped by closely spaced blows of variously shaped hammers, without heating. **123**

Hammonton glass, from one of the better known of the numerous New Jersey glassworks established in the early 19th century, noted particularly for flasks of fine quality.

Hanap, a large silver goblet or standing cup with lid, no handles, sometimes in stoneware mounted in silver.

Hanau faience, from the Dutch-founded, mid 17th-century workshop in Hanau, Germany, difficult to place owing to its similarity to Dutch and other German styles and absence of reliable marks, but noted for narrow-necked jugs with *Vogeldekor* pattern.

Hand-blown glass: see **Free-blown glass**.

Hand candlestick: see **Chamber candlestick**.

Hand cannon, or handgun, prototype of the pistol, consisting of a small cannon mounted on a wooden stock, fired at the touch-hole with a brand.

Hand cooler, a glass egg, like an oval paperweight and with the same range of remarkable colour effects, allegedly intended to maintain a cool hand on social occasions.

Hand glass, a small, portable mirror, the frame of which is extended to form a handle.

Handicraft, any art or occupation done with the hands, using tools but not machines.

Handkerchief table, a small, square, drop-leaf table, hinged from corner to corner so that fixed top and drop leaf are equal triangles; handy for the corner of a room.

Hand screen, a small screen to be held in the hand to frustrate fire or draught, like a non-folding fan.

Hand warmer, a metal box holding hot coals or iron.

Han dynasty, the period in China covering the first two centuries BC and the first two centuries AD. **122**

Hanger, a lightweight shortsword of the late 17th or 18th century, with one cutting edge; also, the strap from which such a sword hung; a chain above the hearth for hanging pots; a rack for hanging clothes, etc.

Hanging, of a cupboard, shelves, etc., fixed to a wall without stand or support; also, of a wardrobe, for hanging clothes.

Hanging clock: see **Falling-ball clock**; also a wall clock.

Haniwa, red earthenware figures, human and animal, placed on tombs in Japan about 500 AD.

Hanley ware, various wares including creamware and others in imitation of Wedgwood's developments, from the Staffordshire pottery, late 18th and 19th centuries; see also **Adams pottery**.

Hanseatic flagon, a pewter vessel of the 14th and 15th centuries, with a pear-shaped body on a generous foot, flat lid, and sometimes having moulded relief decoration on the inside.

Hansesschüsseln, engraved bronze dishes made in Lorraine and the Rhine-land during the Middle Ages.

Hanukkah lamp, an eight-branched silver lamp used in Jewish ceremony.

Hardi, a medieval gold coin, issued in 14th-century France, with a portrait of Edward the Black Prince.

Hard metal, of pewter, the most costly type with a high proportion of tin and 4 per cent bismuth to harden it; not found before about 1700; see also **Britannia metal**.

Hard-paste, 'true' porcelain, made of kaolin and china stone, the secret of which, long known to the Chinese, eluded European potters until the 18th century; also, of earthenware, clay containing no lime, similar to stoneware.

Hardware, articles made of metal.

Hardwood, the wood of broad-leafed, deciduous trees, as distinct from conifers; not all hardwoods are necessarily very hard.

Hare's fur glaze: see **Chienware**.

Harewood, eyrewood, also called silver-wood or greywood, usually sycamore stained a greenish or yellowish grey with ferrous oxide, sometimes other wood so stained, including maple.

Harlequin, a character from Italian comedy who wore a multi-coloured diamond-patterned costume; hence, a diamond pattern, e.g. in inlaid furniture, quilts, etc.; also, a ceramic figure of Harlequin, usually matched with the female figure of Columbine.

Harlequin service, a set of dinnerware or a tea service, etc., each piece being of a different colour; popular in the 19th century.

Harlequin table, a name sometimes applied to a type of Pembroke table.

Harmonica, nowadays a mouth organ, formerly a musical instrument consisting

126 Porcelain teapot. Meissen, about 1740. Decorated by a Hausmaler, probably derived from a factory design. (Victoria and Albert Museum, London)

127 Herrenbøe faience tureen. 1834. The Rococo design is in the French manner. (Musée National de Céramique, Sèvres)

128 Hereke prayer rug. Turkish, 18th century. Numerous inscriptions in various scripts are incorporated into the decoration. (Private Collection, Milan)

129 Chinese headrest. Porcelain with enamel decoration. Ch'ing dynasty, K'ang Hsi period (1662–1722). There is a hole so that it can be filled with hot water in winter. (Musée Guimet, Paris, Grandidier Collection)

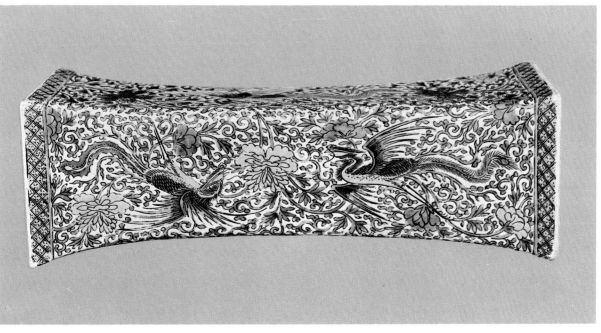

of a series of glass bells, struck with a padded wooden stick, as played by Gluck at a London concert in 1746; various types in the 18th century; see also **Glockenspiel**.

Harmonium, a small, moveable organ, usually with two manuals, in which a reed vibrates in a slot as air is drawn through, on much the same principle as that of the accordion; from about 1800.

Harp, a musical instrument played by plucking the strings, a characteristic shape and hence denoting such a shape in furniture, etc.; see also **Lyre. 124**

Harpsichord, the ancestor of the piano, a keyboard instrument in which pressure on the key moves a quill which plucks the string, or strings; early 16th-century examples fairly simple, 18th-century ones more elaborate, normally with two manuals; superseded by about 1800.

Harquebus: see **Arquebus**.

Harratine, linen or woollen material used for upholstery, coverlets and bed curtains.

Harrington silhouettes, machine-cut silhouette portraits mounted on black silk by Sarah Harrington, English, late 18th century.

Harshang motif, or crab motif, on Persian carpets, a formalized floral motif the outline of which suggests a crab.

Harvard lamp, a late 19th-century oil-burning lamp, adjustable on a vertical rod, sometimes one burner, sometimes two.

Hash dish, a covered silver or pewter dish, sometimes with stand and warming lamp.

Hasp, a hinged, metal lock fastened by a peg (or padlock) through a loop.

Hassock, a stout cushion for kneeling, as in church, upholstered in strong fabric or leather.

Hastener, an open-backed hood of iron or tin sheet which fitted over the joint hard up against the fire bars, used in the 18th century, mainly for speeding up the browning of the meat.

Hat badge, an ornament worn in the hat, popular in the Renaissance, jewelled and enamelled, sometimes called an enseigne.

Hatching, a number of close-set parallel lines, e.g. engraved in silver.

Hatchment, a wooden board with painted heraldic design, showing the arms of a man recently dead, whose death it commemorated.

Hatstand, a piece frequently of pillar-and-claw or bentwood construction for hanging hats and coats in the hall, sometimes with shelf, drawer, mirror, etc.

Hauberk, a suit of chain mail that stopped at the knees; see also **Half armour**.

Haufenbecher, silver or pewter cups that fitted one into the other, rather like modern paper cups, German, late 16th and early 17th centuries.

Haunch pot, a rather mysterious term assumed to apply to the characteristically baluster-shaped pewter or silver tankards of the 16th and 17th centuries.

Hausmalerei, 'home painting', decoration, primarily on German faience and porcelain but also known in other countries, painted by craftsmen working outside the factory, known as Hausmaler. **126**

Hautboy, the old term for oboe.

Haut-relief: see **High relief**.

Havana wood, Cuban mahogany.

Haviland-Limoges, porcelain, stoneware and 'art pottery' made at the Limoges, France, workshop of Charles Haviland in the late 19th century.

Hayburner, a 19th-century American stove, cast iron or brick, made specially for burning hay in the prairie lands where coal was scarce and wood unavailable.

Headboard, a wooden panel at the head of a bedstead.

Headrest, any kind of support for the head, in particular the oriental hollow ceramic version filled with warm water. **129**

Head scratcher: see **Backscratcher**.

Heart-back, a chairback with splat in the form of a heart, seen in some late 18th-century chairs, associated particularly with Hepplewhite.

Hearth tools: see **Fire irons**.

Heathcote pottery, from the Fenton pottery established in the early 19th century, making chiefly Staffordshire blue transfer-printed earthenware and bone china, with views of scenery, etc.

Heath pottery, a term associated with a number of English ceramic wares, notably Staffordshire white stoneware, early Derby porcelain figures, and 19th-century Staffordshire earthenware.

Hedwig glass, cut-glass beakers from the Near East in the early Middle Ages, with thick walls and decoration of animals and other patterns in high relief.

Heftlein, an ornamental, often jewelled, clasp.

Hei-tiki, a Maori pendant and badge of social status, of carved New Zealand jade with inlaid circles of mother-of-pearl resembling staring eyes.

Helical candlestick, a candlestick in which the candle is held in a spiral of wire.

Heliodore, a type of beryl, characterized by its golden-brown colour.

Heliograph, an engraving effected by photographic means, a plate coated with appropriate chemicals being exposed to the light; a technique developed contemporaneously with the similar and more efficient Daguerreotype.

Heller, a common copper coin of various German states in the early modern period, issued in several denominations.

Helm, in armour, a large helmet completely enclosing the head and bolted to back and breastplate; also, a ship's tiller, or thatching for a roof.

Helmet, armour for the head; also, various articles, e.g. coal scuttles, jugs, etc., in the shape of a helmet, particularly the type worn by the Ancient Greeks; popular in the 17th and 18th centuries. **226**

Hematite: see **Haematite**.

Hemispherium, an ancient form of sundial, in which the vertical pointer was situated in the centre of a bowl-like depression with the hours marked around the sides.

Hemp, a coarse material used for ropes and coarse cloth, made from the inner bark of the plant of that name.

Henderson pottery, 19th-century stoneware, including Toby jugs, and many other wares from the factory of David Henderson ('the American Wedgwood') in Jersey City.

Hennin, a tall, conical hat, from the tip of which hung a veil, sometimes multicoloured; a 15th-century fashion carried to such extremes that doors had to be enlarged to allow grand ladies to pass through without stooping.

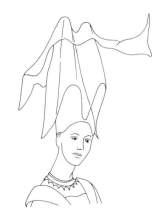

Henri Deux ('Henri II') **ware,** exceedingly rare 16th-century French lead-glazed earthenware with inlaid decoration of variously coloured clays and skilful modelling; also, 19th-century copies.

Hepplewhite furniture, English furniture, especially chairs and settees, in the style of George Hepplewhite (d. 1786), author of a highly influential *Cabinet-Maker's Guide*; the Hepplewhite style is basically Neo-Classical, though less formal than Adam and closer to English tradition than Sheraton.

Heptagonal, seven-sided.

Heraclean knot motif, found in Hellenic and Roman jewellery, a figure-of-eight knot, or reef knot, in gold inlaid with gems, traditionally supposed to guard against injury.

Heraldic, 'of heraldry', usually implying the presence of coats-of-arms on silver, porcelain, etc.; the esoteric vocabulary of heraldry (e.g. argent, gules) sometimes overlaps into the world of antiques.

Herat carpets, from the major carpet-making centre of Herat between the 16th and the 18th centuries, dense wool rugs and carpets of many kinds, Ghiordes knot, characterized by the herati motif in design; see also **Khorassan carpets.**

Herati motif, a design in Persian carpets, originating in Herat but found on many oriental carpets, consisting basically of a rosette enclosed in a diamond.

Herculaneum, a name applied to various articles, particularly certain early 19th-century chairs, the design of which was influenced by the recently excavated city of Herculaneum.

Herculaneum pottery, from the Liverpool pottery established in the late 18th century with Staffordshire workmen, in particular creamware and porcelain tableware, besides other wares similar to contemporary Staffordshire pottery.

Hereke carpets, rare 18th-century Turkish carpets and later copies of fine quality, various designs, frequently on a cream or ivory ground; some Art Nouveau designs for the sultan's palace. **128**

Herez carpets, from the region around Tabriz in north-western Iran, Ghiordes knot, close, stylized patterns in angular forms, mostly quite large (some of 40 sq ft), with a wide range of colours, most frequently on a red ground.

Herm, a bust, normally of the Greek god Hermes, mounted on (most typically) a square pillar; a boundary mark in Ancient Greece, occasionally incorporated in Rococo or Neo-Classical furniture; see also **Term.**

Herrebøe faience, Norwegian faience of fine quality from a short-lived factory near Halden, wares similar to other Scandinavian factories, e.g. bishop bowls, trays, etc., mainly blue-painted or high-temperature manganese colours. **127**

Herrera bed, a type of bedstead originating in Portugal in the 17th century, having an architectural headboard with arcading, bronze mounts and frequently inlaid ivory.

Herringbone, a pattern common in inlay (and tweed), two rows of parallel lines joined roughly at right angles, like a row of arrow heads.

Hessian, a very strong, rough cloth of hemp and jute, used in packing; also, 'of Hesse', as in **Hessian boot,** a high boot with tassels at the top, worn by Hessian troops.

Hessonite: see **Cinnamon stone.**

Hexagonal, six-sided.

Heyne pewter, colonial American pewter by Johann Christopher Heyne of Lancaster, Pennsylvania.

H hinge, a hinge with long vertical leaves, making the shape of an H; also HL hinge, in which one of the leaves is L shaped.

Hickory, a tough and springy wood, native to North America, much used for axe handles, gun stocks, fishing rods, hoops, etc., and sometimes in colonial stick chairs; vulnerable to time and woodworm.

Hiddenite, a very rare gem stone, brilliant green in colour, found only in North Carolina.

Hieroglyph, a written character representing a letter or a word in some esoteric form of writing.

Highboy, a high chest of drawers often in two sections; a lowboy or commode, with chest of drawers on top; an 18th-century American piece, typically with broken-arch pediment and cabriole legs; see also **Tallboy. 64**

High relief, or *Alto relievo*, deeply incised carving in stone or wood panels; also applied to casting in various materials, when the design stands out boldly; see also **Bas-relief. 7**

High-standard, of silver, a high proportion of pure silver, higher than the sterling standard.

High-temperature colours, the colours that could be painted on glazed earthenware before firing and fixed in the furnace that fused the glaze, most commonly cobalt-blue, also used on porcelain before firing; the other colours were manganese purple and, less common, copper green, orange, yellow and a dullish red.

Hilt, the handle of a sword or dagger. **34**

Hind's foot, silver or pewter spoons of the late 17th and early 18th centuries with a double groove in the end of the handle.

Hinge, a jointed device by which a door, lid, etc., opens and shuts. **130**

Hip bath, a portable metal bath, usually enamelled, basically circular with a sloping upward extension for the back, 19th century.

Hip-joint chair, a type of Renaissance X-form chair, often with brocaded seat and back.

Hipped, an out-thrust angle in a curved member, similar to the shape of the rear leg of a horse; also, a cabriole leg extending above the seat; of a roof, sloping upwards at the sides as well as front and back.

Hippocampus, a mythical creature sometimes associated with Neptune, front half horse, rear half fish.

Hippocras bag, a cone-shaped cloth bag used for filtering hippocras, wine flavoured with spices.

Hippogryph, a mythical flying creature, front half gryphon, rear half horse.

Hirado porcelain, Japanese porcelain mainly of the 19th century, fine quality, with scenes painted in an underglaze purplish-blue of boys playing.

Hispano-Moresque, a general term for wares produced by the Moors in Spain, or in their tradition, in particular lustreware, mosaic tiles, large vases, etc., with Eastern motifs often mingling with Western styles; see also **Mozarabic style, Mudéjar style. 132**

Historic, a term applied to glassware, pottery, silver and other articles with explicit historical connections, e.g. commemoration of a historical event.

Historical blue, Staffordshire blue pottery with panels containing transfer-printed scenes, portraits and notable events; also in other colours in the mid 19th century; also known as blue-printed ware.

Hitchcock chair, a fancy chair (various kinds) with caned seat and painted floral designs, associated particularly with Lambert Hitchcock of Hitchcocksville, Connecticut, in the early 19th century.

Ho, a Chinese vessel for heating wine.

Hob, an iron surround to a fireplace, having a flat surface level with the grate; hence, the fireplace itself; also, a hobnail.

Hobby, or hobbyhorse, a wooden toy consisting of a horse's head set on a long stick, or a representation of a horse worn by morris dancers; also, a rocking horse.

Hobbyhorse

130 Hinge for a door. German, 16th–17th century. Engraved and pierced sheet-iron. (Victoria and Albert Museum, London)

131 Porcelain figure, 'Dancer with Cymbals'. Höchst, 1775. Exotic figures were popular in the 18th century. This is probably by J. P. Melchior, the leading modeller at the factory from 1767 to 1779. (Victoria and Albert Museum, London)

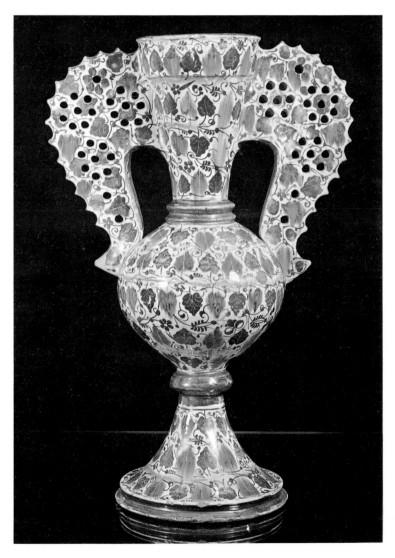

132 Hispano-Moresque lustre-
ware vase. Valencia, 15th century.
Overall ivy leaf decoration.
(Victoria and Albert Museum,
London. Photo: John Webb)

133 Group of pewter holy water
stoups. (Private Collection,
Trieste)

Hobelspanketten, a thick, heavy necklace of gold or silver, usually wound two or three times around the neck, popular in central Europe in the Baroque period.

Hobnail, a short nail with a large head, a metal stud, set in the soles of boots to prolong their life; also, in cut glass, a pattern of four-pointed stars imposed on diamonds.

Hochschnitt, 'high cut', engraving in glass in which the pattern appears in high relief; a technique associated particularly with German glass of the late 17th century.

Höchst ware, 18th-century German faience figures and vessels with fine floral painting, covered dishes in animal form, and early porcelain figures and tableware. **131**

Hock glass, a wine glass especially for white German wine commonly known as hock (from the Hoch Rhein district), usually pale green or yellow with extra-long stem.

Hock leg, on chairs, etc., a cabriole leg with a jutting angle inside the knee; see also **Hipped**.

Hogarth chair, an early 18th-century English chair with vigorously curved back and arms, appearing in scenes by the artist, William Hogarth.

Hohokam pottery, made by the Pueblo Indians of the American south-west, mainly bowls and jars, sometimes with painted outline figures of men and animals.

Holbein carpets, Turkish carpets imported to Europe during the Renaissance, featuring prominently in the work of several contemporary painters, notably Holbein.

Holbeinesque, a style of Victorian pendant brooch with a central stone often en cabochon, surrounded by an oval of enamelled metal inlaid with stones and a small stone hanging below.

Holitsch faience, made in the mid 18th century in Holitsch, Hungary, at first mainly French in inspiration; later products influenced by English developments, notably creamware.

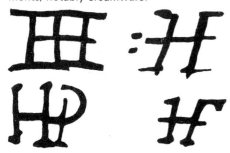

Holland, a type of linen originally imported from the Netherlands, used for linings, coverings, etc.; also, the cloth used for window roller blinds.

Holland and Green pottery, from the Longton pottery during the second half of the 19th century, in particular, fine stoneware often decorated in brilliant colours.

Hollands porceleyn, imitations of Ming porcelain made in the Netherlands during the late 18th century.

Holland stove: see **Dutch stove.**

Hollie point, needlepoint lace associated with ecclesiastical uses in the Middle Ages and later with the Puritans and christening clothes; very fine open-work patterns made with a type of buttonhole stitch.

Hollow-column clock, an uncommon early 19th-century clock with columns that appear to be part of the case but are hollow for the weights to travel up and down.

Hollow-cut, glass or stone cut in a pattern of concave forms.

Hollowed pediment, on a cabinet or clock case, etc., a pediment with concave curves sweeping upward to the central finial.

Hollow-stem, a wine glass in which the bowl opens into a narrow tube in the stem, to drain off sediment; sometimes seen in 18th-century wine glasses.

Hollow-ware, a term used particularly of pewter but also of china, glass, etc., encompassing all vessels such as bowls, cups, etc., as distinct from flatware (plates, dishes, etc.).

Hollywood, hard wood, very pale in colour with small dark flecks, used in inlay; sometimes stained black in imitation of ebony.

Hollywood baronial, a frivolous term to describe certain American furniture of the 1920s and 1930s, characterized by large size, massive turnings, lavish upholstery, etc., usually with a suggestion of Spanish influence.

Holmwood: see **Hollywood.**

Holy water stoup, a small metal vessel like a bowl backed by a panel bearing an appropriate scene in relief, once found in churches; see also **Lavabo. 133**

Honan ware, the name given to Chinese stoneware of the Sung period with purplish-black glaze, thought to be from Honan.

Honduras mahogany: see **Baywood.**

Honeycomb, a term sometimes used to describe a pattern of repeated geometric figures, hexagonal or octagonal, in openwork or embroidery, or a pattern of weave in cloth.

Honey gilding, a technique of gilding ceramics etc., in which powdered gold was mixed with honey and applied before firing, superseded by mercury gilding in the late 18th century.

Honeypot, a jar for honey in the form of a beehive, with the finial on the lid in the form of a bee, found in silver, earthenware, etc., from the 18th century.

Honeysuckle motif: see **Anthemion.**

Honiton lace, the original, top-quality English lace, though imitative of and inferior to Brussels lace in the 16th century; at its best in the early 18th century; best known for pillow lace though needlepoint also made.

Hood, of a long-case clock, the topmost section of the case (enclosing the movement) which can be removed separately, usually having no hinged door as in relatively modern clocks.

Hooded top, of a cabinet, clock case, etc., a top of semicircular shape; see also **Bonnet top.**

Hoof-foot, a leg terminating in a goat's hoof, found on some early 18th-century furniture; also, a less naturalistic hoof of various kinds from earlier periods, including Ancient Egypt.

Hookah, or hubble-bubble, a pipe designed to draw the smoke through water to cool it, originating in the Near East; English examples, from the 18th century, usually silver-gilt.

Hooked rugs, strictly, rugs in which the yarn or strips of tape are hooked through the linen or canvas ground, but commonly applied to rugs sewn as well as hooked.

Hoop-back, any chair, e.g. the ordinary Windsor single chair, in which the top rail forms a curve which descends uninterrupted to the seat, the arms also continuing to form a single back rail.

Hooped can, a pewter or silver vessel, also found in glass, earthenware, etc., with a swelling body like a barrel, its design being clearly based on a wooden model, associated especially with Scandinavia.

Hope chest, a dower chest.

Hop glass, a drinking glass engraved with the leaves of the hop plant; also found on earthenware, including a popular Minton jug; see also **Ale glass.**

Horn, animal horns carved into ornamental forms; also, a drinking vessel made from a horn mounted in silver, associated with northern Europe in ancient and early medieval times; also, a brass wind instrument, often coiled, various types including hunting horns from the 16th century.

Hornbeam, pale, yellowish wood from the tree of that name, tough and hard to work, but occasionally used in furniture, frequently stained; the tree, being amenable to shaping, was popular for formal gardens.

Hornbook, a child's reader consisting of a piece of wood, metal or other hard material in the shape, roughly, of a hand mirror, to which is attached a printed sheet covered by a thin sheet of (transparent) animal horn; genuine medieval examples are rare.

Horn furniture, chairs especially, made from the horns of animals such as stags, bison, etc., a short-lived fashion of the late 19th century.

Horn glazing, small panes of horn used in a window instead of glass.

Horn of plenty: see **Cornucopia.**

Hornpipe, an early reed instrument with a cow's horn at the end of a pipe.

Horse bells, a brass frame in which several small bells hang, attached to the collar of a dray horse.

Horse brasses, small brass ornaments, in the form of a medallion or plaque, attached as decoration to a horse's harness; 'some 2,000 different designs' (Geoffrey Wills); few horse brasses are older than about 1800 and they have

gone on being made continuously since their purpose became redundant.

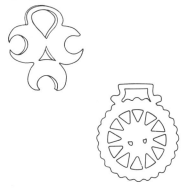

Horse furniture, stands, screens, etc., supported on two legs each having two large projecting feet, frequently in claw form, as in a cheval glass.

Horsehair, from horses' manes and tails, very hardwearing, used sometimes in weaving and in filling cushions and mattresses, mixed with wool or cotton waste.

Horseshoe, a term used to describe the characteristic looped shape of a horseshoe in furniture, e.g. in the backs of certain Windsor chairs; also, a semi-circular dining table; see also **Kidney desk.**

Hotchkiss gun, an early type of machine-gun, named for its inventor; also, a rifle.

Hotel silver, plated tableware especially made for the hotel trade, 19th-century examples often being of rather high quality.

Hot-milk jug, a silver jug that usually matched an accompanying coffee pot, but smaller and lacking the long spout.

Houdon busts, porcelain busts made by various English and European factories after the sculptures by Jean Antoine Houdon (1741–1828), Voltaire being the most popular subject.

Hourglass, a very accurate (and ancient) method of measuring a short period of time, consisting of a glass cylinder or globe nipped in the middle and filled with sufficient sand to trickle from the top section to the bottom in one hour; see also **Powder clock.**

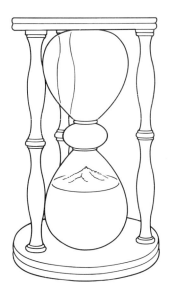

Hourglass clock, a type of Connecticut mantel clock somewhat similar to the acorn clock, the shape of the case suggesting a sandglass, early 19th century.

Hourglass stool, a round-seated, upholstered stool in the shape of an hourglass.

Howard clocks, banjo clocks and other watches and clocks of the mid 19th century by Edward Howard, whose business became the American Waltham Watch Co.

Hubble-bubble: see **Hookah.**

Hubertusburg faience, late 18th- and 19th-century earthenware of fine quality from the centre founded by Frederick Augustus II of Saxony.

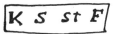

HUBERTUSBURG

Hucche: see **Hutch.**

Hughes ironstone, produced in large quantities at the Brownhills, Staffordshire, pottery of Thomas Hughes in the Victorian period, entirely for export to America.

Huguenot crafts, work done by French Protestants who fled from France after the Revocation of the Edict of Nantes (1685) and settled in the Low Countries, England and America, including many outstanding craftsmen, especially silversmiths and cabinetmakers.

Hull pottery, various types of earthenware from the 19th-century pottery at Hull, Yorkshire.

Humming top, a popular 19th-century toy, a top, usually tin, that emits a musical hum as it spins.

Humpen, a cylindrical glass beaker with silver lid, German or Swiss, usually enamelled or engraved, often with armorial or religious design, some a few inches high, some 'required an effort to lift' (E. M. Elville); see also **Willkomm.**

Hunt board, a sideboard with drawers, made in the American South for stand-up meals after the hunt.

Hunting carpets, outstanding and rare Persian carpets in which figures of hunters and animals being hunted are found among flowers, leaves and arabesques. 134

Hunting chair, an overstuffed armchair with a section that pulls out in front to convert it into a kind of day bed.

Hunting cup, a small silver cup, without handles, such as might have been safely handled by a mounted huntsman, to give him spirit for the chase; also, goblets with hunting scenes engraved.

Hunting table: see **Hunt board.**

Hurdals Verk glass, from the Norwegian factory operating in the late 18th and early 19th centuries, successor to the Nøstetangen works, producing a wide variety of vessels.

Hurd silver, made by a family of 18th-century American silversmiths working in Boston.

135 Inclined plane clock. Late 17th century. When it reached the bottom, the clock was simply placed again at the top. (British Museum, London)

134 Detail of a hunting carpet. Persian, 16th century. (Musée des Arts Décoratifs, Paris)

137 Silver inkstand. English, made
by Isaac Liger about 1705. Drum-
shaped inkpot with hinged cover,
punch-pierced pouncebox and a
depression for pens and wafers.
(Private Collection)

136 Hydrogen clock. Made in
Trieste by Pasquale Andervalt,
about 1820. The pressure of the
gas raised it, when the gas was
exhausted, zinc dropped into acid,
releasing more hydrogen. (Private
Collection, Rome)

Hurdy-gurdy, originally, a lute- or guitar-shaped musical instrument in which the function of the bow was performed by a wheel turning and the finger-stopping operated by a keyboard; more recently, a barrel organ.

Hurricane lamp, any oil-burning lamp designed to protect the flame from draught or wind.

Hurricane shade, a glass shade for a candle, basically cylindrical in shape but often with slightly S-curved sides, from the mid 18th century.

Husk, a stylized flower form, like a wheat husk or a bluebell, found as a moulding descending chair legs or among swags and garlands in Neo-Classical design; see also **Bell-flower.**

Hutch, a small cupboard or chest for storing food, usually on legs, with pierced door for ventilation, often backed with coarse cloth; from the Middle Ages; also called a hucche.

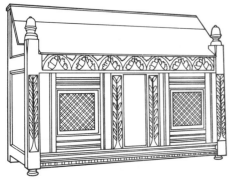

Hüttenglas, glassware made by the traditional method, blown, shaped and decorated by the glassworker.

Hyacinth bowl, or vase, for growing hyacinths indoors, some coloured glass, some earthenware with relief decoration of hyacinths.

Hyalith, black glassware, often with designs in gold, made at Nove Hrady in southern Bohemia in the first half of the 19th century, inspired by Wedgwood's basaltes.

Hydraulic bed, a water bed.

Hydria, a Greek water jug or pitcher with narrow neck and two handles, earthenware or bronze.

Hydrofluoric acid, the only acid that effectively attacks glass (and ceramic glazes), therefore used for etching in glass.

Hydrogen clock, worked by the pressure of hydrogen gas. **136**

Hygrometer, an instrument for measuring humidity, incorporated in many barometers from the late 18th century.

Hyksos pottery, prehistoric pottery from the Near East in the late Bronze Age, mainly bowls and pitchers, of graceful form, often with elegant linear decoration.

Hylton pottery, early transfer-painted earthenware and lustreware from the pottery of that name near Sunderland, late 18th and early 19th centuries, first makers of Wear Bridge jugs; see also **Sunderland pottery.**

Hypsometer, an instrument for calculating altitude, consisting of a metal vessel for water with a lamp for heating it and a thermometer to register the temperature of boiling point.

Ibrahimabad carpets: see **Feraghan carpets.**

Ice-cream dish, a wide-mouthed glass cup on a short, thick stem, sometimes with matching plate; a type made since the 17th century, not always for the implied purpose.

Ice glass, glassware with the appearance of cracked ice, usually either crackled by sudden changes of temperature in the furnace or sprinkled with small pieces of broken glass while the vessel is still hot so that they are melted on; techniques used sporadically since the Renaissance.

Iceland, a large box or cupboard of ash or similar wood, metal-bound and perhaps lined, for keeping ice, found in rural areas of the eastern United States.

Iceland spar, a variety of the mineral calcite, named after the site of the quarry that chiefly supplied it, rather soft but startlingly transparent and used in optical experiments, prisms, etc., in the 17th century, large crystals sometimes being cherished as ornaments.

Ice pail, a small bucket, silver or other metal, sometimes footed, usually with two ring handles and a removable top with central cavity for a wine bottle, which rested in ice.

Icon, a religious painting of Orthodox Christianity, Biblical figures and scenes painted on wooden panels since the earliest years of the Byzantine Church; later, on metal, with jewelled ornamentation.

Iga ware, 17th-century Japanese stoneware jars and vases of deliberately rough appearance, in accordance with the traditions of the cult of the tea ceremony.

Illite, a clay of particularly smooth consistency used as a slip to impart a glossy surface to some types of earthenware.

Illuminated, of manuscripts, decoration of the writing, most commonly the initial letter, with gold, silver and other colours as a pattern of tracery or figures and scenes; also used sometimes of glass engraved and silvered, or just painted.

Ilmenau porcelain, from the German centre where the first porcelain factory, making figures somewhat inferior to other factories in Thuringia, was established during the late 18th century, later associated with the more important factory at Volkstedt.

Image toys, Staffordshire earthenware figures, later known as chimney orna-

ments and sometimes fairly crude, sold by pedlars.

Imari, a decorative style originating in Japanese porcelain made for the European market in the late 17th or 18th century and subsequently much imitated, in China as well as Europe; characterized by rather obtrusive patterns in strong colours; see also **Gaudy.**

Imbricated, overlapping in the manner of tiles or shingles on a roof, a term describing several kinds of 19th-century decorative work, e.g. buttonwork where the buttons overlap each other, and carving or moulding of such form.

Impasto, a pattern in low relief achieved by the application of paint in very thick layers, as seen on some early maiolica; a term more frequently encountered in oil-painting.

Impression, a print from a plate, stone or block, etched or engraved.

Imprint, in books, the name of the publisher or printer, formerly placed at the end of the book, since the 17th century more often at the foot of the title page; see also **Colophon.**

Ince & Mayhew furniture, supplied though not necessarily made by the prominent London firm of cabinetmakers in the second half of the 18th century, or resembling a design in their catalogue; similar to Chippendale.

Incense boat, a silver or silver-gilt vessel shaped like a boat (pointed at the ends), on a foot, sometimes with hinged lid, for incense in Christian ritual.

Incense burner: see **Censer, Pastille burner.**

Incense clock, or incense seal, an ancient time-measuring device in China, in which a tight-packed trail of incense is laid in an arrangement of grooves inside a pierced metal box; various types; see also **Fire clock.**

Incidit, appearing (often abbreviated) on prints, meaning 'engraved'.

Incised, cut or engraved; in particular, a pattern of fluting on a wine glass stem in spiral form, a style originating in Venice.

Inclined-plane clock, a clock that provides its own power by rolling down a slope; early 17th century. **135**

Inclusion, a mark of various kinds visible (not always with the naked eye) in precious stones, caused by accidents of crystal growth, a particle of some other substance, a healed crack or fault, or a hollow containing gas or liquid.

Incroyable, a term applied to several articles of furniture and fashion distinguished by their oddity, including a reading chair of the back-to-front type, the exaggerated style of men's dress in post-Revolutionary Paris, etc.

Incrusted: see **Encrusted**.

Incunabula, the earliest examples of any article, in particular the earliest printed books, i.e. those printed in the 15th century, and the earliest wood-block prints, from the same period.

Incuse, a design sunk into the surface, like intaglio, most frequently used in connection with coins and medals.

India, or Indian, of carpets, wallpaper, china and other wares, often meaning imported from the East, not necessarily India, by the East India Co. during the 17th and 18th centuries.

Indian, the figure of an American Indian, a popular decorative device in the 18th century, sometimes symbolizing America; see also **Cigar-store Indian, Dummy board**; also, an Indian's head or mask, found in glass and pottery and carved on furniture in the same period and later.

Indian-back, a hoop-backed, 17th-century Dutch chair with central splat carved in oriental fashion.

Indian carpets, in particular, hand-made carpets from the late 16th to the early 19th century, based on Persian forms but with greater naturalism and more open ground; a few high-quality carpets were designed by Europeans.

Indian flowers, a type of floral decoration in porcelain and earthenware, derived from oriental (Japanese rather than Indian) design and first employed at Meissen.

India rubber: see **Caoutchouc**.

Indigo, a dark blue dye obtained from the leaves of the indigo plant, used in carpets and other textiles.

Indiscret, a type of upholstered sofa popular in France in the mid 19th century consisting of (usually) three linked armchairs at angles to each other so that the occupants, leaning on their right arms, would find their heads in close proximity.

Inescutcheon, a small shield appearing as part of the heraldic device on a large one.

Ingle, originally a fire, subsequently a fireplace; hence, **inglebench** and **ingle-seat,** a seat by the fire; **inglecheek,** the jamb of a fireplace; **inglenook,** the corner beside the chimney.

Ingot, a block of metal, commonly oblong, made in that shape for ease of carriage and storage, usually referring to gold or silver.

Inkhorn, a cow's or other animal's horn, the standard vessel for ink until about the 16th century, often with metal mounts.

Inkle, linen tape or braid in various colours worn as a trimming on clothes in the 16th century, also on uniforms; the term was also employed for embroidery.

Inkwell, or inkstand, a container for ink which, in the 18th century, was often an elaborate silver piece with a tray for quills and vessels 'for the Ink Viall, another for the wafers, and another for the sand' (1746) plus, perhaps, a candle-holder. **137, 138**

Inlay, decoration of flat surfaces in furniture by cutting a shallow pattern and filling it with wood of contrasting colour, or shell, ivory, metal, etc.; see also **Marquetry. 163**

Inro, a small box for medicines, tobacco and other small necessities, worn by the Japanese attached to the belt by a toggle (netsuke). **139, 190**

Instrument case, a case for surgeon's instruments, usually metal and dating from the Middle Ages, or a case of leather, wood, metal, etc., for geometrical instruments; see also **Canteen**.

Insufflated, of glass, blown.

Intaglio, incised carving as opposed to relief, the design being cut out rather than the surround, as in a seal; also found frequently in glass and jewellery.

Intarsia, a form of inlay popular in Renaissance Italy, employing a variety of differently coloured woods inlaid to form a picture.

Intrados: see **Soffit**.

Iolite, an extremely rare gemstone, a variety of the mineral cordierite, which changes colour (violet, light blue, pale yellow) according to the angle it is looked at.

Ionic, the second order of Greek architecture, characterized by fluted columns with capitals in the form of scrolls and plain moulded bands around the base.

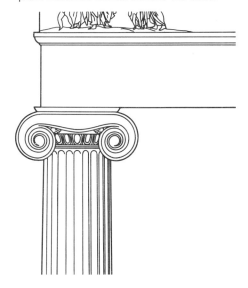

Iridescent, reflecting light in many colours, a property of certain gemstones and of some types of glass, including glass that has been buried for centuries and

undergone some physical degeneration; see also **Lustre**.

Iridium, a rare metal sometimes alloyed with platinum to give it hardness.

Iridized, a glittering surface, like lustre, given to glass by applying a metallic overlay while the glass is hot.

Irish Chippendale, a term applied to Irish mahogany furniture of the mid 18th century exported to England, copying contemporary English designs, with carved lion's masks, diamond patterns with carved scrolls, etc., no connection with Chippendale.

Irish porcelain: see **Belleek porcelain**.

Iron, a metal in use since prehistoric times and frequently used for ornamental purposes, being comparatively easy to work when heated; especially popular for garden furniture in the 19th century; see also **Cast Iron**.

Iron clocks, the earliest European household clocks; see **Gothic clock**; also, a type of Connecticut clock of the mid 19th century with cast iron front, painted and sometimes inlaid.

Iron red, a red pigment made from an iron oxide which can be fired on earthenware or porcelain at the same temperature as the glaze; see **High-temperature colours**.

Ironstone, fine stoneware, patented by Charles James Mason of Lane Delph, Staffordshire, in the early 19th century, originally including glassy slag from iron furnaces, very hard and tough, brilliantly coloured and very popular, thus imitated by many other potteries.

Ironwood, wood from several species of tree, including one used in shipbuilding in China, also a type of hornbeam.

Isfahan carpets, rare carpets of fine quality, late 16th and 17th centuries, from the royal manufactory in the former Persian capital, usually silk incorporating gold and silver thread; also, modern carpets, since about 1900, in traditional floral designs usually with a central medallion and high standard of workmanship.

Isinglass, a pure form of gelatin derived from the swim-bladders of certain fish, notably sturgeon, used chiefly in brewing, jelly-making, etc., but with a number of other uses in the arts, e.g. to give extra lustre to silk, as the basis of a form of plaster, and (dissolved in acetic acid) as a glue for repairing glass and china.

Isleworth pottery, bone china from a Liverpool factory in production about 1800, or earthenware similar to contemporary Staffordshire or Worcester models and Welsh ware from the town in Middlesex in the early 19th century.

Islim, a floral design of serpentine lines in Persian carpets.

Isnik ware, from the great pottery-making centre in Asia Minor (Turkey) dating back to the 13th century or

138 Inkwell. Persian, Khorassan,
13th century. With engraved
decoration in silver of hunting
scenes. (Metropolitan Museum of
Art, New York)

139 Vermilion lacquer inro.
Japanese, 17th century. Decorated
in gold lacquer with a sparrow on a
branch; finished with overlays of
silver and lead. (Museo Orientale,
Venice)

140 Ivory lid of a case. Dieppe workshops, 18th century. Dieppe became an important European centre of ivory carving; this piece is decorated in the Louis XV style. (Musée de Dieppe)

141 An immortal meditating in a grotto. Chinese, Ming dynasty (1368–1644). Nephritic jade, inspired by Taoism. (Metropolitan Museum of Art, New York)

142 Jacobean carved oak chair with arched stretcher. About 1675. (Victoria and Albert Museum, London)

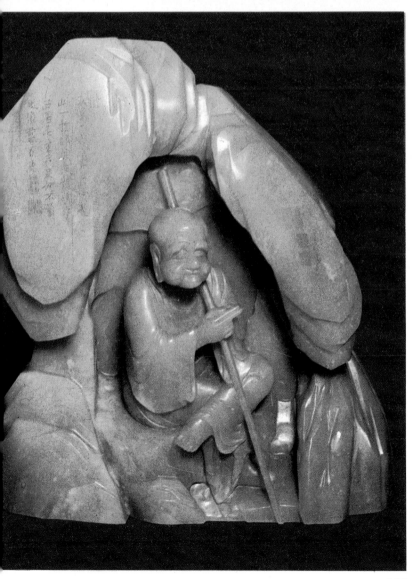

142

141

earlier; in particular, several types made in the Renaissance period and later, including Miletus ware and varieties of a hard, white earthenware with underglaze painted decoration, mainly in blue.

Istoriato, narrative painting, associated with early Italian maiolica.

Italian Comedy figures: see **Commedia dell'arte figures**.

Italian quilts, embroidered with a raised pattern in thickish cord.

Italian walnut, imported to England about 1800 from southern Europe; see **Grenobles wood**.

Ivory, a hard organic material from the tusks of animals, chiefly elephants; it can be carved and polished and has been used ornamentally since ancient times, also used often in inlay. **23, 50, 140**

Ivory nut, a palm nut about the size of a hen's egg, carved by sailors and others.

Ivory porcelain, a development from parian in the mid 19th century, the colour of ivory when unglazed.

Ivory-tinted earthenware, a highly successful Copeland ware in the 19th century.

Ivorytype, a coloured photograph made by placing a light-toned photograph over a hand-coloured picture, a device of photography's early years.

Ivorywood, a type of Australian hardwood, light in colour and apt for carving.

Jacaranda, a Brazilian hardwood from several varieties of tree, used particularly in Portuguese chairs of the 17th and 18th centuries.

Jacinth, or hyacinth, a precious stone, a variety of zircon, reddish-brown in colour; in ceramics, the colour of that stone.

Jack, a name given at different periods to a great variety of disparate objects, including a leather mug or tankard, a leather or chain-mail tunic, a small ship's flag, a copper vessel for straining hops in brewing, a roller towel, and numerous machines for lifting, e.g. a spit jack for raising or lowering a joint over the fire, etc.; see also **Jacquemart**.

Jackboot, a boot that rises up to and sometimes above the knee.

Jackfield ware, from the Shropshire pottery established in the mid 18th century, in particular jet or shining black wares, sometimes with moulded decoration and gilding, also figures; later made at many Staffordshire potteries.

Jack-in-the-box, a toy consisting of a box from which, when the lid is released, a clown-like figure springs up with arms gesticulating; origins old and obscure.

Jackwood, from a Far Eastern tree related to the breadfruit, fine-grained and yellow in colour, sometimes used in cabinetmaking.

Jacobean period, the reign of James I in England (1603–25). **142**

Jacobite glass, an 18th-century English wine glass engraved with Jacobite (supporters of the exiled Stewart dynasty) emblems, including portraits of Prince Charles Edward and more enigmatic devices of various kinds such as a rose (? England) with two buds (? the Old and Young Pretenders); forgeries numerous; see also **Amen glass**.

Jacobus, an English gold coin worth 25 shillings struck in the reign of James I.

Jaconet, a fine, closely woven cotton material like coarse muslin, originating in India, used for scarves and children's clothes in the 18th century; also called nainsook.

Jacquard weave, elaborate woven patterns made possible by the loom invented by J. M. Jacquard (1752–1834); hence **Jacquard coverlet,** the name given to a flowered coverlet professionally woven mainly in the first half of the 19th century with the aid of the new loom.

Jacquemart, or jack, in old tower clocks, a human figure that strikes the hour at the appropriate time.

Jade, a semi-precious stone, most frequently green but also occurring in many other colours including white, red and black, much used for ornamental carving in the Far East, particularly Burma and China, and (a different variety) by the Aztecs and their predecessors. **141**

Jadeite, the Burmese variety of jade; see also **Nephrite**.

Jakobakanne, a tall, slender mug with slightly curved sides and high-set handle in light-brown stoneware, German, 15th century.

Jalousies, shutters or blinds as seen on houses in Mediterranean countries, with sloping wooden slats to admit air while excluding some light.

Jamaica wood, West Indian mahogany.

Jamb, the vertical element at either side of a door, window or fireplace; also, a leg; hence, in armour, plates protecting the legs.

Jamestown glass, from the two earliest glassworks in colonial Virginia, both short-lived, founded in the first years of the colony; only fragments are definitely known to survive

Janina motif, occurring in the borders of Turkish carpets, a stylized pattern of leaves and fruits, two roughly circular shapes being joined by stems to a serrated, leaf-like form.

Janus, the Roman god with two faces, front and back, appearing on Roman coins, also in Renaissance and Neo-Classical decoration, often as a double mask.

Japan, the type of varnish used in japanning, consisting basically of natural asphalt (black japan) or of transparent copal oil; see **Japanned**.

Japanese style, in furniture, spindly forms and fretwork in wood and metal, influenced (sometimes remotely) by Japanese models after the reopening of Japan to the West in the late 19th century; also, lacquer work and decorative styles in ceramics in more direct imitation of the Japanese from the mid 18th century.

Japanned, lacquered, the decoration of furniture and metal wares, particularly tin-plate, with layers of varnish before painting, gilding or engraving; a technique inspired by (though different from) oriental imports of the 16th and 17th centuries; see also **Lacquer**.

Japonaiserie: see **Japanese style**.

Jardinière, a stand on which flowers or a potted plant were displayed, in every conceivable style and material, most frequently porcelain or earthenware; sometimes applied to the actual pot or vase without the stand, also known as cache pot. **144**

Jarrah wood, from an Australian tree of the eucalyptus family, a dark reddish-brown.

Jarrito, a small glass pitcher or vase, with applied or moulded ornament in relief, Spanish, 17th and 18th centuries, showing Moorish and Venetian influence.

Jasmine pipe, a pipe with a long slender stem of jasmine, 'highly prized by the Moors and the Turks' (1911).

Jasper, a quartz stone similar to chalcedony, occurring in various colours, sometimes striped or spotted, as in bloodstone; used for jewellery and carved ornaments. **143, 207**

Jasperware, a very fine, hard, Wedgwood stoneware developed in the late 18th century, naturally white but at first produced in a number of different muted colours, later with coloured slip; used particularly for ornamental wares with applied relief in white; widely imitated in England and Europe and numerous refinements introduced; also, red stoneware produced by Böttger at Meissen. **288**

Javanese motifs: see **Batik design.**

Jelly glass, a cone-shaped vessel on a short stem or convex foot, sometimes with two handles or matching saucer; various types since the 18th century.

Jennens & Bettridge ware, articles of papier-mâché from tea trays to cabinets, often inlaid with shell, made chiefly in the first half of the 19th century by a notable Birmingham, England, firm.

Jenny Lind, of furniture, 'country' furniture factory-made in the late 19th century, painted with flowers, etc. and based on 17th-century styles; also, a large variety of other articles named after the immensely popular Swedish soprano (1820–87).

Jerga, narrow strips of coarse homespun woollen fabric sewn together for use as floor coverings in the American West, sometimes bright plaids and stripes, 19th century.

Jeroboam, now a large wine bottle, formerly a large goblet or drinking cup.

Jersey glass, products of the numerous glassworks, including the Jersey Glass Co., operating in New Jersey in the early 19th century, especially early pressed glass.

Jersey porcelain, from the Jersey Porcelain & Earthenware Co. owned by David Henderson in the early 19th century; no authenticated examples apparently exist.

Jesuit china, Chinese porcelain of the 17th and early 18th century made for export to the order of French Jesuit missionaries, with Christian religious scenes such as the Crucifixion.

Jet, a very hard, very black form of lignite (in effect, coal), carved for jewellery, buttons, etc., and often imitated in black glass.

Jetware, red-bodied earthenware covered with a dark blue glaze and fired to blackness in the furnace, popular in Staffordshire in the 19th century; see also **Jackfield ware.**

Jetwood: see **Ebony.**

Jever faience, rare, tin-glazed earthenware from the north German factory operated by a former Meissen employee in the late 18th century, including some notable figures and bowls.

Jever

Jewelled porcelain, porcelain inlaid with foil-backed glass drops like gems, a technique originated at Sèvres in the late 18th century, popularized in England by Copeland and others in the mid 19th century.

Jeweller's rouge, colcothar, a brownish-red powder derived from a peroxide of iron, used in polishing gems and glass.

Jewellery, ornaments for personal adornment made from or including precious metals and/or precious stones, usually having some social significance (if only as an indication of wealth).

Jewel moulding, on furniture, a decorative frieze with forms shaped like cut gems.

Jew's harp, a semicircular metal instrument with a springy blade of metal attached at one end; held in the teeth and the springy part twanged with the finger, it emits a musical note the pitch of which can be varied.

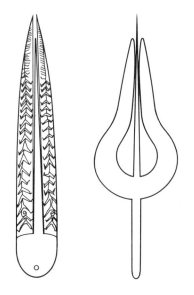

Jigsaw work, fretwork, as in jigsaw puzzles.

Jingall, a small, portable cannon, fired from a stand.

Jingling johnny, a musical instrument of distant Turkish origin consisting of a staff surmounted by a crescent from which many small bells are suspended, jingling when shaken.

Joey, a small tumbler or wine glass, like a dram cup.

Johannes, a Portuguese gold coin current in the 17th century.

Johnson mirrors, based on the mid 18th-century designs published by Thomas Johnson of London, perhaps made by him.

Joined, of a chest, stool, etc., made with a typical joiner's frame, with mortise-and-tenon joints held firm by wooden dowels; 16th and 17th centuries.

Joinery, an activity midway between carpentry and cabinetmaking, concerned with smaller items (including furniture) than the carpenter, and largely dependent on the making of good joints.

Joint holder, an implement, metal or wood, for holding the roast steady while carving, e.g. a metal handle that could be slipped over the bone and tightened by a screw, or a split rod in which the bone was wedged; 19th century.

Joint stool, a joined stool.

Jolly boat, a coaster in the form of a boat on castors, late 18th or 19th century.

Jona, or joney, a Staffordshire earthenware flatback figure, in particular a dog.

Joram, a large cup, tankard or bowl (usually earthenware), for drinking joram, a kind of spiced ale.

Jordan, a large bowl or pot, such as a chamber pot.

Joshaghan carpets, from a village in central Iran, characterized by designs made up of rather small, stylized, floral forms, often set in a diamond, with a central medallion; warm red and blue the dominant colours.

Jousting chest, a wooden chest in medieval style with carved relief scenes of jousting and other festivities, apparently a fairly recent invention.

Judy lamp, a betty lamp.

Jufti, a double knot, Sehna or Ghiordes, in oriental carpets, in which four threads of the warp, rather than two, are involved in each knot, reducing the density of the pile by half.

Jug, any vessel with some kind of lip or spout for pouring liquid into another vessel, with or without a lid.

144 Porcelain jardinière decorated
by J. P. Ledoux. Sèvres, 1758.
(Musée du Louvre, Paris)

143 Jasper vase with mask on
spout, mounted in gold. Bohemian,
1608. (Kunsthistorisches Museum,
Vienna)

145 'The court jesters Fröhlich and Schmiedel' by Johann Joachim Kändler. Meissen, 1741. (Porzellan-sammlung, Dresden)

146 Kazak carpet. Caucasian, 19th century. The two large motifs which occupy the centre are found exclusively in Kazak carpets; they possibly represent stylized eagles. (Private Collection, Milan)

Jugendstil, the German term for Art Nouveau.

Jug head, stopper or cork surmounted by a wooden or china bust, sometimes of a recognizable individual.

Julep cup, the name given to an American silver tumbler or beaker having straight sides that taper inwards towards the base, sometimes given as prizes; late 18th or early 19th century.

Jumeau dolls, fine quality china dolls made at the Jumeau factory in France from the middle of the 19th century; also, imitations of inferior quality made in many countries.

Jumping jack, a toy consisting of a cut-out wooden figure with jointed limbs suspended from a rail between parallel bars which performs acrobatic movements when activated by a string.

Jungfrauenbecher, a large silver cup in the shape of a girl in contemporary (16th- to 17th-century) dress holding a cup, pivoted on two handles, above her head, so that when the girl is held head downwards there are two cups, her hollow skirt forming the second; both were to be drained at wedding feasts.

Juniper wood, from various members of the juniper family, occasionally used ornamentally and for articles like cigar boxes, most varieties having a strong fragrance; also occurring in Ancient Egyptian furniture.

Jute, coarse cloth used for coverings, canvas, etc., made from the fibres of the jute plant, formerly grown chiefly in northern India.

Juvenilia, works such as paintings, writings, etc., made by an artist in his youth; also, various articles, including books, specially produced for children.

Ju ware, rare Chinese stoneware made for a short period in the 12th century, elegant forms with a pale, blue-grey glaze, slightly crackled.

Kabistan carpets, Caucasian carpets, a variety of Shirvan, often decorated with peacocks and other animal forms.

Kabyle pottery, made by a North African people, often with applied patterns in black showing Islamic influence.

Kailyard prints, 19th-century prints of Highlanders, Highland scenes, etc., of little artistic worth.

Kakemono, a Japanese wall picture, frequently painted on silk, mounted between rollers.

Kakiemon, a type of decoration on porcelain, notably Meissen and Chelsea, derived from Japanese ware of the 17th century, painted by a family of potters of this name at Arita, characterized by asymmetrical designs leaving plenty of open space, and distinctive colour scheme of dull red, turquoise, yellow and blue.

Kalardasht rugs: see **Luristan rugs.**

Kala-taing, a Burmese term for a Western-type chair, the occupant of which has his feet on the ground rather than sitting cross-legged.

Kaleidoscope, an optical toy in the shape of a cylinder, containing mirrors and coloured fragments of glass which, viewed through the eyepiece, form an endless variety of patterns as the tube is shifted.

Kaliang ware, a type of 15th-century pottery made in Thailand, including figures of men and animals, covered with a dark brown glaze.

Kamassi boxwood, a light brown African hardwood sometimes used in cabinetmaking.

Kändler porcelain, early Meissen porcelain made during the 40-odd years in which Johann Kändler was model master; see **Meissen. 145**

K'ang, a low platform, usually with openwork sides, for lying on, but sometimes furnished with low tables, etc.; Chinese.

Kangaroo, a small sofa or chaise longue with the open end curved upward so that the legs of a recumbent occupant would be slightly raised; 19th century.

K'ang Hsi period, the reign of that emperor in China (1662–1722), which saw a minor renaissance in the art of porcelain making.

Kaolin, or petuntse, a refractory white clay formed by the decomposition of granitic rocks, an essential element in the making of hard-paste, or 'true', porcelain.

Kap-kap, a type of ornament formerly worn by several Pacific Islands peoples, made from seashells decorated with tortoiseshell and hung on a cord.

Karabagh carpets, from the southern Caucasus bordering on Iran, Ghiordes knot, all-wool, mainly influenced by Persia but also some French-inspired floral designs; the ground is almost invariably dark red or dark blue and the motifs in brighter colours.

Karaj carpets, including runners up to 10 ft long, from northern Iran not so far from (and similar to) Tabriz, a common design being three medallions with the central one larger, also other Caucasian and Persian motifs.

Karat, a measurement of precious metals; see **Carat.**

Karatsu ware, 16th- to 17th-century pottery made in Kyushu, Japan, by Korean potters, in pale-coloured glazes, sometimes decorated with feathering.

Karrusel, the trade name of a late 19th-century watch that incorporated an improved method for preventing time-keeping errors due to changing positions.

Kas: see **Kast.**

Kashan carpets, from the long-established centre south of Teheran, fine-quality rugs and carpets, often with a central medallion (the design of which

may be suggested again in each corner) on a dense floral-patterned ground; also silk 'story' carpets in which the story is written in the borders and illustrated in the field; mainly since the late 19th century.

Kashan pottery, from the major Persian centre, examples dating back to the 12th century at least, especially lustre wares, wall tiles, enamelled ewers, and occasional figures; generally less distinguished, and Chinese-influenced, from the 15th century.

Kashkay carpets, a variety of Shiraz carpets, of particularly fine workmanship.

Kashmir: see **Cashmere.**

Kassel porcelain: see **Cassel porcelain.**

Kast, or kas, a Dutch cupboard, in particular a large, carved or painted wardrobe on ball feet, with drawers and/or shelves, found in the Hudson and Delaware valleys; 17th and 18th centuries.

Kastrup faience, from a Copenhagen factory founded in the mid 18th century and in operation for 20 or 30 years, notable for the rather large size of some groups and vases.

Kast-stel, a set of five Dutch delftware vases, three baluster-shaped and two relatively straight-sided, to adorn the cornice of a cupboard; late 17th and 18th centuries.

Kazak rugs, woven by nomadic peoples in the central Caucasus, Ghiordes knot, highly formal geometric designs of medallions, octagons, stars, diamonds, zig-zags, etc., colours mainly red, blue and cream. **146**

Keene glass, from one of two factories in Keene, New Hampshire, in the 19th century, including bottles, window glass and various types of glassware as well as particularly interesting off-hand articles.

Keep, a safe, particularly one for keeping food; also, the stronghold of a castle.

Keeper, a retaining clasp, latch, bar, etc.; in particular, a ring worn to keep another ring, such as a wedding ring, on the finger.

Kelim rugs: see **Khilim rugs.**

Kelley, kelei, keleghi, etc., a large Persian carpet about three times as long as it is wide; see also **Kenare.**

Kellinghusen faience, mainly unpretentious earthenware with floral designs in high-temperature colours, from the Holstein centre, late 17th to 19th century.

Kellogg prints, 19th-century American lithographs published by a well-known firm with headquarters in Hartford, Connecticut; fairly numerous.

Kelsterbach porcelain, 18th-century figures from the factory founded by former workers at Meissen and imitating Meissen styles; some tin-glazed earthenware was also produced before porcelain took over.

Kelt, or kelter, a coarse cloth made of a mixture of black and white wool.

Kenare, in Iran a runner or side carpet, flanking the central carpet (kelley) and about half its width.

Kennedy porcelain, from a factory in Burslem, Staffordshire, noted for impressed pictures in porcelain in the late 19th century; see also **Lithophane.**

Kensington glass, a variety of early American glass tableware, now possibly all lost, made by the Philadelphia Glass Works, similar to Amelung glass; or from another glassworks operating in Kensington during the mid 19th century.

Kent mirror, a looking-glass of Neo-Classical, 'architectural' design, popular in the mid 18th century and named after the contemporary English architect, William Kent.

Kentucky dulcimer, a stringed instrument similar to a zither but played with a bow.

Kentucky rifle, or Pennsylvania rifle, developed in colonial America from European models by German and Dutch colonists, with a long barrel and relatively small calibre; late 18th-century examples often elaborately decorated with inlay, etc.

Kerchief, or coverchief, originally a cloth covering a woman's head; later, one covering the neck.

Kerf, a cut or saw-mark, e.g. the serrations in a board for baking bread.

Kerki carpets, from the region around Bohkara, very formal designs usually employing the gul motif.

Kerman, carpets from the region around the town in south-east Iran, an ancient centre of carpet making, densely woven cotton and wool in a great variety of floral designs frequently with a central medallion, sometimes of Western influence, the pattern of the ground often repeated in the borders; also, Persian pottery from this region. **148**

Kermanshah carpets, from the region around the town in western Iran, Sehna or Ghiordes knots, harmonious design of many colours.

Keros, a type of earthenware beaker, South America.

Kersie, or kersey, a fine, twilled woollen cloth of East Anglian origin.

Kettle, a metal vessel for boiling water, **147.** In furniture, the characteristic shape as seen in late 18th-century commodes; also, a type of medieval helmet with a brim.

Kettledrum, a large drum, often of brass with rounded base, as seen, for instance, in mounted military bands (or the orchestral tympanum), popular since the 17th century; also a glass bowl on a foot, of kettledrum shape.

Kettle stand, a type of occasional table, often of pillar-and-claw type, with an openwork metal gallery or other retaining device to hold the kettle safely.

Kewblas, a type of art glass produced in the late 19th century at Somerville, Massachusetts, in which milk glass is overlaid with coloured glass topped by a clear coating.

Keybox, any box for keeping keys in, frequently decorative metalwork, sometimes a small glass-fronted cabinet attached to the wall near the door.

Keyhole work, a decorative pattern based on a motif in the form of a keyhole, e.g. an inlaid band on a frieze, a pierced brass gallery, etc.

Key pattern, a geometrical pattern of straight lines and right angles, like the plan of a maze, as seen on the frieze of a cabinet, derived from Greek architecture; also known as Greek key; see also **Fret.**

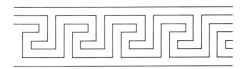

Key plate, or escutcheon plate, the metal or ceramic plate, often elaborately decorated, around a keyhole. **149**

Khalichen, a term describing an oriental carpet measuring approximately 5 × 8 ft and usually implying especially good quality.

Khamseh carpets, Hamadan carpets of above-average quality, usually with a central medallion.

Khilim rugs, kelim, kilim, kisilm, etc., oriental rugs or hangings originally made by and for nomads; flat woven and weft faced like tapestry; mostly bold geometric patterns.

Khilin, a motif found in oriental carpets based on an animal (apparently a deer) of Chinese origin.

Khirbet Kerak ware, a type of Bronze Age pottery of remarkable elegance, found in the Near East.

Khorassan carpets, from a large region in north-east Iran, design frequently based on the herati motif, sometimes identifiable by a tripling of the weft thread every few rows.

Khotan carpets, from a centre of distribution in Sinkiang, often with Chinese motifs and unusual colour combinations, wool pile, Sehna knot; see also **Samarkand carpets.**

Kian ware, Chinese pottery from Kiangsi in the Sung period, with resist designs and slightly marbled glaze.

Kibble, a large wooden pail, used in mining to carry ore to the surface.

Kibitkas, tents used by the nomadic peoples of Turkestan, round, supported on a wooden frame, and hung with carpets.

Kick, a cone-shaped indentation in the bottom of a bottle or decanter made before the late 18th century; sometimes on earthenware vessels of various kinds also.

Kidderminster carpets, made at the centre in Worcestershire since the early 17th century; originally cheap floor coverings, moquette carpets from the mid 18th century.

Kiddush cup, a silver goblet, for wine, used in Jewish ceremonies.

Kidney desk, or dressing table, etc., a shape that became popular for such pieces in the late 18th century, sometimes called 'horseshoe'.

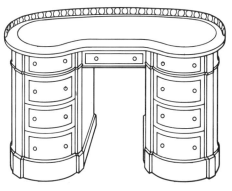

Kiel faience, highly valued wares of many kinds in almost-white tin-glazed earthenware, with vigorous and varied flower painting, from a Holstein factory in operation during the second half of the 18th century.

Kilim rugs: see **Khilim rugs.**

Kimberlite, the hard, blue-grey, perioditic rock found in South African diamond mines.

Kimono, a long, loose Japanese robe with wide sleeves, popular in the West since the Art Nouveau period.

Kinetoscope, an early type of motion picture projector.

King silhouettes, in particular, those drawn by an odd character named William King of Salem, Massachusetts, with his 'patent delineating pencil', late 18th and early 19th centuries.

147 Silver tea kettle and lamp. English, made by William Grundy, 1753. An apron conceals the lamp, while the pear-shaped body is decorated with Rococo scrolls, flowers and shell motifs. (Victoria and Albert Museum, London)

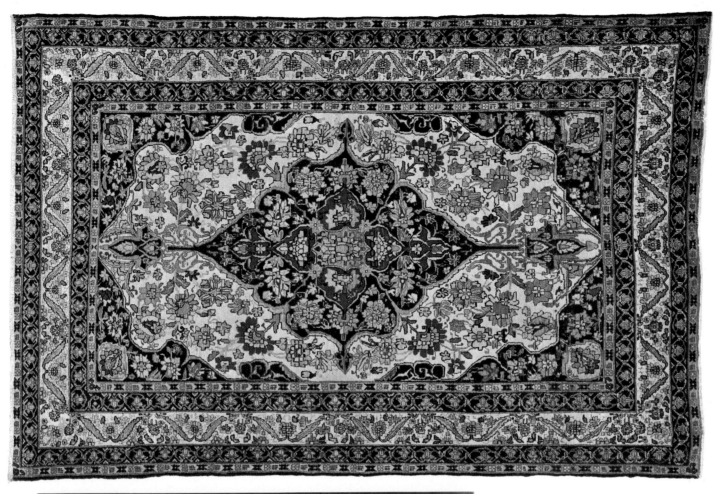

148 Kerman carpet. Persian, 19th century. (Private Collection, Milan)

149 Wrought iron key plate. Spanish, 17th century. (Victoria and Albert Museum, London)

King's Lynn glass, tableware and bottles from the town in Norfolk, England; in particular, wine glasses and tumblers with a pattern of broad, shallow grooves around the bowl, thought to originate in Norfolk in the 18th century.

Kingwood, or violet wood, a dense, sometimes dark purple wood, related to rosewood, imported from Brazil from the 17th century, used for inlay and veneer.

Kinrande style, Japanese porcelain covered with a deep coloured glaze and rich gilt decoration over the glaze.

Kip, the name of several disparate articles, including a reed basket used for trapping fish, a lodging house and thence a bed, a measure of weight, soft leather from a young animal.

Kirman, Persian carpets and pottery: see **Kerman**.

Kirshehir rugs, from central Turkey, usually all-wool and mainly rather small, prayer rugs being common, formal in design and somewhat sombre, relatively primitive in conception and execution.

Kist, a chest or, more particularly, a coffer in which money or jewels were kept.

Kit, a large container or basket, in particular a wooden, hooped tub with a lid in which milk or butter was carried; also, a very small violin, carried by 18th-century dancing masters.

Kit-Kat glass, a baluster-stemmed wine glass, early 18th-century English, so named for their appearance in portraits by Sir Godfrey Kneller of members of the aristocratic Kit-Kat Club.

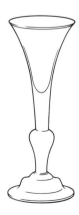

Kitsch, a very useful (and therefore hard to define) term covering works of art and ornament that would once have been considered—and by many connoisseurs still would be—cheap and/or in bad taste.

Klismos, an ancient Greek chair with sabre-curved legs and a comparatively shallow, curved backrest on three posts, revived in the Neo-Classical period.

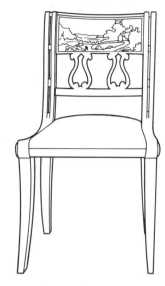

Klondike, a form of the card game patience, or solitaire; also the object of a Canadian gold rush (1896); hence, colloquially, a bargain or a successful financial coup; also, a light modern chair with fitted cushions forming back and seat.

Kloster-Veilsdorf porcelain, from the Thuringian factory founded in the second half of the 18th century; early works closely imitative of Meissen.

Knag, a protrusion, like a knob on a stag's antlers; specifically, a peg or hook.

Knee, in furniture, the outward curve of a cabriole leg, in the 18th century often decoratively carved and sometimes with applied ornament; also, any shape suggesting a knee, as in certain pewter jug handles, etc.

Kneehole desk, a desk with a cut-out portion to accommodate the knees of the person seated at it, thus implying the absence of a hinged or sliding writing surface; see also **Pedestal desk**.

Knick-knack, a frippery, trifle, trinket, of any kind.

Knife case, or box, for table knives, usually in wood, silver-mounted, since the mid 18th century, recognizable by its characteristic shape of bowed front and top sloping steeply up from front to back, though other shapes also occur, e.g. vases; see also **Knife tray**.

Knife cleaner, a device for cleaning non-stainless steel knives, various types in the 19th century, usually involving rotary motion but sometimes simply a box with compartment for abrasive cleaning material.

Knife tray, or box, a wood or metal tray with sides and central dividing board with slot handle.

Knitting sheath, a cylindrical container for holding knitting needles.

Knocker latch, a doorknocker in handle form which, when lifted and turned, raises the latch.

Knop, a protuberance or swelling, as seen on the stem of a wine glass; also, a knob or finial of roughly ball-like form.

Knorpelwerk, decorative carving on Baroque (particularly German) furniture consisting of vaguely scroll-like forms suggestive of malformed flesh or mutant fungi; see also **Auricular decoration**.

Knot, in sheet glass, the central bulge or bull's eye; in wood, a protrusion or irregularity causing changes in the grain, sometimes used for decorative effects in furniture; in handmade carpets, the method of tying the pile to the warp threads.

Knotty pine, knot-ridden pine boards formerly painted over when used for furniture to conceal the blemishes, more recently considered chic when stripped.

Knowles ware, from the 19th-century factory in East Liverpool, Ohio, which among other wares produced the thin and highly translucent lotus ware; also, English stoneware; see **Brampton stoneware**.

Knuckle arm, on a Windsor chair, an arm rail terminating in a down- and inward-curving scroll form.

Knuckle duster, or brass knuckles, a backstreets weapon dating from the 19th century, consisting of heavy metal reinforcements for the fist, basically four joined rings that slip over the fingers.

Knuckle joint, a type of hinge in which a pin, attached at either end to the moving part, pivots inside a cylinder; in metal or wood.

Knulling: see **Knurled**.

Knurled, knotty or gnarled; or decorated with a pattern of ridges, flutes, knobs; of a foot in seat furniture, an inverted scroll curling inwards in the manner of a half-clenched fist; see also **Whorl**.

Koban, a Japanese gold coin, oval in shape, current from the 16th to the 19th century.

Kokowood, from a Far Eastern tree, particularly the Andaman Islands, a dark brown hardwood with pronounced markings, used chiefly for veneer.

Kokplank, a wooden gingerbread mould, Dutch.

Kolbuszowa furniture, 18th-century Polish furniture named after a contemporary workshop, in Rococo and later styles, distinguished by stylized marquetry patterns; mainly desks and cabinets.

Königsberg faience, from two short-lived Prussian factories at Königsberg in the second half of the 18th century, blue-painted earthenware and creamware.

Kopek, a Russian coin issued in various denominations since the 16th century, silver or copper.

Korean style, in ceramics, Kakiemon style.

Kornilov porcelain, fine-quality Russian porcelain from the St Petersburg (Leningrad) factory in the first half of the 19th century, distinguished by brilliant colours and gilding; later, mass-produced wares largely for export.

Kosta glass, from the Swedish glass-works founded in the mid 18th century; the most notable early products now surviving are chandeliers; still the centre of the Swedish glass industry.

Kotosh ware, ancient Peruvian pottery with a greyish body and engraved decoration, often painted red after firing.

Kovsh, a Russian silver vessel for pouring a measure of drink, like a shallow gravy boat with high, looped handle; late 18th- and 19th-century examples more ornate and made for non-utilitarian purposes.

Kowlstaff: see **Cowlstaff**.

Krater, a rather large, two-handled bowl or jar, as wide or wider at the mouth than at any other point, the mixing bowl of Ancient Greece, a popular form in pottery throughout history.

Kraut board: see **Cabbage cutter**.

Krautstrunk, a type of German glass jar or beaker of the late medieval period decorated with prunts, which resemble the stalk (or *Trunk*) of a cabbage (*Kraut*).

Kreussen stoneware, from an old-established pottery centre in Bavaria, including 17th-century tankards with applied relief and bright enamel painting, sometimes with pewter mounts.

Kreuzblume, 'cross flower', a term applied to the four finials on top of Gothic clocks, towers, gables, etc., usually foliated. ▶

Kreuzer, or kreutzer, a copper or silver coin of low value, several types, current in Germany from the 16th to the 19th centuries.

Kris, a heavy dagger with a wave-like blade from Malaya.

Krishna spoon: see **Buddha spoon**.

Krummhorn: see **Crumhorn**.

Ku, a Chinese vessel for tasting wine.

Kuang, a Chinese vessel for storing wine.

Kuan ware, a type of celadon ware of the Sung dynasty, reproduced in later ages, having a greyish porcellanous body covered with a number of glazes of varying tints, usually crackled. **150**

Kuan Yin, a female version of the original Indian Bodhisattva of total compassion, to whom Buddhists pray in sickness or trouble.

Kuba rugs: see **Kabistan carpets**.

Kubachi ware, from north-western Iran, 16th and 17th centuries, mainly dishes, painted with figures and animals and naturalistic floral patterns in underglaze colours.

Kuei, a Chinese vessel for storing sacrificial food.

Kufic, Cufic, a type of decorative Arabic writing, more angular than Nashki, found on some oriental carpets and on Islamic pottery.

Kula rugs, mainly nomadic rugs from the town in western Turkey, similar to Ghiordes and other Turkish rugs, a difference discernible to experts being the (usually) exclusive use of wool; see also **Graveyard rugs**.

Künersberg faience, unusual Bavarian faience of the mid 18th century, high-quality painting sometimes in the style of Du Paquier porcelain, Rococo figures in the French manner, and coffee pots painted with sporting scenes, etc.

Künersberg

Kungsholm glass, from the notable Swedish glassworks, late 17th to early 19th century, mainly very elaborate pieces showing Venetian and later German influence, including stems in the form of

Kreuzblume

the king's initials and other patriotic emblems engraved.

Kunzite, a rare, pinkish-blue gemstone, a variety of spodumene, first discovered about 1900 and occasionally used in jewellery.

Kurfürstenhumpen, a large German glass beaker painted with the figures of the Holy Roman Emperor and the imperial electors, 17th century or earlier; see also **Humpen**.

Kurk, sheep's wool of good quality.

Kussenkast, a large Dutch cupboard, late 17th or early 18th century, in architectural style with decorative inlay.

Kutahya ware, Armenian pottery made under Ottoman rule in the 17th and 18th centuries (and probably earlier), painted designs on a very white body with clear glaze, often European in style but also some Islamic tiles.

Kutani porcelain, Japanese porcelain chiefly of the 18th century, mostly indistinguishable from Arita porcelain.

Kuttrolf: see **Guttrolf**.

Ku Yüeh Hsüan style, extremely delicately enamelled and cameo glass, 18th-century Chinese, often showing European influence, named after the outstanding practitioner.

Kuznetzov porcelain, from the major Russian enterprise which accounted for more than half the total Russian production by about 1900.

Kwaart, a final lead-glaze coating on delftware, adding extra brilliance to the finish.

Kwachō, Japanese prints of birds and flowers.

Kyanite, a rare precious stone, blue, difficult to cut owing to its tendency to split along the length of the crystal.

Kyanized, wood treated to prevent decay, a process named after the 19th-century inventor, John Kyan.

Kylix, Cylix, a wide, shallow cup or bowl with two handles, on a foot, from antiquity.

Kyx, a stopper or bung of a barrel.

Labarum, a banner, as carried by the legions of the Roman Empire.

Labelled, of glass, bottles, decanters, etc., engraved with the name of their contents and often with appropriate decoration such as vine leaves; on furniture, clocks, etc., labelled with the maker's name.

Labrador stone, or labradorite, a variety of feldspar found in Labrador, grey with flashes of red, gold, green, etc., used in jewellery.

Labret, a type of jewellery found in several primitive societies, usually a disc, wood, gold, stone, etc., inserted in the lip or ear lobe, distorting the face.

Labrum, a flange, edge or rim, e.g. of a basin.

150 Kuan ware bowl. Chinese, from Chekiang, Southern Sung period (1127–1279). The crackle reveals the delicate dark clay body. (Percival David Foundation of Chinese Art, London)

151 Lacquer tray. Chinese, 16th–17th century. The red and black lacquer is worked like cloisonné, the areas being separated by silver wires. (Camelia Blakemore Warner Fund, Cleveland Museum of Art, Cleveland, Ohio)

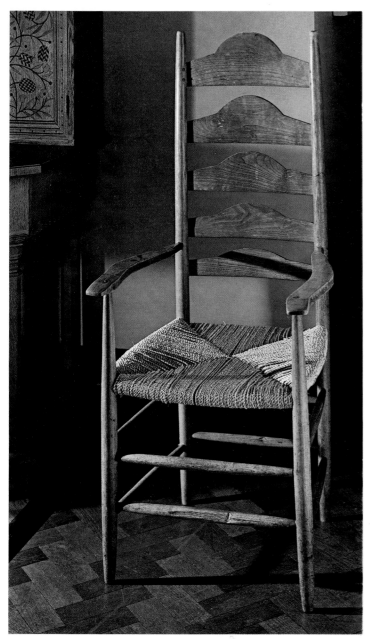

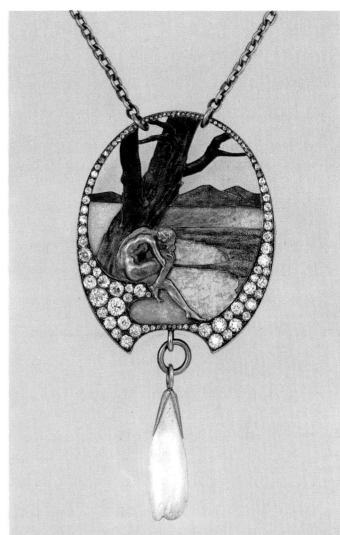

153 Necklace and pendant in gold,
enamel and diamonds and pearls,
by the French artist, René Lalique.
(Museum für Kunsthandwerk,
Frankfurt)

152 Ladderback chair designed by
Ernest Gimson about 1865 for
Morris & Co. (Victoria and Albert
Museum, London)

Laburnum wood, hard, pinkish-yellow wood with darker flecks, often cut on the slant for use in parquetry and oyster veneer from the late 17th century.

Labyrinth, a type of fretted pattern of straight lines and right angles suggesting a maze or labyrinth; see also **Fret**.

Lacca, lacquer, used on furniture, the Italian version of the 18th century being much thinner than the lacquer used in northern Europe.

Lacca contrafatta, thin Italian (particularly Venetian) varnish applied to furniture previously decorated with paint and cut-out, stuck-down paper figures.

Lace, fine openwork fabric of linen, cotton, wool, metal, e.c. threads, either embroidered with a single thread (needlepoint) or with several threads on bobbins (pillow lace); a complex and outstanding art in Europe from the Renaissance to the 19th century; also, a ribbon, as in shoe-lace.

Lace glass, a speciality of Venetian glass, a latticino design of fine coloured and transparent threads, the decorative network being formed first and enclosed in layers of glass applied from either side; see also **Lacy glass, Latticino**.

Lacemaker's globe, a globular glass vessel, typically with narrow neck and large conical foot, which was filled with water and placed before a lamp to concentrate the light.

Lacerna, a short woollen cloak.

Lacework, decoration on ceramics, glass, etc., resembling lace; in particular, actual lace coated in slip and applied to porcelain, the lace being consumed on firing but leaving its framework.

Lacquer, a type of gum or varnish applied to wood or metal in several coats, which can be carved, painted or gilded; originally an oriental technique, imitated in Europe from the late 16th century; see also **Japanned**. 58, 70, 139, 187

Lacy glass, associated particularly with Sandwich pressed glass, a pattern of stippled dots looking like lace, as background, to add brilliance to the design and perhaps conceal slight faults in moulding.

Ladder-back chair, having several narrow, horizontal slats between the posts to form the chair back, particularly a high back; originally a 'country' piece, but adopted by Chippendale and others; also

applied to 17th-century high-backed chairs with elaborately carved horizontal rails. 152

Ladik prayer rugs, well-known rugs from the Turkish centre, characterized by a foreshortened mihrab or niche, below which are three small niches, point downwards and terminating in stylized tulip forms.

Ladle, a large serving spoon, typically with cup-shaped bowl and upright handle, for serving punch, soup or other beverage.

Lady Jane, or Dame Jane, a demijohn.

Lady's chair, a small upholstered armchair with low seat and high back; 19th century.

Lafayette ware, any article, particularly glass bottles and flasks, celebrating the visit of the Marquis de Lafayette to the United States, scene of his former exploits, in 1824.

Lageniform, shaped like a bottle, implying in particular straight sides.

Lair, a ewer, particularly an elaborate silver example.

Lajvardina, medieval Persian pottery, with painting in black, red and white over a cobalt-blue glaze, pots, jars, bowls, etc.; see also **Mina'i ware**.

Lalique glass, made by the notable French artist, René Lalique (1860–1945), or at the factory bearing his name from about 1910; art glass of many kinds; also **Lalique jewellery**. 153, 154

Lambeth delftware, English (London) tin-glazed blue and white painted wares from the early 17th century, including products of the Lambeth pottery founded somewhat later; also, late 19th-century wares from the Doulton factory imitating the techniques of old Italian maiolica.

Lambrequins, lacy decoration as seen particularly on book covers, also on ceramics and drapery (e.g. pelmets), a stylized pattern of swags, festoons and pendants with a suggestion of oriental influence. 226, 257

Lamé, in armour, a thin plate; also, cloth woven from (or including) gold or silver thread.

Laminated, covered with a thin layer of (originally) metal, or built up with a series of layers, as in plywood.

Lamp, originally a metal or glass vessel filled by oil or fat for burning a fibrous wick; see **Argand lamp**.

Lampas, a fabric similar to damask, embroidered and used for upholstery.

Lamp clock, either a Carcel lamp, in which a clockwork pump supplied oil to the wick, or a lamp with a glass reservoir on which the hours are marked, the time indicated by the falling level of the oil. 155

Lamp screen, a moveable metal shield which is attached to the chimney of a glass lamp.

Lancashire chair, a late 17th-century armchair found chiefly in the north of England; the term usually implies a type of heavy Windsor chair or ladder-back; also known as Derbyshire chair; see also also **Yorkshire chair**.

Lancaster glass, jugs, bottles and flasks in coloured glass, including some examples of historical significance, made at the Lancaster, New York, glassworks established in the mid 18th century.

Lance, a light spear with a wooden shaft and iron or steel spike, as carried by cavalry.

Lanceolate, shaped like the head of a lance, tapering at each end; in particular, curved, spiky leaf forms in oriental carpets.

Lancet, an arch, window, etc., tapering to a point at the top, as in late Gothic architecture; hence lancet top, lancet clock.

Landau, a type of convertible carriage, a four-wheeled vehicle with a fold-back hood at either end.

Lander process, a mid 19th-century technique that speeded up transfer-printing of coloured pictures on ceramics, using a number of plates each bearing one part of the design and one colour.

Landscape rugs, also lampshades, mirrors, etc., embroidered, painted, engraved or inlaid with a landscape scene, an especially popular form of decoration in the late 18th and early 19th centuries.

Landscape panel, a wood panel in which the grain runs from side to side rather than top to bottom.

Lane Delph, 18th-century Staffordshire pottery, some of which was decorated by Wedgwood, also green-glazed ware; some early Wedgwood creamware was enamelled at Lane Delph.

Lange Lijsen, or Long Elizas, the slender and graceful female figures found on Chinese porcelain and extensively copied in Dutch and English blue-painted porcelain wares.

Lang yao, a rich red glaze on Chinese porcelain; see **Sang-de-boeuf**.

Lantern, any container for a candle or lamp designed to shield the flame from draughts.

Lantern clock, a development of the Gothic clock in the early 17th century. perhaps suggesting a lantern or possibly a corruption of latten, meaning brass; a weight-driven wall clock with bell under a canopy, usually with brass fretwork; the type has continued to be imitated intermittently since the 17th century. **156**

Lanthorn, a lantern, originally having horn rather than glass panes.

Lapidary work, the technique of gem-cutting.

Lapis lazuli, an opaque stone of a characteristic deep blue, occasionally gold-speckled as a result of the presence of iron pyrites, formerly used sometimes for inlay as well as small carved ornaments. **157**

Lapped edge, in Sheffield plate, concealment of the copper edge by extending the silver plate so that it overlapped the tell-tale copper, or by applying a separate strip of silver.

Laqabi ware, medieval Persian pottery with carved decoration and many-coloured glazes, kept apart by raised or engraved borders; chiefly large dishes, often with Kufic inscriptions.

Larch, light reddish-brown or yellowish wood, sometimes used in place of pine in furniture construction, but notoriously liable to warp.

Larin, small pieces of silver in loop shape used as currency in the Middle East during the 16th and 17th centuries.

La Rochelle faience, chiefly late 18th- and 19th-century faience, very similar to better-known centres such as Rouen, including some historical scenes and Chinoiserie figures.

La Rochelle

Lasting, probably short for 'everlasting', a stout woollen cloth woven with a double or treble thread; sometimes also a type of satin.

Latch, a lock operated by turning a handle or pressing a lever; various types.

Latchet, an ornamental pin in Celtic (particularly Irish) jewellery, consisting of a chased metal disc with serpentine pin, which would not easily pull out when thrust through folds of a garment.

Lath, a thin, narrow strip of wood; in particular such strips used to support the plaster in a ceiling or a wall.

Lath-back, a Windsor chair, English rather than American, in which the vertical sticks in the back are narrow, flat boards, not turned spindles.

Latten, hammered metal similar to brass, sometimes with a small amount of iron; a term often applied to any metal in thin sheets.

Lattice, an openwork structure of wood or metal strips (laths) crossing to form a pattern of small squares or diamonds, as in lattice windows. **41**

Latticework, any kind of decoration or construction in the form of a lattice; in furniture, most frequently fretwork in diamond pattern; see also **Latticino.**

Latticino, decorative glass in the Venetian manner, consisting of thin threads, usually white but sometimes other colours, within the glass; a technique introduced in the 16th century; see also **Filigree, Lace glass. 158**

Lattimo, opaque white glass, or milk glass.

Laub- und Bandelwerk: see **Leaf- and strapwork.**

Laurel, an Indian variety, dark brown in colour, used for cabinetmaking; the leaves feature in Neo-Classical decoration particularly in wreaths and swags; also, an early 17th-century English coin worth one pound, bearing a portrait of the king crowned with a laurel wreath.

Lavabo, in Christian ritual, a vessel for washing the hands, typically a shallow basin with a backplate decorated in relief with a religious scene, sometimes with cistern and faucet above.

Lavallière, in jewellery, a simple pendant of mounted stones.

Lava ware, a hard, glazed stoneware made with slag from iron furnaces, used for cheaper tableware in the second half of the 19th century, usually blue or purplish.

Laver, a large basin for washing hands or feet.

Lawn, a delicate linen material, finer than cambric, used for shirts and, in particular, the sleeves of a bishop's robe; also, various cotton muslins.

Lay metal, or ley metal, a cheap form of pewter, an alloy of tin and lead in proportions of 3 to 1, used only for inferior vessels such as chamber pots until the early 19th century.

Lazulite: see **Lapis lazuli.**

Lazy-back, a device for suspending a kettle over a fire, with a handle so that the kettle could be tipped to pour without being touched.

Lazy Susan, or dumb waiter, a series of (usually three) circular trays on a central pillar and tripod base; various elaborations on this basic pattern in the 19th century; see also **Dumb waiter.**

Lazy tongs, wooden or metal tongs with extending handles for a woman wearing crinoline to reach objects that her bulky skirts otherwise prevented or to reach objects without moving from her chair.

Lead, very soft, heavy grey metal with extremely low melting point, not too easily corroded; at various times used for outdoor statuary and even furniture, also gargoyles.

Leaded diamond, window panes of diamond shape set in lead, chiefly 16th to 17th centuries; see also **Lattice.**

Lead glass, the discovery of the English glassmaker, George Ravenscroft, glass containing lead-oxide which gave an extra brilliance, universal by about 1700 and accounting for the high quality of English glass in that period.

Lead glaze, containing powdered lead, the first really efficient glaze for clay pottery, known in the ancient Near East nearly 4,000 years ago.

Leading, in printing, the space between lines of type.

Leaf- and strapwork, of Laub- und Bandelwerk, a Baroque ornamental border predominantly of leafy scroll forms, often framing a scene, associated with early German porcelain.

Leaf-scroll, in furniture, a carved scroll like a curling leaf.

Leafwork, a term usually applied to naturalistic ornament in low relief, e.g. carved on 17th- and 18th-century furniture.

Leatherwork, any decorative work on leather, e.g. in book binding.

Le Creusot glass, late 18th- and early 19th-century French glass from the glassworks near Sèvres.

154 'Senlis' vase designed by René
Lalique, about 1925. (Marie-Claude
Lalique Collection, Paris)

155 Pewter lamp clock. Italian 17th
century. As the oil was used up,
one could tell the time of day by
measuring the level against the hour
indicated down the side. (Private
Collection, Milan)

156 Typical brass lantern clock.
Made by the English clockmaker,
Edward Webb, 1688. (Science
Museum, London)

157 Lapis lazuli vase mounted in
gilt bronze. Italian, by Bernardo
Buontalenti and Giacomo Bilivert,
1583. (Museo degli Argenti,
Florence)

Lectern, the reading desk on which the Bible is placed in a church; wood, or, typically, in the form of a brass eagle whose wings provide the support; also known as a book desk.

Leech jar, an earthenware jar, often baluster-shaped, with two handles and pierced lid, for holding leeches (used medicinally until quite recently), sometimes inscribed with the name of its contents.

Leeds ware, a variety of earthenwares from the Yorkshire city since the 18th century, most notably creamware, often recognizable by characteristic handles of two interlaced bands or lacy openwork; reproduced more recently.

Left-hander dagger, the fencing dagger, held in the left hand to supplement the rapier in the right, characterized by a large, sometimes curved crossguard.

Legend, a motto or inscription.

Leg-of-mutton, in women's dress, a sleeve puffed out at the shoulder.

Leg rest, a support, such as a stool, for the feet; sometimes an upholstered support shaped to fit the calf comfortably, 19th century.

Lehn ware, turned and carved small wooden vessels and boxes, hand-painted, made by Joseph Lehn of Lancaster County, Pennsylvania, in the 19th century.

Leithner blue, in porcelain, a pigment named after a chemist of that name, developed in the late 18th century at the Vienna factory.

Lekythos, a type of Greek jar or urn, associated with funeral offerings, straight-sided, curving in towards the foot and sharply shouldered, with handle and narrow neck, frequently painted on a white ground.

Lemon finial, a finial of lemon form as seen most typically on andirons, cheval screens, sometimes chair posts.

Lemon squeezer, an instrument of silver or other metal in which the lemon (or lime or orange) is placed in a saucer-shaped depression and squeezed by opposed wooden handles, from about 1800.

Le Nove, 18th-century porcelain from a factory near Venice and similar to contemporary Venetian porcelain; maiolica was also made at Le Nove.

Lenticular, or lenticel, having the form of a lens, i.e. with convex sides; in particular, the pendulum bob of a long-case clock.

Lenzburg faience, from a Swiss factory founded in the mid 18th century, generally imitating contemporary French patterns; also, enamelled stoves from a later factory in the same town.

Lesghistan rugs, woollen rugs from the eastern Caucasus, Ghiordes knot, sometimes as much as 10 ft long, but only up to 3 ft wide; stylized, often Persian-influenced motifs and fairly bright colours.

Les Islettes faience, from a factory in Lorraine, late 18th- and 19th-century faience in traditional style, including popular historical pieces.

Letter rack, a silver stand with vertical divisions, somewhat like a tall toast rack, from the late 18th century; also made in other media such as papier-mâché in the 19th century.

Letton silhouettes, early 19th-century cut-out portraits by a travelling American artist.

Levigation, the process of straining clay by diluting with water so that intractable lumps sink.

Lewin bird prints, late 18th-century prints of British birds, drawn, engraved and painted by William Lewin.

Lewis, a three-piece iron jack for shifting heavy stones; shears for cutting fabric; an air-cooled machine-gun used in the First World War.

Ley metal: see **Lay metal**.

Libbey glass, from the late 19th-century glassworks in Toledo, Ohio, noted for cut- and pressed-glass wares of many kinds and high quality.

Liber, the inner bark of a tree, particularly lime, used in ancient times for paper; also plaited as mats, notably in Russia whence they were exported to England in the 19th century.

Liberty glass, late 19th-century American cut and pressed glass from several glassworks in New Jersey and the Mid West.

Liberty print, printed cotton and silk fabrics from the East, also fabrics in Art Nouveau designs (some by William Morris), supplied by the well-known London store.

Library candlestick, an adjustable candlestick, frequently with two sockets, and a metal screen to shade the light.

Library steps, a short flight of folding steps, for access to high shelves, sometimes ingeniously convertible into an armchair or table, made from the early 18th century.

Library table, a flat-topped writing table or desk, particularly a large pedestal desk, wide enough for two people sitting opposite each other, from the early 18th century also known as partner's desk.

Lichtenhayn tankard, a type of German pewter tankard of the 18th century with ball-shaped thumbpiece and cut-card decoration.

Liège glass, made since the 16th century, at first in Venetian style, hard to distinguish from other, neighbouring centres.

Lift-handle, a pendant, drop- or pivoted handle, such as a drawer pull, that hangs down and is raised before being pulled.

Lighthouse clock, a mantel clock in the form of a lighthouse, the dial being enclosed by a glass 'lantern', early 19th century, rare.

Ligneous marble, marble that looks like wood, or vice-versa.

Lignum vitae, a very hard wood from South America and the West Indies, dark brown or blackish, used occasionally in furniture in the 17th century but chiefly in articles requiring special strength, such as machinery.

Ligron ware, lead-glazed earthenware and stoneware from a French factory notable for ingenious if grotesque high-relief figures of people and animals.

Lilihan carpets, from one of the numerous villages in the region of Hamadan, stylized floral motifs in striking colours; see **Hamadan carpets**.

Lille faience, from the late 17th century, fine tin-glazed ware resembling Delft but decorated in patterns associated with Rouen, also Chinese figures in Baroque style, etc.

Lily-pad: see **Picot**.

Limbach porcelain, late 18th- and 19th-century Thuringian porcelain imitating Meissen as closely as possible, also somewhat primitive early figures; still operating.

Limed, of oak furniture, treated with lime, not polished.

Lime glass, containing powdered limestone, used mainly for bottles and cheaper glasswares from the mid 19th century, lighter than lead glass.

Limewood, a sweet-smelling, pale yellow or cream, relatively soft wood with amenable grain, much used in carving; also for turning, but seldom for construction except the American variety, known as basswood; see also **Liber**.

Limited edition, of books, a relatively small number printed, each volume usually numbered and often with the author's signature.

Limned, drawn or painted; in particular, painted in watercolours.

Limoges enamels, painted enamel on copper plate, in colour or sometimes *en grisaille*, from the most important centre of the art in western Europe from the Middle Ages; religious scenes in Gothic style (16th century) and Renaissance designs (16th to 17th centuries). **219**

Limoges porcelain, hard-paste porcelain similar in style to Sèvres with which there was some co-operation in the late 18th century, Limoges possessing the clay; also, 19th-century European wares in imitation of Limoges enamels; in America, a general term including French-imported and domestic porcelain; see also **Haviland-Limoges**. **160**

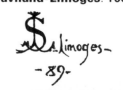

Lincoln, a name applied to a great variety of late 19th-century American articles commemorating Abraham Lincoln, sometimes (as in certain mugs) bearing his likeness; also, a type of open-armed rocking chair supposed to have been favoured by the president.

Lindenwood: see Limewood.

Line engraving, a print from a copper (or other metal) plate on which the design is incised with a sharp instrument.

Linen, cloth woven from spun flax fibres and widely used for clothes and coverings since the Stone Age, a notable product of Ireland since the 17th century; also, collectively, linen clothes, particularly shirts or bed sheets.

Linenfold, carved ornamentation in imitation of folded cloth set on end, found on wooden panels in chests, settles, etc., in Tudor furniture.

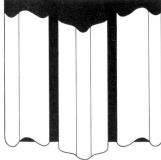

Linen press, an early (17th-century) form of English cupboard, with shelves; also a wooden screw-down press for damp linen, sometimes a part of the cupboard.

Linen smoother, a glass instrument used to smooth linen or rub down floors, consisting of a thick, solid disc with a vertical handle, knopped or banded.

Linsey-woolsey, a standard household cloth since the Middle Ages, a mixture of wool and linen, and sometimes cotton; also, woollen quilts, not necessarily of this material.

Linthorpe ware, late 19th-century English art pottery including highly original designs of many kinds, from a pottery near Middlesbrough, Yorkshire, especially celebrated for brilliant glazes.

Linzioletto, a white cotton shawl that covered the head and descended to the waist, a 17th-century Venetian fashion.

Lion, an animal that features in decorative art in one form or another more often, perhaps, than any other; e.g. lion-mask doorknockers and cabriole legs, lion's-paw feet, lion money-boxes, etc.

Lion period, a term occasionally applied to the early Georgian period in regard to English furniture, when lion forms, particularly a lion mask on the knees of cabriole legs, were popular.

Lionne style, in women's dress, a 19th-century French fashion for women of masculine cast, influenced by the English riding habit—stocks, leather gloves, etc.

Lion's paw, a form of footing in furniture found in many ancient civilizations and periodically adopted in more recent times, e.g. during the 'lion period' **47, 221**

Lip, or lip spout, the V-shaped indentation on the rim of a jug, so-called to distinguish it from the long tubular spout of, for instance, a teapot.

Liquid gold, a relatively cheap form of gilding china, used in the late 19th century, gold being dissolved or suspended in an oily liquid and brushed on; liable to wear off quickly.

Liquor chest: see Cellaret.

Lira, an Italian silver coin; also, a stringed musical instrument, the ancestor of the viola, played at the shoulder (lira da bracchio) or between the knees like a cello (lira da gamba).

Liripoop, the tail-piece of an academic hood.

Lirlkrug, a pewter jug of late 18th-century Bohemian origin with ogee-curved body, straight cylindrical spout and screw-down top with a loop handle.

Lisbon maiolica, Portuguese tin-glazed earthenware (possibly not, or not invariably, from Lisbon) made from the early 17th century, blue-painted, Chinese-influenced designs.

List, or listel, a strip or band, usually bearing an inscription, date, etc., a term used primarily in architecture.

Lit à lange, an 18th-century French bed, with a tester less than the full length of the bed.

Lit à l'antique, a bed with a single headboard of any Classical design, about 1800.

Lit à la turque, a bed with matching carved boards at head and foot, late 18th century.

Litchfield ware, early colonial American pottery from Litchfield, Connecticut; simple earthenware vessels, slip-decorated.

Lit de parade, a bedstead of considerable grandeur, such as that from which regal instructions might be issued to the assembled court, 17th to 18th century.

Lit de repos, a day bed.

Lit droit, a simple bedstead, of plain or painted wood, 18th to 19th centuries.

Lit en bateau, a bed with a frame that curved up to form the ends like a boat, early 19th century; *en corbeille,* somewhat similar, basket-shaped.

Lithograph, a print from a porous stone block on which the design is drawn in a special kind of greasy chalk.

Lithophane, a picture in porcelain clearly visible only when held to the light, made possible by the translucency of porcelain, the entire design being created by variations in thickness achieved by a tricky and enormously lengthy process developed in the early 19th century; also known as Berlin transparencies.

Lithotint, a lithograph in which the design was made with a brush; also, a coloured lithograph.

Lithyalin, a type of opaque, coloured glass, typically marbled blue and green, developed in Bohemia in the early 19th century.

Little folks' work, a form of (needless to say) Victorian embroidery, very simple, on squared canvas.

Littler's blue, a brilliant blue found as background on Longton Hall soft-paste porcelain, named after the factory's manager.

Liverpool lamp, a type of Argand lamp, silver or brass, with an adjustable disc over the wick to extend the circle of the flame, hanging or standing, early 19th century.

Liverpool pottery, delftware from a large number of potteries in Liverpool, particularly in the first half of the 18th century, most notably blue-painted punch bowls; also, earthenware since the mid 17th century and porcelain from the mid 18th century; see also **Soapstone. 161**

Livery board, a sideboard or table, 17th century.

Livery cupboard, a type of cupboard used for storing food, during the 16th century perhaps kept in a bedroom, some having open shelves, without doors, in one section; see also **Court cupboard.**

Livery pot, a flagon.

Loadstone, a piece of magnetic iron ore, in a metal frame, used for magnetizing compass needles, or as a curiosity.

Lobated, having a rounded, petal-like edge. **187**

Lobby chair: see Hall chair.

Lobby chest, a small chest of drawers, late 18th century.

Loblolly wood, Central American pine.

Lobster-tail helmet, a 17th-century cavalry helmet with faceguard like an American football player's and a ribbed neckpiece like a lobster's tail.

Lock, a device for fastening a door, lid, drawer, etc., operated by a key. **162**

Locker, a box or chest with a lock, nowadays usually one of a set.

Locket, a small, flat, silver or jewelled box worn on a chain around the neck and containing a portrait miniature.

Log-cabin bottle, a glass bottle in the form of the favoured pioneer residence, made in America before the Civil War and often copied in recent times.

Loggerhead, a stout post in the stem of a whaleboat; also, a round pewter inkwell, with sides sloping outwards from the rim.

Logwood, Central American dyewoods, so called because they were imported in logs.

Long arm, or shoulder arm, a gun fired from the shoulder.

Long-barrel: see Kentucky rifle.

Long-case clock, or grandfather clock, any pendulum clock in which the pen-

158 Latticino glass cup and cover. Murano, mid 16th century. (Museo Vetrario, Murano)

159 Looking glass with engraved figure of Winter. Mid 18th century. (Museo di San Martino, Naples)

160 Porcelain teapot. Ponyat, Limoges, about 1870. Derived from an 18th-century shape. (Musée des Arts Décoratifs, Paris)

161 Liverpool delftware plate. About 1750. The free painted decoration is influenced by earlier Dutch designs. (Victoria and Albert Museum, London)

dulum is encased in a tall box, with hood often of architectural form, first made in the second half of the 17th century. **165**

Long chain, in particular, a gold chain worn around the neck and hanging to the waist, 19th century.

Long Eliza: see **Lange Lijsen**.

Longton Hall porcelain, salt-glazed stoneware and soft-paste porcelain, including some early figures, from a factory in the Staffordshire centre operating for about ten years only, about 1750.

Looking glass, a mirror in a decorative frame. **159**

Loop-back, a type of Windsor single chair in which the back is framed by a single loop, with no horizontal interruptions between seat and top; see also **Balloon-back, Hoop-back**.

Loo table, a circular table on a pillar suitable for playing the 19th-century card game called loo, in which up to eight people participated.

Lopers, the wooden runners that support the writing surface of a slant-topped desk.

Lord rocker, a rocking chair in which the seat only rocked, pivoting in a stationary stand, 19th century.

Lost-wax process: see **Cire perdue**.

Lotus blossom, various decorative motifs based on the flower, found in Egyptian embroidery and glass of the 2nd millennium BC, on oriental carpets, in European Neo-Classical ornament, etc.

Lotus ware, a form of American Belleek, a frail, pearly porcelain made at the Knowles factory in East Liverpool, Ohio, in the late 19th and early 20th centuries.

Louis, a French gold coin of the 17th and 18th centuries, various types issued.

Louis XIV, the period covered by the king's reign (1643–1715) and the style of the decorative arts during the age, roughly equivalent to the Baroque. **163**

Louis XV, the period covered by the king's reign (1715–74) and the style of the decorative arts during the age, roughly equivalent to the Rococo. **31**

Louis XVI, the period covered by the king's reign (1774–93) and the style of the decorative arts during the age, roughly equivalent to Neo-Classical. **165, 212**

Louis XVI à l'Anglaise, English furniture, or English-influenced designs, in France during the reign of Louis XVI, particularly the Sheraton style.

Louisville glass, from the Kentucky glassworks, mainly flasks and bottles in various colours, mid 19th century.

Lounge, or lounging chair, an easy chair with a long seat, virtually impossible to sit upright in, from the early 19th century.

Louvre, an opening such as a door or window, for ventilation, covered by horizontal boards slanting out as in a Venetian blind.

Love seat, a small settee just big enough for two people; the term is sometimes

also applied to a conversation chair or confidante.

Love spoons, carved wooden spoons, presented as love tokens; Welsh.

Loving cup, or courting cup, a fairly large two-handled cup, usually on a foot and without a lid, but made in every changing style since the 16th century in silver and china; see also **Posset pot**.

Lowboy, a low chest of drawers, usually two layers, on four legs; often matching a highboy; made from about 1700. **52**

Lowdin porcelain, soft-paste porcelain from Bristol, England, about 1750, from a factory previously owned by a man named Lowdin and subsequently absorbed by Worcester.

Lowestoft ware, porcelain made at Lowestoft, England, in the second half of the 18th century, similar in type to Bow porcelain; also, a term widely applied to Chinese wares made for export to the West.

Low-poster, a bed with low posts at head and foot, no drapery.

Low relief: see **Bas-relief**.

Low-temperature colours, enamel colours on glass and ceramics, fired on at a relatively low temperature, and thus not necessarily at the time and place of manufacture; see also **Enamel**.

Loza fina, faience-fine or creamware.

Lozenge, a pattern of diamond or rhomboid forms; also, the boteh motif in oriental carpets.

Lübeck cupboard, a type of 18th-century, North German cupboard or dresser, with drawers in the lower part, doors in the upper, elaborately carved and sometimes gilded.

Lucerne hammer, a weapon similar to a halberd, the horizontally projecting blade being replaced by a hammer head.

Ludwigsburg porcelain, late 18th- and early 19th-century porcelain from a factory patronized by an enthusiastic duke of Württemberg, noted especially for small, sometimes humorous figures, three-legged pots and jugs and restrained colours; some tin-glazed earthenware was also made.

Lug, a projecting flange, knob, tab, etc., e.g. the wing of a wing chair, or the handle of a porringer; also, an L-shaped bracket to support a shelf.

Luminescence, the mysterious glow of certain gems, such as rubies, which results from the absorption of light rays beyond the range of the visible spectrum.

Lunette, ornamental band or moulding in which the dominant motif is a repeated half-moon form, variously embellished; found particularly on 18th-century dressing tables, commodes, etc.

Luneville faience, from a factory in Lorraine which made faience-fine in the late 18th century.

Lung-ch'uan ware, celadon ware of the Sung period, fine stoneware in strong but elegant forms covered with a lustrous blue-green glaze.

Luristan bronzes, from the region in Persia in the late Bronze Age, various art objects of cast bronze finished with engraving; also repoussé work.

Luristan rugs, from south-west Iran, Ghiordes knot, high quality materials, seldom over 8 × 5 ft, made by nomadic peoples with simple abstract patterns, based on floral forms.

Lustre, a thin metallic film (gold or copper for red, platinum for silver, etc.) applied to the surface of ceramics, giving a lustrous, sometimes iridescent effect, a speciality of Hispano-Moresque decoration, seldom imitated with complete success elsewhere before the 19th century; sometimes applied to glass; also, a chandelier with glass pendants; the reflection of light from a precious stone. **132, 164**

Lustring, a shiny, corded silk material used in upholstery from the late 17th century and later for women's dresses.

Lute, a stringed musical instrument, very ancient, with a neck and generally pear-shaped body; many variations in the 4,000 years of its existence. **166**

Lyons faience, from the French pottery centre, including early tin-glazed wares resembling Italian maiolica, blue and white and monochrome yellow wares.

Lyons silk, from the leading centre of silk weaving in 18th- and 19th-century France. **167**

Lyre, a musical instrument, the ancestor of all modern stringed instruments, known in Ur (Mesopotamia), basically a horse-shoe-shaped implement, the strings running from the body to a horizontal bar between two arms; a motif popular during the Neo-Classical period; hence **lyre-back,** a late 18th-century chair with back in the form of a lyre. **4**

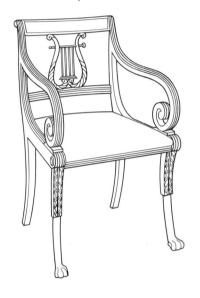

Lyre clock, a close relative of the banjo clock, the case suggesting the shape of a lyre, often with scroll-like leaf forms at the curves of the base; early 19th century. **169**

Lyrichord, an immediate predecessor of the piano in England, in which small wheels driven by clockwork were brought into contact with the strings by pressing the keys; probably the prototype only made (last heard of in the late 18th century).

Macaroni style, a contemporary name for Art Nouveau (with its elongated coiling forms), adopted by those who did not care for it; also, the extravagant, frilly style of dress adopted by rich young Englishmen in the mid 18th century, 'long curls and spying glasses' (Horace Walpole).

Macassar wood: see Zebrawood.

Mace, originally a medieval club like a pole-axe, carried on horseback; subsequently a silver or occasionally gold staff of civic authority, often topped by a crown and finial. **170**

Macramé, a type of lace, originally Italian and used for ecclesiastical vestments. Made basically by knots of various kinds and therefore simple in design;

later used for furnishings, dress trimmings and ornamental fringes. Currently enjoying a popular revival as a craft.

Maculated, of prints, spotted, stained, or otherwise spoiled.

Madder, a crimson dye obtained from the root of a plant of the same name, used in some Persian carpets.

Madeira stove, a free-standing, cylindrical stove, 19th century.

Madeira wood: see Canary wood.

Madeley porcelain, soft-paste porcelain in the manner of old Sèvres, but unmarked, produced at the Shropshire pottery of Thomas Randall in the early 19th century; also bone china similar to Coalport.

Madhen rugs, prayer rugs from western Turkey, made chiefly for export to the West.

Madras, silk or cotton fabrics printed in bright colours, in particular handkerchiefs that were sewn together and used for mats, coverings, etc.; hence the more recent multicoloured, patchwork Madras jacket.

Madras carpets, Indian carpets, some of large size, made for European export in the late 19th and early 20th centuries.

Magascope, a magic lantern.

Magdeburg faience, from the north German city, 18th-century faience including vases and jars with a kind of latticework outer casing, in high-temperature colours.

Magic lantern, a very old (18th century) machine for projecting a picture painted on glass, or, more recently, a photographic slide; 19th-century types more elaborate, some able to create an illusion of movement by rapidly changing slides.

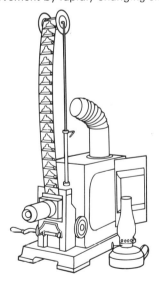

Magnum, a large bottle (now two imperial quarts) of wine, or a large glass or bumper of wine or spirits.

Mahal carpets, from western Iran, similar to Hamadan, but notably soft and not very dense; Ghiordes knot, floral and geometric designs.

Mahoganized, wood treated to look like dark mahogany.

Mahogany, the most popular wood in cabinetmaking since the early 18th century, originally chiefly from the West Indies; in fact, a very large number of similar woods, generally a warm or rosy brown, hard and durable, easily worked and adaptable as to colour, etc., very dark mahogany usually being comparatively recent. **64**

Maidenhead, a type of early spoon, the handle terminating in a female bust, probably representing the Virgin Mary; see also **Virgin spoon.**

Maigelein, a glass or metal beaker, basically cylindrical in form, with fluted decoration, central Europe, 16th century or earlier.

Mail armour, commonly called chain-mail armour, made of interlocked metal rings, in use from ancient times to the 17th century; sometimes applied to other forms of armours, e.g. 'mailed fist'.

Maiolica, tin-glazed earthenware of (chiefly) Italy and Spain, particularly in the 16th and 17th centuries, though made much earlier and extensively reproduced ever since, essentially the same as faience and delftware. **93, 164**

Maize glass, pressed glassware with relief patterns of ears of corn (wheat as well as maize), popular in the Middle West in the late 19th century.

Majolica, an alternative spelling of maiolica; more particularly, a pale brown stoneware with decoration in high relief developed by Minton in the mid 19th century, tin-glazed and enamelled in rich colours; also applied to other 19th-century wares more or less resembling Italian maiolica, but not necessarily tin-glazed.

Makkum pottery, tin-glazed earthenware, especially tiles of various kinds, from a factory in Friesland, Holland, 18th century.

Malachite, a rich green (owing to the presence of copper) veined stone found mainly in Russia, sometimes in huge columns, and used there occasionally for panelling and furniture as well as jewellery; also, 19th-century pottery with glaze resembling malachite.

Malaga work, golden lustreware in Hispano-Moresque style, from the centre in Valencia which also produced various other wares, from the 14th century.

Malayer carpets: see Feraghan carpets.

Malleated, beaten out into a thin leaf or foil, as in hammered gold leaf.

Mallet decanter, a type of glass decanter of the early 18th century, hexagonal or octagonal body, abrupt shoulder and long neck with a collar below the mouth.

Malling pottery: see Wrotham pottery.

Maltese clocks, made by a family named Pisani, in Malta, from the early

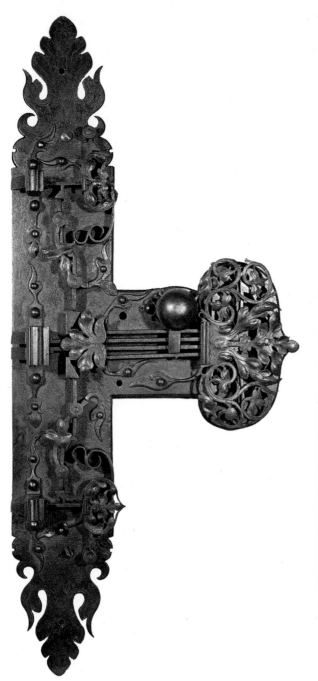

162 Lock for a casket. German, 17th century. Finely pierced, embossed and engraved. (Victoria and Albert Museum, London)

163 Louis XIV cabinet. Attributed to the French cabinetmaker, Gaudron; late 17th century. Inlaid with wood and ivory, the cabinet is typical of the Baroque style. (Victoria and Albert Museum, London)

164 Lustreware maiolica plate.
Valencia, 15th century. A rich effect
is produced by the combination of
stylized natural and geometric
panels. (Hispanic Society of
America, New York)

165 Louis XVI long-case clock by
Balthazar Lieutaud (d. 1780).
Veneered in oak and ebony and
with gilt bronze mounts; this clock
is particularly interesting because it
shows sidereal and terrestrial time,
the date and it has a barometer
below the dial. (Wallace Collection,
London)

19th century, fairly simple clocks, early examples having only one hand.

Maltese lace, a type of lace originating in Malta but found elsewhere, black or white silk, usually in fairly simple abstract patterns.

Mammy's rocker, a wide-seated rocking chair of Windsor type with a railing along part of the front of the seat, so that mother and baby could rock without the latter falling off; 19th century.

Manardi maiolica, from the workshop of the Manardi brothers, at Angarano in northern Italy; including plates decorated with the meeting of Christopher Columbus and Queen Isabella, also landscapes and pastoral scenes.

Manchester velvet, a cheap variety of velvet, cotton not silk, for upholstery, curtains and hangings, about 1800.

Mandarin china, rather grand Chinese porcelain exported to Europe in the late 18th century and subsequently imitated, with subjects (usually figures) framed in panels and enamelled in red, pink and gold.

Mandarin silk, or wool, dyed an orange colour by means of dilute nitric acid which effects a chemical change in the fibre.

Mandolin, a small lute, popular particularly in Italy and known since the Middle Ages, usually with metal strings; also, a type of musical box, sounding like a mandolin.

Mandore, or mandola, a musical instrument similar to a mandolin but with gut strings, plucked with the fingers, probably older than the mandolin.

Mangle, a variety of machines for extracting water from laundry, in particular a pair of wooden rollers turned by a crank and mounted in an iron frame, 19th century, often ornate.

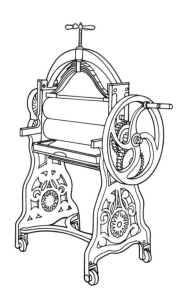

Manière criblée, a technique in making wood-block prints during the Renaissance (and later in other prints), breaking up solid areas of black by dotting.

Manifer, an armour-plated glove for the left hand, in jousting armour particularly.

Manila, or manilla, Philippines hemp used in rope-making; a type of paper; a metal bracelet worn in parts of tropical Africa and apparently used as money; a silk shawl.

Manises lustreware, Hispano-Moresque pottery very widely distributed in 15th-century Europe and perhaps the original 'maiolica', sometimes made outside Valencia by travelling potters from Manises.

Manivelle, a type of Swiss-made toy musical box, often with mechanical figures, crank-operated by hand.

Mannerist, a style in art, in particular the style in 16th-century Italy bridging the Renaissance and Baroque periods, still influenced by Classicism but striving for greater movement and feeling, applied especially to small bronzes of the period.

Mannheim gold, a 3 to 1 alloy of copper and zinc with an appearance very close to the gold it was designed to imitate.

Mantel, a wooden shelf, in particular the shelf above a fireplace; hence **mantelpiece,** the ornamental structure around a fireplace incorporating a shelf as its chief feature. **168**

Mantel clock, a shelf clock or bracket clock; in particular, a clock with an ornamental case, 18th century or later, perhaps designed to form the centrepiece of the mantelshelf. **168**

Mantel mirror: see Chimney glass.

Manteltree, the beam supporting the chimneypiece; also, a wooden rack for drying clothes, attached to the beam.

Mantel valance, an embroidered cloth draped over a mantel.

Mantilla, an embroidered silk shawl, covering head and shoulders, worn particularly in Spain and Mexico.

Manton, an English sporting gun made by a gunsmith of that name in the late 18th or early 19th century.

Man trap, a large spring-operated, toothed, iron trap, like a bear trap, for catching poachers.

Mantua glass, early 19th-century Stiegel-type glass in various colours, also bottles, etc. from a glassworks in Mantua, Ohio.

Manwaring chair, a chair of the Chippendale period with an openwork back splat of scroll-like forms and straight, square-section legs, taken from a design of the London cabinetmaker, Robert Manwaring.

Manx table, a tripod table with three legs of human form like the legs in the Isle of Man's badge.

Maple, several types of wood from the numerous species of maple, paleish and close-grained, particularly the American sugar maple with its 'bird's eye' motif, popular for veneers in the 19th century, and the so-called curly maple with wavy stripes; much used in early American furniture; in England, sometimes meaning sycamore.

Marble, a strong, handsome, crystalline limestone, in various colours, usually mottled, taking a high polish; used in architecture and sculpture (especially the fine white Carrara marble), also for table tops, etc. **172**

Marbled, or marled, having the appearance of marble, i.e. mottled in contrasting colours, as in certain ceramic glazes, wooden surfaces or, very frequently, the endpapers of books up to the early 20th century, which were made by pressing the paper on to colours stirred about with a stick.

Marble glass, 19th-century pressed glassware marbled in swirls of (usually) purple and white, made at several English and American glassworks; see also **Purple slag.**

Marcasite, an opaque, brassy stone, a crystallized form of iron pyrites, used for ornaments and inexpensive jewellery in the 18th and 19th centuries.

Marcella, a cotton cloth with a quilted diaper pattern, originating in Marseilles, used for coverings of various kinds.

Marche pied, a portable short stepladder or footstool.

Margariti, 'pearls', small glass beads that look like pearls, made at Venice since the late Middle Ages and used as currency in Near Eastern trade during the Renaissance period; they were made by specialist craftsmen.

Marieburg ware, soft- and hard-paste porcelain from the 18th-century factory near Stockholm, largely derivative in style; also, tin-glazed earthenware and creamware from the same factory, including skilfully modelled figures. **174**

Mark, on silver, china, glass, etc., a name or symbol usually out of sight on the bottom of the article, signifying its maker; not a universal practice in most areas, and ease of forgery makes them an unreliable guide for the non-expert.

Manwaring chair

Marked pontil: see **Pontil mark**.

Marlboro' leg, in furniture, especially tables, a leg of square section, usually slightly tapered and ending in a somewhat larger square foot, late 18th century.

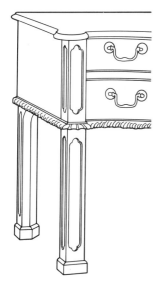

Marline spike, a slightly curved iron spike, sometimes with a handle like a screwdriver, for separating the strands of a rope.

Marquetry, an ornamental pattern on flat surfaces of furniture made by fitting together pieces of differently coloured woods, shell, ivory, metal, etc., into a single sheet which is applied to the surface; see also **Boulle work, Inlay**.

Marquise, a term applied to several articles in French furnishings, in particular a wide, upholstered armchair, of the 18th century. **175**

Marriage chest: see **Dowry chest**.

Marriage cup, made to commemorate a wedding; in particular, a Venetian glass cup or goblet, often bearing portraits of the happy pair in enamels, 15th and 16th centuries. **171**

Marriage plate, celebrating a marriage with suitable inscription, sometimes merely with appropriate initials added to an ordinary plate, ceramic or pewter.

Marrow scoop, a kind of long, narrow silver spoon, often scooped at both ends, for extracting the marrow from meat bones, made in several versions from the early 18th century.

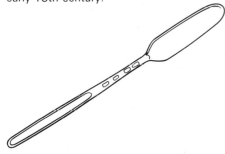

Marseille faience, from several potteries in the French city, since the second half of the 17th century, notable especially

for colourful enamels (late 18th century) painted with great skill; porcelain was also made at Marseille; see also **Veuve Perrin faience**. **173**

Martel de fer, a medieval horseman's weapon, a short-handled pick-axe, for use against armour.

Martha Gunn jug, an 18th-century toby jug modelled on a well-known character in the seaside town of Brighton.

Martha Washington chair, a high-backed armchair with upholstered back and seat, open wooden arms and turned front legs, in late 18th-century style.

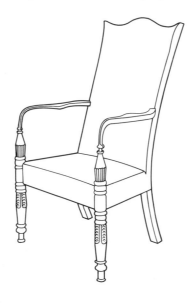

Martha Washington worktable, a sewing table in Sheraton style with small compartments and drawers, fluted legs.

Martingale brasses, horse brasses (a martingale being part of the harness).

Martin lacquer: see **Vernis Martin**.

Martin ware, salt-glazed stoneware made by the four idealistic Martin brothers near London in the late 19th and early 20th centuries, often with asymmetrical decoration in the Japanese manner; no two pots alike.

Marver, the polished metal or marble plate, set in a frame on which blown glass vessels are shaped; hence, marvering, smoothing out.

Mary Gregory glass, cheap glassware painted with figures, children playing, etc., mostly made in Europe in the late 19th century, once ascribed to a woman who worked at the Sandwich glass works, Massachusetts.

Maryland pottery, stoneware and earthenware from several potteries in or near Baltimore, since about 1800, including well-known printed dishes of historical interest from the factory of Edwin Bennett.

Mascaron, a Rococo ornament based on a human (or animal) mask; see also **Mask**.

Mascle, a lozenge-shape, in heraldry a hollow diamond form; hence, a plate in armour of overlapping scales.

Maser: see **Mazer**.

Mask, the representation of a human (or animal) face, found particularly in primitive art, **23**; used in decoration particularly in the Baroque and Rococo periods, found for instance with plaster swags and garlands, carved on protruding joints such as the elbows of chair arms, in door knockers, bosses, etc. **7, 143**

Mason china, from the Staffordshire pottery of Charles James Mason, including early 19th-century bone china and, most notably, Mason's ironstone; see also **Ironstone**.

Masonic silver: see **Guild silver**.

Massachusetts clock, in particular an early 19th-century shelf clock (half-clock) of box-on-box construction, made by such notable Massachusetts clock-makers as the Willard family.

Massachusetts furniture, from this important centre of American furniture making, which produced characteristic pieces from the early colonial period and later. **64**

Massachusetts tea table, Queen Anne style rectangular tea table with slender cabriole legs and pad feet, the restrained curve being repeated in the delicately scalloped skirting, characteristic of Massachusetts and the Connecticut River valley.

Mass dial, a type of sundial sometimes seen cut in a stone on the wall of a medieval church, indicating the times of Mass.

Masterpiece, originally an example of his craft submitted by a workman seeking the status of master craftsman from the guild; hence, a particularly outstanding piece.

Matapan, a medieval Venetian coin, similar to the ducat, but silver, not gold.

Matchlock, a gun that fires by moving a lighted match (wick) into contact with the powder in the priming pan, in use from the early 15th century; superseded by the wheel-lock and flintlock.

Maternity bowl, a name given (somewhat obscurely) in particular to a type of relief-decorated pewter bowl, with cover and flat handles, made in Europe in the 17th and 18th centuries.

167▲

166 Soprano lute. Italian, 17th century. Inlaid with ebony, ivory and mother of pearl. (Castello Sforzesco, Milan)

167 Example of Lyons silk with motifs popular during the Empire period, including swans, the emblem of the Empress Josephine. (Malmaison)

168 Mantelpiece in Marie Antoinette's boudoir at Fontainebleau. The gilt bronze decoration includes a bow threaded with flowers, and quivers of arrows. The andirons are decorated with Classical arms. The mantel clock and candelabra are in the style of Clodion. (Château de Fontainebleau)

168

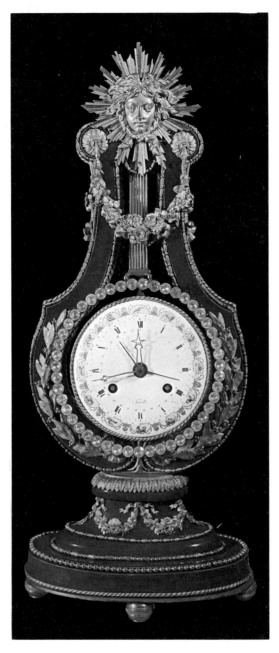

169 Clock in the shape of a lyre, signed Kinable. Late 18th century. Sèvres porcelain case and painted enamel face. (Victoria and Albert Museum, London)

170 Mace. Italian, perhaps Genoese?, 16th century. Typical war hammer much used by cavalry in hand to hand fighting and tournaments. (Dal Pozzo Collection, Milan)

Matrix, a place in which something is contained; hence, the mass of rock in which precious stones or metal are found, the recess cut in stone for a brass tablet, etc.

Matted, a pitted or punch-marked surface, e.g. as background to a design in relief in silver; a matt (non-shiny) surface.

Mauchline ware, mainly small or souvenir items in wood, featuring prints of Highland scenery, tartan patterns, etc., 19th century.

Maud, a woollen plaid shawl.

Maundy pence, small silver coins in denominations up to fourpence, traditionally distributed to the poor by the English monarch on Maundy Thursday; special issues struck since the mid 18th century.

Maw pottery, from a factory in Broseley, Shropshire, making among other wares imitation maiolica tiles, in the second half of the 19th century.

Maximilian armour, a name given to the elaborate, fluted, German Renaissance armour, after the Emperor Maximilian I (1494–1519).

Mazarine, deep royal blue, sometimes varying slightly in tone, found on Sèvres and some English soft-paste porcelain and bone china as ground colour; also, a silver strainer that fitted inside a meat dish or, more commonly, a double-bottomed dish for fish, the upper level pierced; from the 17th century.

Mazer, or maser, a wooden drinking bowl, varying in shape, dating from the Middle Ages, in England usually made of maple (or sycamore), later mounted in silver, sometimes having a single handle like a porringer. **180**

Mazlaghan carpets, Persian carpets distinguished by the frequent presence of a jagged outline, like an irregular zigzag, to the field; otherwise similar to the Hamadan type.

Mazzochio, a woman's head-dress of Renaissance Italy, winding round the head, with a long pointed tailpiece that could be wound round the neck for extra protection.

Meakin ironstone, from the Tunstall, Staffordshire, works of James and George Meakin, ironstone china much exported to America.

Meander, or Greek fret, the pattern made by a straight line, turning at right angles, as seen in a Classical Greek frieze; see also **Fret, Key pattern.**

Measure, a flagon or jug, pewter, brass or other material, containing a set quantity of liquid, e.g. one quart, used in inns.

Mecca rugs, a term sometimes applied to Muslim prayer rugs, not necessarily having any physical connection with the holy city of Islam.

Mechanical furniture, any furniture incorporating some kind of machinery, e.g. spring-released drawers and secret compartments, automatically extruding writing surfaces in desks, and various

ingenious pieces that convert into something completely different.

Mechanical toys, birdcages with metal birds that 'sing', pictures that appear to move, various clockwork devices such as dancing girls on musical boxes, etc.

Mechlin lace, at one time a general term for Flemish pillow lace, confined to true Mechlin in the 18th century; patterns and ground made together, very fine thread, often with a flat, shiny thread outlining the pattern; though expensive, very popular in 18th-century England.

Medallion, a large medal with design in relief, or any roughly circular or square motif in decoration, e.g. in oriental carpets. **178**

Medallion fan, a fan with three medallions, the central one larger, painted on the silk; a popular pattern in the late 18th century.

Medicine chest, a box fitted with compartments and jars containing lotions, drugs and other cures for disease. **177**

Medici porcelain, the result of efforts, patronized by the Medici duke of Tuscany, to reproduce Chinese porcelain in 16th-century Italy, the body containing powdered glass and sand and somewhat translucent; influenced by contemporary maiolica as well as oriental porcelain; rare.

Medullary rays, in timber, lines that radiate outwards from the centre crossing the rings, sometimes seen in oak.

Medusa, in Greek mythology a female creature with snakes for hair, whose head appears particularly in Neo-Classical decoration, and on shields to commemorate the stratagem by which she was killed.

Meerschaum, a softish, easily carved mineral (a silicate of aluminium), naturally almost white, widely used for the bowls of tobacco pipes, often in most elaborate forms, during the 18th and 19th centuries.

Megri carpets: see **Melas carpets.**

Mehrschichtenglas, multi-layered glass made by a relatively cheap process developed in early 19th-century Bohemia, engraving through one or more layers of which produced striking effects; see also **Flashed glass.**

Meigh pottery, a vast variety of wares from the Staffordshire pottery run by the Meigh family, especially Charles Meigh, best known for his popular stoneware jugs in Neo-Gothic style, mid 19th century; see also **Minster jug.**

Meillonas faience, late 18th-century wares from the factory in Ain, influenced by the style of Marseille, high-quality enamel painting.

Meissen, the first successful European true porcelain and the outstanding porcelain of the 18th century, beginning about 1710 though the body was not perfected for some ten years; also known as 'Dresden'; copied with greater or less success by virtually every porcelain factory in Europe; still going strong; see also **Kändler porcelain, Böttger porcelain. 126, 145**

Meissonier style, the Rococo style in France at its most elaborate, silver based on the designs of the court silversmith, Justin Aurèle Meissonier (1695–1750).

Melanite, a type of garnet, black, occasionally found in jewellery.

Melas carpets, or Milas, Meles, etc., Turkish carpets from the town south of Izmir (Smyrna), rather loosely woven wool rugs and carpets, often similar to Caucasian carpets in design, floral patterns usually confined to borders only, some distinguished by the predominance of a coppery yellow colour. **179**

Melbourne creamware, from an 18th-century Derbyshire pottery the products of which have only been identified comparatively recently.

Melée, in the diamond trade, a term for small stones varying in size, often rose-cut and mounted around a larger stone in jewellery.

Mell, mall, maul, etc., a hammer or club, particularly a ceremonial mace, chairman's hammer, etc.

Melodeon, or American organ, a double-keyboard, free reed instrument that worked on a similar principle to that of the accordion, foot-pedals operating the bellows; popular from the mid 19th century.

Melon bulb: see **Bulb.**

Melon pattern, in silver, a scalloped form in the body of a vessel such as a teapot, about twelve lobes to the total circumference, characteristic of the Rococo revival of the early 19th century.

Memento mori, a reminder of mortality, e.g. an article made in the form of a skull; see also **Memorial ring.**

Memorial ring, or mourning ring, worn in memory of some departed soul, sometimes black-enamelled, or engraved with a romantically sombre device, or even containing a lock of hair, 18th and 19th centuries.

Mendlesham chair, a type of 19th-century Windsor armchair in which the back was squared off with two flat (not turned) horizontal rails at top and bottom with a row of balls between them.

Mennecy porcelain, from a French factory also making faience, first established in Paris but operating at nearby Mennecy-Villeroy during the mid 18th century, similar to Chantilly; noted especially for cane-heads, snuff-boxes, etc.

Menorah, a candelabrum used in Jewish worship.

Menuisier, the approximate French equivalent of the English carpenter or joiner; see also **Ébéniste.**

Mercery, all types of cloth, as sold by a mercer; also, sometimes, small household articles of various kinds.

Mercury gilding: see **Fire gilding.**

Mercury twist, in a wine glass, an air-twist stem of special brightness.

Merese, in glassware, a small disc or collar where the bowl of a glass joins the stem, or between parts of the stem.

Méridienne, a type of day bed or couch, 18th-century French, curving up at the end, sometimes at both ends, to form scrolled head- and foot-boards.

Merino, a thin, twilled, woollen cloth from the wool of the merino sheep (originally a Spanish animal), sometimes mixed with silk, used for clothing.

Merletto, lace (Italian).

Merryman plates, English delftware plates in a set of six or eight, each bearing one line of a humorous verse, e.g. 'But if his wife do frown/Then merriment goes down', first made in the late 17th century.

Merrythought, or wishbone, the forked bone in the breast of a fowl, sometimes made in porcelain or glass as an ornament or lucky charm.

Meshed, 19th-century Persian carpets from the old-established city of Meshed, Khorassan; Sehna or Ghiordes knot, usually with central medallion and snaky (islim) floral decoration, bright colours; also, Persian blue-and-white pottery.

Metal, in particular, the material of glass.

Metope, in the Doric order, the blank, square block which alternates with a triglyph (grooved); see **Doric.**

Metropolitan slipware, simple, 17th-century lead-glazed slipware found in London, of obscure origin, sometimes bearing admonitions of a Puritan cast, e.g. 'Remember God'.

Meubles, 'moveables', i.e. furniture, especially cabinets and cupboards etc.

Mezza-maiolica, Italian lead-glazed earthenware with engraved designs in white slip on a red body, sometimes with added splotches of green and orange, 14th to 17th centuries; see also **Sgraffito.**

Mezzero, an embroidered silk shawl, associated particularly with Genoa.

Mezzotint, a print from an engraving using tonal gradations rather than line, a kind of minute cross-hatching being scratched on the copper plate and the resulting burr scraped away to gain lighter tones; especially popular with English painters from the 17th to the 19th centuries.

Mica, aluminium silicate, the outstanding quality of which is its perfect cleavage, i.e. splitting into paper-thin, transparent sheets, used in lanterns and (in Russia) windows.

Miers miniatures, black-painted profile portraits on card or plaster medallions, also silhouette brooches, by John Miers and his son, of Leeds and London, early 19th century.

Mignonette box, a small, pierced box, of terracotta or similar material, for the fragrant petals of the garden flower.

Mignonette lace, a form of pillow lace, made from the 16th century, light and fine, named after the flowers of the plant of that name.

Mihrab, a prayer niche, pointed at the top, a common motif in Islamic art, particularly in prayer rugs, all of which (by strict definition) have a central mihrab. **107**

Milan maiolica, 18th-century maiolica from several Milanese potteries, notably that connected with the Clerici family; including chinoiserie plates and figures influenced by German porcelain.

Mildner glass, late 18th-century Bohemian glass decorated by a technique similar to Zwischengoldglas but confined to a small area, in gold, silver, enamel, or even painted parchment, named after the foremost practitioner of the art.

Miletus ware, early Islamic pottery, painted in blue and green on white slip with transparent glaze, first found at Miletus; 14th to 15th centuries; see also **Isnik ware.**

Miliarense, a small silver coin issued by the Emperor Constantine in the 4th century.

Military furniture: see **Camp furniture.**

Milk glass, or milchglas, lattimo, porcelain-glass, etc., opaque white glass somewhat resembling porcelain; an effect achieved by adding tin oxide, often decorated in the manner of porcelain in the late 17th and 18th centuries, though made earlier in Venice; popular for pressed ware in the late 19th century. **176**

Milkwood, willow.

Millefiori, 'thousand flowers', the highly decorative technique in glass, notably paperweights, achieved by drawing out threads of variously coloured glass and cementing them together to make each flower-like cane; a technique known in ancient Egypt and Rome, rediscovered in 16th-century Venice, and perfected in the mid 19th century. **13, 182**

Millefleurs, meaning the same as millefiori but applied to floral decoration in ceramics, embroidery, etc.

Mills & Deming furniture, made by a prominent firm of New York cabinet-makers in Hepplewhite and Sheraton styles, about 1800.

Millville glass, from a number of glass-works in the New Jersey town, from the late 18th century, attractive curiosities as well as much window glass, tableware and bottles.

Mimosa, a family of shrubs related to the acacia, the larger varieties of which were occasionally used for cabinet-making in America.

Mina'i ware, a type of early Persian pottery with enamel, over-glaze colours, scenes of court life, hunting, etc.

Mina-khani, or mina-chané, a motif in oriental carpets, four flowers at the points of a diamond with a fifth flower in the centre, repeated all over the ground.

Miner's candlestick, a pewter candlestick from the mining region of Saxony in the form of a figure of a miner who holds the candle socket; from the 17th century.

Ming dynasty, the period in China from 1368 to 1644, which encompassed the development of Chinese porcelain and the beginning of the export trade to Europe; 'Ming vase' is a phrase that seems to embody the ultimate in priceless objects of art; genuine examples rather rare. **22, 27, 141, 181**

Miniature, in particular, a small portrait, often painted on ivory, vellum or copper, also, an illumination, i.e. in a manuscript, etc. **196**

Miniver, spotted grey and white squirrel's fur, used for the trimmings and linings of coats and cloaks in the Middle Ages.

Minne tapestries, woven from the late 14th century in homes and convents, depicting scenes inspired by the courtly love tradition, chiefly South German.

Minster jug, a very popular pattern in the second half of the 19th century, patented by Meigh of Hanley, a stoneware jug in the Gothic style, with figures of the apostles framed in arches in high relief; the name is sometimes applied to other designs of the same type.

Minton china, from the pottery established at Stoke-on-Trent by Thomas

172 ▲

171 Commemorative glass marriage
cup with enamel decoration.
Murano, late 15th century.
(Kunstgewerbemuseum, Cologne)

172 Marble statue of Madame de
Pompadour portrayed as the Venus
of the Doves. French, by Etienne
Maurice Falconet (1716–91).
(Samuel H. Kress Collection,
National Gallery, Washington)

173 Marseille faience vase and dish.
French, 18th century. (Musée
National de Céramique, Sèvres)

173

174 Marieberg faience tureen.
Swedish, 18th century. This piece is
derived from a French pattern.
(Musée National de Céramique,
Sèvres)

175 Louis XV marquise by Nicolas
Heurtat, 1720–71. (Private
Collection)

Minton in the late 18th century and by the mid 19th century 'the most influential in England' (G. B. Hughes), originally creamware and other earthenware, then (most notably) bone china, and after about 1850 a variety of other wares including fine copies of Renaissance maiolica.

Mir carpets, old Persian carpets from the district of Feraghan, Ghiordes knot, characteristically employing an angular version of the boteh motif, probably the origin of this pattern; dark blue or dark red ground, now rare.

Mir-i-bota: see **Boteh motif**.

Mirror, plate glass (sometimes metal in medieval times) polished and silvered (since the 16th century) on the back to reflect with up to 95% effectiveness. **122, 159**

Mirror clock, a clock incorporating a looking glass, particularly a rectangular New England wall-clock of such a type in the early 19th century; also, a 16th-century astronomical clock with a mirror, supported by a figure of Hercules.

Mirror painting, a painting on the back of a mirror, the reflecting layer of metal first being scraped off where necessary; see also **Glass picture**.

Misericord, a small bracket-like ledge under the tip-up seat in the choir stalls of a church, especially a monastic church, to give some support to the standing worshipper, often combined with anti-Establishment carvings; also a dagger used to inflict the coup de grâce to a defeated opponent. **253**

Miser's purse, a stocking purse secured by a moveable metal band, popular in the 19th century.

Missal, strictly, a book containing the service of the Roman Catholic Mass; more generally, a prayer book, especially if illuminated; often richly bound, with hammered silver, etc.

Mission furniture, a term applied to imitations of early Spanish-American furniture which was often made by Indians under Spanish direction; rather heavy, unfinished.

Mitre, in cabinet-work, a joint characteristic of mouldings in which the two joined members are cut at half the angle of the joint, i.e. at 45° in a right angle; hence, **mitred**, **mitreboard** (a cutting board for 45° cuts); **mitrewheel** (for engraving glass); also, various types of

head-dress, including a turban and the hat worn by a bishop.

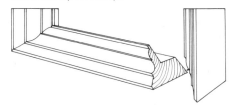

Mixed-twist, the stem of a wine glass with air twists of different colours, often opaque-white and transparent.

Mob cap, a close-fitting linen cap worn by women indoors in the 18th and 19th centuries.

Mocha stone, a variety of chalcedony with green inclusions in the (often remarkably exact) form of ferns, leaves and mosses.

Mocha ware, early 19th-century earthenware in which spots of colour were applied to bands of wet and porous slip before glazing, spreading like inkspots on blotting paper to create an effect like mocha stone.

Moderator lamp, a mid 19th-century improvement in oil lighting in which a spring brought wick and fuel into contact.

Modern Movement, the change in styles marked approximately by World War I, with emphasis on functionalism and new materials and influenced by contemporary developments in the arts such as Cubism; see also **Bauhaus**.

Modern style, Art Nouveau; see also **Modern Movement**.

Modillions, a series of ornamental projecting brackets below the cornice in the Corinthian order of architecture; also on cabinets, etc. in 'architectural' style.

Mohair, the wool of the Angora goat usually mixed with cotton or silk, or a garment of such material, soft and silky; imported in England since the 17th century, occasionally used in upholstery.

Mohs' scale, a scale indicating the hardness in stones from 1 (talc, very soft) to 10 (diamond, very hard), devised by the Austrian mineralogist Friedrich Mohs in the late 19th century.

Mohur, an Indian coin current from the 16th to the 19th centuries, various types and shapes, some square.

Moiré, a watered or clouded silk, or other lustrous material such as mohair; also *moiré métallique*, metal with a shimmering, watered appearance, achieved by lacquering.

Moko pottery, a form of inexpensive mocha ware, in which various coloured slips were slapped on with a brush before glazing, 19th century.

Molded: see **Moulded**.

Molding: see **Moulding**.

Molinet, a stick, usually wood with silver mounts, for stirring chocolate in a chocolate pot.

Mon, a Japanese emblem or heraldic badge, signifying some kind of social or professional status.

Mondscheinglas: see **Moonlight glass**.

Money-box, or money-bank, a small box with a slit for inserting coins, or as a container for a tip, made since the Middle Ages in a variety of forms and media.

Monkey orchestra, porcelain figures of monkeys dressed as itinerant musicians, originated at Meissen and copied at Chelsea and elsewhere.

Monk's table, a long oak table; see also **Refectory table**.

Monochord, a medieval musical instrument, ancestor of the clavichord, originally a sounding board with a single string, later with several strings.

Monopodium, 'one-foot', applied particularly to early 19th-century stands or small tables with a central column, or a table leg in the form of a lion's head and body descending to a single foot.

Monotype, a print made from a design painted in oils on the metal plate, one impression only being normally possible; also, a type-setting machine invented in the late 19th century.

Monster pearl, a Baroque pearl.

Monstrance, a silver or gilt vessel usually with glazed apertures for the bread in the Roman Catholic Mass; also, a 17th-century German clock, silver or gilt, resembling the vessel.

Monteith, a large silver (later also china and glass) bowl with a scalloped edge from which wine glasses were suspended to cool in iced water, from the late 17th century; often with detachable rim and lion-mask drop handles, **183**; also, spotted cotton handkerchiefs made by a firm of that name in Glasgow, 19th century.

Montelupo maiolica, Tuscan maiolica distinguished for the bold sweeps of the painting, covering the whole surface; from a number of potteries, 15th to 17th centuries. **184**

Montereau ware, earthenware and faience-fine, 18th and 19th centuries, from the French factory specializing in wares of English type.

Month clock, a clock that will run for 32 days without rewinding.

Montpellier faience, from the 16th century, mainly wares similar to neighbouring centres such as Marseille; some late 16th- and 17th-century drug jars in the Italian style are thought to be from

Montpellier, a centre of the medical profession.

Monumental brass, a flat, engraved brass figure, often nearly life size, placed as a memorial in church from the Middle Ages to about 1700; see also **Brass rubbing**.

Monument candlestick, or lamp, a silver candlestick or lamp in the form of a Greek, usually Corinthian, column.

Moon, in porcelain, a small area like a grease spot on paper that has greater translucency when the piece is examined against the light, caused by a minor imperfection in the body.

Moon dial, a dial on a clock-face, common on 18th-century long-case clocks, showing the phases of the moon; useful in times when streets were unlit.

Moon lantern, a globular, horn-paned brass lantern on a pole, a development from the cresset.

Moonlight glass, or Mondscheinglas, blue, semi-opaque glass developed by Gallé in the late 19th century; see also **Gallé glass**; also, a lustrous, pearly glaze in ceramics.

Moonstone, one of the most alluring of gem stones, a variety of feldspar with a shimmering pearly glow once believed to wax and wane with the moon, opaque and therefore usually cabochon-cut, originally coming mainly from Ceylon.

Moonstone glass, milk glass.

Moore pottery, the product of several potteries operating under that name, e.g. Victorian lustreware from a Sunderland factory, or art pottery by Bernard Moore of Longton, about 1900.

Moorfields carpets, English hand-knotted carpets from the works in Moorfields, London, in the second half of the 18th century, including some designed by Robert Adam.

Moquette, a plush cloth of wool or linen or cotton that looks like silk, used since the Middle Ages for coverings of all kinds and for upholstery, hard wearing.

Moravian work, in embroidery, fine muslin embroidered with (mainly) floral patterns in white thread, early 19th century.

Mordant, a substance used as a fixative in dyeing cloth or in certain forms of gilding, or the liquid that 'bites' into the plate in etching.

Moreen, a twilled cotton-and-wool fabric resembling damask, sometimes watered, used for curtains and cushions and for women's dresses; see also **Moiré**.

Moresque, decoration in Moorish or Arabian style; see **Arabesque, Hispano-Moresque**.

Morez clock, a type of clock of simple appearance (though complicated movement), made in Morez, Franche Comté, from the early 18th century, somewhat resembling a Gothic clock in general structure.

Morgan & Saunders furniture, English Regency furniture by a well-known London firm which introduced several innovations, particularly in mechanical furniture.

Morganite, a translucent, pinkish stone, a variety of beryl, named after J. Pierpont Morgan, who had a famous collection of pink beryl.

Morion, a helmet worn by infantry in the 16th and 17th centuries, a tall domed shape with a small all-round brim, sometimes (especially in Spain) curving up to a peak front and back and with a half-moon crest; also, a smoky brown quartz.

Morning star, a late medieval weapon, carried on horseback, a flail or club the business end of which was basically a metal globe mounted with blades or spikes.

Morocco, soft leather used in bookbinding (and for other purposes), originally the skin of a Moroccan, or North African, goat, now any goatskin. **25**

Morris chair, a Victorian easy chair with pads on the arms and a reclining back adjustable by a supporting bar that fits a series of grooves along the extended arms; also, a cane-seated armchair with slender, turned members, an adaptation of the Sussex chair. **186**

Morris design, reflecting the influence of William Morris (1834–96), responsible for hand-woven carpets, the Morris chair, etc., who, more importantly, 'revolutionised the public taste in domestic art' (Art Journal, 1896); a chief progenitor of the Arts and Crafts movement and thence Art Nouveau. **185, 186**

Morse, a gold and/or jewelled clasp or buckle for a cope.

Mortar, a basin, most commonly stone or metal but also wood, in which a substance is pounded with a pestle; an ancient vessel, still in common use.

Mortar candle, a short thick candle that would burn for a long time without attention, as used in food- and teapot-warmers.

Mortise-and-tenon, a type of joint in woodwork in which a rectangular cavity (mortise) in one section receives a projecting plug (tenon) on the other; sometimes held fast by a dowel; also mortice-and-tenon.

Mortlake pottery, from the long-established centre in south-west London, chiefly utilitarian stoneware and earthenware, also delftware similar to Lambeth and art pottery from a studio in operation about 1900.

Mortlake tapestry, from the factory founded in Mortlake, south-west London, in the early 17th century, manned for a time by Flemish weavers, rare Baroque tapestries and table covers.

Mortuary chair, a name sometimes given to a 17th-century chair with relief carving of a man's head, said to be that of the late King Charles I, in the back.

Mosaic, pictures or patterns formed by cementing together small pieces of appropriately cut, differently coloured stone, chiefly in floors; an ancient technique especially popular with the Romans; also, a similar effect in glass; in porcelain, a dense diaper pattern, typically surrounding panels.

Mosque lamp, an enamelled glass Islamic lamp, of vase form, on a foot, the lamp being suspended inside; the finest examples from the 14th century or earlier; a motif in oriental prayer rugs. **203**

Moss agate, a form of chalcedony, basically a pale reddish or yellowish stone but with green inclusions that look like tiny plant forms; virtually identical in appearance with mocha stone.

Moss oak: see **Bog oak**.

Mote spoon, a long-handled teaspoon with pierced bowl for skimming out tea leaves, and barbed handle for clearing the clogged spout of a teapot; see also **Straining spoon**.

Mother-of-pearl, the inner shell of certain shellfish, notably oysters; a hard, but brittle, shimmering, iridescent material, frequently used for inlays and for small objects such as dessert-knife handles, fan mounts, buttons, etc. **187**

Mother-of-pearl glass: see **Phoenix glass**.

Mother-of-pearl ware, various ceramics with an iridescent effect, usually in the glaze; see also **Pearlware**.

Motif, the basic theme or pattern in any form of decoration, e.g. a floral motif in a carpet with a pattern of flowers.

Motley, the cap-and-bells, many-coloured dress of a court jester.

Moton, in armour, a small plate protecting the armpit.

Mould-blown glass: see **Blown-moulded glass**.

Moulded, strictly, shaped in a mould, as in cast metal; also, of wood, plaster, etc., carved, usually implying relief; sometimes sculpted or modelled; see also **Moulded glass**.

Moulded glass, pressed glass or, more strictly, blown-moulded glass, the metal being pressed into the mould by air pressure.

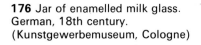
177▲

176 Jar of enamelled milk glass.
German, 18th century.
(Kunstgewerbemuseum, Cologne)

177 Medicine chest. Italian, 1742.
In one of the little drawers are the
credentials of a Dr Pierro Martino.
Four pewter jars in the front row
are for pomades, the others, of
glass, with beautiful pewter lids,
are for liquid medicaments.
(Private Collection, Trieste)

178 Medallion with relief of Louis
XIV. By Jean Varin (1604–72).
(Musée Carnavalet, Paris)

178

179 Melas carpet. Turkish, 18th century. Decorative motifs include carnations and diamonds. (Private Collection, Varese)

180 Mazer bowls. English, 1510 and about 1460. Spotted maplewood mounted in silver. (Worshipful Company of Goldsmiths, London)

Moulding, an ornamentally shaped band, chiefly wood; in particular, such a band along the length of a wall-ceiling junction, around a panel, or on a cornice.

Moulins faience, from the town in central France, notable for very elaborate Rococo designs, influenced by Rouen.

Mount, most commonly, a metal fitting applied to an article in another medium, e.g. brass handles, locks and other fittings on furniture, silver lids and bases on stoneware jugs, etc.

Mount Vernon glass, notably blown-moulded bottles, from the glassworks established at Mount Vernon, New York, in the early 19th century and which later moved to Saratoga.

Mount Washington glass, from the 19th-century factory founded in Boston, later moving to New Bedford, Massachusetts; all types of glassware particularly art glass such as Peachblow and Burmese.

Mourning jewellery, bearing the initials of the departed, sometimes concealed under a stone as in such pieces worn by Royalist ladies to commemorate Charles I; see also **Memento mori, Memorial ring**.

Mousseline, a cloth similar to muslin; silk or wool, used in women's dress.

Moustache cup, a tea cup specially made for gentlemen with large moustaches in the late 19th century, having a pierced lip inside the rim which allowed the tea to reach the mouth while holding it off the moustache.

Moustiers faience, highly valued faience from one of the chief pottery centres of southern France, from the 17th century, especially notable for distinguished blue-and-white painting often with engravings by Jean Bérain, also for high-temperature colours (chiefly purple and yellow), imaginative grotesques, etc.; see also **Bérain style. 24**

Mouton, a gold or silver coin of Renaissance France, so-called because it bore a type of the Lamb of God.

Movement, in clocks and watches, the entire works.

Mozarabic style, the style of art created by the Christians and Jews who remained in Spain during the Arab occupation of the Middle Ages, including religious art showing Arab influence; see also **Hispano-Moresque, Mudejar style**.

Mozetta, a type of cape with a small hood, as worn by important figures in the Roman Catholic Church.

Ms., the abbreviation for manuscript, a hand-written work, particularly one before the invention of printing.

Mucronate, tapering to a sharp point; see also **Lanceolate**.

Mud carpets: see **Khorassan carpets**.

Mudéjar style, the style of art created by the Muslims who remained in Spain after the Christian Reconquest, who were skilled in the use of brick, tiles and plaster and introduced the Islamic horseshoe arch into Christian art; see also **Hispano-Moresque, Mozarabic style**.

Mudjur rugs, prayer rugs from central Turkey, characterized by unusually wide borders; central ground most frequently dark red.

Muffineer, a caster for sprinkling sugar or cinnamon on muffins, in America a particularly tall vessel with pierced-dome top, in England usually a small caster (perhaps intended for pepper); from the early 18th century; also, a dish for muffins, with cover.

Muff, a fur cover for the hands, like a bag open at both ends, covering the clasped hands up to the wrists.

Muffle colours, in ceramics, colours fired in a muffle kiln, i.e. at a relatively low temperature, including all enamel colours.

Muff warmer, a hand warmer held inside a muff.

Mug, a type of tankard with no lid, in particular a small tankard, basically straight- or convex-sided like a barrel, but many variations in the 19th century.

Mulberry, hardwood from several trees of this family, usually golden brown with darker streaks, tough and heavy, used in joinery and occasionally for veneers in the early 18th century.

Mule chest, a chest with a layer (or two layers) of drawers in the bottom, a 17th-century piece usually oak, carved and/or panelled; also made in later styles.

Mullions, vertical elements, stone or wood, dividing a window (particularly a Gothic window); see also **Muntins**.

Multiformia, convertible furniture such as a cheval screen that could be turned into a small table or a lampstand, 19th century.

Muntins, the vertical wooden elements dividing panels in doors and furniture.

Muntz's metal, an alloy of copper and zinc developed in the early 19th century and used particularly for ship's hulls, being little affected by salt water and antipathetic to barnacles and teredo worms.

Mural, a wall painting (not a fresco).

Mural clock, a wall clock.

Mural nomad, the term preferred by the architect Le Corbusier for a tapestry, logical but unpopular.

Murano glass, Venetian glass, so-named for the island on which the Venetian glass industry was established in the 13th century. **158, 171**

Murphy bed, an iron bedframe with fold-in legs at the foot and hinged at the head, which is fixed; to be raised to a vertical position and concealed by doors during the day.

Murrhine glass, or murrini, made by the Romans, perhaps containing murra, which is thought to have been a type of fluorspar; also, a type of mosaic glass made of variously coloured canes; or, a trade name for a type of late 19th-century art glass; see also **Millefiori. 188**

Muscadin style, the style in dress in late 18th-century France in reaction to the severity of the Revolution; slashed coats, striped breeches, lace and ribbon trimmings.

Mushroom, an implement for darning socks, also various other articles of mushroom shape, e.g. a garden stool, a knop on a wine glass stem, a glass bottle stopper, a paperweight containing coloured canes bunched like a mushroom, etc.; see also **Linen smoother**.

Mushkabad carpets, from central Iran, between Feraghan and Hamadan, mainly rather small, with stylized floral design.

Musical chair, a children's chair, originally Swiss, 19th century, which played a tune when sat on, operating on the same principle as a musical box; see also **Music chair**.

Musical glasses, a series of glass bowls that, when struck, emit a note of the chromatic scale; also, glasses played by rubbing a wetted finger around the rim; see also **Harmonica**.

Music box, any ornamental box that plays a tune, usually when the lid is opened setting in motion a revolving cylinder in which projecting pins strike metal leaves, sounding a note; a principle evolved from clockwork; innumerable types in the 19th century.

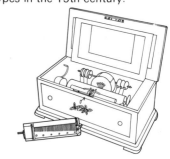

Music chair, a term sometimes applied to lyre-back chairs in the Neo-Classical period.

Music stand, either for bearing the sheet music while being played, of which highly ornamental types were made in the 18th and 19th centuries; or a rack for storing sheet music; see also **Canterbury**.

Music stool, a revolving, circular, padded stool, chiefly 19th century; also a stool, often with a rise and fall mechanism, incorporating a compartment for sheet music below a padded lid.

Musk apple, a small pierced globe, silver or other metal, containing sweet-smelling herbs, carried by fastidious persons during Renaissance times; also, an early watch of this shape, worn on a ribbon with the dial on the base.

Musket, a term generally applied to old firearms fired from the shoulder, having a smooth (i.e. not rifled) barrel; specifically, the heavy wheel-lock weapon, first fired from a rest, in use from the late 16th century.

Musketoon, a small musket or blunderbus.

Muslin, a very fine, gauze-like cotton cloth originating in the Near East, a term now used rather widely of virtually any fine, transparent cloth.

Mustard pot, a small pot, often silver with a hinged lid, spoon and (usually) a blue glass container inside, also porcelain, from the 18th century (earlier, mustard was served dry in a caster). **66, 189**

Mutule, a series of projecting brackets under the cornice in the Doric Order; see also **Modillions**.

Mysterious clock, a clock, usually in some highly ornamental form, with no visible means of support—or rather movement, the works being concealed in some ingenious manner so that their existence is not apparent to the casual glance.

Nabeshima, Japanese porcelain of fine quality, especially in the first half of the 18th century, apparently made only for persons of high position; dishes, etc. in enamel colours combined with underglaze blue designs.

Nacre, mother-of-pearl.

Nacreous lustre, mother-of-pearl glaze, as on Belleek porcelain, etc.

Nacrework, embroidery on velvet or similar stuff incorporating small pieces of mother-of-pearl, often with gold thread.

Nailhead decoration, in furniture, nails in visible positions having decorative heads, e.g. securing upholstery to the frame; also, carved relief decoration, usually mouldings, of small squares, resembling nail heads.

Nailsea glass, from the famous Bristol glassworks founded in the late 18th century, notable for bottle-glass wares of various kinds and for a wide variety of toys and curiosities, e.g. rolling pins, walking sticks, etc.; the name is commonly applied to such articles made elsewhere.

Nain carpets, fairly modern rugs and carpets from a village in central Iran, Sehna knot in very high density (up to 600 to the square inch), naturalistic decoration frequently in an all-over pattern.

Nakers, or nacaires, the kettledrum.

Name chest, a travelling chest on which the owner's name is painted or carved.

Nankeen, originally a Chinese cotton cloth of a natural yellowish colour, also grown in other places or, in Europe, dyed to imitate Nankeen.

Nankin china, exported from the Chinese port of Nankin in the late 18th and 19th centuries; particularly the blue-and-white wares much imitated in England, e.g. in the well-known willow pattern.

Nankin yellow, a yellowish glaze found on certain Chinese blue-and-white porcelain.

Nantgarw porcelain, the brilliantly white, highly translucent soft-paste porcelain made at Nantgarw, near Cardiff, by William Billingsley in the early 19th century; production was small and economic necessity dictated a change to bone china.

NANT-GARW C.W

Nap, the surface or pile of certain cloths.

Napery, household linen, napkins, etc.

Napier's bones, a simple calculator traditionally invented by John Napier of Merchiston (1550–1617), consisting of sticks of bone (or ivory, wood, etc.) divided among numbered compartments.

Napkin holder, a ring, usually silver, for a rolled up napkin, or one of various gadgets known since the 17th century for attaching a napkin to a collar or skirt front.

Napkin press, a small linen press.

Napkin ring: see **Napkin holder**.

Naples porcelain, from the royal factory founded in the late 18th century with the intention of rivalling Capodimonte (recently removed to Spain); soft-paste porcelain, rather glassy; notably Classical figures.

Nappy dish, a china plate or shallow bowl, often scalloped, placed under a drinking cup to prevent the foam from strong ('nappy') ales running over on to the table top.

Nashiji, Japanese lacquerwork.

Naskhi, a cursive form of Arabic writing; some of the foliation taken over from Kufic.

Naturalistic decoration, designs faithfully following natural forms, by contrast with stylized designs; in particular, an early Victorian style associated in painting with the pre-Raphaelites and noticeable in furniture, ceramics, silver, etc. as extremely elaborate and detailed representations of flowers and leaves.

Nautilus, or argonaut, a large nacreous seashell, occasionally used as a vessel, mounted in silver, in the late Middle Ages; also, china in the form of a nautilus shell made in England in the late 18th century.

Navette: see **Nef**.

Necessaire, or vanity box, a box, sometimes papier mâché in the 19th century, for toilet articles.

Necklace, originally (presumably) a ribbon or collar of lace, but more commonly any ornamental chain, e.g. a string of pearls, worn around the neck. **153**

Neck ring, a heavy band around the neck, as worn in pre-Roman Britain or in parts of Africa; also, in glass decanters, a ring around the neck in one of many forms which to connoisseurs are evidence of date.

Needlecase, a small flat box for needles, kept inside a needlework basket, ivory or other material.

Needle gun, an early 19th-century German invention, the first gun in which the cartridge was fired by the impact of a needle.

Needlepoint, lace worked with a needle and single thread and predominantly in buttonhole stitch, the pattern first being made on parchment backed by cloth, probably originating in Renaissance Italy; see also **Pillow lace**.

Needlework, any fabric sewn or embroidered with a needle; of carpets, the

181 Ming vase with decoration
painted in enamels and blue
underglaze. Chinese, Ming dynasty,
16th century. (Musée Guimet,
Paris, Grandidier Collection)

182 Two millefiori vases. French,
about 1845–50. (Corning Museum
of Glass, Corning, New York)

183 Silver punch bowl, called a monteith. English, made by Samuel Wastell, 1704. (S. J. Phillips Ltd., London)

184 Montelupo maiolica plate. Italian, about 1630. (Victoria and Albert Museum, London)

term is often applied to early European imitations of oriental carpets in cross stitch and tent stitch. **193**

Nef, or navette, a medieval vessel of precious metal, most frequently silver gilt, usually made for use on a dining table to hold napkins, salt, etc., in the form of a ship, including every detail of sails and rigging and sometimes even figures of the sailors, perhaps the outstanding examples of the medieval goldsmith's art.

Négligé, a loose gown worn by women at informal moments; also, a type of necklace, particularly one of differing, single stones.

Neo-Classical style, the revival of Classical design in the late 18th century, which was encouraged by the excavations at Pompeii and Herculaneum and by reaction against the excesses of Rococo; it went through many phases and embraced rather different fashions in different countries; see also **Greek Revival**. **4**

Neo-Gothic, the revival of the Gothic style in the 18th and 19th centuries; see also **Gothic Revival**. **117, 285**

Neo-Jacobean style, a term sometimes applied to Victorian furniture in the style of the 17th century.

Nephrite, one of the two forms of jade, usually green but also other colours, including a greyish white; see also **Jadeite**. **141, 211**

Nest of drawers, a very small chest of drawers, such as might stand on a dressing table; see also **Collector's cabinet**.

Nest of tables, three or four side tables in diminishing sizes that fit one inside the next when not in use.

Netsuke, small Japanese carved ornaments, originally made as a kind of button with cord attached to a bag and hung from a belt, typically wood, jade or ivory. **190**

Network, an openwork fabric, like a fishing net, a ground for lace or embroidery; also, any decorative pattern, e.g. in relief on earthenware, suggesting a net.

Neudeck porcelain, mid 18th-century porcelain from a factory that moved, after a few years' production, to Nymphenburg.

Nevers figures: see **Verre de Nevers**.

Nevers faience, from a number of potteries in the French town, including 16th-century wares closely resembling Italian maiolica; later, characteristically French faience often decorated with pastoral scenes—a style associated particularly with Nevers. **191, 295**

Nevers glass: see **Verre de Nevers**.

New Amsterdam glass, from two 17th-century glassworks in the Dutch colony that became New York, of which no authenticated examples appear to exist.

New Bremen glass, good-quality tableware from an 18th-century Maryland glassworks; see also **Amelung glass**.

New Canton porcelain, soft-paste porcelain from the factory at Stratford-le-Bow, London, founded in the mid 18th century; see also **Bow**.

New Chelsea porcelain, from the Longton, Staffordshire, factory established in the early 20th century, making reproductions of old porcelain.

Newcastle glass, from the long-established Tyneside centre of English glassmaking; in particular 18th-century enamelled glassware and certain designs associated with Newcastle, e.g. a type of drinking glass with a cone-shaped bowl and heavily knopped stem; see also **Beilby glass**.

Newcomb pottery, Art Nouveau earthenware from the pottery established by the college of that name in New Orleans, about 1900.

New England glass, in particular glassware from the early 19th-century glassworks of that name near Boston, run by Deming Jarves, including pressed and cut glass and Baccarat-style paperweights.

New Forest pottery, early British pottery, dating back to Roman times, dark reddish brown ware with trailed white decoration.

New Hall porcelain, from the Staffordshire pottery founded in the late 18th century by a combine of potters who purchased the recipe for hard-paste porcelain from Bristol and made it for some years before changing to bone china.

New Hampshire mirror clock: see **Mirror clock**

New Jersey glass, usually a general term embracing the products of the innumerable glassworks, mainly in southern New Jersey, from the late 18th century; see also **South Jersey glass**.

New Orleans lace, the famous, decorative cast ironwork seen on the balconies of New Orleans (though chiefly made elsewhere).

Newry glass, Irish flint glass from a factory operating in the late 18th and early 19th centuries.

New stone china, the trade name for a type of Spode stoneware containing potash feldspar, introduced in the early 19th century.

Nickel, a hard silvery white metal, resistant to oxidation, frequently used in a copper alloy as a substitute for silver.

Nickel silver, an alloy of 75% copper and 25% nickel, used in cutlery and coins.

Niderviller faience, from the factory in Alsace-Lorraine founded in the mid 18th century, elegant forms and delicate floral painting, also small faience figures rivalling the finest porcelain.

Niello, a kind of black enamel consisting of metal alloy used for filling in engraved designs in silver (or other metal), especially popular in Russia.

Night clock, designed for telling the time in the dark, typically with a pierced dial through which shone the light from a lamp, placed behind the clock. **192**

Night commode, a close stool.

Night latch, a spring-operated bolt turned by a handle on the inside or a key from the outside, as in a modern Yale lock.

Night light: see **Fairy lamp**.

Night table, a small side table with cupboard containing a chamber pot, or a washstand with the same convenience.

Night-watchman jug, a popular pattern of Toby jug, of a watchman with his lantern.

Nipple, a small protuberance like the nipple of a breast, e.g. for the percussion cap in a muzzle-loading gun.

New Hall porcelain

Nipt diamond waies, a 17th-century phrase describing the decorative effect in glass of pinching together thick vertical ribs of glass into a diamond pattern; see also **Pincered**.

Noble metals, precious metals, i.e. gold, silver, platinum and their alloys.

Nodding figures, figures with nodding heads, usually made of porcelain, and popular in Victorian times, originated in China; see also **Pagodes**.

Noggin, a small drinking cup, sometimes implying a quarter-pint measure.

Nomad rugs, oriental prayer rugs and carpets made by nomadic peoples rather than in established villages, and thus often made on a primitive loom—often no more than a pair of beams laid on the ground with the warp stretched between.

Nomisma, a Byzantine gold coin from about the 11th century, irregular in shape.

Nonmineral gems, materials other than stone or metal used in jewellery, especially amber, coral, ivory, jet, pearl and shell.

Nonsuch chest, a Tudor chest with inlaid decoration suggestive of the famous (but long-vanished) palace of that name, probably of Flemish rather than English make.

Norfolk latch, the name given to a common type of iron latch in which the handle was soldered on to a large escutcheon plate, basically a narrow vertical rectangle, pierced near the top for the latch; see also **Suffolk latch**.

North pistols, made by the American gunsmith Simeon North; in particular, those made for the U.S. Navy about 1800.

Northwood School, a term sometimes applied to the followers of John Northwood, the British artist who revived the art of making cameo glass in the second half of the 19th century.

Norton pottery, in particular, Bennington earthenware and stoneware from the pottery founded in the late 18th century by John Norton.

Norway rugs, double-weave upholstery materials made in Norway in the 19th century.

Norwich glass, Norwich cut: see **King's Lynn glass**.

Norwich pottery, possibly the earliest English delftware, made by the Flemish potter who was subsequently established in Lambeth, but no authenticated examples are known.

Norwich silver, in particular, plate made for Norfolk churches after the Reformation, of which much still survives.

Nosing, a general term describing a rounded or half-rounded edge, as in a stair tread.

Nöstetangen glass, 18th-century Norwegian glass from the glassworks established under royal patronage, manned largely by German and English (Newcastle) glassmakers, but evolving a distinctly Norwegian style in fine tableware.

Nostril jewellery, precious stones worn in the side of the nose, pierced for the purpose, chiefly by Indian women.

Nottingham stoneware, early (17th century) brown, salt-glazed stoneware mugs, pots, etc. made by James Morley among others, with engraved and pierced decoration and generally elegant form.

Novelties, curious or unusual articles, particularly in glass, e.g. Nailsea glass; also, trinkets, puzzles, mechanical devices, souvenir items, etc. in any medium.

Nove: see **Le Nove**.

Nulling: see **Gadrooning**.

Numismatics, the study (and/or collection) of coins.

Nun's cloth, a woollen dress material, typically but not necessarily black, similar to bunting.

Nuppenbecker, a claw beaker in medieval German glass, or any glass beaker decorated with prunts (nuppen). **60, 206**

Nuremberg egg, the name given to an early South German watch worn around the neck, apparently the result of a mistranslation of the German 'little clock' (*Eichen* for *Ührchen*).

Nuremberg kitchen, a 19th-century German toy to encourage housewifely virtues, a miniature fitted kitchen complete with copper or pewter pans, etc.

Nuremberg pottery, a variety of wares from the Middle Ages, especially 18th-century faience which evolved a distinctive style, notably in blue-on-white floral decoration and scenes based on engravings with characteristic hatching. **195**

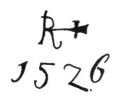

Nursing chair, a term sometimes applied to virtually any low-seated chair, whether or not designed for a nursing mother.

Nutmeg grater, a cylindrical container, originally silver, for nutmeg, with a grater immediately below the lid at one end and a separate compartment for the powdered spice; similar to but smaller than a snuff grater.

Nutria fur, from the coypu, used in hats as a substitute for beaver in the 19th century.

Nymphenburg porcelain, 18th-century porcelain from the factory near Munich, notable especially for the extraordinarily vital figures modelled by Franz Anton Bustelli, whose work marked 'a period of supreme fulfillment in porcelain modelling' (S. Ducret). **65, 194**

Nyon porcelain, from a factory near Geneva founded in the late 18th century and producing a good white body with conventional Rococo decoration in the south German manner.

Oak, a paleish brown hardwood very widely used for early furniture in Europe, especially the 17th century, sometimes called the 'oak period'; thereafter superseded by less intractable woods; the best English oak furniture was made of imported timber; see also **English Oak**. **142**

Oak-leaf jars, a name given to the two-handled drug jars of Renaissance Florentine maiolica with low-relief decoration in blue and background pattern of oak leaves.

Oban, a Japanese gold coin worth ten of the Koban, current from about 1700.

Obelisk, a four-sided pillar, tapering slightly as it rises and usually chamfered to a point at the top.

Objet d'art, a work of art.

Object of vertu, a work of beauty, rarity or antiquity, perhaps a small box, ornament or miniature made of precious

186 The Morris chair. Designed by
William Morris about 1883.
(Victoria and Albert Museum,
London)

185 Chintz designed by William
Morris. Mid 19th century.
(Victoria and Albert Museum,
London. Photo: John Webb)

187 Cosmetic box. Chinese, 18th century. Cinnabar lacquer inlaid with an elegant floral motif in mother-of-pearl. (Compagnie de la Chine et des Indes, Paris)

188 Bowl of murrhine glass. Venetian, 19th century. (Museo Vetrario, Murano)

metals and decorated with enamels and jewels. **196**

Obol, a small silver coin, Greek, various types and denominations.

Obsidian, a hard volcanic glass, black or dark green with a metallic sheen, sometimes resembling bottle glass; carved as ornaments, jars, etc., and occasionally found in jewellery.

Obverse, the front, e.g. of a coin, medal, etc., the opposite side to the reverse.

Ocarina, a curiosity among wind musical instruments, consisting of an earthenware egg-shaped body with a pipe emerging from the side (like the spout of a pot) with mouthpiece; Italian in origin.

Occasional table, a small side table, games table, etc., which may be easily moved about the room when required; numerous kinds since the 17th century.

Ochsenkopf, 'ox-head', in German glass, an enamelled beaker picturing the wooded mountains of that name; made in the 17th century; also known as Fichtelgebirge glass.

Octagonal, eight-sided.

Octavo, the commonest size of book, roughly eight inches high, so-called because each printed sheet makes eight leaves (16 pages).

Oeil de boeuf: see **Bull's eye.**

Oeil de perdrix, 'partridge's eye', a random pattern of small bright blue circles surrounded by darker dots found as background decoration on some porcelain; also, a pattern in pressed glass, a dotted ground in lace, etc.

Oenochoe, a type of jug, known in ancient Egypt, the basis of a common form of jug to this day, i.e. swelling slightly outward from flat base to sharply rounded shoulder, with relatively narrow neck, wide lip, and generous looped handle.

Off-hand glass, curious, decorative and sometimes useful objects made by the glassmakers outside their normal work from superfluous metal; see also **End-of-day glass.**

Offprint, in books, a section of a large book printed (from the same type) as a separate small book.

Ogee, the 'line of beauty' or cyma recta, an inward-outward curve like a slender S that appears in a Classical moulding; hence, **ogee bowl,** of a wine glass, etc., a common form also seen in a bottle, cabriole leg, etc.

Ogee clock, a term employed in particular to describe a common variety of 19th-century New England shelf clock the front of which is framed by an ogee moulding.

Ogival, ogive: see **Ogee.**

Oignon watch: see **Onion watch.**

Oil and vinegar frame, a silver stand containing small bottles for olive oil and vinegar; see also **Cruet.**

Oil clock: see **Lamp clock.**

Oil cloth, a textile fabric made waterproof by treating with oil, particularly canvas table coverings so treated; from about 1800.

Oil gilding, an early form of gilding, in which gold leaf was in effect glued on with a preparation containing oil and gum arabic, cheap but not durable, generally superseded in the late 18th century.

Oil lamp, any oil-burning lamp, since ancient times; more specifically a lamp of the Argand type.

Oil sink, in clocks and watches, a dished depression over an arbor in the back plate of the movement, for oil.

Oil spot, in porcelain, a small silvery spot in the glaze.

Ointment jar, a lidded vessel for healing or cosmetic unguents.

Old English silver, a reference to pattern rather than date, characterized by sharply narrowing spoons and handles turned down at the ends.

Oldfield ware, brown, salt-glazed stoneware from a pottery at Brampton, Derbyshire, 19th century.

Olerys style, in Moustiers faience, polychrome decoration in the Spanish style introduced by Joseph Olerys who had run a factory at Alcora (Spain) in the mid 18th century.

Olivewood, hard, rather intractable, greenish yellow wood with dark wavy markings, sometimes used for veneers and boxes from the 17th century.

Olivine, an olive-green stone found in volcanic rock and meteorites, usually very small, used in jewellery; see also **Demantoid garnet.**

Ombre table, a three-sided card table for playing the three-handed game of that name, popular in the 18th century.

Omega pottery, early 20th-century English pottery designed by Roger Fry and other artists associated with what is known as the Bloomsbury circle.

Omnium, a stand of shelves; see also **What-not.**

On-glaze, or over-glaze, of decoration on ceramics, applied after glazing and fixed by a subsequent firing normally at a lower temperature.

Onion foot, on furniture, a foot similar to a bun foot, flattened at the bottom and with an upward curve at the top.

Onion watch, a name applied chiefly to French watches of the late 17th and early 18th centuries, which were particularly thick after the introduction of the balance spring.

Onlaid, similar to inlaid, particularly of leather in bookbinding, so thin that no recess is necessary to allow a level surface.

Onyx, a variety of quartz, usually black striped with white and/or other colours, used in jewellery, e.g. cameo brooches; also **onyx marble,** a type of marble, banded like onyx and sometimes called oriental alabaster. **197**

Onza, a Spanish gold coin, or doubloon, current in the 17th century.

Opal, a precious stone, characteristically white and iridescent but especially valuable in its black variety and also occurring in a transparent orange form, subject to deterioration in time due to dehydration.

Opal glass, or opaline glass, a fine white or coloured glass, frequently green, popular in the 19th century, especially in France. **199**

Opaque-white glass, glass somewhat resembling porcelain, containing tin oxide; see **Milk glass.**

Opaque-twist, in the stem of a wine glass, a spiral twist of opaque white glass, often combined with other colours.

Open-back chair, any chair with an openwork back, particularly one of the so-called Derbyshire or Yorkshire type, having no vertical members except at each end.

Open-twist, turned chair or table legs consisting of two separate intertwined spirals, also seen in balusters, late 17th century; see also **Barley-sugar twist.**

Opus Anglicanum, early English needlework worked in a characteristic variation of cross-stitch, extremely fine, used in embroidering details in ecclesiastical vestments particularly.

Orange glass, Williamite glass; also, a small glass dish for an orange.

Orange jumper, a popular creamware figure of a stablehand dressed in orange, made at the Don pottery in the early 19th century.

Orangewood, a fruit wood occasionally used in Portuguese and Spanish furniture.

Orders, in Classical architecture, the basic types of columns and entablatures, i.e., Doric, Ionic, Corinthian, Tuscan and Composite.

Orfray: see **Orphrey.**

Organ, a musical instrument comprising sets of pipes sounded by compressed air, played at a keyboard. **198**

Organ clock, a clock in which the hours are sounded by pipes operated by bellows like an organ, known since the 16th century.

Organdie, a very fine type of muslin, used for trimming dresses, etc.

Orient, a term used to describe the lustre of a pearl; geographically, the world east of Suez, more particularly the Far East.

Oriental carpets, hand-knotted carpets and rugs made in the Near East (and China) since ancient times, originally by nomadic peoples, mainly in long-established stylized designs; first imported to Europe in the Middle Ages and immensely popular since the 15th century.

Oriental lacquer: see **Japanned, Lacquer.**

Oriental style: see **Chinoiserie, Japanese style.**

Original engraving, painted and engraved by the same person.

Orleans porcelain, produced at the French factory from the mid 18th century to the early 19th.

Ormolu, strictly, gilt bronze, but sometimes applied to alloys imitating gold, gilded or not; characteristic of the best French gilded furniture of the 18th century and particularly associated with Baroque and Rococo clocks; see also **Bronze doré. 48**

Ormosia, a family of hardwood trees furnishing a variety of woods used in Chinese furniture.

Ornament, an article the chief or only purpose of which is decorative rather than useful, hence the term 'ornamental furniture' for chairs too beautiful and uncomfortable to sit on, tables of such delicate form that nothing should stand on them, etc.

Ornamented, decorated; more specifically (particularly in glass and ceramics) applied decoration in relief.

Orpharion, a stringed musical instrument similar to the cittern, with as many as nine pairs of strings, popular in the 17th century.

Orphrey, cloth embroidered with gold and/or silk, associated particularly with priestly vestments, altar cloths, etc.

Orpiment, or yellow arsenic, a yellow pigment.

Orrefors glass, modern Swedish art glass. **200**

Orrery, a mechanical instrument that ► shows the relationship between Earth, moon, sun and planets, named after an early owner of such a device in the early 18th century.

Orris: see **Arras.**

Orthoclase, a type of feldspathic precious stone, which includes moonstone among its varieties.

Orvieto maiolica, from one of the earliest Italian centres; plates, drug jars and jugs, with Gothic decoration, surviving from the 14th century.

Os de mouton, 'ram's horn', a gently scrolled form suggesting the horns of, perhaps, a buffalo rather than modern breeds of sheep, seen in the legs and stretchers of some late 17th-century French chairs.

Ostensory, a silver vessel for a holy relic, etc.; see also **Monstrance.**

Ostrich-egg cup, the egg of an ostrich, mounted in silver, a curiosity of the 17th century.

Ottingen-Schrattenhofen faience, chiefly 18th-century wares with floral decoration in high-temperature colours, from the south German centre.

Ottoman, or ottomane, originally a richly upholstered bench, originating in the Ottoman empire; a term used more widely in the 19th century to include various shapes and sizes of overstuffed seat with or without back, including a round pouffe.

Ottoman pottery: see **Isnik ware.**

Ottweiler porcelain, figures, dishes, etc., from a pottery in the German town established in the second half of the 18th century and at one time under French control; also faience.

Oude Loosdrecht porcelain, Dutch porcelain from the late 18th century, noted particularly for painting of peasant scenes and landscapes, otherwise generally similar to contemporary German porcelain.

Oushak carpets: see **Ushak carpets.**

Outside decorator, in glass and porcelain, an independent craftsman who painted wares made elsewhere; see **Hausmalerei.**

Ovenware, or oven-proof ware, ironstone dishes, 19th century; also any other ware that withstands the heat of an oven.

Over-glaze: see **On-glaze.**

Overlay, in glassware, two or more layers of metal, usually of different colours and engraved to reveal the layer underneath; see also **Cased glass.**

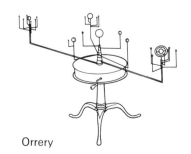

Orrery

Overmantel, the area above the shelf on a chimneypiece, particularly when consisting of some built-in feature such as a mirror or panelling.

Overstuffed, of seat furniture, heavily padded; now sometimes applied to upholstery that continues over the sides of the seat and is fastened on the bottom, obscuring all wood from view.

Ovolo, a convex, quarter-circle moulding, occurring for instance on a bracket, pediment, etc.

Owl-head spoon, a silver spoon with owl-head finial, from the 16th century.

Owl jug, or Eulenkrug, a jug in the form of an owl with detachable head serving as a cup, made in tin-glazed earthenware in Germany in the 16th century, later in stoneware.

Oxblood glaze: see **Sang-de-boeuf.**

Oxbow front, a curved front seen in certain New England cabinets, suggesting the shape of the collar (bow) worn by draft oxen.

Ox-eye cup, one of numerous names given to small, plain, two-handled silver cups known from the early 17th century and surviving mainly in ancient English educational institutions.

Oxford flagon, a type of pewter flagon or jug with convex sides, domed lid and a strainer in the spout, from about 1700.

Oyster veneer, an effect like oyster shells achieved by cutting small-sectioned timber at a slant across the grain, so that the growth rings appear wider and oval, found chiefly on panels, drawer fronts, etc. from the late 17th century, perhaps originally a Dutch technique.

Ozier pattern, like rushwork or basketwork, in particular, a subtle relief pattern used in early Meissen and other European porcelain.

189 ▲

190

189 Porcelain mustard pot.
Bourg-la-Reine, 1756. (Musée des
Arts Décoratifs, Paris)

190 Inro with netsuke. Japanese,
17th–19th century. The inro is of
plain gold lacquer on a wooden
framework, with scene of rocks and
waves and Mount Fuji in the
distance. (Museo Orientale,
Venice)

191 Nevers faience jug. Late 17th
century. An early example of the
motif of flowers on a bright blue
background. (Victoria and Albert
Museum, London)

192 Night clock. Probably central
Italian, about 1680. Ebonized wood
case. A small lantern inside the
clock throws a reflection of the
face against the nearest wall on
which the time can be read.
(Private Collection, Milan)

193 English needlework carpet.
19th century. A typically Victorian
design, the squares contain floral
motifs and are separated by lions
rampant. (Mayorcas Collection,
London)

Pace eggs: see **Pasch eggs.**

Paddle-and-anvil pottery, the method of making clay pots without a wheel, by shaping the vessel against an anvil with blows from a wooden paddle.

Pad foot, on furniture legs, a rounded foot similar to the club foot, the two terms often interchangeable.

Padouk wood, a dark reddish brown Far Eastern wood something like rosewood, very hard and heavy, sometimes used by European cabinetmakers in the 18th century.

Paduasoy, a relatively stiff, hard-wearing, corded silk material, probably made originally in Padua, used chiefly for clothes in the 18th century.

Pagoda, a Chinese tower with projecting curved roofs at each storey, appearing frequently in Chinese-style ceramics and influencing furniture design in the late 18th-century Chinese fashion; also, various small gold coins of southern India up to the 18th century.

Pagodes, Chinoiserie porcelain figures of old men, seated, sometimes with separately made head set on a bar resting in slots inside the shoulders so that the head nods gently when tapped; also, a pagoda.

Paillons, or paillettes, small pieces of bright metal foil or other material incorporated in decorative patterns in embroidery or in lacquered boxes, papier mâché, etc.

Paintbrush foot, in furniture (mainly chairs), a Spanish foot.

Painted furniture, specifically, furniture painted with designs of some kind, as in the Adam style and later; also, imitations of oriental lacquer; see also **Fancy chair.**

Paisley pattern, in cloth a pattern based on the boteh motif like a lozenge with a tail, common on Paisley shawls.

Paisley shawl, soft woollen or silk and woollen shawls in various colours, originally made at Paisley, near Glasgow, in imitation of cashmere.

Paktong, an alloy of copper, nickel and zinc, made in China and imported to England in the late 18th century, used chiefly for hearth furniture, candlesticks, etc.

Palace letters, found on furniture made in the French royal furniture factories, indicating the palace to which the piece belonged.

Palas: see **Khilim.**

Palette, or pallett, a wooden board for a specific purpose, e.g. for an artist to mix his paints, for a potter to stand his wares, for a bricklayer to carry his plaster.

Palimpsest, a monumental brass that has been turned over and engraved on the reverse; a parchment or ms. on which the original writing has been obliterated and replaced.

Palissy ware, pottery in the style of the famous 16th-century French potter, Bernard Palissy, with very realistic, high-relief ornament of insects, reptiles, etc., reproduced in many places in the 19th century. **202**

Palladian style, in architecture, the Neo-Classical style of the Italian architect Palladio (1518–80), adopted widely in England for country houses in the 18th century by Adam and others.

Painted furniture

Paisley pattern

Pallash, a single-edged sword with a long straight blade, various types, 18th to 19th century.

Pallisande, rosewood.

Pall-mall, a wooden club or mallet for striking the ball in a 17th-century game of that name; also, the alley in which the game was played (hence the well-known London street).

Palmette, a decorative motif in the form of a stylized palm leaf, of Egyptian origin, occurring for instance in late 18th-century furniture and in oriental carpets.

Panache, a headdress of feathers, the plume of a plumed helmet; also, a tassel or fringe.

Pan, a wide, shallow, flat-bottomed vessel, usually metal and with a handle; see also **Pot.**

Pancheon, a wide, shallow bowl for milk, in wood, clay or metal.

Panderma carpets, from a town in western Turkey, including many modern reproductions of old Persian designs in which sometimes even the effects of wear and tear are painstakingly imitated. **203**

Pandore, a lute- or cittern-like musical instrument of about the 16th century, the precise form of which remains a matter of surmise since no examples have been positively identified.

Panel, a rectangular element, most typically on a door, which is either raised or (more commonly) recessed, and usually framed by a moulding; any design framed in a rectangle, e.g. a printed scene on porcelain, etc.

Panel-back chair, a Tudor chair with a panel set in the back, or any chair with some type of decorative element in the back framed in a panel.

Panel-cutting, glass cutting with the flat surface (rather than the circular edge) of the grinding wheel, an 18th-century technique.

Panelled construction, mainly of chests, consisting of a stout framework with thin panels set between the vertical and horizontal members.

Panharmonicon, a type of harmonium or 'mechanical orchestra' as demonstrated by J. N. Maelzel about 1800, apparently incorporating free-reed pipes.

Panier, a basket; also, the wide skirt supported on a whalebone framework, an 18th-century fashion carried to extremes when ladies had to turn sideways to pass through a door.

Panoptyque, or panopticon, an epidiascope, i.e. capable of projecting non-translucent images.

Pantin glass, art glass of various kinds made at the French centre from the second half of the 19th century.

Pantograph, a machine used by 18th-century portrait miniaturists, silhouette-cutters, etc., to reduce a life-size image to the size required.

Pap dish, or cup, etc., a shallow bowl or cup with a spout for feeding liquid foods to babies or invalids.

Paper knife, for opening letters or the uncut pages of books, a blunt-bladed knife, frequently silver or ivory, often with a handle scarcely thicker than the blade.

Paper ware, papier mâché articles, or, more frequently, pressed paper; see also **Clay ware.**

Paperweight, in particular a glass article, usually hemispherical in shape and heavy, containing brilliantly coloured designs, most often millefiori; originally a French speciality, but soon copied elsewhere, 19th century. **13**

Paperweight clock, a small clock in a glass case with metal base, about 1900.

Paper filigree: see **Quillwork.**

Papier mâché, a material consisting basically of mashed paper, combined with a binding agent and various other substances, which hardens when dry; used for mouldings in the early 18th century, trays and boxes in the late 18th century and furniture in the 19th century, this progress reflecting improvements in its manufacture; see also **Clay ware. 201**

Papier peint: see **Wallpaper.**

Pappenheimer, a large, two-edged sword of the early 17th century, named after a German commander in the Thirty Years' War.

Pap-warmer, or food-warmer, a cup and cover on a hollow stand containing a lamp or candle, usually earthenware, from the 18th century.

Papyrus, the writing material of ancient times, made of strips of the 'paper rush' (papyrus) in several layers, each layer laid at right angles to the one above, soaked, pressed together and dried; also used in furniture making by the Egyptians for decorative elements and small pieces such as footstools, small tables, etc.

Paragon, an outstanding example of any article, in particular a precious stone; also, a woollen material used for coverings in the 17th century.

Parasol, a gaily coloured umbrella carried by ladies for keeping off the sun, fashionable in the mid 19th century.

Parcel gilt, partly gilded, describing, for instance, 18th-century furniture in which decoratively carved elements are gilded and other areas left plain; also common on silver articles, from early days.

Parchment, the chief material for writing until the late Middle Ages, prepared from the skin of animals, chiefly sheep or goats; still used occasionally for special documents and for painting; see also **Vellum.**

Parchment pattern, fluted carving in Tudor furniture, usually in panels; see also **Linenfold.**

Parian ware, a type of porcelain resembling fine white marble developed in England in the mid 19th century and used mainly for figures, small copies of Classical sculptures being much favoured.

Parison, or paraison, the mass of molten metal taken from the glass furnace and inflated and marvered (smoothed) on the end of the blow-pipe.

Paris porcelain, from a large number of factories, making soft-paste porcelain until the late 18th century, thereafter chiefly hard-paste; both in the manner of Sèvres; faience was also made at many Paris potteries, whose history is somewhat entangled. **118, 205**

Parliament clock: see **Act of Parliament clock.**

Parlour chair, a term used rather loosely of a single chair with upholstered seat, more particularly a chair intended for the dining room, from the late 18th century.

Parquetry, similar to marquetry except that the pieces of wood are straight-sided and the decorative effect is achieved by contrasting lines of the grain, as in parquet floors.

Parson and clerk figures, various anti-clerical earthenware ornaments in the shape of a minister, the worse for drink, aided by his clerk; English, early 19th century.

Partizan, a type of spear or pike, ending in a curved, triangular head; see also **Halberd. 214**

Partner's desk, a term usually implying a pedestal desk, large enough for two people to sit opposite each other.

Partridge eye: see **Oeil de perdrix.**

Partridge wood, a Brazilian hardwood with red and brown streaks like the plumage of a partridge, used as an inlay wood in the late 17th century.

Part-size mould: see **Pattern-moulded glass.**

Partworks, books issued in instalments, weekly, monthly, etc., from the 19th century.

Parure, a set of jewellery, comprising (for example) necklace, pendant and bracelet; made since the 16th century.

Pasch eggs, pace eggs, or *oeufs de Paques,* coloured Easter eggs, made of china, glass, papier mâché, etc.

Paschal candlestick, a large marble candlestick, several feet high, with Easter scenes carved in relief: medieval, north Italy.

Pasguard, in armour, an extra plate protecting the left elbow in tilting armour.

Passementerie, originally, lace; subsequently, decorative textile trimmings of all kinds, e.g. braid, ribbons, tassels, etc., the making of which was a specialized craft.

Passe partout, a cut-out cardboard frame, e.g. for a picture; hence, the sticky fibrous tape used in cheap framing of pictures, tablemats, etc.

Passglas, a tall, cylindrical glass beaker marked off into sections, each mark representing the measure to be drunk by one man during a toast; German, from the 16th century. **206**

Paste, in jewellery, imitation gem stones (especially diamonds) made of glass; also, the body of porcelain; see also **Body.**

Pasteboard, a thin board made by pasting together a number of sheets of paper or card, used for instance in bookbinding.

Paste print, a print made from a metal plate coated with an adhesive ink allowing application of gold leaf or other colours, a Renaissance technique.

Parson and clerk figures

194

195

194 Group of 'Lovers' by Francesco Antonio Bustelli. Nymphenburg, mid 18th century. (Bayerisches Nationalmuseum, Munich)

195 Nuremberg faience jug. 1826. A 19th-century copy of a popular 18th-century design derived from Dutch art. (Musée National de Céramique, Sèvres)

196 Small box decorated with an enamelled miniature mounted in gold. (Musée Cognacq-Jay, Paris)

197▲

198

197 Onyx cameo brooch representing an eagle. German, mid 13th century. (Schatzkammer, Munich)

198 Positive organ. Made by Diego Evans, London, 1762. (Museo Municipal de Musica, Barcelona)

199 Opaline glass dish with undulating edge. Venetian, 18th century. (Museo di San Martino, Naples)

Pastiche, or pasticcio, a work of art imitating another style, or a medley of styles; or a work by several hands; also, a forgery made by using parts of several genuine works.

Pastiglia, in Italian furniture, relief ornamentation in plaster, frequently gilded; see also **Gesso, Stucco.**

Pastille burner, a vessel of various shapes and sizes, e.g. a model cottage in earthenware, for burning a plug of incense; popular in the late 18th and early 19th centuries.

Patch box, a small box like a jewellery box, often china, containing the false 'beauty spots' (silk patches) affected by fashionable ladies in the 18th century.

Patch figures, a term applied to early English porcelain figures that have an unglazed patch on the base where they rested during firing.

Patchwork, the technique, primarily in making quilts, of sewing together small patches of differently coloured and patterned cloth; an outstanding domestic craft in America.

Pâte de verre, or pâte de riz, 'glass paste', a late 19th-century technique in glassmaking, in which figures, vases, etc. were moulded from a paste containing powdered glass and fired like pottery; a similar technique was used in ancient Egypt.

Paten: see **Ciborium.**

Patera, in Neo-Classical design, a round or (sometimes) oval decorative motif, carved, inlaid, painted, etc., frequently resembling a flower or rosette, based on the form of an ancient Greek dish. **69**

Paterna pottery, Hispano-Moresque pottery with abstract, Islamic designs or European scenes, from the region of Valencia, 13th century and later.

Paterson revolver, the original Colt pistol, made at Paterson, New Jersey, in the first half of the 19th century.

Pâte sur pâte, 'paste on paste', low-relief decoration in white slip on porcelain before firing and glazing, a technique first used in Europe at Sèvres in the 19th century, also associated particularly with Minton in England and Rookwood in America.

Patina, the appearance of a surface affected by time, e.g. on furniture after many years of polishing; more specifically, the greenish cast on bronze caused by oxidation. **35**

Patten, originally, a wooden shoe; also, overshoes of various kinds, e.g. raised on a high metal rim; the word was also applied to a bag in which shoes were carried.

Pattern-moulded glass, blown-moulded glass in which the pattern is impressed in a small ('part-size') mould before being blown to full size.

Pattypan, a small round metal dish with scalloped rim for meat pies (patties).

Pauldron, in armour, a shoulder plate.

Pavé, 'paved', a term used in jewellery to describe close-set stones as in paving, concealing the metal setting.

Pavilion, in jewellery, the lower part of a faceted diamond (or other stone) which in a ring or brooch is held by the mount.

Pavillon, a French gold coin of the 14th century showing the king enthroned in a Gothic pavilion.

Pavis, a large shield to protect the bearer from arrows.

Paw foot, a furniture leg terminating in an animal's paw, most commonly a lion's, also sometimes a dog's, found in various periods; in Neo-Classical furniture frequently gilded.

Pax, a holy tablet, bearing a Crucifixion scene, with a handle on the reverse so that it could be presented for worshippers to kiss; wood, silver, etc.

Peachbloom, a glaze found on some Chinese porcelain; see also **Peachblow.**

Peachblow, a type of late 19th-century American art glass in various colours more or less peach-like, first made by the New England Glass Co.; resembling certain Chinese porcelain glazes.

Peale silhouettes, small hollow-cut portraits made in large numbers by Charles Willson Peale (1741–1827), master of many trades and proprietor of a Philadelphia museum; other members of his family, including his son Rembrandt, worked in the same craft.

Peardrop handle, a drop handle in the shape of a pear, brass or glass.

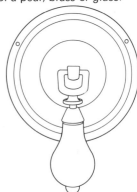

Peardrop moulding, arcaded moulding in which the divisions between the arches swell into pear-shaped terminals.

Pearl, an organic gem formed in oysters (and other molluscs) around an irritant; usually white and iridescent, smooth and round; cultured pearls, artificially instigated, are indistinguishable from natural pearls to the naked eye; see also **Baroque pearl.**

Pearling, a lace trimming on clothes.

Pearlware, a Wedgwood innovation of the late 18th century, similar to creamware but with greater whiteness of body and used particularly for blue transfer-printing; see also **Queen's ware.**

Pearwood, a light pinkish-yellow fruitwood sometimes used in early English veneer, also in country furniture and for carved ornaments, being easily worked.

Peasant ware, pottery made for local use, often with rather crude relief decoration; see also **Redware, Slipware.**

Pebbled ware: see **Agate ware, Marbled.**

Péché mortel, a couch, 18th century.

Pe de pincel: see **Spanish foot.**

Pedestal, originally, the support for a column; a solid stand, usually four-sided, for a bust, lamp, jardinière, etc.

Pedestal clock, a brass clock of basically Gothic type set on top of a four-sided pillar, for easy visibility; a 16th-century south German speciality.

Pedestal desk, a large writing table supported by two pedestals, containing drawers, on either side of an open knee hole.

Pedestal seat, a stool or chair with a single leg (as in many modern easy chairs of steel construction), or a type of porter's chair—basically a cushion on top of a box.

Pedestal table, a table with a single, central support culminating in a wider base or foot; see also **Pillar and claw**.

Pediment, the upward-sloping or scrolled piece on top of a cabinet, bookcase, clockcase, etc.; a term often used more loosely to describe the horizontal moulding on the top of such pieces. 64

Peep show, a box containing cut-out figures and scenery arranged in perspective which, viewed through an aperture, gave an impression of three dimensions.

Pegasus: see **Winged horse**.

Pegged furniture, with joints held by wooden dowels rather than iron nails; in particular, chests etc. that could be taken apart by removing the pegs holding them together.

Peg tankard, a type of silver or pewter tankard dating from the 17th century with small pegs attached at regular intervals inside (sometimes outside) to mark the amount of beer drunk.

Pelisse, originally, a fur coat; also a long cloak of any material, 18th century.

Pell, leather or parchment.

Pelmet, a horizontal strip across the top of a window, obscuring the curtain rail, frequently made of the same material as the curtains, often scalloped or fringed.

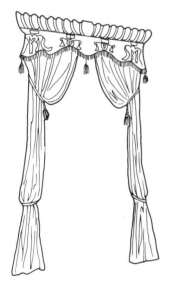

Pembroke table, a side-table with two short drop-leaves, supported on hinged brackets; usually oval or with rounded corners; popular since the mid 18th century; also called a flap and elbow table.

Pen box, a small, lidded box for writing instruments; see also **Penner**. 204

Pencil cedar, a reddish brown softwood, sometimes used in American cabinet-work for structural parts under little or no strain, such as the sides of drawers.

Pendant, 'hanging', thus any form of suspended ornament e.g. in crystal chandeliers; also, in jewellery, an ornament hanging from a chain around the neck. 153

Pende carpets, rugs and carpets woven by nomadic peoples of western Turkestan, Sehna knot, predominantly deep red, blue and natural colours; see also **Bokhara carpets**.

Pendeloque: see **Pendant**.

Pendulum clock, any clock (generally a long-case clock) driven by a rod with a weight (bob) on the end which swings back and forth under the influence of gravity; made since the mid 17th century.

Pendulum watch, an aberration of certain watchmakers of the late 17th century who did not understand that the principle of the pendulum, which so improved time-keeping in clocks, could not be applied to watches.

Penner, a cylindrical silver (or other metal) case for quill pens, sometimes with a seal at the end, a knife blade, and/or an inkwell; from the 17th century.

Penn glass, allegedly from the first glassworks in Philadelphia, perhaps making bottles, but none are known to have survived.

Pennington pottery, made in Liverpool, England, by the Pennington brothers in the 18th century, including blue-painted delftware punchbowls; later, soft-paste porcelain, and decoration of Worcester figures.

Pennsylvania chest, an early American type, usually on bracket feet and sometimes with a pair of drawers in the base, decoratively painted; see also **Dowry chest, Pennsylvania-Dutch**.

Pennsylvania-Dutch, or Pennsylvania-German, the style in the decorative arts of the early German settlers in Pennsylvania in which various European 'peasant' styles mingled; painted softwood furniture, wood-carving in almost medieval forms, lead-glazed redware pots and dishes, etc.

Penny, the standard British coin since the early Middle Ages, originally silver, copper since the 18th century; also, various other copper coins.

Pennybank, a money box.

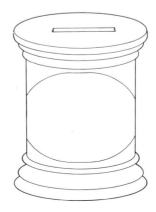

Penrhyn marble, slate.

Penrose glass, from an Irish glassworks in Waterford established in the late 18th century.

Pen tray, a narrow tray, silver or glass, for quill pens, usually part of an inkstand but sometimes made separately, from the 18th century.

Penwork, in furniture, linear designs in black, made with a pen against light-coloured surround, fashionable in the early 19th century.

Pepperbox, a small caster for pepper; see also **Muffineer**, 66; also, an early 19th-century repeating pistol with five or six barrels which revolved after each shot.

Pepper caster: see **Pepperbox**.

Perambulator, a pedometer, a device with a wheel that, run along the ground, registered distance travelled on a dial; also, a baby carriage.

Percale, a stiff cotton cloth with a matt finish, imported from the East in the 17th century and subsequently manufactured in Europe, block-printed and sometimes used for coverings.

Percussion lock, a firearm fired by the striking of a percussion cap, since the early 19th century.

Perforated: see **Pierced**.

Perfume burner, a vessel, usually urn-shaped and in silver or ceramic, for heating a variety of pleasant-smelling materials, chiefly 18th century though made much earlier; see also **Censer, Pastille burner**. 207

Perfume sprinkler, a glass, metal or ceramic vessel, often with many spouts, for dispersing scented water around the house, during processions etc.; originally from the East, since early times; see also **Almorrata**. 5

Peridot, olivine.

Perlwerk: see **Beading**.

Pernambuco wood: see **Brazilwood**.

Perpendicular style, the late Gothic style in architecture and reflected in furniture, characterized by more slender forms, more elaborate tracery, less naturalistic patterns, some based on drapery.

Perpetual calendar, a device, usually part of a clock, for registering the date automatically on a slowly turning dial

200 Cut-glass decanter and flask. By the Swedish glassmaking firm, Orrefors, 1925. (Musée des Arts Décoratifs, Paris)

201 Papier-mâché cellaret. English, about 1860. (Victoria and Albert Museum, London)

202 Oval dish attributed to Bernard Palissy. Decorated with fish, lizards, a snake, shells and plants, all in high relief. (Victoria and Albert Museum, London)

203 Panderma prayer rug. Turkish, 19th century. A mosque lamp hangs in the mihrab, which is bordered with carnations. (Private Collection, Milan)

throughout the year, being adjusted to take account of the different lengths of months and, in rare cases, of leap years too; also, a clockwork calendar that shows on what day Easter (or any other feast) will fall on any year, a task so complex that it 'has only been done four times in the whole history of horology' (H. Alan Lloyd).

Perpetual motion clock, a clock which is kept permanently wound up by making mechanical use of changes in atmospheric pressure. **208**

Persian carpets, known by the names of individual producing or marketing centres, renowned in Europe since the Renaissance and distinguished by their complex floral designs, in contrast to geometric Turkish and Caucasian patterns.

Persian embroidery: see **Resht embroidery**.

Persian knot, in carpets; see **Sehna knot**.

Perspective, in particular, the Renaissance art of making pictures with a startlingly realistic three-dimensional effect with inlaid wood.

Peruke, a wig.

Pesaro maiolica, Italian maiolica from the ducal capital of Urbino, wares in the changing styles from the Renaissance to the 19th century.

Pesaro 1771.

Peso, a gold or silver Spanish coin current since the 16th century; more recently a silver coin of most Spanish-speaking countries.

Petit-feu colours: see **Low-temperature colours**.

Petit point: see **Tent stitch**.

Petit porcelain, from a 19th-century French factory at Fontainebleu, notable for figures in revived Rococo style, elaborate clock cases, etc.

Petronel, the short carbine, or arquebus, carried by cavalry in the 16th and early 17th centuries and fired with the butt against the chest.

Petuntse: see **Kaolin**.

Pew group, a lead-glazed earthenware ornament of two or three figures seated on a pew, English, early 18th century, frequently reproduced later.

Pewter, an alloy of tin with a relatively small amount of lead and sometimes antimony, copper or brass, various types according to period and cost; either dull like lead or highly polished like silver; very widely employed throughout the Middle Ages and up to about 1900, associated chiefly with relatively inexpensive (i.e. compared with silver) household wares but also used for elaborate ritual vessels. **209**

Pewter feather, a sample of the medieval pewterers' wares, a strip of metal stamped with the town's coat of arms or other insignia, indicating to potential customers the quality of the metal.

Pewter touch: see **Touch**.

Phaeton, a light and 'sporting' four-wheeled carriage with a high seat, drawn by a pair of horses.

Pharmaceutical jar: see **Drug jar**.

Phenakistoscope, a trade name for one of many types of 19th-century magic lantern, which projected pictures set in a disc that, being revolved, gave an impression of movement.

Philadelphia chair, a Windsor chair.

Philadelphia Chippendale, late 18th-century furniture made by various Philadelphia cabinetmakers in the Chippendale style, notably highboys.

Philadelphia glass, in particular, glassware from an 18th-century glassworks in Kensington, Philadelphia; no examples can be identified for certain.

Phillumeny, collecting matchbox labels.

Phoenix, the mythical bird which, being consumed by fire, rises again from its own ashes, a symbol of immortality; featuring in Classical and Renaissance decoration particularly.

Phoenix glass, made by a Pittsburgh company of that name in the late 19th century, notably cased milk glass known as mother-of-pearl glass.

Phoenixville pottery, in particular, 'majolica' wares, from a pottery in the Pennsylvania town in the second half of the 19th century.

Phonograph, the earliest type of gramophone or record-player.

Phrenological inkwell, in the shape of a human head and marked with the areas believed to be significant by phrenologists, 19th century.

Phyfe furniture, made in the workshop of the famous New York cabinetmaker, Duncan Phyfe, in the late 18th and early 19th centuries, in contemporary European styles. **79**

Physionotrace, a tracing machine used by silhouette portraitists and others, such as St-Memin, in the late 18th and 19th centuries to achieve an accurate and speedy likeness.

Pichet, a small tankard, usually pewter, slightly pear-shaped and sometimes footed, French, 16th to 18th centuries.

Picot, in lace, a decorative edging of small loops; also, a looped relief decoration in glass, sometimes called 'lily-pad', distinctly Art Nouveau in effect though characteristic of mid 19th-century American glass.

Pictorial flask, a glass flask or bottle bearing an enamelled scene, e.g. of hunting, made chiefly in the second half of the 19th century.

Pictorial lace: see **Stumpwork**.

Picture clock, any clock with a picture of some kind on the case; in particular, curiosities of the 18th and 19th centuries in which the clock dial was set in an appropriate place, normally the church tower, in a picture of a village scene.

Picturesque, a term with several different meanings; nowadays, visually attractive 'like a picture'; formerly, almost the opposite, i.e. design based on the study of art, as in some Rococo and Neo-Classical decoration; also, especially of landscape gardening, natural as opposed to formal.

Pi disc, a disc with a hole in the centre, a burial object from the Far East, emblem of heaven, usually made of jade. **211**

Piecrust dish, an earthenware pie dish with a cover in the form (and colour) of a pastry topping.

Piecrust table, a round-topped side-table, usually of pillar-and-claw type, with a narrow rim boldly scalloped in alternate concave and convex curves separated by straight sections; popular since the mid 18th century.

Pied de biche: see **Hind's foot**.

Pier, a structural support such as a buttress, the section of a wall between large windows, or a square column.

Pierced, openwork in hard materials, especially silver and other metals, but also wood, porcelain, etc.; any pattern that is cut right through the material; see also **Cut-card**. **73**

Pier glass, a tall mirror on the wall between windows, sometimes combined with a pier table.

Pier table, a side-table, usually semi-circular, designed to stand against the wall between windows, thus frequently made in pairs (or more), often the subject of the most accomplished art of Louis Quinze ébénistes; see also **Console table**.

Pietà, in Christian art a work of piety, usually a representation of a woman, representing the mother of Jesus, mourning over her dead Son.

Pietra dura, a type of mosaic used for table tops, made of small pieces of coloured stone including gem stones, associated particularly with Renaissance Florence.

Pigeon hole, a small open compartment in a bureau, so-called for its resemblance to the hole in a pigeon coop; hence 'pigeon holes' a humorous term for the stocks in the 17th century.

Pigeonwood, tropical American wood of obscure type, resembling the plumage of the pigeon, used in early 18th-century furniture.

Piggin, a small wooden milk pail, perhaps used as a measure.

Pike, a long spear carried by foot soldiers in the 16th and 17th centuries.

Pilaster, a flat-sided column attached to and projecting from a wall, decorative rather than structural, adopted from Classical architecture and fairly fre-

quently employed in case furniture since the Renaissance. **47**

Pile, in carpets, the loops made by the knotted threads; similarly, in cloth, the nap, especially of soft, thick fabrics like velvet; also, a javelin, a post driven into the ground supporting a structure of some kind, etc.

Piled cups, or beakers, drinking vessels that fit one inside another.

Pilgrim bottle, a flask or bottle in the shape of a globe flattened at the sides, as in its descendant, the canteen, and with ring handles on each shoulder for a carrying cord; made in every conceivable medium since ancient times both as functional and decorative vessels.

Pilgrim furniture, a term occasionally applied to the earliest New England colonial furniture, some of it probably made in England; see also **Brewster chair**.

Pilgrim's sign, a metal medallion distributed to pilgrims at various medieval shrines, fakes being perhaps more common than the genuine articles; see also **Billy and Charley**.

Pilkington pottery, early 20th-century English art pottery remarkable for effects achieved with various coloured glazes, associated with the Lancashire glass factory still operating.

Pillar and claw, the commonest form of construction in small round tables, from about 1800, a central supporting column on a tripod, the feet of which are generally of curved, scroll-like form.

Pillar and scroll, a form occurring in cabinets and, more particularly, certain early 19th-century shelf clocks, having a scrolled pediment and a column at each corner of the face.

Pillar carpets, long, narrow carpets for cladding columns.

Pillar clock, the hour being indicated by a pointer moving along a vertical scale; also, a clock in which pillars (Classical columns, twist-turned pillars, etc.) form a prominent part of the case.

Pillar moulding, in glass, ribs raised in relief on a vessel, made by hand while the metal is still soft, a form of decoration found on Roman glass.

Pill box, a small box, often highly decorated for carrying pills. **210**

Pillow lace, or bobbin lace, made with a number of threads, variously plaited, at a time, the threads being held on bobbins; used particularly for pillow covers; the basic form of lace other than needlepoint.

Pill slab, a slab of marble or glazed earthenware for mixing apothecaries' wares, sometimes bearing insignia of the guild.

Pincered, in glass, relief decoration (e.g. pillar moulding) made with pincers while the metal is hot and soft, rather than in a mould.

Pinchbeck, an alloy of copper and zinc invented by Christopher Pinchbeck in the early 18th century as a substitute for gold,

which it resembles, in watches, jewellery, etc.

Pinched glass, shaped with hand tools; see also **Pincered, Quilling**.

Pincushion, a small padded cushion for holding loose pins safely; hence, **pincushion seat**, a small padded seat on a stool or chair.

Pine: see **Deal**.

Pineapple ware, 18th-century yellow-and green-glazed pottery in the shape of the fruit; see also **Cauliflower ware**.

Pine-tree shilling, the oldest silver coin in North America, minted in Massachusetts in the mid 17th century.

Pinking: see **Pouncework**.

Pin lock, the oldest type of lock, wooden, in which the bolt-latch was held in place by pins that were raised by turning a key; known in ancient Egypt.

Pinnacle, the highest point of (chiefly) a building, a finial; more strictly, a conical or pyramidal roof on turrets, etc. in Gothic architecture.

Pinten, small stoneware tankards, German, from the early 16th century.

Pinxit, or pinx., on an engraving, 'he painted', indicating the name of the original artist; see also **Del**.

Pinxton porcelain, from the short-lived factory (about 1800) established by William Billingsley near Nottingham, making soft-paste porcelain in the manner of Derby.

Pipe, a large barrel or cask, traditionally equivalent to two hogsheads, for wine.

Pipe clay, a fine white clay used for making tobacco pipes and as a cleaning agent, e.g. for white canvas or webbing.

Pipe dryer, pipe kiln, etc., wrought iron stands, commonly consisting of circular bands linked by two staves, for cleaning and drying churchwarden pipes.

Pipe rack, a wooden stand, in various forms, often a disc mounted on a pillar and base, with holes for tobacco pipes.

Pipe stopper, a small tool with a flat, round end for pressing tobacco into a pipe bowl, made in many media and a variety of amusing or curious forms since the 17th century; see also **Smoker's companion**.

Piping, reeding.

Pipkin, a small earthenware pot or metal saucepan.

Piqué-work, a term describing several forms of decoration, in particular miniature inlay, typically of specks of gold in tortoiseshell, in small articles such as snuff boxes and jewellery; also, a type of stiff, ribbed cotton cloth with raised pattern.

Pirlie-pig, a money-box.

Pistol, a small gun with curved stock for one hand only. **83, 106, 291**

Pistole, a small gold coin, originally issued in Spain about 1600.

Pistol handle, a knife handle curved like that of a pistol.

Pitcher, a large jar or jug, in particular a vessel of baluster form with a narrow neck and handles placed like ears. **112**

Pitkin glass, small bottles or flasks of generally oval form with moulded ribbing, associated with a Connecticut glassworks in operation about 1800.

Pitschen, small pewter tankards or jugs, German, 18th century.

Pittsburgh glass, products of the prosperous Pittsburgh industry under way before 1800 and leading the country thanks to technical forwardness; notable especially for early pressed glass of outstanding quality both in the metal and execution of the ware. **217**

Place's stoneware, the product of a Yorkshire artist of the 18th century whose experiments in mixing different clays had a strong influence on the development of Staffordshire pottery.

Plackart, in armour, an extra, reinforcing plate over the cuirass.

Plaid, a woollen material in checked or tartan pattern, as worn traditionally in the Scottish Highlands.

Plancher, a floorboard.

Planchette, a heart-shaped wooden board on small wheels with a hole for a pencil, which when the fingers of several people are placed on it may inscribe words apparently without conscious direction.

Plancier, the strip below a cornice.

Planetarium: see **Orrery**.

Planetenkrug, German stoneware jugs and tankards, from the 15th century, decorated with personalized representations of the planets in enamels.

Planewood, an almost-white, tough, but rather soft wood, used for inexpensive furniture in the 18th century, often painted.

Planished, in metalwork, smoothed by hammering with a rounded hammer.

Planked, of furniture (particularly oak chests, etc.), constructed from plain boards, not panelled.

Plaque, an ornamental plate on a wall or inlaid in furniture; see also **Medallion, Patera. 212**

Plaquette, a small plaque, particularly one bearing a religious or domestic scene sometimes found on old pewter, etc.

Plasma, a variety of quartz, green, once used for carved ornaments, also jewellery; see also **Chrysoprase**.

Plaster, a composition of lime and sand, or gypsum, which can be moulded when damp, hardening as it dries; see also **Plaster of Paris**.

204 Pen box. Persian, Khorassan, 1210. Bronze, decorated with silver inlay showing extremely stylized animals and script. (Freer Gallery of Art, Washington)

205 Porcelain plate. Paris, 1860. (Musée des Arts Décoratifs, Paris)

206 Green Passlas with prunts. German, early 16th century. (Kunstgewerbemuseum, Cologne)

206

207 Louis XVI perfume burner.
By Paul Gouthière (1732–1814).
The red jasper vase is supported on
a gilt bronze tripod decorated with
satyr's masks, grapes and a coiled
serpent. (Wallace Collection,
London)

208 Pendulum clock. English, by
James Cox, 1772. Worked by
atmospheric pressure and known as
a perpetual motion clock. (Victoria
and Albert Museum, London)

Plaster of Paris, powdered and calcined gypsum which, mixed with water, forms a mouldable paste; extensively used for relief decoration in furniture, e.g. as a basis for gilding, and for modelling, repairs, etc.

Plasterware, figures cast in plaster of Paris, often small-scale copies of well-known sculptures, sometimes rather crudely painted, from the early 18th century.

Plastics: see **Bakelite, Celluloid.**

Plata, silver (Spanish).

Plate, originally solid silver; subsequently, silver-plated metalware, chiefly copper; see also **Sheffield plate, Electroplate.**

Plate armour, made of steel sheets, as distinct from mail; from the 14th century a fully enveloping suit.

Plateau, a tray or a set of fitting trays, often mounted on small feet, which stood on the fashionable late 18th-century dining table, bearing a centrepiece, épergne, cruet, candlesticks, etc.; see also **What-not.**

Plate glass, sheet glass polished on both sides for use in mirrors, windows, etc.

Plate mark, in printing, a line made by the edge of the plate sometimes discernible in engravings.

Plate money, large, square copper coins, the size of plates, current in 17th-century Scandinavia.

Plate pail, a wooden container or rack for carrying dinner plates between the dining room and the kitchen.

Plate pewter, pewter flatware (plates and dishes) made of an alloy of tin and copper in proportions of about 3 to 1 in the 17th century and earlier.

Plateresque, i.e. 'in the manner of silver (*plata*)', a description applied to the marquetry and relief patterns of Spanish furniture in the Renaissance period.

Plate warmer, a stand of various kinds for holding plates near the fire.

Platform rocker, a rocking chair that rocks on a stationary base, first made in the 19th century.

Plating, coating base metals with silver or gold; see also **Electroplate, Gilding.**

Platinum, a precious metal, more costly, harder and whiter than gold and unknown before the 18th century, sparingly used in jewellery.

Playing card, one of a set or pack of cards used in various games of chance and skill, from the Middle Ages; see also **Tarot card.**

Pleated, cloth folded at one end into triple thicknesses, like a Z, and pressed, flowing free at the other end, as in a pelmet or valance; a term also applied to a relief pattern of apparently overlapping vertical strips in other media.

Plinth, a base, usually square or rectangular, originally in a Classical column, subsequently in any case furniture that stands flat on the floor, without feet; also, the square base of a vase, the pedestal for a sculpture, or for a bronze figure, for example.

Plique à jour, in jewellery, a pattern of differently coloured enamels set in wire, having an effect like a stained-glass window in miniature; see also **Cloisonné.**

Plumet, a pear-shaped lead weight with a loop at the top, as used by fishermen to plumb the depth; also, a silver implement of this form used in the 18th century for obscure purpose, perhaps fastening the buttons on tight-fitting gloves.

Plum-pudding wood, a type of mahogany that has irregular black spots like the fruit in a plum pudding; a similar effect may be seen in other woods, e.g. maple.

Plum wood, a strong, heavy fruit wood, dark red shading to yellow, used quite widely in English furniture before the 18th century.

Plush, a material of silk, wool and/or cotton with a soft and luxuriant pile, almost like fur, used for upholstery particularly in Victorian times (especially in red) but has been known since the Middle Ages.

Pluvial, a long cloak of ritual significance; see also **Cope.**

Plymouth porcelain, very early English hard-paste porcelain made at Plymouth for a short period by William Cookworthy (who moved to Bristol in 1770), many imperfections (soon to be overcome and merely enhancing its rarity value), rather crude under-glaze blue painting in Chinese style. **213**

Plywood, made of three or more very thin boards or veneers glued together, the grain in each sheet going in contrary directions to prevent warping; chiefly a 20th-century technique.

Pocket bottle, a hip flask.

Pocket watch, any watch between the original pendant type and the invention of the wrist watch and many since.

Point d'Angleterre, Brussels lace (not English).

Point d'Hongrie, a zig-zag pattern in embroidery, widely employed for upholstery.

Point lace, needlepoint (rather than pillow lace).

Poison bottle, a small bottle in blue glass, often with a bright-cut design in relief, the distinctive colour and design adopted to prevent disaster due to mistaken identity.

Poitrel, in armour, a breastplate, particularly one worn by a horse rather than its rider; also, a bodice.

Pokerwork, a pattern in wood burnt out with a hot poker, a popular domestic craft in the 19th century.

Pole arms, cutting or thrusting weapons on longish handles such as spears. **214**

Pole-axe, a long-handled axe carried by foot soldiers in the Renaissance period, usually with a hammer head opposite the axe blade.

Pole glass, a tall beaker with a foot and trailed spiral decoration, perhaps suggesting a barber's pole, German, 16th to 17th century.

Pole medallions, in oriental carpets, a decorative pattern of small medallions with a pole running down the centre, usually in the ground around the central motif, e.g. in Hamadan carpets.

Pole screen, a firescreen mounted on a pole, usually with tripod or pillar and claw base, from the late 17th century.

Poleyne, a long, pointed shoe worn in the Middle Ages, apparently originating in Poland; also, a term in armour for a plate guarding the knee or lower portion of the leg.

Polish, in wood, the application of beeswax, linseed oil, etc., laboriously rubbed into the surface for a smooth shiny finish; also, such a finish achieved more easily by some type of varnish, as in French polish; in stone or glass, rubbing with a very fine powder, sometimes to melt a thin layer of the mineral which hardens to a perfectly smooth surface.

Political flask, a bottle or flask bearing a portrait of a presidential candidate or an appropriate slogan, associated with American elections since the early 19th century; see also **Gin bottle.**

Pollarded wood, the timber of trees that have been regularly lopped, tending to produce denser grain and stronger wood.

Polonaise carpets, rare and luxurious Persian carpets, chiefly 17th-century, probably from Kashan, distinguished by comparative freedom of design, usually floral, silk; the name arising from an error due to Polish ownership of a collection of such carpets exhibited at the Paris exhibition of 1878.

Polychrome, many colours; in porcelain, usually referring to low-temperature enamel colours; also, pottery in variously coloured slips; in particular, a type of 10th-century Byzantine ware (mainly surviving in fragments) with under-glaze enamel colours.

Polygonal, many-sided.

Polyopticon, a cheap type of magic lantern.

Pomade bottle, various types of bottle and jar, since the 16th century, made for a scented ointment applied to the skin, or oil for the hair.

Pomander, a small, pierced, usually spherical box, frequently silver, sometimes gold, ivory, etc., containing sweet-smelling herbs in divided compartments, hung around the neck or from the wrist, etc., by a chain, mainly before the 18th century; see also **Musk apple, Vinaigrette.**

Pomegranate, a fruit that appears frequently in decoration, particularly oriental, being a symbol of plenty. **231**

Pommel, a knob or finial, particularly the knob at the end of a sword hilt, or at the front of a saddle. **34**

Pomona glass, late 19th-century art glass originated by the New England Glass Co., pale yellowish orange, with a frosted appearance achieved by etching and floral decoration; chiefly mould-blown vases, jars, etc.

Pompadour, the style associated with the ascendancy of Mme de Pompadour in the Louis XV period, in particular the hairstyle in which the hair is rolled back off the forehead; also, a bright pink colour, in upholstery and ceramics; furniture in Turkish style; a floral design (or modelled flowers) in porcelain; a similar, pink-and-blue design in embroidery, etc. **228**

Pompeiian style, early Neo-Classical design influenced by the discoveries made at Pompeii.

Pongee, a type of Chinese silk.

Poniard, a dagger, especially a small dagger with narrow, needle-like blade, easily concealed.

Pontil mark, a rough mark, approximately circular, on the bottom of glass vessels, made by the removal of the pontil rod (attached to the bottom of the glass to remove it from the blow-pipe), found on all glass before about 1750, but not usually after about 1850.

Pontypool ware, japanned metal, from the late 18th century, made at Pontypool, Monmouthshire or (usually spelled Ponti-pool) in the English Midlands.

Poplarwood, a very pale yellow or greyish, rather soft wood with close grain, of the white and black (not Lombardy) poplar, sometimes stained and used in early inlays and later for floorboards, waggons, etc., requires careful drying.

Poplin, formerly a fine, corded, silk-and-wool material, associated particularly with Dublin, used for clothes and, some varieties, for upholstery.

Poppyhead, a carved finial in Gothic woodwork, frequently of plant-like form and topped with an acorn, found most typically on the gabled ends of pews in medieval churches.

Porcelain, the most generally admired ceramic, not made in Europe until the 18th century, but known in China nearly a thousand years earlier; see also **Bone china, Hard-paste porcelain, Soft-paste porcelain.**

Porcelain de Paris: see **Paris porcelain.**

Porcellanous, 'like porcelain', a term applied to relevant types of glass or stoneware.

Porcellein-glas, opaque-white glass, superficially similar to porcelain; see **Milk glass.**

Porphyry, a hard feldspathic rock, generally red, used ornamentally and for table tops since ancient Egypt; also, a red colour, like porphyry; hence, porphyry porcelain, etc.

Porringer, a small, shallow, silver basin with a single handle, in England usually called a bleeding bowl; also, a two-handled vessel of similar form to a mug, but often with a lid; see also **Caudle cup, Posset pot. 216**

Porron, a glass vessel something like a vase with a long, tapering spout, from which wine can be poured down the throat without touching the mouth, Spanish, 17th and 18th centuries.

Portable barometer, mounted on a turned wooden pillar with tripod feet of brass, current about 1700.

Portable sundial, known from the 16th century and probably older, made in wood, ivory etc., a flat case the lid of which raises to a vertical position, with a rod to cast the shadow and compass to place the dial in the correct position; other types also known, e.g. the shepherd's sundial.

Porter's chair, a straight-backed leather-covered armchair, sometimes a wing chair; see also **Hall chair.**

Portfolio stand, in appearance a large rectangular box on a stand, the sides of which open out to a horizontal position to permit inspection of documents, etc.; see also **Print cabinet.**

Portland vase, a Wedgwood jasperware vase modelled on a famous Roman cameo-glass vase in the British Museum; see also **Northwood school.**

Portmanteau, a term describing an article that fulfills two or more separate purposes, e.g. convertible furniture; also, a type of travelling bag that opens into two more or less equal parts, or a clothes rack.

Portobello ware: see **Pratt ware.**

Portrait, a representation, usually in paint, of a real person; hence, **portrait flasks, portrait medallions,** etc.

Portuguese leg, on furniture of the second half of the 17th century, a turned leg with a large bulb or knop towards the top and often a square section where the stretchers are fitted.

Posset pot, a china (particularly delftware) pot with two handles and domed lid, similar to a caudle cup but distinguished from it (and from other similar vessels, e.g. loving cup, porringer) by the presence of a spout; for a hot, spiced, alcoholic drink called posset; 17th and 18th centuries.

Posy holder, a portable vase, for carrying a posy of flowers; made in many shapes and media, including silver, in the 19th century.

Pot, a term used rather vaguely in various periods, covering virtually any type of hollow ware of which the height is greater than the width; also, a round, 17th-century steel helmet, like a large skullcap.

Potash glass, made with potash, derived from wood ash, rather than soda, as a fusing agent; better for engraving, not so amenable to moulding; characteristic of much German glass.

Potato ring, a dish ring, specially Irish.

Pot belly, a pewter measure of swelling, bombé shape; also, a 19th-century stove of similar form.

Pot board, the lowest shelf of a cupboard or dresser.

Pot cupboard, a small cupboard on four legs, sometimes with drawers, for a chamber pot.

Potemkin glass, late 18th-century Russian glassware from a factory that supplied the imperial court and for a short time also produced commercial tableware.

Pothook, an iron hook for hanging a pot or kettle over the fireplace.

Potiche, an oriental vase, in particular the familiar baluster-shaped vase, sometimes with lid, which was a traditional form in Chinese porcelain, often reproduced in the West.

Potichomania, a 19th-century fashion for decorating plain glass vessels with designs from oriental porcelain printed on paper and glued to the inside of the glass.

Pot lace, lace with a motif in the form of a two-handled jar, associated particularly with Antwerp.

Pot lids, white eathenware lids for pots containing fish paste, hair oil, etc., with colourful printed scenes, from the mid

209 English pewter teapot and sugar bowl. Marked Sheffield, 18th century. (Private Collection, Trieste)

210 Pill box in the Art Nouveau style. Silver with three stones. (Private Collection, Trieste)

211 Ritual Pi disc. Chinese, Warring States period (481-221 BC). Off-white nephritic jade with stylized mythical animals in high relief. (William Rockhill Nelson Gallery of Art, Kansas City)

212 Small Louis XVI mahogany cupboard with Sèvres biscuit plaques. By Etienne Avril (1748–91). (Château de Fontainebleau)

19th century, originally chiefly by Pratt of Fenton; recently a very popular collector's item and thus much reproduced; see also **Pratt ware**.

Pot-metal, a metal of which pots were made, including a copper-lead alloy and cast iron; also, stained glass that is coloured all through, not enamelled.

Potpourri jar, a porcelain, glass, silver, etc. jar, sometimes with pierced lid, for a potpourri—a sweet-smelling mixture of dried flower petals, herbs, etc.

Potsdam glass, from the famous glassworks near Berlin founded in the late 17th century, notable for the early development of a rich ruby-red glass, often expertly engraved, and for milk glass that survived the challenge of Meissen porcelain.

Potsherd, a broken fragment of pottery, as found on archaeological sites.

Potstone, a variety of soapstone, easily worked and resistant to heat, used for a variety of household vessels since prehistoric times.

Pottery, strictly, clay vessels made by a potter on a wheel, but used more often of earthenware and stoneware (not porcelain) generally.

Pottle, a large earthenware, pewter, etc. pot for ale, containing about a posset (half an imperial gallon).

Pouch table, a small worktable or sewing table, frequently round or oval, with a wooden top and rim above a pleated bag, early 18th century.

Poudreuse, a dressing table, French, 18th century.

Pouffe, a large, round cushion with no visible framework, or an upholstered stool, popular from the early 19th century.

Pouncebox, a small cup, caster or box, glass, silver, etc., containing pounce—a powder sprinkled on parchment after writing; frequently incorporated in an inkstand; see also **Pumice. 137**

Pouncet box, a small decorative box with pierced lid or sides, usually round, with compartments for herbs, similar to a pomander but straight-sided.

Pouncework, in silver, a decorative ground of small, chased dots, like grains of sand, from the 16th century.

Poupard, a doll without legs, often mounted on a stick, popular in Victorian times; some with jointed arms and heads, some talking, etc.

Powder blue, under-glaze decoration on porcelain achieved by blowing the pigment (in powdered form) through gauze on to the greased surface of the biscuit, giving an effect of very fine grains; originally a Chinese technique.

Powder clock, a series of hourglass flasks in a frame which indicate the quarters, halves and three-quarters of an hour. **215**

Powder flask, or powder horn, originally an animal's horn, later many other shapes and materials, for carrying gunpowder for muzzle-loading guns. **220**

Prague porcelain, in particular, 19th-century porcelain produced in great quantity on the decline of old centres like Vienna and Meissen; also, early 20th-century pottery influenced by contemporary art movements such as Cubism.

Prase, a green, translucent, quartz stone, inferior to the better-known variety, chrysoprase.

Pratt ware, late 18th- and early 19th-century English earthenware decorated with distinctive high-temperature colours (yellow, brown, blue and green) perhaps originated by Felix Pratt of the Fenton, Staffordshire, pottery, but made in many places.

Prayer rugs, Islamic rugs used for daily prayers, with the central design in the form of the mihrab or niche, made in most carpet-making regions of the Muslim world. **203**

Première partie, marquetry in which the pattern in brass is set in a tortoiseshell ground, rather than the other way round; see also **Boulle work**.

Press, a large cupboard or wardrobe, particularly for linens.

Press bed, a bed that folds up and is stored in a cupboard during the day, an arrangement known in the 17th century.

Press book, a term applied to a book of interest for the place or manner of its printing, e.g. by small or private presses.

Pressed flowers, real flowers dried and pressed, frequently between the pages of a book, and sometimes arranged as flat posies, mounted on cloth; a popular hobby in the 19th century.

Pressed glass, glassware formed in a mould by mechanical pressure rather than by blowing, an early 19th-century invention first exploited by the great American glassworks; see also **Sandwich glass. 217**

Preuning ware, lead-glazed jugs and other ware, of exceedingly fine quality in decoration (frequently religious scenes) made in a prominent Nuremberg workshop in the 16th century.

Pricket, in a candlestick, a spike instead of a socket for the candle; also, a spiked fence, etc.

Pricking, a raised pattern made with the point of a needle, particularly on early silver.

Prie-dieu, an upholstered single chair with a low seat and padded armrest on the back, suitable for kneeling on, 19th century; also, a tall medieval desk with wooden knee rest, after which the chair was named.

Prince-of-Wales chair, a late 18th-century English chair with a carved representation of the three-plumes crest of the Prince of Wales on the back.

Prince's metal, a copper-tin alloy, a late 17th-century imitation of gold similar to Pinchbeck and likewise named after its alleged inventor, Prince Rupert (1619–82).

Prince's wood: see **Kingwood**.

Print, an impression, usually from an inked metal plate, woodblock, etc., bearing the design.

Print cabinet, a chest for large prints, often with very shallow, wide drawers, sometimes with a slant top, 19th century.

Printed porcelain: see **Transfer-printed**.

Printies, circular hollows cut in glass, a pattern dating from about 1800; sometimes seen in Baccarat paperweights, cut through a cased layer of coloured glass to the clear glass behind.

Prism cutting, in glass, found on a stepped foot of a wine glass or neck of a decanter, V-shaped rings of decreasing size making a zig-zag outline, late 18th and 19th centuries.

Prisoner-of-war work, in particular ornaments, notably model ships and wooden boxes, carved by French prisoners in England during the Napoleonic wars, often astonishingly delicate and accurate.

Profile, a term employed for profile portrait miniatures in which details are painted in, as distinct from cut silhouette portraits.

Profile perdu, a portrait in which the subject's face is turned away by more than 45°.

Projection clock, a type of night clock with a lamp behind the dial which, when the lamp was lit, was projected on to the wall or ceiling; known since the early 18th century.

Promethean, an early 19th-century fire-lighting device, consisting of a roll of paper with a percussion cap at the end which, being struck, lit the paper.

Protoporcelain, stoneware approaching the character of porcelain, in particular the feldspathic, glazed stoneware of the Han dynasty.

Provenance, the recorded ownership through the years of a work of art, which may establish its authenticity.

Providence glass, glassware, including early pressed glass, from a short-lived factory in Providence, Rhode Island, in the first half of the 19th century.

Prunk Uhr, the name given to a type of Baroque south German clock of highly elaborate design, including moving figures, complicated chime and so much ornamentation that the actual dial is almost lost.

Prunts, applied round blobs on glass vessels, notably medieval German glass, sometimes modelled into decorative shapes; see also **Claw beaker**. 60, 206, 223

Prussian decanter, a type of glass decanter popular about 1800, rounded body sloping inwards slightly from shoulder to base, often with mushroom stopper and usually heavily cut.

Psaltery, a medieval stringed instrument somewhat like a zither, but plucked not struck, the strings being stretched across a soundbox, usually approximately triangular, held in front of the chest or resting in the lap.

Psyche mirror, a cheval looking glass.

Pudding dish, a plain bowl or basin, round or oval, sometimes in silver, since the 18th century.

Puginesque, in the manner of Augustus Pugin, the immensely influential architect and designer who was the leading advocate of the mid 19th-century Gothic revival in England. 285

Pulse watch, a late 17th- or 18th-century watch, made to order for doctors, with a seconds hand on a separate dial and a lever for stopping the watch.

Pulvinated, curving outwards, like a cushion (Latin, *pulvinus*), a term applied in architecture to a frieze with a convex curve.

Pumice, a glassy, porous stone, used as a mild abrasive in polishing metal, or, ground into a powder, for finishing felt hats (pouncing).

Punch bowl, a large, footed bowl, typically in silver with two ring handles, for serving the wine-based drink called punch, from the 17th century; also occurring in glass, delftware, porcelain, etc.; see also **Monteith**. 183

Punch box, a jack-in-the-box.

Punched work, relief decoration in metalwork made by hammering with a punch bearing the design, a somewhat primitive method sometimes used in silver before about 1650, common on coins; see also **Repoussé**.

Punch ladle, a ladle with cup-shaped bowl sometimes found in silver with matching punch bowl.

Punch pot, a large china teapot, sometimes of spherical form (the lid being a segment of the sphere), and occasionally accompanied by a stand containing a lamp, for serving punch, 18th century.

Punto in aria, a type of extremely delicate needlepoint lace.

Punty mark: see **Pontil mark**.

Purdah, a curtain or veil, in particular one screening women from male view, as used in the East.

Purdonium, a coal scuttle, particularly one with a lid and metal liner, 19th century.

Purfle, an ornamental border, as of a garment; hence, an ornamental crest on a roof, etc., or ornamentation in wood that resembles lace or drapery; in particular, an inlaid border on the back of a violin.

Puritan furniture, a term sometimes applied to certain early 17th-century English pieces, but more commonly to early American colonial furniture; see also **Pilgrim furniture**.

Puritan spoon, an English, 17th-century silver spoon, with a relatively wide and untapered handle squared off and notched at the end.

Puritan watch, the name given to certain English watches of the first half of the 17th century, oval in form and strikingly plain by comparison with the generally elaborate decoration of the period.

Purled, twisted or plaited like wire or thread; in glass, a lacy, diaper pattern.

Purpleheart, a tropical American hardwood that turns purple when cut, used for inlays and banding in the second half of the 18th century.

Purple lustre, 19th-century Staffordshire lustreware varying from pink to mauve to purple, achieved by the application of purple of Cassius (containing tin and gold) over the glaze.

Purple of Cassius: see **Purple lustre**.

Purple slag, a waste product of steel furnaces, used by glassmakers from the mid 19th century to make purplish marble glass, press-moulded.

Purse, made in many forms through the centuries, in particular silver-link purses of the 18th century; silver frames of earlier canvas purses survive, the fabric having long rotted; see also **Miser's purse**.

Putto, a nude figure of a small chubby boy, a favourite motif of the Baroque period. 124

Puzzle cup, a cup so made, in one way or another, that it was difficult to drink from; see also **Puzzle jug**.

Puzzle fan, a fan on which different pictures are visible according to the angle from which it is viewed, an 18th-century curiosity.

Puzzle jug, an earthenware jug, perhaps best known in delftware, from the 17th century, jokingly designed so that it was impossible to pour successfully by someone who did not know the trick; a common type having a pierced neck and three or four spouts connected with the body of the jug by a tube through the handle, the liquid being extracted by syphoning through one spout while blocking off the others; see also **Cadogan teapot**.

Puzzle ring, in jewellery, three gold rings mounted with precious stones that could be worn independently but also fitted together, whereupon they formed a symbolic religious motif not apparent when the rings were separated; 16th and 17th centuries, central European.

Pyrography: see **Pokerwork**.

Pyrope, a type of garnet, deep but vivid red, perhaps the commonest type used in jewellery, being inexpensive, refractive, and of good colour, usually faceted.

Pyx, in the Middle Ages a chest or coffer; subsequently, a valuable metal box, usually silver, containing the bread in Christian ritual, eventually replaced by the monstrance. 219

Quadrans, a bronze coin of the Roman empire.

Quadrant, a quarter circle; in particular a navigational instrument of that shape for calculating the elevation of a star, used in medieval Europe and probably invented by the Arabs; also, various articles of quarter-circle shape, e.g. a drawer with a curved front and two sides meeting at an angle which swings out on a pivot.

Quadriga, a chariot drawn by four horses in line abreast, a recurring motif in Classical and Baroque design. 218

Quadrigatus, a Roman silver coin, bearing a Janus portrait, with a quadriga on the reverse.

Quadrilobed: see **Quatrefoil**.

Quaich, a silver drinking cup of medieval Scottish origin, a shallow bowl with two flat handles; probably originally wooden, its form sometimes suggesting staved construction; surviving examples mainly of the 17th or early 18th century.

Quail pattern, in English (particularly Worcester) porcelain, a design of a pair of quail (or partridge) in a landscape, derived from a Japanese original.

Quaint, a word applied particularly to a style in English furniture in the late 19th century, characterized by an exaggeration of the style of Art Nouveau—writhing forms, abundant surface decoration, frequent pierced work, etc.

Quaker chair, a name given to a simple, balloon-back, cane-seated, 19th-century chair.

Quarter clock, a clock that strikes every 15 minutes.

Quartering, in furniture, a type of veneer used, for instance, on largeish panels or table tops, four pieces of the same or similar grain being arranged

213 Porcelain figure of a woman. Plymouth. The soft modelling and colours are typical of English production. (City Art Gallery, Plymouth)

214 Italian pole arms. On the left a partisan; on the right a corseca. (Purcelli-Guerra Collection, Gavirate)

215 Powder clock. Italian, 1720. Ebony and ivory. The four flasks show the quarters, halves and three-quarters of the hour. (Science Museum, London)

216 Small two-handled cup usually called a porringer. English, made in York, 1668. Embossed and chased in the Dutch manner. (Victoria and Albert Museum, London)

symmetrically, usually so that the line of the grain in all the four quarters points toward the centre of the surface.

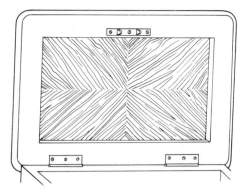

Quarter-round: see Ovolo.

Quartetto, a nest of four tables fitting one inside the next in ascending order of size, found in most drawing rooms about 1800.

Quarto, the size of a book of which each leaf (i.e. two pages) represents one quarter of the printed sheet, usually about 9–10 inches high.

Quartz, a hard, siliceous stone, occurring very widely in a great variety of forms including amethyst, jasper, onyx, etc. as well as rose quartz, smoky quartz (named for their appearance).

Quatrefoil, a form based on four leaves or a four-petalled flower, found in Gothic tracery and sometimes as a small window with the four lobes separated by cusps; also applied to various articles, in particular a mid 18th-century decanter having a body in this form.

Quattrocento, a term sometimes used to describe the 15th century, especially in relation to the arts in Italy.

Queen Anne style, the style in English furniture, architecture, etc. in the reign of Queen Anne (1702–14) or, less strictly, in the early 18th century, a period that witnessed considerable changes, characterized by curved rather than straight forms and generally greater elegance (e.g. introduction of the cabriole leg), growing preference for walnut rather than oak, increased use of upholstery, more restraint in carving, etc.; also the equivalent style in America which lasted until the mid century. **64**

Queen's Burmese, a late 18th-century English version of American Burmese glass, widely copied.

Queen's ware, an improved, harder type of creamware developed by Wedgwood and rapidly adopted by other 18th-century English potters.

Quern, a hand mill for grinding pepper, etc.; also, a mill for grinding corn in the home, the stone turned by hand.

Quicksilver, mercury.

Quill, a pen made from a bird's feather (usually a goose), the end cut into a point (with a penknife).

Quilling, on glass, trailed ornament worked into a pattern like teeth by nips with the pincers at regular intervals.

Quillon, one of the branches of the crossguard of a sword. **34**

Quillwork, or filigree paperwork, narrow strips of twisted, varicoloured paper glued edge-down to a wooden or cloth ground, sometimes incorporating various other materials, used to decorate household articles, including furniture; popular in the 18th century as a domestic craft, though a similar form of decoration was known in the 15th century.

Quilt, a mattress or bed cover consisting of two layers of cloth with a thicker layer of wool padding in between, stitched through in lines up and down and across, forming large squares (sometimes other patterns), decorated with embroidery or patchwork; an outstanding craft in the 17th and 18th centuries particularly; other material, including clothes, was sometimes quilted.

Quimper faience, from a factory in Brittany established in the late 17th century, producing close imitations of Rouen production in the 18th century.

Quinarius, a Roman silver coin worth half a denarius and similar to it, bearing a V, from the 3rd century BC.

Quincento, the 16th century; see also **Quattrocento.**

Quinton, or quinte, a musical stringed instrument of the violin family, with five strings, French, 17th century; there was a treble and a tenor version (quinte).

Quire, a quantity of paper, usually 24 sheets.

Quirk, a narrow groove sometimes found as the final element in a curved moulding, dividing it from the adjacent flat surface.

Quizzing fan, an 18th-century fan for a coy lady, with two peepholes permitting clandestine inspection of the scene while the observer herself remained screened.

Quoin, a cornerstone in a building, or the corner of a room; also, the imitation of corner stones in furniture, e.g. on certain 18th-century English long case clocks.

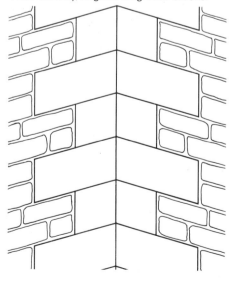

Rabbeted, a type of joint in woodwork; see **Rebate.**

Rabinet, or robinet, a small cannon with pear-shaped barrel.

Rack clock, a clock that is powered by its own weight, late 17th-century German examples being suspended between notched pillars; various types; see also **Gravity clock.**

Radiant, a diamond or other brilliantly reflecting stone.

Raeren ware, jugs and drinking vessels of various kinds in coloured clay or, particularly, dark-brown glazed stoneware, from the Rhineland centre, chiefly late 16th century.

Rag bolt, an iron pin or staple with barbed prong to hold it fast in wood.

Rag doll, a doll made of cloth and stuffed with rags, known since ancient times.

Rail, a horizontal member in furniture, e.g. in the back of a chair.

Raised pattern, a relief pattern, especially when punched or embossed, or embroidered on cloth.

Raising, the method of making metal vessels, especially silver, by heating and hammering into shape on a wooden anvil, once the usual method for jugs, tankards, etc.; see also **Planished.**

Raku ware, Japanese tea bowls in pottery of a calculatedly rough appearance, sometimes black-glazed, undecorated, from the 16th century.

Ramekin, an individual mould for preparing and serving soufflés and cheeses.

Ramie, a fibre derived from a Far Eastern plant, woven into cloth and sometimes used as a substitute for silk.

Ramified, formed in a number of dividing branches, as of a candelabrum.

Ramrod, an iron rod attached to the barrel of a muzzle-loading gun, for ramming the charge down the barrel.

Ram's foot, a cleft hoof surmounted by frilly, wool-like carving, found occasionally in furniture.

Ram's head, a decorative device of Classical times, often employed in Adam-style furniture.

Ram's horn, such a curved form found on the handles of bowls, the thumbpiece of metal tankards, the arms of chairs, etc., chiefly an 18th-century device.

Randolph furniture, in particular, the work of Benjamin Randolph of Philadelphia in the Revolutionary period, noted especially for elaborately carved chairs in a style that has been called 'Chippendale-Gothic'.

Range, a large, cast-iron kitchen stove with an oven on one or both sides of the fire and space on the top for several saucepans to cook at once.

Rap, or rappen, small copper coins of low value, 18th and 19th centuries, in particular an Irish coin or token (rap) of no official value used in lieu of genuine coins.

Rapier, a thin sword with three- or four-sided blade, for thrusting rather than cutting, first used in the Renaissance period, the gentleman's duelling weapon. **222**

Rasp, or rape, a small implement in various forms and materials with a serrated surface for shredding tobacco or spices.

Ratafia glass, a name sometimes given to a narrow-bowled English wine glass of the late 18th century, with one continuous line from rim to foot, supposedly for drinking the liqueur called ratafia; see also **Flute glass. 1**

Rat foot, a term sometimes applied to a ball and claw foot when the claw is of notably skinny, ratlike proportions.

Ratona, a small, low table of a type popular in Spanish America in the late 18th century, with heavily carved frieze and legs.

Ratskanne, a Rhineland stoneware jug with swelling body on a high foot, a similar shape being found in pewter, about the 15th century.

Rat-tail, a characteristic pattern in silver spoons of the late 17th and 18th centuries, having a raised band on the underside of the bowl tapering to a point; also, various other articles incorporating an element in the shape of a rat's tail, e.g. rat-tail hinge.

Rattan, a cane made from the stem of the rattan palm; see also **Bamboo.**

Rauenstein porcelain, Thuringian porcelain, chiefly in imitation of Meissen, from the late 18th century.

Ravar carpets: see **Kerman carpets.**

Ravenscroft glass, late 17th-century glass from the London Glass Sellers' Co.'s glassworks at Henley-on-Thames, Marked with the raven's-head seal of George Ravenscroft (1618–81), whose use of a lead flux revolutionized English glassmaking.

Raynes, or rennes, fine-quality linen of the 15th and 16th centuries, originally imported to England from Rennes, Brittany.

Razor case, a flattish box, often similar to a small knife box, for holding 'cut-throat' razors, sometimes with compartments for other shaving accoutrements.

Reading chair, in particular, a back-to-front chair of the 18th century in which the occupant sat facing the back, resting his book on a slanted book rest, perhaps with candlesticks attached; see also **Cockfighting chair.**

Reading stand, a stand with a sloping surface on which to rest a book; see also **Lectern. 224**

Real, a standard Spanish silver coin from the Renaissance onwards, bearing the royal arms.

Ream, a measure of paper (20 quires); also, to enlarge with a reamer, a tool like a drill.

Rat-tail

Rebab, an ancient stringed musical instrument of the Near East, with no neck, plucked; also, later instruments played with a bow; see also **Rebec.**

Rebate, in woodwork, a joint formed by cutting a recess to fit the end of the member to be joined, e.g. tongue-and-groove boarding; also, a rectangular groove or cavity.

Rebec, a medieval stringed instrument of the violin family (played with a bow), with narrow pear-shaped body and usually three strings, probably derived from the oriental rebab.

Récamier sofa, a Neo-Classical sofa or daybed with curved ends, as appears in a famous portrait of Mme Récamier by J-L. David; see also **Lit en bâteau.**

Recessed, set back, like a panel in a door.

Reclining chair, a 19th-century single (no arms) chair with upholstered back and seat in one continuous curving piece.

Recto, the right-hand page of a book; see also **Verso.**

Redan, a notched edge, like the teeth of a saw, similar to dentils.

Red-figure, the technique of Attic potters from the 6th century BC in which the ground was painted black and the figures left in the red body of the clay, with details added in black.

Redingote, a single- or double-breasted, long-skirted coat which became fashionable in 18th-century France, adapted from the English 'riding coat'.

Red stoneware, the medium of popular, imported Chinese teapots in the 17th century and thus widely imitated in Europe, often appearing as a prelude to true porcelain, notably at Meissen and Fulham (London); see also **Böttger porcelain, Elers redware, Rosso antico.**

Redware, red clay pottery, usually of a primitive kind, often with incised patterns and sometimes ornamented with coloured slips.

Reeding, ornament composed of narrow, vertical, convex bands, the opposite of fluting (and often combined with it).

217 Milk jug and comfit jar in pressed glass. Pittsburgh, about 1830. (Corning Museum of Glass, Corning, New York)

218 Fragment of Byzantine silk serge fabric. 8th century. Medallion with a quadriga design. (Aachan Cathedral treasure)

219 Enamel Pyx. Limoges school,
13th century. Champlevé
decoration of rosettes. (Museo
d'Arte de Cataluña, Barcelona)

220 Powder flask. German, mid
17th century. Wood, inlaid with
bone. (Gallini Collection, Milan)

Refectory table, a long dining table, usually oak, vaguely associated with the refectory of a monastery, and especially popular since the 19th-century Gothic Revival; traditionally accompanied by benches.

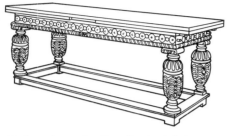

Refraction, the 'bending' of light rays passing through a lens, prism, etc., a phenomenon that accounts for the brilliant effect of cut gems.

Regal, a portable organ from the late Middle Ages, some examples being so small (with pipes an inch long) that they folded up like a suitcase; still made in the 18th century.

Régence, a term sometimes used of the decorative arts in France during the minority of Louis XV (1715–23), a transition between the Baroque and Rococo. **293**

Regency style, the style in English furniture, etc. in the early 19th century (strictly 1811–20, the period of the Regency of George IV), roughly corresponding with the French Empire style, characterized by stricter adherence to Classical forms, darker woods, wide use of brass mounts (especially with Egyptian motifs) and a revival of oriental influence; also called English Empire style. **44, 221, 245**

Reggivaso, a vase- or candlestand of the 18th century often in the form of a black male figure, especially popular in Venice.

Registration mark, on 19th-century English china, a diamond-shaped mark with a large R in the centre and figures or letters in the corners giving the date of registration of the pattern at the patent office; also found on other articles of patented design in the same period.

Regulator, an extremely accurate clock, used for checking others.

Reichsadlerhumpen, a large German glass beaker of the late 16th or 17th century enamelled with the imperial Habsburg double-headed eagle; see also **Humpen**.

Reinicke figures, mid 18th-century Meissen porcelain figures modelled by Peter Reinicke under the supervision of J. J. Kändler.

Relief, ornamentation raised from the general level; see **High relief, Bas-relief**.

Religieuse, a French clock of the late 17th century, with a wooden case usually inlaid with great delicacy but otherwise of relatively simple appearance.

Reliquary, a medieval casket or other container, usually of silver or gold and sometimes with gems, containing some item of religious significance such as the bones of a saint.

Remarque, in engraving, a mark at the edge of a print to indicate the approximate stage at which it was made, usually confined to early impressions; also, any inserted illustration in a print that is separate from the main design.

Remington firearms, by the famous New York gunsmiths established in the mid 19th century, best known for rifles and Civil War revolvers, also makers of, among other arms, a frightening pepper-box pistol.

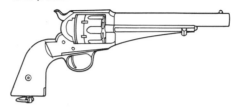

Remington prints, 19th-century coloured prints of the paintings of the American West by Frederick Remington; models of his Bronco Buster sculpture were also widely produced.

Renaissance period, the revival of Classical art and ideas in 15th-century Italy (and somewhat later in the rest of Europe) combined with a marked growth of new techniques and (apparently) a remarkable outburst of talent, which marks the end of the Gothic period and introduces the modern era of comparatively rapid change in styles and methods.

Rendsborg faience, high-temperature blue-painted ware from a Danish factory founded in the mid 18th century, which later converted to faience-fine, black basaltes and other wares.

Reichsadlerhumpen

Reniform, kidney-shaped; see **Kidney desk**.

Rennes faience, from a number of 18th- and 19th-century potteries in the French centre, mainly in the style of Rouen and Marseille enamel painting.

Rennes
ce. 12. 9bre
1763

Rent table, a late 18th- or 19th-century table, basically circular (octagonal, etc.), with drawers all the way round; see also **Drum table**.

Rep, a thickly corded material of silk and/or wool, or cotton, used in upholstery and curtains, in silk mainly for clothes.

Repeater, a semi-automatic rifle; also, a clock which repeats its most recent strike when a lever is operated.

Repository, a large combination-piece incorporating desk, bookcase, clothes cupboard, etc., 18th century, but known primarily from pattern books rather than actual examples; also, any place of storage.

Repoussé, relief decoration on metal made by hammering or punching the metal from the back against some resilient material such as pitch or leather. **110**

Reproduction, a deliberate and exact copy of an earlier work or style, not made with intent to deceive; see also **Fake. 69**

Reredos, a pierced screen of stone or wood separating the choir from the nave in a church, or a screen or curtain behind the altar; also, a fireback.

Reserve, areas left untouched by the colouring (glaze, etc.) in a design; see also **Resist**.

Réseau, a net, used particularly of the ground in lacemaking.

Resht embroidery, a combination of embroidery and patchwork made at the Persian centre in the 18th century, very tiny patches of cloth in bright colours, with gold and coloured threads in chain stitch embroidering the patches; floral and other patterns.

Resist, a material that repels colouring matter (e.g. a textile dye), or ink (in engraving), etc., applied to that part of the design which is to remain uncoloured; see also **Resist-lustre**.

Resist-lustre, in ceramics, a decorative effect most frequently found in silver lustre, the design being painted in a greasy resist medium before application of the lustre (or glaze), the latter being burned off the resist areas during firing.

Restoration, a term sometimes used to describe the period in England immediately following the restoration of Charles II to the throne in 1660.

Restored, of furniture, an old, damaged piece that has been renovated, the important question being how much is original and how much new?

Retable, or retablo, a painting on a wooden panel, usually religious; or, the decorative (painted, carved, etc.) panel or panels behind the cross on an altar.

Reticella, or Greek point, an early form of needlepoint lace developing from cutwork, in which the outline of the pattern was first made with strong thread and the solid areas then stitched in.

Reticello, in glass, a rim or edging made of threads of glass of different colours twisted together like a rope, found in Roman glass; also, lace glass; see also **Latticino**.

Reticulated, a network of similar figures, as in Gothic tracery; also, diaper pattern.

Reticule, a small, loosely woven, net-like bag; sometimes, any small bag and especially one intended to be kept inside a larger bag or a workbasket; also, a papier-mâché or metal case shaped like a Greek vase, fashionable in Paris about 1800.

Reval faience, late 18th-century faience from a short-lived factory in the town in Estonia, chiefly rather coarse-bodied ware in contemporary Scandinavian style.

Rheinsberg faience, from a north German factory founded in the late 18th century, wares similar in type and quality to Magdeburg.

Rhenish, from the Rhineland in south-west Germany. **60, 290**

Rhinegraves, voluminous knee breeches, gathered at the waist, fashionable in the late 17th century.

Rhineland stoneware, tankards, jugs, etc. in blue-grey or brown stoneware, often relief-moulded, made in various Rhineland centres as early as the 12th century but most notably about the 16th, unglazed before about 1500, afterwards salt-glazed; the result of rich local deposits of siliceous clay; much reproduced. **290**

Rhode Island chair, several early New England chairs, including a Windsor chair with a pronounced curve of the lower part of the leg, and an arrow-back spindle chair.

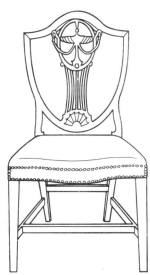

Rhodian pottery: see Isnik ware.

Rhodium, a very hard, white metal similar to platinum and equally expensive, occasionally used for electroplating silver (and tips of steel pen-knibs), sometimes alloyed with platinum.

Rhodochrosite, a softish manganese stone, light red in colour sometimes with dark bands, and easily carved for small ornaments, also used in jewellery.

Rhodonite, a pink or reddish stone with black markings, opaque and harder than rhodochrosite, used mainly in jewellery.

Rhomboid, having four sides, the opposite sides parallel, but no right angles (hence, not square or rectangular).

Ribband-back chair: see **Ribbon-back chair**.

Ribbed, ornament of narrow bands in relief, especially in glass; also, the parts of a curved, supporting framework, e.g. the ridges in a Gothic stone vault.

Ribbon-back chair, a Chippendale chair with openwork back carved in the form of interlacing ribbons. **56**

Ribbonwork, ornament in the form of ribbons, often combined with flowers, occurring frequently in French Rococo furniture, also in ceramics, tapestries, etc.

Ricasso, the untapered section of a sword blade near the hilt, at one time a separately made piece of metal.

Rice-grain porcelain, an ornamental device in porcelain consisting of perforations filled with clear glaze, looking like rice grains, forming a pattern; known in China and Persia in the 16th century or earlier.

Rice paper, a fibrous material originally made in China from the soft core of an oriental tree; edible.

Richelieu work, a 19th-century form of embroidery similar to old cutwork, the pattern outlined in buttonhole stitch on a linen ground and the remainder of the ground subsequently cut away.

Ricketts glass, early 19th-century cut glass and bottles made by a firm of that name in Bristol, England, bottles often bearing seals of wine merchants who ordered them.

Ridgway china, a variety of wares from a 19th-century pottery in Hanley, Staffordshire, including blue-painted earthenware, 'stone china', lustreware, porcelain, etc.

Riesener furniture, by a French cabinetmaker of that name in the second half of the 18th century, patronized by the court, 'the greatest cabinetmaker of the period' (Yvonne Brunhammer). **74**

Rifling, spiral grooves, particularly inside the barrel of a gun to impart spin to the bullet, a principle known to Renaissance gunsmiths but not generally adopted until the 19th century.

Rigaree, applied decoration of glass with close-set, narrow, vertical bands, sometimes in different colours.

Rimonim, the small silver bells attached to the Scroll of the Law in Jewish ritual.

Rimu, a New Zealand softwood, brown to red, with varied markings, sometimes used for veneers.

Ring handle, a brass or silver handle in the form of a circle, frequently held in the mouth of a lion mask in the late 18th and 19th centuries.

Ringkrug, a German stoneware vessel made like an upright, hollow ring with a hole through the middle, from the 16th century. **290**

Ring stand, a small stand of metal, glass, etc., a slender cone shape or with a number of branches like a tree, for hanging finger rings.

Ring sundial, a sundial consisting basically of a circular metal band inclined toward the sun, which shines through a hole in the ring on to a scale marked with the hours on the inner surface opposite.

Rippled, a wavy rim on glass, pottery, or furniture (e.g. the edge of a table).

Rising sun, a decorative motif found on some late 18th-century furniture, a fluted semicircle, flat edge down, somewhat similar to the more widely known shell motif.

Rittenhouse clocks, late 18th-century American clocks by David Rittenhouse (1732–96) of Philadelphia, who made long-case clocks, orreries, and scientific instruments of outstanding quality.

Roan, soft sheepskin leather used as a cheap substitute for morocco in bookbinding about 1800.

Robinia wood: see Acacia.

Rocaille, 'rockwork', as in gardens and fountains, the origin of the term Rococo, decoration of stones, shell forms, etc.; see also **Rococo style**.

Rock crystal, the perfectly clear, colourless variety of quartz that glassmakers strove to imitate, used for carving since the Middle Ages (and for crystal balls); see also **Crystal. 111**

Rocking chair, originally (about 1700) a simple stick armchair the legs of which were set in long, curved rails; subsequently, any chair that rocks backward and forward.

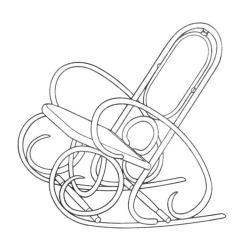

Rockingham ware, in England, the products of a Yorkshire pottery operating from about the mid 18th to the mid 19th century, first maker of the Cadogan teapot, other wares similar to Leeds, with characteristic purplish-brown 'Rockingham' glaze, also bone china of fine quality with luscious enamels and much gilding; in America, dark-brown, often mottled, glazed earthenware, made at Bennington and various other 19th-century centres.

Rockwork, designs in pebbles as in Japanese gardens, on the base of porcelain figures, etc.; see also **Rocaille**.

221 Regency sofa in gilded wood with lion's-paw feet. English, about 1805. (Victoria and Albert Museum, London)

222 Rapier with basket hilt. Spanish, second half of the 17th century. The work of the Toledo swordsmith, Thomas De Ayala. (Don Juan Institute of Valencia, Madrid)

223 Wine glass, called a rummer.
Rhenish, about 1600. This type was
very common in the Rhine valley, a
great wine-producing area.
(Kunstgewerbemuseum, Cologne)

224 Rotating reading stand in the
Art Nouveau style. Designed by
A. Charpentier in 1901. (Musée des
Arts Décoratifs, Paris)

Rococo style, in European art and design the style prevalent roughly from 1730 to 1760, developing from Baroque and merging into Neo-Classical, associated particularly with France; characterized by boldly curving, even contorted forms and profuse decoration of shells, scrolls, flowers, etc., and by asymmetry of design (the most marked departure from Baroque) that derived from oriental influence; never fully accepted in England, except perhaps in (French-influenced) porcelain; a Rococo revival occurred in the early 19th century. **232**

Rodney decanter, a type of decanter associated with Admiral Lord Rodney (1719–92); see **Ship's decanter.**

Rods, in glass, narrow cylinders of metal with a colourful, decorative pattern in cross section; see also **Canes.**

Roemer: see **Rummer.**

Rogers group, late 19th-century figure groups in plaster, after the folksy models of the New York sculptor John Rogers (1829–1904), sold in large numbers yet no longer common.

Röhrken, German tankards, typically in pewter, of the 17th and 18th centuries, characterized by their slender, almost cylindrical form, widening toward the mouth, usually with hinged cover.

Roll-back chair, an early 19th-century chair in which the back is curved over in a scroll-like form, seen also in the arms of contemporary sofas.

Rolled gold, a thin gold plating on base metal, heated and spread with a roller.

Rolled paperwork: see **Quillwork.**

Rolling-ball clock: see **Ball clock.**

Rolling pin, a wooden cylinder about 12 in. long with a handle at either end for rolling pastry, frequently made in glass from about 1800, often hollow as containers or merely decorative.

Roll-over arm, in an upholstered armchair, a scroll-form arm giving a comfortable, curved armrest.

Roll-top desk, having a quarter-circle, roll-back cover of narrow strips of wood on a flexible backing such as canvas, which slides in grooves; see also **Tambour.**

Romanesque, the style, primarily in architecture, in medieval Europe up to the 12th century, usually known as Norman in England, characterized by the round arch of Roman style, superseded (particularly in north-western Europe) by the Gothic style.

Roman-pillar, relief decoration on glass and ceramics of narrow, vertical bands, convex curved, a form of reeding (like reversed fluting).

Roman spindle, a simple, Windsor-type chair, with a broad, slightly kidney-shaped rail and turned spindles in the back.

Roman striking, in clocks, the use of two bells of different tones, one striking the Is and the other the Vs, so that no more than four notes sound at any hour, a late 17th-century invention.

Romayne work, in Renaissance furniture, a decorative device consisting of a human head, frequently in profile, in a circular panel or roundel.

Rondel, a disc, e.g. a circular cross-guard in a dagger.

Rondiste, in a cut gem stone, the rim around the base.

Rookwood pottery, late 19th-century pottery from a Cincinnati studio, perhaps the most distinguished 'art pottery' of the period, each piece made individually, notable especially for floral decoration in coloured slips, strongly influenced by Japanese design.

Rope turning, the form of twisted rope imitated in wood; see also **Cable moulding.**

Roquaille: see **Rocaille.**

Roquetta: see **Barilla.**

Rorstrand ware, 18th-century faience, mainly in high-temperature colours, from a factory near Stockholm, notable for several innovations including transfer-printing and characteristically Swedish vessels imitated from silver; from the late 18th century, creamware and other English-type wares.

Rosary, a string of beads, often attached to a cross and sometimes of precious materials, used by Roman Catholics as an aid to memory when praying; also, a counterfeit coin of medieval England.

Rose bowl, a silver or glass bowl similar to a punch bowl in which flowers or rose petals floated, late 19th century; also used as a finger bowl.

Rose-cut, a pattern in cut diamonds, a flattish hemisphere made up of triangular facets rising to a central point, first used in the early 17th century.

Rose du Barry, rose Pompadour, the name deriving from English confusion over the names of Louis XV's mistresses.

Rosenberg silhouettes, black-painted profile portraits on glass by a German-born artist working in Bath, England, about 1800.

Rose-engine turning, patterning or smoothing of pottery on a lathe before the clay is fully hardened, before firing.

Rose Pompadour, a deep pink, admired by Mme de Pompadour, originally employed as a ground colour on Sèvres porcelain in 1757. **228**

Rose quartz, a pale pink to red, transparent, relatively uncommon variety of quartz, occasionally used in carving, also in jewellery usually *en cabochon.*

Rose's Coalport, soft-paste porcelain; see **Coalport.**

Rosette, an ornamental motif in the form of a stylized rose, as in much Tudor decoration, oriental carpets, etc.

Rosewood, from various tropical trees of the same family as kingwood (and sometimes identified with it), a hard and durable wood, dark brown with purple tint, strongly marked, very popular in the 18th and early 19th centuries, chiefly in veneers. **245**

Rosso antico, a type of polished red stoneware originated by Wedgwood in imitation of ancient Greek vases, often gilded, adopted by various other potteries, sometimes used for copper lustre in the 19th century.

Roubilac figures, English porcelain figures modelled after the works of the French sculptor Louis François Roubilac (1705–63).

Rouble, a Russian silver coin similar to the English crown, first issued in the early 18th century bearing a portrait of Peter the Great.

Rouen faience, from the famous pottery centre in Normandy, in production in the mid 16th century and at its peak in the early 18th, influential throughout France particularly with the lace-like designs known as lambrequins and *style rayonnant,* notable also for the presence of red among its high-temperature colours and enormous variety of articles; soft-paste porcelain was also made at Rouen in the late 17th century. **226, 257**

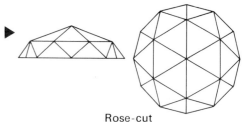

Rouge de fer, in ceramics, a rust-coloured glaze.

Roundabout chair: see **Burgomaster's chair.**

Rose-cut

Roundel, any circular ornament; see **Patera, Romayne work**.

Rout chair, a cheap, painted chair of light construction, rushwork seat, etc., used for large assemblies in the late 18th and early 19th centuries.

Rowels, spurs, in the form of a disc with projecting spikes; a term sometimes used of starlike patterns.

Royal Crown Derby, bone china and earthenware of fine quality made by a firm of that name founded at Derby in the late 19th century, which subsequently absorbed other Derby potteries; see also **Derby**.

Royal Doulton, Doulton stoneware from about 1900.

Royal Worcester, porcelain from the original Worcester factory from about 1790.

Rozenburg pottery, late 19th- and 20th-century pottery from the Hague; in particular, vessels influenced by traditional Indonesian designs and outstanding Art Nouveau vases.

Ruby, a precious stone used in jewellery, identical with sapphire with the important exception of its ruby-red colour, can be synthesized effectively; see also **Corundum**.

Ruche, or ruching, a decorative device in needlework, particularly on a trimming or border, similar to box pleats, the material being gathered at intervals and held by a line of stitching.

Ruckers instrument, a keyboard musical instrument, particularly a harpsichord, made by an Antwerp family of that name from the late 16th century.

Rudder, in furniture, a term sometimes applied to butterfly-tables, the leaves somewhat resembling the shape of a boat's rudder.

Rudd's dressing table, a fitted dressing table of the late 18th century with many drawers and compartments and several adjustable mirrors for all-round self-inspection.

Ruff, a large collar of stiff, fluted, white linen, sometimes projecting almost to the shoulders, worn in the late 16th and early 17th centuries.

Rug, originally, coarse woollen material used for coverings or cloaks, since the 19th century a small carpet.

Ruin room, a curious affectation of the Italian upper classes in the mid 18th century, a room furnished to look like Roman ruins with broken columns, armless statues, etc.

Rule hinge, the type of hinge seen in a folding ruler and on flap tables from about 1700, allowing a full 180° movement and permitting no gap when the flap is open.

Rule joint, a joint, as in a drop-leaf table, cut so that no gap appears between the two members.

Rummer, or roemer, originally a German wine glass of the 16th and 17th centuries with convex bowl, thick stem usually decorated with prunts, and short foot made up of coils of metal, usually green; widely copied throughout Europe; English 18th-century versions (rummer) very variable in form, often straight-sided. **223**

Runnel, a drainage gutter, a groove in a meat platter, etc.

Runner, a long narrow carpet as used in corridors, or flanking a larger carpet in the traditional Persian plan; also, a loper in a writing table, a groove or bearing for a moving part in furniture, etc.; also, a curved rail of a rocking chair and hence, the chair itself.

Running-dog motif, somewhat similar to the key pattern, common in the borders of oriental carpets, an angular hook form frequently combined with a triangle. **246**

Running footman, or sideboard, a stand of three or four rectangular trays, similar to a tea trolley, sometimes standing flat, sometimes on castors.

Rupee, a standard Indian silver coin from the 16th century, issued in various types and shapes, including square.

Rushlight, the stem of a rush steeped in oil and used as a substitute for a candle.

Rushwork, plaited rushes made since prehistoric times, very common for the seats of cheaper chairs in the 18th and 19th centuries.

Russelbecher, a medieval German glass beaker similar to a claw beaker, the 'claws' being particularly elongated, suggesting an elephant's trunk.

Russia leather, fine red leather from young calves with a pleasant smell resulting from tanning in willow bark and further treatment with oil-bearing woods; also, various imitations of this originally Russian product.

Rustic, of furniture, chairs and tables resembling the natural forms of trees and plants, sometimes with legs and chair backs made from unplaned branches, a feature of the 18th-century Gothic revival; also, country furniture.

Rusticated, in furniture, woodwork given the appearance of masonry by grooves carved like the divisions between bricks.

Rya carpets, the shaggy, hand woven carpets made in Finland from the Middle Ages, sometimes with figures of people and animals, sometimes religious or symbolic patterns.

Ryal, or rial, an English gold coin originally worth half a sovereign (ten shillings), later 15 shillings, current from the 15th to the 17th centuries, bearing a rose.

Sabbath lamp, the hanging lamp, usually silver, used in Jewish ceremony.

Sabicu, a tropical American hardwood somewhat similar to rosewood in appearance, found occasionally in veneers from the late 18th century.

Sabot, a wooden shoe like a clog, hollowed from a single piece of wood; in armour, a plate over the instep; a term also applied to various articles shaped like a shoe and to detachable cup feet on the legs of furniture.

Sabre, a one-handed sword with a single cutting edge, usually but not necessarily curved, for cutting rather than thrusting. **225**

Sabre leg, on furniture (chiefly chairs), a leg with a bold outward curve like a sabre, a popular form in ancient Greece, revived in the Neo-Classical period; sometimes only one pair, the other legs being straight, turned members; see also **Regency style**.

Sack, originally a bag containing a fixed quantity of wool; also, a mattress, or a long piece of draped cloth, from collar to ground, at the back of a gown or robe.

Sackback chair, an American hoop-backed Windsor chair.

Sackbut, a medieval wind instrument, brass, the ancestor of the modern trombone, with sliding tube; early examples straight, later S-shaped or coiled.

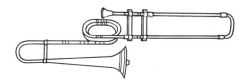

Sacristy chest, a large, carved oak chest as found in medieval churches, containing vestments, altar cloths, etc.

Saddle bottle, a round-bottomed bottle, metal, earthenware or glass, with a ring at the neck, slung from a saddle; see also **Pilgrim bottle**.

Saddlecloth, a small, squareish rug laid on the back of a horse or over the saddle, known from prehistoric times through Near Eastern archaeological excavations, embroidered with initials etc. of owners of carriage horses in the 19th century.

Saddle seat, the type of wooden seat common in Windsor chairs, slightly hol-

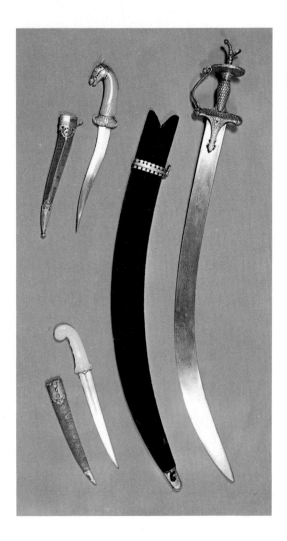

225 Two 19th-century Moghul daggers and an 18th-century sabre. (Wallace Collection, London)

226 Rouen faience water-jug. French, about 1680. The helmet shape was a popular motif. (Musée des Arts Décoratifs, Paris)

227 Porcelain teapot. St Petersburg, late 18th century. Part of a service destined for the noble family indicated by the monogram. (Victoria and Albert Museum, London)

228 Vase of soft-paste porcelain. Sèvres, about 1760. Rose-pink, called rose Pompadour, was produced at Sèvres for the first time in 1757; the combination of pink and green in 1759. (Musée des Arts Décoratifs, Paris)

lowed to fit the human rear and rising to a gentle ridge at centre front.

Sadiron, a solid, cast-iron smoothing iron for linen etc., sometimes found with metal stand for heating over coals.

Sadler & Green ware, transfer-printed earthenware and porcelain by the Liverpool, England, originators of the process, who decorated wares made by various English potters in the later 18th century.

Sadware, non-precious metalware, especially pewter flatware (as distinct from hollow-ware); also, certain cast-iron articles; see also **Sadiron**.

Safavid dynasty, the ruling house in Persia, 16th to 18th centuries, which witnessed (and was largely responsible for) a notable renaissance in Persian art, particularly carpets and ceramics.

Safe, a portable chest, usually metal, with pierced door, for keeping food; also, a strongbox, of heavy iron or steel, designed to survive natural disaster and frustrate thieves.

Saffron, a plant of the crocus family that provides a vivid yellow dye, formerly used in carpets, etc.

Saffron teapot, a small silver teapot, similar to an ordinary teapot in everything except size, for saffron tea, mainly 18th century.

Saff rugs, Turkish prayer rugs, patterned with mihrabs, the pile usually silk.

Sagger, the fire-clay box in which pottery is placed to protect it from direct contact with the flames in the kiln.

Sailor's charm, a name that seems to have described glass rolling pins and perhaps other whimsies.

St-Amand-les-Eaux faience, 18th-century earthenware from the factory of the Fauquez family in northern France, noted especially for lacy white decoration on a pale grey glaze; soft-paste porcelain also made.

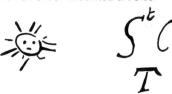

St-Clement faience, from a factory in Lorraine associated with Luneville, making a type of faience-fine from the fine local clay in the late 18th century.

S. Clement

St-Cloud, faience in the manner of Rouen and (particularly) soft-paste porcelain, mainly in the first half of the 18th century, from the famous factory near Paris under the patronage of the duc d'Orléans, noted especially for brilliant use of enamel colours in Kakiemon style, sophisticated blanc-de-chine imitations, and small silver-mounted articles.

St-Germain lamp: see **Student lamp**.

St Ives pottery, the work of a 20th-century pottery founded by Bernard Leach, making wares in Japanese and old English styles, vastly influential on modern hand-made pottery not only in England but indirectly West Africa, Japan, etc.

St-Louis glass, from the factory in Lorraine founded in the late 18th century and associated with Baccarat in the 19th, making cut glass of the English type and, in the 19th century, a pioneer of pressed glass and coloured glass of several kinds; see also **Opal glass, Paperweight**.

St-Mémin prints, portraits and views from the engravings of the prolific French artist, Charles Févret de St-Mémin, at work in New York and Philadelphia in the early 19th century; see also **Pantograph, Physionotrace**.

St-Omer faience, late 18th-century ware from a factory south-east of Calais, styles generally similar to Rouen (whence the factory's director came), noted for particularly lively Rococo decoration.

St Petersburg porcelain, wares mainly in the French Rococo style, large ornamental pieces, close copies of oil paintings, original Russian peasant figures, from a factory under imperial patronage, late 18th and 19th centuries. **227**

St-Porchaire earthenware: see **Henri Deux ware**.

St-Vérain stoneware, French Renaissance stoneware, characteristically dark blue, best-known for tiles; still made in the traditional style after 1700; see also **Beauvais pottery**.

Salad bowl, a small, silver or glass, fluted bowl from about 1700, assumed to be for salad at least in some cases; see also **Strawberry dish**.

Saladière, a salad dish.

Salad scissors, an implement like a large pair of scissors culminating in spoon or fork forms, for serving salad one-handed, made since the late 19th century.

Salad servers, similar to salad scissors but in two separate pieces (spoon and fork); from the late 18th century.

Salamander, an iron implement like a long-handled paddle, heated in the fire and applied to loaves during baking to make a browned crust; also, an iron poker for igniting or burning some substance; also, the reptile of that name sometimes represented in decorative arts, e.g. salamander legs on a chair.

Salamander ware, a term sometimes applied to oven-proof stoneware.

Salem chair, a name sometimes applied to several different chairs associated with Salem, Massachusetts, including a Windsor rocking chair with comparatively low back and an early 18th-century chair with openwork splat and pronounced 'ears' in the back.

Salem secretary, a combination piece associated with the cabinetmakers of

Salem, Massachusetts, about 1800, basically a glazed cabinet on a sideboard, usually having a central drawer that pulls out to reveal a writing compartment.

Sallet, in Renaissance armour, a helmet descending to the level of the nose in front, extending farther at the back (to protect the neck); see also **Barbute**.

Salt, a salt cellar, particularly a very large silver one which had a social significance in the Middle Ages (and later); made in a variety of shapes, sometimes incorporating pepper casters, in the 16th and 17th centuries; usually glass lined or gilded since the early 18th century. **66**

Salt caster, or salt cellar: see **Salt**.

Salt glaze, generally used on stoneware (which vitrifies at too high a temperature for lead glazes), ordinary salt being thrown into the kiln to fuse with the clay, forming a hard clear glaze, usually slightly pitted; see also **Stoneware**. **290**

Saltire, in heraldry a diagonal (St Andrew's) cross, hence such a form in furniture and decoration, particularly stretchers of a chair running diagonally and crossing in the centre, a common form in the late 17th century.

Salute, a French gold coin of the late Middle Ages, showing the Virgin Mary and archangel.

Salver, a large flat plate or dish, commonly silver but also any other suitable material, for placing underneath other dishes, often on small feet or a central stem. **232**

Samadet faience, from a factory in south-west France in operation from the mid 18th to early 19th century, known particularly for its monochrome green and Chinoiserie grotesques.

Salem chair

Samarkand carpets, from Sinkiang (China) and distributed through the market of Samarkand, wool pile on cotton warp, Sehna knot, rather loosely knotted but famous for exquisite design and colours (especially creams and yellows), common motifs being three central medallions, a flowering pomegranate tree, geometric fret or meander borders. **231**

Samarkand pottery, in particular an early Persian red-bodied ware, including Chinese-influenced slipware, lustreware, etc. of about the 10th century; also, various later Persian wares.

Samarra ware, a remarkable type of prehistoric Near Eastern pottery, dating from the 4th or 5th millennium BC, characterized by stylized painted designs on a creamy slip.

Sambo clock, a 19th-century American clock representing a negro playing a banjo. **230**

Samovar, an urn for making tea, Russian, usually copper, sometimes silver, containing a tube filled with burning coals to keep the water on the boil. **229**

Sampan, a light boat of the type still seen in the Far East, propelled by a single sculler in the stern, with a mat covering on the after-deck, sometimes figuring in decoration in oriental style.

Sampler, a small piece of embroidery, originally as a sample of the worker's skill or a record of a particular pattern, later (from the 17th century) chiefly made by children as an exercise, showing the letters of the alphabet, figures, the Lord's Prayer, etc., and in the 19th century appalling verses, e.g. 'Elizabeth Hide is my name/And with my needle I work the same/That all the world may plainly see/How kind my parents have been to me'.

Samples, any articles, sometimes small-scale, or parts of articles made by craftsmen as a token of their ability, often demanded by prospective customers since the Middle Ages; also called travellers' samples, especially china and glass, in the 19th century.

Sanctuary lamp, a hanging lamp, usually silver, for the sanctuary of a church, typically bowl-shaped, rare in England before the 19th century though no doubt common before the Reformation; the term is also sometimes applied to glass votive lamps and to hanging mosque lamps.

Sandalwood, a sweet-smelling wood from several Indian trees, its oil once believed to have medicinal properties, used in India for small ornamental articles.

Sand-blasted, a late 19th-century technique in which a surface, typically glass but also many other materials, is bombarded with particles of sand, a decorative effect being created by masking certain areas or by varying the intensity of the blasting; also, for cleaning stone buildings, etc.

Sand box, a small box, made in many forms and materials since the Middle Ages, with a perforated top, for sprinkling sand on to ink writing before the days of blotting paper; see also **Pouncebox.**

Sandburning, a technique in marquetry to impart a dark or grainy effect to the surface by dipping the wood into hot sand, in use in the second half of the 17th century.

Sanderson furniture, in particular that made by the brothers Sanderson of Salem, Massachusetts, about 1800, including fine carving by Samuel McIntire; much exported, especially to the South.

Sanderson silver, rare 17th-century American silver by Robert Sanderson (1608–93) of Boston, partner of John Hull, makers of Pine Tree shillings and of various articles such as tankards, porringers, etc.

Sandglass: see **Hourglass.**

San Domingo mahogany: see **Spanish mahogany.**

Sand picture, known chiefly as a 19th-century pastime though made much earlier, sand in various colours, sometimes natural, sometimes dyed, being affixed to a sticky surface of canvas, wood or other material in a pattern that formed a picture, usually a view.

Sandwich glass, from the Boston & Sandwich Glass Co. founded by Deming Jarves in 1825 in Cape Cod, Massachusetts, making almost all types of glass,

pioneering many patterns (e.g. Sandwich loop), early pressed glass and coloured glass of Bohemian type.

Sang-de-boeuf, 'oxblood', a deep, rich-red, high-temperature glaze found on Chinese ceramics from the Ming period and later, imitated in Europe in the 19th century. **236**

Santaline, a red pigment obtained from sandalwood.

Santa-Maria, a type of pinkish, Central American hardwood formerly imported from British Honduras.

Santos, holy pictures, i.e. of saints, made by the indigenous inhabitants of the Spanish-influenced areas of North America from local materials; see also **Bulto, Retable.**

Sapphire, the varieties of the precious stone corundum in colours other than red (ruby), typically but not exclusively blue, as hard as any stone except diamond and treasured since prehistoric times; capable of synthesis.

Saraband carpets: see **Seraband carpets.**

Sarab carpets, from the village near Ardebil, producing fine carpets of similar type, in modern times especially stair carpets.

Saracenic, a term applied to the late 19th-century fashion for furnishings in the Moorish or Turkish manner—oriental carpets, ottomans, pouffes, etc.

Sarcanet, a fine silk fabric of Near Eastern origin, used especially for linings of clothes from the late Middle Ages, and somewhat later for bed hangings and coverings.

Sarcophagus, in ancient times a stone tomb or coffin; hence, various pieces somewhat in the shape of a sarcophagus, such as a chest, cellaret; see also **Coffin.**

Sardonyx, a quartz stone similar to onyx but banded in brown and white (rather than black and white).

Sari ware, a type of Persian and Near Eastern unglazed pottery found at Sari and other places, mainly bowls and dishes decorated with birds, flowers, etc., about the 10th century.

Sarreguemines faience, reproductions of old maiolica and other wares from the French factory in Lorraine operating from about 1800.

MAJOLICA SARREGUEMINES 702P

Saruk carpets, from the centre south-west of Teheran, densely knotted, high-quality carpets, mainly traditional Persian

230 American 'Sambo' clock. About
1850. (British Museum, London)

229 Silver samovar by Friedrich
Wilhelm Sponhotz. Danzig, about
1775. (Germanisches
Nationalmuseum, Nuremberg)

231 Samarkand carpet. Mongolian, 19th century. A rare silk carpet with the ancient pomegranate motif over the central field. (Private Collection, Milan)

232 Silver salver with cartouche by José Coelho Sampaio. Portuguese, about 1760. Influenced by French Rococo. (Museu Nacional de Arte Antigua, Lisbon)

designs, often with central medallion, herati motifs, etc., similar to Kashan carpets, Sehna knot, sometimes rather strong colours; recently, Western-influenced designs intended for export.

Satin, a fabric, traditionally silk, with a brilliant, glossy texture, dull on the back, an effect achieved by weaving long weft threads on the surface, durable but hard to clean, used in upholstery etc. since the Renaissance; a term also used to describe a lustrous finish in other materials, e.g. silver.

Satinade, satinette, satin-cloth, etc., cheap varieties of satin, sometimes silk, sometimes wool and cotton or cotton and silk.

Satin glass, a type of late 19th-century art glass in which the final satin-like finish was achieved with the fumes of hydrofluoric acid.

Satinwood, from several varieties of tropical hardwood trees, particularly a West Indian variety, generally yellow in colour with strongly marked grain, but variable; very popular for veneer with English cabinetmakers in the second half of the 18th century. **240**

Satsuma ware, early Japanese porcelain and earthenware from the region in southern Japan often showing the influence of Korean craftsmanship; see also **Arita porcelain, Karatsu ware.**

Satyr, in Classical mythology a supernatural creature, human with animal connections (e.g. goat's legs), associated with unbridled lust and thus commonly figuring in erotic art; appearing quite commonly in 18th-century art and design, frequently as a mask on pottery or carved on furniture. **207**

Sauceboat, a long, low, narrow, footed jug more or less the shape of canoe or rowboat, a standard shape for sauces since about 1700, originally having a lip at each end with handles at the side, footed and often with matching spoon; most notable in silver; see also **Sauce tureen.**

Saucepan, a metal vessel with straight handle, frequently kettle-shaped before the 19th century, made in its familiar form since about 1800, when usually copper with tinned interior.

Saucer, since the mid 18th century a small plate under a teacup, but originally a small shallow basin containing sauce of some kind placed on the dining table; see also **Trembleuse. 233**

Saucer-edge, a raised edge on a circular surface such as a round table.

Sauce tureen, a lidded sauceboat. **115**

Saut de lit, a bedside table, often with ewer and basin.

Sautoir, in jewellery, a chain with a pendant or scent bottle reaching to the waist, a French fashion of the early 19th century.

Save-all, a candlestick designed to burn the stubs of candles, wasted in an ordinary candlestick.

Saveh carpets: see **Hamadan carpets.**

Saveh ware, medieval Islamic pottery, especially lustreware, notable for its characteristic check pattern representing foliage.

Savery furniture, the work of the notable Philadelphia cabinetmaker, William Savery (1721–87), or, more generally, fine Philadelphia Chippendale-style furniture of the late colonial period.

Savonarola chair, a term sometimes applied to an X-form chair in the Italian Renaissance style, perhaps on the grounds that Savonarola probably sat on one.

Savona ware, from the town west of Genoa, the pottery of which was mainly blue-painted, tin-glazed earthenware imitating Chinese designs, mingling with the compendiario style from Italy farther south but not classed as maiolica in the traditional Italian manner; 17th and 18th centuries.

Savonnerie carpets, extremely fine French carpets and tapestries from the works founded in the early 17th century, at one time operating from a former soap factory (savonnerie), Western designs and oriental techniques (Ghiordes knot), taken over by Gobelins in the early 19th century. **102, 235**

Sawbuck, or sawing horse, a support with X-form ends for sawing timber, hence a table of similar construction as found in early American colonial furniture.

Saw clock: see **Gravity clock.**

Saw mark, on furniture an indication of age; when a circular saw is evident, signifying a date not much before 1800.

Saw-tooth, a term used to describe a decorative border or moulding in the shape of the teeth of a saw, like a half-diamond pattern or zig-zag.

Sax, an early medieval sword, particularly one with a short, wide, tapering blade, double-edged (similar to the Roman sword), but also applied to one-edged blades.

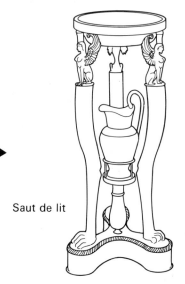

Saut de lit

Say, or sayette, a term applied to more than one type of cloth, including silk for bed hangings and a wool or wool-and-silk cloth of stout character used for cloaks.

Scagliola, various forms of imitation marble, originally (as developed in Italy about 1600) a mixture of plaster and glue to which chips of coloured marble were added, popular for mosaic table tops in the 18th century; also, plaster coloured and inlaid, and various other alternatives in the 19th century; see **Pietra dura.**

Scale pattern, a design in relief resembling the scales of a fish found chiefly on Rococo furniture, also painted on ceramics, usually as a border, including Greek vases, Renaissance maiolica, Worcester porcelain, etc.

Scalloped, particularly of an edge or rim in wood, silver, glass, embroidery, etc., a series of convex curves or semicircles as on a scallop shell; or a representation of such a shell, a popular device in the 18th century. **183, 250**

Scape, in architecture, the shaft of a column; also, a view as in 'landscape'.

Scaphe dial, a sundial in which the hours are marked on the inside of a cup-shaped depression.

Scarab, a precious stone such as an emerald in the form of a scarab beetle, an insect of symbolic significance to the ancient Egyptians, often worn as a ring with a seal on the underside; also found on tapestries in Egyptian tombs.

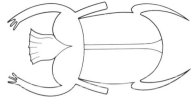

Sceatta, an Anglo-Saxon silver coin copied from late Roman types.

Sceaux faience, the product of a pottery near Paris producing high-quality faience that imitated contemporary Sèvres porcelain, notable for brilliant Rococo decoration of birds, flowers, etc. in enamel colours; mainly late 18th century, 'the last flowering of the art of faience in France' (Jeanne Giacomotti).

Scenic furniture, also rugs, etc., decorated with landscape scenes.

Scent apple: see **Musk apple, Pomander.**

Scent bottle, a small bottle of rock crystal, glass or silver, usually a flattened pear shape and round-bottomed for carrying on the person, from the 17th century or earlier.

Schaper glass, German glass enamelled in black, 17th century, named after a prominent craftsman, Johann Schaper of Nuremberg, who specialized in landscapes on beakers; see also **Schwarzlot.**

Schiavona, a type of sword with a straight, two-edged blade and basket hilt of interlacing metal bands, developed in northern Italy in the 17th century.

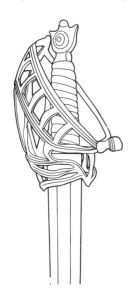

Schiller, a many-coloured glow caused by interference (of light waves) seen in certain gems, notably moonstone.

Schimmel eagle, a carved wooden eagle (among other creatures), some with detachable wings and painted, by the travelling wood-carver of Pennsylvania, William Schimmel, mid 19th century.

Schist, a crystalline rock that tends to cleave in parallel planes; see **Mica**.

Schläger, a light sabre with narrow flexible blade, as used formerly by German students in their ritual duels.

Schleswig faience, in particular the ware of a Danish factory in the second half of the 18th century owned by Johann Rambusch and his son, making chiefly manganese-painted faience which did not infringe the monopoly of Store Kongensgade, and noted also for distinguished Rococo modelling.

Schmelzglas, the various types of white glass and marbled glass that imitated stones such as agate, aventurine, onyx, opal, etc., a Venetian speciality in the Renaissance, later widely reproduced, with many new types in the 19th century.

Schnabelkanne, a characteristic vessel of 16th-century Rhineland stoneware, a footed jug with a narrow, cylindrical neck and a long, straight spout, decorated in relief; similar vessels were made in pewter.

Schnelle, a type of Rhineland stoneware tankard, tall with straight sides tapering inward towards the top, usually with pewter lid, hoops around top and bottom and decoration in relief; associated particularly with Siegburg, 16th century.

Schooner, a term applied to various drinking glasses, nowadays a waisted wine glass on a short stem used particularly for sherry, also a tall ale glass or measure.

Schrenkeisen rocker, a type of platform rocking chair, 19th century.

Schrezheim faience, from a Bavarian factory founded in the mid 18th century, noted for large pieces, especially figures by the sculptor J. M. Mutschele.

Schwanhardt glass, German (Nuremberg) glass, engraved by Georg Schwanhardt and his sons in the 17th century, excellent in drawing and execution and setting the standard for an outstanding school of glass engravers, sometimes working on remarkably thin glass.

Schwarzhafner ware, the black 'ironstone' pottery made in southern Germany and Austria in the late Middle Ages.

Schwarzlot, in ceramics and glassware, painting in black, creating an effect similar to an engraving, found on early European porcelain, notably Vienna; sometimes applied to plain white porcelain at a date considerably later than that of manufacture.

Scimitar leg: see **Sabre leg**.

Scissors, a term applied to various articles in the form of the well-known cutting tool, including folding X-form furniture.

Scissorwork, pictures made from cut-out pieces of variously coloured paper, in particular silhouette portraits, usually cut from black paper and mounted on white.

Scold's bridle, a metal cage incorporating a gag that fitted over the head and prevented speech, imposed on scolding women in the Middle Ages (and later).

Sconce, a candlestick (later a lamp) to be mounted on the wall, sometimes on a bracket, frequently with at least two candle-holders, perhaps best known in silver or brass in the 18th century but made in many materials; sometimes, simply a candlestick. **234**

Scoop, a rounded coal scuttle or hod, or a small shovel like a trowel, the two often matched in the 19th century; also, a laterally rounded spoon or ladle, such as certain sugar spoons, apple corers, etc.; also, a form of fluting carved on Renaissance furniture.

Schnelle

Scoop-back, applied to a chair with curved, form-fitting back, like a spoon-back but usually restricted to chairs with solid, upholstered backs.

Scorched paperwork, a 19th-century homecraft in which patterns were made on paper with a needle heated at a lamp; see also **Pokerwork**.

Scotch box: see **Mauchline ware**.

Scotia, a concave moulding or recess in the form of a half circle; see also **Cavetto**.

Scott chair, a late 19th-century single chair in 17th-century style with fringed, upholstered seat and spiral-turned members.

Scramasax, a single-edged broadsword with short straight blade, a standard weapon in early medieval Europe; see also **Sax**.

Scrapbook, an album compiled of pictures, coloured paper, pressed flowers, photographs, in fact any images that appealed to the (Victorian) compiler, sometimes a family album.

Scraped lithograph, a print made from a plate wholly covered with greasy lithographic chalk, the design obtained by 'scraping' relevant portions off.

Scratch carving, a simple form of decoration found on old country furniture, a design made in lines cut by a knife; also, incised decoration in pottery, the incisions sometimes being filled with pigment before firing; see also **Sgraffito**.

Scratch dial, a sundial cut in the stone of a wall, frequently seen on old churches.

Screen, any piece of furniture designed to block draughts, heat or, sometimes, excessive light, may be large standing pieces, hand-held like fans, or adjuncts to other articles (e.g. lamps); see also **Cheval, Firescreen. 238**

Scribing, in furniture, the shaping of a member to fit exactly an irregular surface in close juxtaposition, e.g. a bookcase shaped at the back to fit a moulding.

Scrim, a type of rough cloth or canvas, as used under the frame of upholstered armchairs and sofas.

Scrimshaw, the art of engraving and carving in whalebone, whale teeth and walrus tusk, a popular activity with sailors, and sometimes amazingly intricate and clearly worked with tools more sophisticated than jack-knife and sail-needle.

Script: see **Calligraphy**.

Scriptor, a variation of scrutoire, a term applied in particular to a drop-front writing cabinet on a stand.

Scrivener's desk, a tall, square-sectioned pedestal with slant-topped desk on top, at which the scrivener stood to enter records of financial transactions.

Scroll, a curving or spiral form, common in Baroque design particularly, the basic

233 Silver saucer dish. English, by William Maundy, 1636. Sometimes called a strawberry dish, decorated with stylized flowers and beaded punchwork. (Private Collection)

234 Louis XVI gilt bronze sconce in Neo-Classical style. (Musée des Arts Décoratifs, Paris)

235 Savonnerie carpet. French, 18th century. (Catan Collection, Paris)

236 Porcelain vase with sang-de-boeuf glaze. Chinese, Ch'ing dynasty, K'ang Hsi period (1662–1722). (Musée Guimet, Paris, Grandidier Collection)

form being the volute in an Ionic capital, **69**; also, a document, usually of legal or ceremonial importance, wound on two sticks.

Scroll arm, a curved, open arm (of a chair) that curls over and in at the end then outward and down to the seat, characteristic of the Rococo period.

Scroll foot, on the legs of furniture a foot that curves inward or outward in scroll form; see **Knurled**, **Spanish foot**.

Scroll leg, a leg on a table or stand, usually squareish in section, the overall form of which is in the form of an S (or scroll), characteristic of late 17th-century and early 18th-century furniture.

Scroll pediment, on 18th-century cabinets, bookcases, etc., particularly, a broken pediment turning inwards at the centre in scroll forms; see also **Swanneck**.

Scrowled, scrolled.

Scrutoire: see **Escritoire**.

Scuttle: see **Coal scuttle**.

Scudo, a silver coin of the Vatican, first issued in the Renaissance period, bearing a portrait of the pope; similar coins issued in various Italian states; see also **Escudo**.

Scyphus, a large earthenware drinking cup, usually with two handles and no stem.

Seal, a stone with a device carved in *intaglio*, mounted in metal (often a ring) for stamping an impression (typically in wax to 'seal' a document), usually the personal monogram, coat of arms, etc., of its owner; similar devices used since ancient times; also, a raised mark showing owner's (or maker's) name on early glass bottles.

Seal box, a shallow box, sometimes silver, often with curved sides, in which an important seal was kept.

Seal plate, articles of silver made from the melted-down metal of a (usually royal) seal that had become obsolete.

Seal spoon, a silver spoon dating from the late 15th or early 16th century terminating in an engraved seal, usually hexagonal; probably not made after the 17th century.

Seat furniture, a portmanteau term like 'case furniture' and 'stand furniture' including all types of furniture made for sitting on.

Seaweed marquetry, a pattern found chiefly on English walnut furniture, resembling the curly fronds of certain seaweed; see also **Endive**.

Secession, the Art Nouveau style in Vienna, after the firm set up by the artists Klimt and Olbrich.

Sechiello, a silver pail or wine bucket, Italian, from the 17th century.

Secrétaire, or secretary, a term encompassing a great variety of chiefly 18th-century desks, bureaux, cabinets, etc. that contain a writing compartment, often in the form of a pull-out drawer, the front of which lets down to provide a flat surface; with cabinet or bookcase on top; the term is used interchangeably with **Escritoire**.

Secrétaire à abattant, a drop-front secretary on a cupboard or stand, usually of rather plain lines but with surfaces often decorated with all the panache of the ébénistes in the Rococo style.

Secrétaire à capucin, a table that converts into a writing desk.

Secrétaire à cylindre, a cylinder or roll-top desk.

Secretary: see **Secrétaire**.

Secret compartment, a small drawer or compartment the existence of which is not evident to the casual glance, often opened by a concealed catch of some kind, made since the 17th century; see also **Mechanical furniture**.

Section, in construction, the plan of a member as if it were cut through the middle, showing its profile or outline.

Sector, an instrument similar to a geometric compass, basically two hinged arms (like a folding rule) marked with scales and sights, for measuring distance by triangulation, usually brass, from the early 17th century.

Sedan chair, a chair in a small carriage slung between two rails, which could be carried by two 'chairmen' in the manner of a stretcher, a common form of transportation in early 18th-century cities. **239**

Sedan clock, a carriage clock of the type resembling a large watch with bow-shaped handle.

Seddon furniture, made by the firm founded by George Seddon in London in the mid 18th century, probably the largest furniture-making establishment in England in the early 19th century, though authenticated survivals are uncommon.

Sedelium, a seat or throne, particularly the priest's seat in the chancel of a church.

Sedjadeh, a Persian carpet measuring approximately 5 ft by 8 ft; see also **Khalicheh**.

Seed embroidery, large seeds, such as maize, cucumber, etc., sewn into embroidered patterns of flowers; or sewn into a chain, as a necklace.

Seeds, the tiny bubbles sometimes seen in old glass, resulting from faults in manufacture—usually insufficient heat in the furnace; also, very small pearls.

Seersucker, a striped linen or cotton material, originally white, in which the stripes are puckered, originating in India, now known as a popular American, cotton material.

Sehna carpets, from the town in Kurdistan that gave its name to one of the main carpet-making knots, very fine carpets with extremely dense, short pile, various traditional Persian decorative motifs (e.g. herati, boteh), frequently with central medallion, sometimes bright colours; paradoxically, Ghiordes knot common.

Sehna knot, or senneh, the Persian knot in carpet-making, in which the wool pile is looped under and over one warp thread and under the adjacent one; see also **Ghiordes knot**.

Seichur carpets, Caucasian rugs and carpets similar to Shirvan, characterized by a pattern like a diagonal cross made up of repeated figures.

Self-coloured, of one colour all over, in particular the natural colour of the material.

Self-pouring teapot, a 19th-century conversation piece, occurring in silver plate, in which the depression of a lever pumped the tea through the spout, making it unnecessary to raise or tilt the pot.

Selour: see **Celure**.

Selvedge, or selvage, the strip of material at the ends of a carpet or any piece of woven cloth to prevent fraying.

Semiprecious stone, a gem stone of high but not the highest rank, often defined as those with a hardness less than 7 on the Mohs scale (i.e. softer than quartz), but as other considerations such as rarity, colour, etc. are effective, not to be treated literally.

Sen, a small Japanese copper coin, various types, first issued in the early Middle Ages.

Senneh: see **Sehna carpets, Sehna knot**.

Septagonal, seven-sided.

Sequin, a small bright object, usually of metal, used to ornament cloth, particularly women's evening dresses; formerly, gold coins of various kinds current in Venice and the Near East, from the 17th century.

Seraband carpets, from the area around the town south-west of Teheran, carpets and, more commonly, narrow rugs of the kelley type, characteristically with the boteh-mir (or mir-i-bota) motif, Ghiordes or Sehna knot; see also **Mir**.

Serge, a strong, twilled, fabric, silk or wool, frequently used for upholstery from the late 17th century, also for military uniforms, etc. **120**

Sergeant's cloth: see **Serge**.

Sermon glass, a sand glass used by preachers (perhaps still used) to measure the length of their sermon.

Serpent, an early bass wind instrument, wooden but with brass mouthpiece, named for its coiling shape, rather harsh in tone, popular in the 17th century but obsolete by the early 19th (though still heard occasionally).

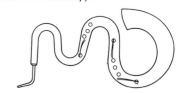

Serpentine, a curving form generally like a flattened S, associated particularly with the fronts of certain late 18th-century cabinets and similar pieces having a central convex curve flanked by concave curves; also describing various other effects, e.g. the curved X-form stretchers sometimes found on late 17th-century chairs; also, a semiprecious green stone very similar to jade (and sharing its colour variations), used for ornamental carvings, sometimes in imitation of jade; see also **Verde antico**. **237**

Serpentine fluting, a moulding of alternate convex and concave curves.

Serpentine horn: see **Snake horn**.

Serrated, indented, especially of rims of metalware; see also **Saw-tooth**.

Serrated leaf motif, a decorative pattern found in the borders of Caucasian carpets. **242**

Serving table, a side table.

Sestertius, a Roman silver coin, one quarter of a denarius, of the 3rd–4th centuries BC; reissued under the early empire as a brass coin with portrait of Augustus and his successors.

Settee, a seat in general similar to a sofa, the difference lying in the later date of sofas (from the mid 18th century) and their more comfortable construction; long seats with chairbacks (not upholstered) being classed as settees; see also **Confidante**.

Settle, the predecessor of the settee, a plain, high-backed wooden seat, with arms, sometimes built-in, for two or more people, often with a chest below, the seat forming the lid; made since the early Middle Ages but rare before the 17th century.

Settle table, a combination piece similar to a chair table.

Severe style, a term often applied to Italian maiolica of the early 15th century, in which form and decoration were subordinated to function, with painting in primary colours, but 'severe' only by comparison with the later 'beautiful style'.

Sévigné brooch, a type of jewelled brooch in the form of a bow, with pendants, popular in the 17th century and named after the famous French letter-writer, Mme de Sévigné.

Sèvres, the finest European soft-paste porcelain, from the factory south-west of Paris founded (originally at Vincennes) in the mid 18th century, under government control since its early years, when particularly notable for rich painting and gilding (especially on vases), and biscuit figures; more versatile hard-paste evolved in the late 18th century; forgeries of early Sèvres very numerous. **29, 228, 241, 280**

Sewing table, a small table with (originally) a sewing machine mounted on it, with a cast-iron frame of ornamental form, a popular item nowadays in sitting rooms and restaurants; also, a small worktable containing sewing materials. **298**

Seymour furniture, fine furniture in Neo-Classical styles from the workshop of John Seymour of Boston in the late 18th and early 19th centuries.

Sgabello, or sgabelle, an early wooden stool or single chair, the back being a single board pierced and/or carved, sometimes with three legs, sometimes including a chest under the seat.

Sgraffito, 'scratched', a term usually applied to a form of decoration on pottery, in which a design is incised in a coloured slip to reveal the contrasting colour of the body underneath, frequently white on red; see also **Mezza-maiolica**.

Shade, a silhouette portrait painted or cut in solid black; also, a glass lampshade or domed cover for ornaments.

Shadow clock, any time-keeping device that works by registering the length of a shadow cast by the sun.

Shadowless lamp: see **Sinumbra**.

Shaft-and-globe, a descriptive term applied to glass decanters, bottles, etc., with rounded bodies and long necks, characteristic of the 17th century.

Shag, a long, coarse pile on a cloth, or cloth (usually woollen) having such a pile (hence, also, shredded tobacco).

Shagreen, sharkskin or a similar material (perhaps originally, roughened ass's hide), almost invariably dyed green, popular in the 18th century as a covering for knife boxes, sword handles, and similar articles.

Shah Abbasi carpets, oriental carpets bearing a pattern associated with the great period of Persian carpet-making in the reign of Shah Abbas (1587–1629), in particular the harshang motif.

Shaker furniture, the articles (including metalwork, textiles, etc.) made by Shaker communities in America, the style of which, reflecting their religious beliefs, raises 'country' furniture to a high art; plain, clean, simple forms ('there is no dirt in Heaven'), natural local woods (notably maple), impeccable line and proportion, devoted care apparent in small details and, not least, a strong individuality and willingness to adopt new forms.

Sham, false, not what it pretends to be; applied particularly to carved drawer fronts where there are no drawers, thick-walled dram glasses that contain less than an honest dram, etc.

Shammy: see **Chamois**.

Shang dynasty, in archaic China the first period of known civilization, about 1500–1050 BC. **299**

Shank, on a button, the metal ring or other form of fastening on the back; also, the stem of any object, e.g. a wine glass, tobacco pipe, oar, etc.

Shantung, a soft, undressed, undyed silk originally from the Chinese province of that name, much imported from India in the 19th century, chiefly for women's dresses.

Shape watch: see **Form watch**.

Sharpe ironstone: see **Swadlincote pottery**.

Sharps rifle, a development from the Hall rifle by Christian Sharps of Philadelphia about 1850, a single-shot, breech-loading weapon with improved action; other guns from the same maker, from whom came the term 'sharpshooter'.

Shaving bowl: see **Barber's bowl, Shaving dish**.

Shaving chair: see **Barber's chair**.

Shaving desk, a toilet table, of any type.

Shaving dish, a shallow basin, elliptical in outline, sometimes silver with a matching ewer.

Shaving mug: see **Barber's mug, shaving pot**.

Shaving pot, a term usually describing a straight-sided metal mug with removable handle, on a stand with oil-burning heater, from the late 18th century.

Shaw furniture, in particular, authenticated examples by the Annapolis cabinet-maker, active in the Revolutionary period, or from a 19th-century Boston firm.

Shawm, a medieval woodwind instrument, ancestor of the oboe, but producing a louder, rougher note; many types, obsolete by about 1700.

Shaw stoneware, English 18th-century white stoneware associated with Ralph Shaw of Burslem, in which decoration was incised in a brown slip over the white glaze.

Sheared edge, on early Sheffield plate (silver-plated on one side only) revealing a strip of copper at edges, i.e. around a rim or foot, etc.

Shearer furniture, from the designs of a late 18th-century London cabinet-maker, Thomas Shearer, responsible for innovations concerning the sideboard and dressing table, regarded by Sheraton as superior to Hepplewhite.

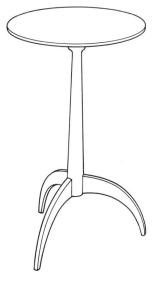

Shaker furniture

237 Vase of serpentine mounted in gilt bronze. Made by Pierre Gouthière (1732–1814) for the Duc d'Aumont. (Musée du Louvre, Paris)

238 Screen designed by the French painter and designer, André Mare, 1922. Lacquer over parchment and bronze. (Michel Mare Collection, Paris)

239

240

239 Sedan chair which belonged to Charles of Bourbon (Carlos III of Spain). (Capodimonte Museum, Naples)

240 Satinwood cabinet in Sheraton style with walnut and amboyna banding and medallions. English, about 1790. (Victoria and Albert Museum, London)

241 Porcelain lidded sugar bowl. Sèvres, 1758. The piece is typical of the Sèvres factory. (Musée des Arts Décoratifs, Paris)

Sheep's head clock, a type of late 17th-century lantern clock, with an extra-large dial that hid the case almost entirely from view.

Sheet glass, for windows, mirrors, etc., glass made in sheets by one of several processes, including casting (especially when large or thick plate glass was required); see also **Broad glass, Crown glass.**

Sheffield plate, silver-plated copper, cheaper and stronger than solid silver, made by the method invented in Sheffield, England, in the mid 18th century (though not necessarily manufactured there), in which silver sheets were fused to copper sheets (usually on both sides) and rolled, the thickness ratio being generally about 1 to 12; decorated in much the same ways as solid silver though deep engraving was ruled out; see also **Electroplate.**

Shekel, various ancient Near Eastern coins, particularly a silver coin issued in Palestine in the first centuries BC and AD during the Jewish rebellions against Roman rule, named for its weight, bearing religious emblems; also, a general term for money.

Shell, a common ornamental form, usually the type that represents the well-known oil company, seen in silver butter-dishes (sometimes an actual scallop-shell), carved on furniture, etc., especially in the Rococo period; see also **Conch, Scalloped. 140, 250**

Shellac, thin layers or 'shells' of lac, a resinous substance deposited on trees by a certain insect, varying in colour from red to orange to dark brown and used in furniture varnishes from the 18th century, also as dye and in sealing wax; see also **Cochineal.**

Shell-back chair, a term sometimes applied to late 18th-century chairs with a shell form carved in the back.

Shellwork, various types of decorative work incorporating shells of interesting shapes and colours, sometimes combined with paper filigree in the late 17th century; or large shells mounted in silver as ornaments, vases, sconces, etc.; or shells embedded in plaster covering boxes, mirror frames, etc.

Shenandoah Valley pottery, earthenware generally of fairly simple type, such as slip-decorated redware, from a number of potteries in the Shenandoah valley towns, notably that of the Bell family; from about 1800.

Shepherd's ring, the gold ring worn by medieval abbots; see also **Bishop's ring.**

Shepherd's sundial, a small, portable shadow clock, bearing seasonal, hour-marked scales with vertical pillar to cast a shadow, in use since Roman times.

Sheraton style, strictly, furniture based on the designs published by Thomas Sheraton in London between 1790 and 1805, though more generally applied to

English furniture of the period; more refined than Hepplewhite, showing a preference for straight lines and gentle curves, with generally light, elegant forms, often influenced by Louis XVI design, manifesting an occasional liking for gadgetry; no pieces by Sheraton himself are known. **240**

Sheveret: see Cheveret.

Shield, a protective plate (metal, leather, etc.) carried to ward off blows in battle, various types from ancient times; a common motif in decoration in the form known from heraldry, basically a downward-pointing isosceles triangle with curved sides.

Shield-back, a popular form for a single chair in the Hepplewhite style, the frame of the back curving up and outward from a central point near the seat with the top rail curving up to the centre.

Shilling, an English silver coin, worth 12d. (5p), first issued in the 16th century, with royal portrait.

S hinge, a metal hinge each leaf of which is shaped like an S.

Shino ware, Japanese stoneware from the late medieval period onwards, mainly tea-bowls etc., often thickly glazed or decorated in various slips with designs painted in reddish brown.

Ship glass, a drinking glass with an abnormally thick base and short sides, hard to tip up, from the 18th century.

Ship-in-bottle, a model of a ship inside a bottle, 19th-century sailor's work, the model being passed into the bottle with masts lowered then drawn into position by a thread.

Ship's decanter, a glass decanter with a wide, heavy base (for extra stability at sea) and sharply sloping sides, from the late 18th century.

Shiraz carpets, nomadic rugs and carpets distributed through Shiraz in central-southern Iran, often all-wool, Sehna or Ghiordes knot, variable density and quality, decoration usually simple geometric motifs, basic pattern often two or three large diamonds in line; see also **Kashkay carpets.**

Shirred, in needlework, puckered, strong threads being sewn along the material and pulled tight, drawing it into small folds, a technique used in making certain patchwork rugs; see also **Caterpillar rugs.**

Shirvan carpets, Caucasian carpets from the town on the shores of the Caspian Sea, especially smallish rugs of varied colours and designs, frequently of Persian derivation, the central design often made up of a line of small geometric figures, Ghiordes knot. **242**

Shoe piece, a bar at the base of a chair back into which the central splat was slotted, a separately made member on most chairs of the relevant type before the late 18th century.

Shōji, a lightweight, paper-covered, sliding panel in Japanese houses; see also **Fusuma.**

Shooks, staves for a barrel made up in packs for ease of handling; hence, the parts of other containers that can be disassembled for transport.

Shooting plate, a pewter plate awarded to the winner of a shooting contest, a popular prize in Germany from the late 18th century.

Shore pottery: see Isleworth pottery.

Short ale glass: see Dwarf ale glass.

Shortsword: see Smallsword.

Shoulder, in a vase, jar, etc., the angle where the body begins to slope inward toward the neck.

Shoulder yoke: see Yoke.

Shovelboard, a table, or a board placed on a table, for playing the game better known as 'shove-ha'penny', in which a coin is propelled by a blow across the polished surface to a desired spot, since the 16th century and no doubt earlier.

Shovel spoon, a spoon of shovel shape for salt, sugar, etc., in various forms.

Show bottle, or show jar, a glass or china vessel for use in shops in various decorated forms, sometimes made to fit one inside the next; see also **Drug jar, Pot lid.**

Showcase, a cabinet in which the sides as well as the front, and sometimes back and top, are glazed, for displaying ornaments, since the 17th century; see also **Specimen table. 243**

Showpiece, a particularly outstanding example of a craft; see also **Masterpiece.**

Shrub jar, or beaker, etc., a vessel for serving or drinking shrub, a fruit drink usually laced with rum, 18th century.

Shu, a straight-sided Japanese silver coin, various types and values, from the 16th century.

Siamese twins, commemorations in English pottery of various biological mishaps, late 17th and 18th centuries.

Sick couch, a bed incorporating an adjustable headrest; a day bed.

Sick feeder: see Spout cup.

Sickle hook, a curved metal hook of the type often found in cupboards for hanging cups.

Sideboard, a side table, which evolved into a distinctive piece of furniture in the late 18th century, typically D-shaped, the curve of the D containing a central drawer or drawers flanked by cupboards (for bottles); upper sections, often including mirrors, common from the mid 19th century; see also **Buffet, Court cupboard, Running footman**. 245

Sideboard pedestal, a pedestal usually surmounted by a vase and acting as a cupboard or cellaret, supplementing a side table, popular in early Neo-Classical furniture.

Sideboard plate, a term applied to silver grand enough to be displayed on a sideboard, particularly chargers and large flagons, often made in connection with a special event (a royal visit, a military campaign, etc.) and accordingly engraved; see also **Garnish**.

Sideboard table, a term sometimes used for a sideboard without cupboards and drawers; see also **Side table**.

Side chair, a single, i.e. armless, chair, particularly one of a set of chairs that included one or more armchairs; see also **Carver**.

Side table, a narrow rectangular table for serving food or displaying silver or china, which evolved into the sideboard in the 18th century.

Siegburg stoneware, perhaps the oldest Rhineland salt-glazed stoneware, from before 1400, and source of several basically cylindrical forms such as the Jakobakanne, in Renaissance times produced in a notably white body.

Siege, a seat, especially one of some ceremonial importance such as a throne.

Siège meublant, a side chair, placed against the wall in a salon or gallery, not seriously intended for sitting on and thus highly ornamental, from the late 17th century.

Siena maiolica, early Italian Renaissance maiolica, pavement tiles and other wares, sometimes with geometric, Moorish-influenced patterns, and strong colours including the dark orange named after the city.

Sifter, a silver sugar spoon with perforated bowl; see also **Straining spoon**.

Sigillata, of pottery, relief decoration formed in a mould impressed with pattern, a technique of ancient Rome.

Sigillated, stamped or impressed, as with a seal.

Signature, in book binding, a section of pages (normally a multiple of eight) sewn through the centre, a number of which make up the book, often labelled with a letter or letters at the foot of an inside margin.

Signet ring, a finger ring, usually a stone mounted in gold, with a coat of arms cut in intaglio, serving as a seal or mark of identification, examples known in ancient Egypt.

Signpost barometer: see **Diagonal barometer**.

Sile carpets: see **Soumak carpets**.

Silent-striking clock, any clock containing a device that permits shutting off the strike.

Silenus figure, the mythological, goat-like minor god represented in art since the Renaissance, including a popular 19th-century stoneware jug, usually as a fat bald figure in company with satyrs.

Silesian stem, in a wine glass, a heavily moulded stem, four-, six- or eight-sided, tapering out from the foot to a sharply defined 'shoulder', early 18th century.

Silex, rock crystal.

Silhouette, a portrait or scene in outline only; in particular, outline portraits drawn from the shadow cast by the sitter, filled in with black paint or cut out in black paper and mounted on a white ground, popular with many variations in technique from the late 18th century, made in large numbers, sometimes by travelling artists, sometimes with the aid of machines.

Silhouette china, especially dinner services, decorated with silhouette portraits or scenes, early 19th century.

Silica, the basic constituent of glass, derived from flint, sand, etc.

Silicon ware, a vitreous stoneware, variously coloured, made by Doulton and others in the late 19th century.

Silk, a soft and lustrous cloth woven from the thread produced by the cocoon-spinning silkworm, strong as well as beautiful, made in China over 4,000 years ago, said to have been smuggled to the West in the 6th century and widely used in clothing and furnishings.

Sillón de fraileros, perhaps the best-known type of Spanish chair (sillón), a 16th-century armchair with seat and back panel typically in leather, early examples often folding, with front-to-back stretchers only; many later variations.

Silver, articles made of this precious white metal (its colour only described by its own name), harder than gold and therefore more versatile (though subject to tarnishing), being cast, engraved, etched, embossed, etc., used since pre-Classical times for all kinds of metalware, usually as an alloy containing a small amount of copper; see also **Sterling**.

Silver case, a cupboard supposed to be made specially for the display of silver.

Silver furniture, articles normally made in wood such as chairs and tables, made in solid silver or silver-plated, for the ostentatiously wealthy, mainly in the 17th century.

Silver-gilt, gilded silver; see **Fire gilding, Silvering**. 44, 103

Silvering, on the backs of mirrors, a thin layer of mercury sandwiched between the glass and tin foil, a technique as old as the manufacture of suitably clear plate glass; also, the application of silver leaf or ground silver by methods similar to those used in gilding.

Silver lustre, in ceramics, a silvery, iridescent finish, achieved by platinum (not silver); see also **Lustreware**.

Silverwood: see **Harewood**.

Simmler furniture, early 19th-century Polish (Warsaw) furniture in a light, simple, Neo-Classical style, somewhat similar to the Biedermeier style.

Sincency faience, from a pottery in the local castle, north-east of Paris, in operation from the early 18th to the mid 19th century, staffed largely by workers from Rouen and reflecting Rouen styles, noted for the ability of its painters of Chinese scenes and rather pale colours.

Singeries, decoration of monkeys in various situations, popular in the French Rococo style.

Singing doll, a 19th-century toy that operated on the same principle as a musical box, some quite large and with a considerable repertoire.

Singing kettle, a kettle with a whistle on the spout, sounded by the steam when the water boils; a mid 19th-century innovation.

Sinkiang carpets, in particular, relatively modern, mass-produced carpets of traditional Chinese and Persian design; see also **Samarkand carpets**.

Sinking bowl, an ancient time-keeping device said to be still in use in some areas, consisting of a metal bowl with a small hole in the bottom which, placed in water, takes a set time to sink.

Sinumbra, the trade name of an early 19th-century oil lamp also applied to other lamps that cast no shadow, e.g. the type with a ring reservoir higher than the burner.

Siphon barometer, predecessor of the dial barometer, usually in the form of a narrow, upright rectangle, with mercury tube of constant width turned up at the end like a siphon and vertical scale.

Sistrum, a type of metal rattle, shaped like a stirrup or pear, associated with religious ritual in ancient times.

Sivas carpets, from the city in central Turkey, formerly very good quality rugs and carpets usually of Persian-influenced design, sometimes of notably light colours; see also **Ushak carpets**.

Sixpence, an English silver coin worth six pennies (half a shilling), current since the 16th century.

243 Mahogany showcase in
Chinese Chippendale style.
(B. Vangelisti Collection, Lucca)

242 Shirvan carpet. Caucasian,
19th century. Wine glass and
serrated leaf motif in the border.
(Private Collection, Milan)

244 Sofa with carved mahogany frame. English, about 1835. (Ipswich Museum and Art Galleries, Suffolk)

245 Regency rosewood sideboard. English, about 1820. (Victoria and Albert Museum, London)

Size, a sticky liquid, of gelatin or a similar substance, with various uses for priming or dressing a surface, e.g. before gilding.

Skånska glass, Scandinavian glass-ware from the factory in southern Sweden founded in the late 17th century, notable for simple and unsophisticated design and decoration as well as imitations of contemporary Rococo fashions.

Skeel, a shallow, wooden bowl, for cream.

Skeleton, in furniture, the carcase or frame.

Skeleton clock, any clock in which the movement is visible, usually encased by glass.

Skewer, a wood or metal pin or spike for securing meat while roasting, often made in silver from the early 18th century, in various decorative forms.

Skillet, an ancestor of the modern saucepan, originally a large bronze basin, later a deep, footed, metal bowl with cover and a long handle; also, a footed earthenware bowl, or a shallow frying pan.

Skimmer, a ladle with a shallow, saucer-shaped, pierced bowl, for skimming cream off the milk.

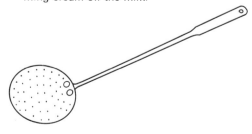

Skirmisher, a name applied to a short-sword carried by foot soldiers in the post-Renaissance era particularly.

Skirt, or skirting, in furniture a horizontal board such as the board around the foot of a wall, or a similarly shaped member in upholstery and furnishings; see also **Apron**.

Skiver, a thin layer of leather pared from (usually) sheepskin, used for book-binding, lining drawers for silver, etc.

Skyphos, a vessel in Greek pottery, a deep basin or cup with almost straight sides and two flat handles at the rim.

Slab-ended stool, a common type dating from the 15th century or earlier, the seat made of a board and supported by two vertical boards at either end, early examples suggesting Gothic architecture.

Slag glass, containing slag from an iron furnace, giving a variously coloured, streaky effect; see also **Agate glass, Marbled glass, Purple slag**.

Slat-back, a chair with wide, flat, horizontal rails in the back, popular from the late 17th century; see also **Ladder-back chairs**. 152

Slate, a tile (originally wood) hence the grey stone used for slating roofs because of its flat cleavage, also used for various other purposes, e.g. billiard tables, chimneypieces; also, a piece of fine slate, usually in a wooden frame, for writing.

Sleeping chair, an easy chair or day-bed with adjustable reclining back, known since the 17th century.

Sleepy Hollow chair, a name given to a type of X-frame 19th-century reclining chair with upholstered back and seat in one continuous curve and open arms, often with footstool.

Slice, a silver server like a blunt knife with very wide blade, sometimes pierced, as used for serving fish; the handle frequently bone, porcelain, etc.

Slickstone, or slicker, a polished stone used for smoothing fabric.

Slider, or slide, a shelf or writing surface that slides out from a recess when in use; also, a coaster.

Sliding table, an extension table, in which a section of the frame pulls out to support the drop leaf, from about 1700.

Slip, in ceramics, clay diluted with water to form a creamy liquid used to decorate earthenware vessels in a manner similar to glazing or as applied, low-relief ornament; see also **Slipware**. 249

Slip-cast, pottery made in a mould rather than on a wheel, slip being poured into moulds of plaster that absorb water from the clay and permit a very thin body and greater versatility of form.

Slip-ended spoon, a silver spoon with thickish handle ending in a flat surface at an angle to the handle, engraved with initials etc., 15th to 17th centuries.

Slipper, a term applied to several articles resembling the shape or otherwise associated with the footwear, including a 19th-century tin bath, a stone-ware hot-water bottle, an upholstered rocking chair, a low chair with high back and upholstered seat.

Slipware, earthenware decorated with slip of fine clay over a different coloured base; an early method found frequently on 'primitive' pottery, usually trailed, later incised or tooled in various ways; see also **Earthenware, Sgraffito**. 249

Slope-front desk, a bureau.

Slug, a small slab of base metal, e.g. the iron block heated at the fire and placed inside a smoothing iron to impart heat.

Small arms, of weapons, those carried by one man—rifles, pistols, etc.

Smallsword, a narrow-bladed, light-weight sword, usually about 30 inches long, as used for duelling since the late 17th century and (nowadays) a part of certain ceremonial dress. 248

Smalt, coloured glass, usually cobalt-blue, ground to a fine powder and used as a pigment in enamels; see also **Zaffre**.

Smaltino, a light blue tin glaze on Italian maiolica.

Smear glaze, a very thin glaze placed in the sagger (often painted on the inside walls), vapour from which settled on the surface of the ware during firing, sometimes used on 19th-century porcelain.

Smith furniture, in particular the designs of George Smith, a London cabinetmaker who published several books of designs in the early 19th century which helped to establish the Regency style.

Smock, a woman's shift or petticoat; also an outer garment of coarse linen traditionally worn by labourers in rural England, and by painters and craftsmen generally.

Smocking, in needlework, a puckered diamond pattern as used (presumably) on smocks: also, a similar effect in pressed glass; see also **Shirred**.

Smoke-jack: see **Spit-jack**.

Smoker's bow, a stick-backed corner chair of the hoop-back Windsor type.

Smoker's companion, a set of implements for cleaning, scraping and generally servicing a pipe. 247

Smoky quartz, a stone found in various smoky shades of brown, popular in jewellery and ornament; see also **Cairngorm**.

Smoothing mushroom: see **Linen smoother**.

Smoothing rod, a tapered stick some-times attached to a bed, for smoothing the sheets.

Smyrna carpets, a range of Turkish carpets originating from Smyrna (Izmir), a former centre for the trade; in particular, carpets made to order for European customers, often of somewhat inferior quality.

Snake foot, a name sometimes applied to the type of foot seen frequently on tripod stands and tables, an elongated oval form perhaps suggesting a snake's head.

Snake horn, an early brass wind instrument with coiling tube; see also **Serpent**.

Snake trailing, applied threads of glass in a wavy pattern, often coloured, seen in some early medieval European glass and probably copied from similar ornament on Near Eastern glass.

Snakewood, a tropical South American hardwood, a dark reddish brown with pronounced markings of rings and irregular, well-defined shapes, used for veneer from about 1700.

Snaphance, or snaphaunce, a type of 16th- and 17th-century flintlock gun in which the priming pan cover had to be raised before firing, or any flintlock in which steel and pan were separately mounted.

Snarling, raised decoration in metalwork, e.g. in a narrow-bodied vessel, with a springy iron tool which, being hammered at the other end, delivers impact by repercussion to the inside of the surface being decorated.

Snowbirds, vertical iron projections on eaves, often in the shape of birds, to prevent snow sliding off the roof.

Snowman figures, a class of mid 18th-century English porcelain figures covered with a thick, obscuring glaze, probably all made at the Longton Hall pottery.

Snowstorm paperweight, a popular type of cheap glass paperweight since the late 19th century which contains flecks of white that drift about in a clear liquid when agitated.

Snuffbox, a small box, early examples often including a rasp or grater for powdering the leaf and sometimes a small silver spoon, made in every conceivable material from solid gold to paper from the 17th to the 19th century.

Snuffer: see **Candle snuffer**.

Snuff grater, or rasp, for powdering tobacco, often silver and of intricate workmanship; see also **Snuffbox**.

Snuff horn, a sheep's horn, silver mounted, for keeping snuff and perhaps leaf-tobacco, from the 18th century; other forms of horn (and hoof) were sometimes similarly adapted.

Snuff mull, a container for snuff, often in the form of a horn, associated with the Scottish Highlands, usually with various accoutrements attached such as a silver-mounted hare's foot for wiping the lips.

Soap box, in particular, the characteristic silver vessel in use in the early 18th century, of ball form including cover, on a circular foot, the cover sometimes pierced.

Soapstone, a steatitic stone with a faintly slippery feel somewhat like jade, used for carving household articles and ornaments (notably by Eskimos), also used in the manufacture of certain soft-paste porcelain, e.g. early Worcester, in place of kaolin.

Sociable chair or sofa: see **Confidante, Love seat**.

Sociable table, a table in the form of a semicircle (sometimes three separate tables fitting together), usually with the centre of the straight side cut out for a round cellaret on a stand, placed in front of the fire at which convivial gentlemen could warm their feet while imbibing, late 18th century.

Socle, a plinth, or a plain, low pedestal on which a vase, sculpture, etc., might stand.

Soda glass, glass containing soda as a flux, creating a light metal somewhat easier to work than glass made with potash, used in most early European glass, notably Venetian.

Sofa, an upholstered seat with back and arms, sometimes overstuffed, for two or more people, from the mid 18th century; see also **Settee**. 221, 244

Sofa bed, a bed that converted by various means into a sofa by day, known since the mid 18th century.

Sofa table, a small table for use by persons seated on a sofa; in particular, an English 18th-century low, narrow table with drawers and drop-leaf ends sometimes placed at the back of a sofa.

Soffit, the flat band underneath a cornice, or the under-surface of an arch; hence, sometimes, a ceiling.

Soft-ground print, the effect reproduced in an etching by drawing with a pencil on a sheet of paper laid over the coated plate, the coating being removed from the plate wherever the pencil has pressed.

Soft-paste porcelain, the result of early efforts to imitate Chinese porcelain, a mixture of white clay and glassy frit, lacking the true feldspathic china stone, difficult to make owing to the precision required in temperature of the kiln; manufactured successfully from the late 17th to the late 18th century when generally superseded by hard-paste porcelain; see also **Bone china**.

Softwood, all timber derived from coniferous trees; see also **Deal**.

Solar clock, a sundial or shadow clock; also, a clock or watch in which a small representation of the sun indicated whether it was day (6 a.m. to 6 p.m.) or night; nowadays a timepiece powered by a photo-electric cell.

Solera, a barrel, especially a sherry cask.

Solid-cast, a term usually applied to bronze objects cast by pouring the molten metal into a simple cast of plaster or stone, as distinct from the cire perdue method.

Solidus, a Byzantine gold coin, first issued in the late Roman empire, current in Europe throughout the Middle Ages, the exemplar of most subsequent gold coins.

Solitaire, a china tea set for one person, often including a tray; see also **Cabaret**; also, a single brilliant-cut (usually large) stone such as a diamond set on its own.

Sölje, a gold brooch traditionally worn in Norway, basically in the form of a circular band variously decorated, sometimes with pendants.

Solo table: see **Games table**.

Sopraportes, decorative elements, such as tapestries or panels, over the doors of a room.

Soudé emerald, a counterfeit gem, two colourless stones such as quartz being cemented together with a green cement that imparts colour to the whole.

Soumak carpets, or Sumak, perhaps the finest of Caucasian carpets, from the region north-west of Baku, exquisitely orderly abstract designs and imaginative colours; flat-woven Soumak carpets are unusual in having a decorative weft thread woven in a kind of chain stitch embroidery. **246**

Soup tureen: see **Tureen**.

South Boston glass, wares of various kinds from a Massachusetts factory associated with the Boston Glass Co., perhaps the original maker of three-mould glass, early 19th century.

South Jersey glass, the products of the numerous glassworks founded in southern New Jersey in the late 18th and early 19th centuries, particularly simple, good-quality free-blown offhand articles, often in tinted metal; a term usually applied to the type and including similar wares made in Ohio and elsewhere.

Southwark pottery, in particular, the first English delftware, subsequently produced at a number of potteries in Southwark, south London, in the 17th century; see also **Lambeth delftware**.

Souvenir, a small article made as a memento of a particular place or event, since the late 18th century, taking many forms and made of many different materials, form and material sometimes having local significance (e.g. Delft windmills from Holland), silver spoons being perhaps the commonest in the 19th century; see also **Goss china**.

Sovereign, an English gold coin worth one pound, first issued in the 15th century, last issued in the early 20th century, bearing a portrait of the sovereign; issued in multiples of two and five in the late 19th century with St George and dragon on the reverse.

Soy frame, similar to a cruet but usually smaller and catering for a large number of bottles, including soy sauce; from the mid 18th century.

Spade-end, a form like the spade in playing cards, in door handles, metal mounts, etc.

Spade foot, on furniture, a leg culminating in a square-section foot with tapering sides.

246 Soumak carpet. Caucasian, 19th century. The geometric medallions and the running-dog motif in the outer border are characteristic of Caucasian carpets. (Private Collection, Milan)

247 Pewter smoker's companion. German, 1760. Tobacco crusher and pipe cleaner with their own tray. (Museen für Kunst und Kulturgeschichte, Lübeck)

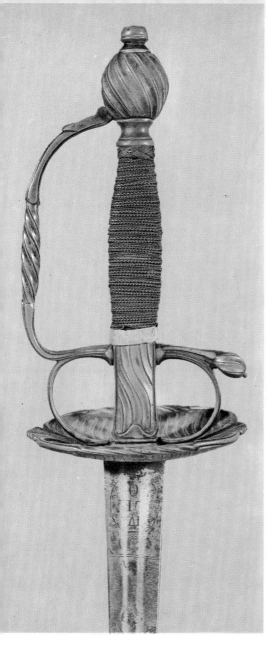

249▲

248 Smallsword. French, about 1700. Ceremonial sword of a French official in the period of the Wars of Spanish Succession. (Private Collection, Milan)

249 Staffordshire slipware plate with a figure of a siren. Second half of the 17th century. Thomas Toft was probably the name of the potter. (Victoria and Albert Museum, London)

250 Small shell-shaped spice or sugar box. English, 1620. The shell form was popular between about 1595 and 1625; typical stamped decoration and a latch fastening. (Ashmolean Museum, Oxford)

250

Spandrels, the corners remaining when a circle is imposed on a square of its own diameter, in particular the corners of a clock face, often decorated with applied or other ornament from the 17th century.

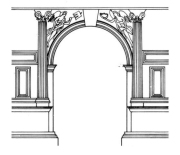

Spangled, covered with glittering specks, e.g. of glass; see also **Vasa Murrhina.**

Spanish calf, in books, a calf-leather binding with border decoration of red and green.

Spanish foot, on furniture, an inward-turning scroll foot with three or four vertical grooves, associated particularly with American 18th-century furniture of fine quality; also called Braganza foot.

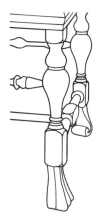

Spanish mahogany, West Indian mahogany from the island of Hispaniola or San Domingo, similar to Cuban mahogany but generally darker in colour and in England less common, usually close-grained and obtained in particularly large sizes.

Spanish point, a term applied to several kinds of lace, especially that made with gold and silver thread, sometimes embroidered with coloured silks, and various early needlepoint laces similar to contemporary Italian lace.

Sparable, a small nail or tack.

Sparking chair, a love seat.

Sparta carpets, or Isparta, chiefly made at Smyrna (Izmir) rather than Isparta, carpets in the Turkish tradition made largely for the European trade, generally of better quality than most Smyrna carpets, often with pale colours.

Sparvers, bed hangings, in particular the type which, fixed to a ring in the ceiling, enclosed the bed in a cone-like arrangement of drapery.

Spatterware, cheap English pottery (later, ironstone china) made for the American market in the first half of the 19th century, with simple, brightly painted designs, ground and borders densely 'spattered' or sponged with colour.

Spatula, a simple instrument like a broad blunt knife-blade, rounded at the end, for various purposes, e.g. spreading; hence, **spatulate,** in the form of a spatula.

Spavin leg, on chairs, a dog leg or (more appropriately because often combined with lion's paw foot in the early 19th century) a lion's leg, seen in Ancient Egyptian and Classical furniture.

Specimen table, a shallow glass case, frequently oblong, on four legs, to contain a collection of various decorative articles such as fans, coins, shells, etc., 19th century.

Speculum, an alloy of tin and copper used in making metal mirrors; also, such a mirror.

Spelter, zinc.

Spencer, a short, waist-length jacket, often velvet, close-fitting and with a high collar, fashionable about 1800.

Spermaceti candle, a candle made of the white, fatty substance derived from sperm whales.

Spessartine, a type of garnet, pale orange to red, often similar to hessonite, rather rare.

Sphalerite, a stone more brilliant than diamond but too soft for general use in jewellery; also, an ore of zinc.

Sphene, a green, yellow or brownish stone with great brilliance but rather soft, rare.

Sphinx, a mythological creature with a human head (and, if female, bust), lion's body and sometimes wings, as found in ancient Egypt and fairly frequently in decorative art since, especially in the Neo-Classical period.

Spice box, a small, internally divided casket or box, frequently silver and footed, with lid most characteristically in the form a shell, from the late 16th and 17th centuries; also, later table containers of various forms for salt, pepper, etc. **250**

Spice cabinet, or box, hanging shelves, etc., a container for small glass or china jars containing spices.

Spider, a three-legged iron or copper pot; a term also applied to very thin legs in a table.

Spider's web, a term applied to decorative effects like a spider's web, e.g. in embroidery, or in certain cane-seated chairs.

Spigot, a tap, as seen near the base of an urn, to extract the liquid contents without tipping.

Spill jar, a jar, pot or other container for wooden spills, placed near the fire for the lighting of tobacco pipes.

Spindle, in furniture a turned member shaped like a spindle, similar to a baluster, but without the characteristic swelling, sometimes found as applied relief moulding; see also **Split baluster.**

Spindle-back, a stick-back or Windsor chair, a term sometimes applied particularly to a type of simple, usually cane-seated chair with vertical spindles (often three in number) linking horizontal rails in the centre of the back.

Spindler furniture, the work of two German brothers who supplied the palace at Potsdam, peerless Rococo craftsmanship, rich marquetry and lavish use of brass mounts.

Spinel, a precious stone, hard as topaz and found in many colours, most desirably a near-ruby red, often described as ruby until relatively recent times, known in several famous historic jewels.

Spinet, a keyboard musical instrument with plucked strings, like a small harpsichord, various types from the 15th to the 18th century. **251**

Spinning wheel, the wooden machine used for spinning fibre into thread, the wheel being operated by a foot pedal with gear to raise the ratio of wheel rotation to pedal movement, found in nearly every house and cottage in the 17th and 18th centuries; hand-operated wheels known since the Middle Ages.

Spiral turning, or moulding, a turned member (e.g. chair leg) with incised spiral pattern, usually applied to shallower pattern than that called 'barley-sugar twist'; also in glass, particularly Venetian glass. **298**

Spirit case, a small wooden chest of fine construction, usually with silver mounts, containing internal divisions for bottles, from the 18th century; see also **Cellaret.**

Spit, an iron bar for suspending meat to roast over the fire, turned by some means to ensure even cooking.

Spitalfields silk, from the leading centre of silk weaving in 18th-century England.

Spit-jack, a mechanical method for turning a spit, e.g. by descending weights on a chain, or in the 18th century by clockwork.

Spittoon, a large bowl or basin, frequently brass, sometimes enclosed in a wooden box like a closestool, associated particularly with the saloons of the American West in the tobacco-chewing pioneer days.

Splashboard, the metal or china backplate behind a washstand, tap, etc.; see also **Lavabo**.

Splat, in furniture, a single vertical member between seat and top rail of a chair, as in most 18th-century dining chairs, pierced and/or carved; see also **Vase-back chair**; also, any narrow, decorative panel.

Splayed leg, in furniture, a leg angled outward from seat to floor.

Splint seat, in a chair, a seat woven of thin strips of wood (generally ash or oak and hickory) about 1/16th of an inch thick and half an inch wide; fairly common in the 18th century.

Split baluster, applied relief ornament consisting of half-baluster (divided lengthwise like a half-column) forms, found on chests, cupboards and sometimes chair backs, mainly in the 17th century.

Split-end spoon: see **Pied de biche**.

Spode, earthenware and porcelain from the Stoke-on-Trent, Staffordshire, firm founded by Josiah Spode the first (1733–97), a pioneer of transfer-printed Staffordshire blue and bone china; subsequently run by Josiah the second and William Copeland and their sons and very successful with stone china, feldspathic porcelain, excellent reproductions, etc., ever since; see also **Copeland**.

Spodumene: see **Hiddenite, Kunzite**.

Sponged, a decorative effect on cheap household china, colour being applied with a sponge offsetting painted birds, cottage scenes, etc.; much exported in the 19th century; see also **Spatterware**.

Sponse, in ceramics, a stencil through which the outline of the design was picked out in dots as a guide for subsequent painting.

Spontoon, a small, short-handled pike or halberd, chiefly 18th century.

Spool-turning: see **Bobbin turning**.

Spoon, the earliest type of implement used in eating (other than knives), usually silver, subdivided into numerous classes by type and period.

Spoon-back, a chair with a slight, form-fitting, concave curve to the back (stiles and splat), a popular form in the first half of the 18th century.

Spooning chair: see **Love seat**.

Spoon rack, a wooden rack for hanging up to a dozen spoons, usually with a box at the bottom for knives and forks, probably required especially for pewter spoons (too soft to be banged about), known since the 17th century, various forms.

Spoon seat: see **Saddle seat**.

Spoon tray, a small decorative tray, usually silver, basically oval in form, for teaspoons in the days before cups and saucers, chiefly in the first half of the 18th century.

Spout cup, a cup, pot, or tankard, with a cover and a spout like that of a teapot, for feeding invalids or infants (probably), known in silver since the 17th century, usually with two handles at right angles to the spout; known in later periods in differing forms.

Spread glass, sheet glass.

Sprig, applied relief decoration, often though not necessarily small flowers, in ceramics, embroidery, etc.; also, a small square-sided nail or tack, or a diamond ornament in the form of a floral spray.

Spring chair, an upholstered chair with coiled springs under the seat, more comfortable than padding; from the mid 19th century.

Spring-driven clock, one in which the movement is powered by a spring.

Spring rocker, a platform rocking chair with two springs in the base which were stretched when the chair was tilted back, from the late 19th century.

Sprinkler bottle: see **Perfume sprinkler**.

Spruce, a common white softwood; also, a term sometimes apparently used to mean 'Prussian'.

Sprung stretcher, or spur stretcher, a bow-shaped stretcher, imparting tension, linking front chair legs, with straight stretchers from the bow to the rear legs, seen on some Windsor chairs.

Spun glass, threads of glass drawn fine enough to be woven into fabric, from the early 19th century; see also **Fibreglass**.

Spur mark, a rough mark sometimes seen on the base of pottery, made by the fireclay supports on which the vessel stood in the kiln.

Spur stretcher: see **Sprung stretcher**.

Squab, a cushion, especially one made for the seat of a particular chair; also, sometimes, an upholstered seat of some kind.

Square, in glassware, a square-sided decanter with very short neck, from the mid 18th century.

Square piano, rectangular in shape, originally the size of an 18th-century clavicord; see **Zumpe piano**.

Square Windsor, a Windsor-type chair with square-sectioned (rather than turned) members, sometimes called a lath-back.

S scroll, a double scroll like an S, often found in combination with C scrolls on early 19th-century furniture.

Stackfreed, a device in early German spring-driven clocks to maintain constant power, in effect a counterspring that retards the mainspring with decreasing pressure as it unwinds; superseded by the fusee.

Staffordshire blue: see **Blue-printed ware**.

Staffordshire china, many types of wares from the numerous potteries of Staffordshire, the centre of the English industry since the early 18th century, particularly lead-glazed earthenware, stoneware, and later developments therefrom; often implying, in particular, figures and models (cottages, etc.). **249**

Staffordshire figures, generally simple earthenware figures of little artistic pretension and cheap, of well-known public figures (foreign and domestic), dogs, etc., produced in very large quantities in the 19th century, sometimes unpainted; see also **Flatbacks**.

Staff weapons: see **Pole arms**.

Stained glass, mosaics of transparent coloured glass; more strictly, glass coloured by coating with silver and copper oxides, then firing, in Bohemian glass often subsequently engraved; also applied to transparent enamelled glass. **252**

Stair button, a metal button that fitted over the head of a nail retaining the stair carpet.

Stake, in metalwork, an anvil of some particular form on which a metal vessel was shaped.

Stalking horse, a flat representation of a horse used by hunters to conceal their approach to their quarry.

Stall, a seat, particularly an enclosed, built-in seat with standing space in a church, generally with gable ends; also, the panelled-off section for one animal in a stable, and a bench for the display of goods for sale.

Stamford ware, early English lead-glazed earthenware, from the 10th century onward, in the van of English ceramic developments throughout the Middle Ages.

Stamped, a design impressed or printed; when applied to marks on ceramics, usually implying printed rather than relief or intaglio; in metalwork, usually hammered from the back.

Stand, for a candle, vase and other ornaments, made in many forms through the ages; see **Canterbury, Pedestal**; also, a frame like a table on which an article of furniture, such as a cabinet, chest, or bookcase, is supported.

Standard, a term with many meanings depending on context; in furniture, a very large Tudor chest as used for removals; or the uprights of a standing mirror, firescreen, etc.; or a candle-stand of pillar form (hence, standard lamp); also, a military flag or banner, an author-

251 Spinet. Made by Benedetto Floriani in 1562. The keys are inlaid with rare woods and ivory. (Castello Sforzesco, Milan)

252 Stained glass window representing 'Spring' designed by E. Grasset in 1894 in the Art Nouveau style. (Musée des Arts Décoratifs, Paris)

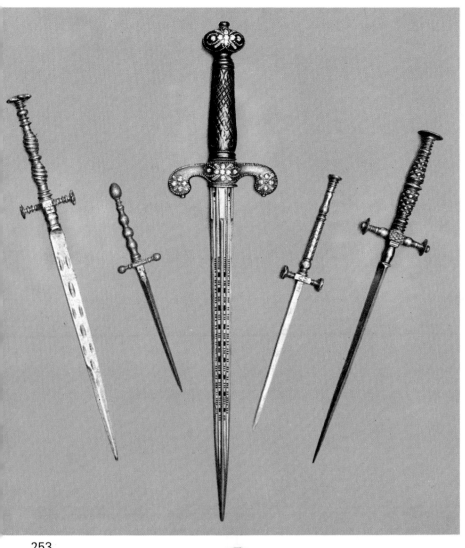

253

254

253 Dagger and four stilettos. Italian, 16th century. The dagger has a characteristic pierced blade; with the stiletto or misericord one dealt the coup de grâce to a defeated opponent. (Dal Pozzo Collection, Milan)

254 Ceramic stove. German, 1773. The fashion for porcelain stoves was Dutch in origin but spread all over northern Europe (except England); this stove was painted by Abraham Leihamer. (Kunstgewerbemuseum, Vienna)

255 Vessel in the shape of a human head with stirrup handle. Northern coast of Peru. (Museo Nacional de Antropologia y Arqueologia, Lima)

ized, legal measure of quantity or quality (as in silver standard), etc.

Stand furniture, a portmanteau term encompassing all types of table, desk, stand, etc., as distinguished from 'seat furniture' and 'case furniture'.

Standing shelves, moveable bookshelves standing flat on the ground, as distinguished from hanging shelves and bookcases.

Standing salt, a salt of particularly ostentatious form, usually 17th-century or earlier, often in a form based on architecture.

Standish, an inkstand, the common term for such a piece before the 18th century. **137**

Stangenglas, a tall, narrow, cylindrical glass beaker on a foot, often decorated with prunts or trailing, German, 16th and 17th centuries; see also **Humpen.**

Stanhope, a light, open, horse-drawn carriage.

Stannary, tinware, named after the tin-mining district in Cornwall.

Stannous glaze, tin-glaze.

State bed, a grand and elaborate bed, lavishly draped, such a bed from which a monarch might conduct state business. **104**

Stater, a gold or silver coin of ancient Greece, a term applied to various different coins; see also **Drachm.**

Statuary porcelain, parian ware, the form of porcelain developed in the mid 19th century and popular for figures owing to its resemblance to marble.

Statuette, a small statue or figurine. **271**

Stave, one of the narrow curved boards of which a barrel was made; also, a staff, rod, or stretcher of a chair.

Steamer chair, the type of deck chair that really was (and is) found on the deck of a ship, a folding chair with long low seat and reclining back, generally of slatted wood, from the mid 19th century.

Steam sideboard, a combined steam boiler and sideboard, with marble top, mid 19th century.

Steatite: see **Soapstone.**

Steel engraving, a 19th-century print from engraved steel plates, harder-wearing than copper and thus giving a larger number of impressions, but less receptive to delicate tooling.

Steening, a brick or stone lining, as of a well or a fireplace.

Steeple clock, a type of Gothic clock characterized by tall tapering finials at the 'eaves' of the case.

Steeple cup, a tall silver goblet or chalice, the cover surmounted by a tall, pointed finial, usually 17th century or earlier.

Steingut, the German version of the improved lead-glazed earthenwares, especially creamware, introduced by Wedgwood in England in the late 18th century, which superseded the traditional faience in many potteries.

Steinkirk, a type of cravat worn by women (sometimes) as well as men, loosely knotted at the throat and threaded through a buttonhole; early 17th century.

Stem, of a wine glass, etc., the shank between bowl and foot.

Stencilled, decorated with a pattern painted through a stencil—a card with the pattern cut out—on furniture (e.g. 'fancy' chairs), ceramics, etc.

Stepped, a term applied to any form resembling a step or flight of steps in outline, especially a right-angle interrupting a curved form as in a moulding or the foot of a wine glass. **294**

Steps, short, moveable flights of stairs in various forms, often combined with a stool, chair or other piece; see also **Bed steps, Library steps, Marche pied, Stepped.**

Stereoscope, a viewing device usually something like a pair of binoculars, in which two slightly different views of the same picture, seen simultaneously through the two eyepieces, gave an impression of three dimensions, 19th century.

Sterling, the standard for English silver, in force with one short interval since before 1300, a proportion of at least 925 parts per 1,000 pure silver, signified by a lion mark; early American silver, though not marked, was usually of the same standard.

Steuben glass, modern American art glass of high quality.

Stevengraph, a picture woven in silk, mainly of contemporary events, by Thomas Stevens of Coventry and his successors, late 19th century, usually a narrow rectangle mounted on white card; an example of cheap (but unique) Victorian ornaments that have recently become major collector's pieces.

Stick barometer, the earliest (from the mid 17th century) type of barometer, a long, vertical glass tube in a narrow wooden case, often with top in similar form to contemporary clock cases and decorative carved terminal ending in a point, mounted on a wall.

Stick furniture, a term applied particularly to chairs of the Windsor type, made up largely of thin, turned members, or spindles.

Stiegel glass, American glass of the type first made by Henry William Stiegel at his two Manheim glassworks in Lancaster County, Pennsylvania, before the Revolution, employing workers from various European glassmaking countries; table glass often coloured and blown-moulded, simple engraving and painted flasks and jars.

Stile, a vertical member forming the side of a frame or in furniture, e.g. on either side of a panelled door, the uprights at either side of a chairback; see also **Rail;** also, a wooden step or steps to assist crossing a fence intended to confine animals.

Stiletto, a small dagger with a narrow but thick blade like a flattened diamond in section, from the 16th century. **253**

Stilt, a term applied to various articles of furniture, including certain chairs, on long, relatively thin legs.

Stilt marks: see **Spur mark.**

Stipple, a process of engraving-cum-etching in which the pattern is made with small dots, the density of which govern light and shade, the dots being enlarged by acid and finished by engraving, a technique especially popular in England, from the 18th century (though practised much earlier); also, glass engraved by a similar use of incised dots, a Dutch speciality in the 18th century.

Stirrup cup, a wine-cup, usually silver or china and frequently in the form of a fox's or hound's head, for a mounted horseman; see also **Hunting cup.**

Stirrup vase, a type of amphora with squareish handles like stirrups; similar vessels were made by Peruvian potters over a period of 2,000 years in the form of globular pots with spout emerging from the centre of the handle. **255**

Stock, a word with many meanings, some of them pertaining to antiques, e.g. a man's collar or breastcloth attaching to the collar; a handle, especially a heavy wooden handle as of a firearm; a pillory (stocks).

Stockelsdorff faience, from a late 18th-century factory in Schleswig-Holstein, notable especially for fine painted stove tiles and trays as well as large vases and centrepieces.

Stockholm faience: see **Rorstrand ware.**

Stockinette, or stockinet, a silk or cotton woven fabric, highly elastic, used mainly for clothes, 19th century.

Stocking purse: see **Miser's purse.**

Stole, a long cloak, also the embroidered band around the neck falling almost to the feet in front, worn by Christian priests in celebrating Mass.

Stollenschrank, a late medieval cupboard or tallboy, with shelf below, carved in the Gothic style, sometimes a corner cupboard.

Stomacher, a waistcoat or bodice; a jewelled piece worn underneath the lace-up bodice by women in the 16th century, hence a large brooch worn on the chest.

Stone china, a 19th-century Staffordshire stoneware developed by Spode, very similar to porcelain at a casual glance, containing petuntse, hard and heavy, a faint bluish cast usually visible in early ware.

Stones, in glass, the name given to small specks of red or black within the metal, the result of imperfect mixing of the batch, sometimes seen in old glass.

Stoneware, a ceramic ware between earthenware and porcelain, fired at a higher temperature than ordinary clay earthenwares and thus impervious to liquids without glazing, but coarser than porcelain and not translucent, though fine salt-glazed stoneware (from the early 18th century) was similar to the porcelain it was designed to imitate; see also **Rhineland stoneware. 290**

Stool, a small seat with no arms or (since the 15th century) back, usually for one person (if more than two, it becomes a bench); or for resting the feet (often made matching an upholstered armchair in the 19th century).

Stop-reeding, ornamental reeding or fluting that forms a decorative band, e.g. on the upper part of a chair leg, but is confined to a limited area of the element concerned, or is interrupted by some other ornamental device.

Stop watch: see **Pulse watch.**

Store Kongensgade faience, from perhaps the outstanding Danish (Copenhagen) factory, enjoying a Danish monopoly of blue-painted ware during the mid 18th century, notable for bishop's bowls, large trays or table tops and other wares.

Stork, an iron replica of the bird, mounted on roofs to encourage nesting; also, a type of metal lamp with a long beak like a stork.

Storr silver, the work of the famous English gold- and silversmith Paul Storr (1771–1844), mainly in Regency style. **44**

Stoup, a basin, particularly a stone basin for holy water, used in Christian ritual, set in the wall of a church; also, a large tankard or measure. **133**

Stourbridge glass, from the glass-making centre in Worcestershire, notably coloured glass for church windows, early English imitations of Venetian glass, and especially various 'art glass' innovations of the 19th century, as displayed in the Stourbridge museum.

Stove tile, in particular, a tin-glazed earthenware tile for stoves, made chiefly in northern Europe from the early 16th to the late 18th century; comparatively few old stoves survive intact; also, an iron plate, usually decorated in relief, from 19th-century iron stoves. **254**

Straddle chair, any chair in which the occupant sat facing the back; see also **Reading chair.**

Stradivarius, a violin (less commonly a viola or cello) made by the unrivalled Italian (Cremona) instrument-maker Antonio Stradivari (?1644–1737), of which a surprisingly large number apparently survive.

Straight-front, a term sometimes applied to standing furniture such as commodes, bookcases, cabinets, etc., with a flat façade.

Straight-sided, applied to a vessel, implying sides that form a straight line from top to bottom (or rim to stem), not necessarily parallel as in a square-section or cylindrical form.

Straining spoon, also known as mote, mulberry, olive, etc., a silver spoon with pierced bowl and long handle, somewhat similar in form (and purpose) to a modern tea strainer, from the early 18th century.

Stralsund faience, Swedish tin-glazed earthenware from a factory in the town now in East Germany in the second half of the 18th century, wares generally similar to Marieberg but notable for extremely large pieces – vases, table-tops, etc.

Strap, any ornamental curved band, engraved, carved, painted, etc., or any structural element like a strap, e.g. handles on Leeds teapots.

Strap-and-leaf, strap-and-jewel, strap-and-tongue, etc., terms relating to various types of ornamental strapwork.

Strap hinge, a hinge with a long leaf stretching across the door for a con-considerable distance; see also **Cross garnet hinge.**

Strapwork, ornamentation, usually chased work on silver, carved low relief on furniture, etc., based on an arrangement of curving bands, 16th to 18th century; see also **Leaf- and strapwork.**

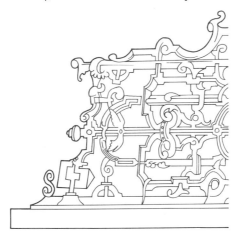

Strasbourg ware, in particular, faience and porcelain from the potteries of the Alsatian city; faience from two 18th-century factories owned by the Hannong family, the first enamel-painted French faience, notable for unsurpassed flower-painting particularly the naturalistic *fleurs de Strasbourg* patterns, as well as lively Baroque figures, certain original Chinoiserie designs, and dishes in animal forms;

porcelain an offshoot of faience production (and bringing both to financial ruin), colours and patterns similar to faience and to Frankenthal porcelain. **38, 256**

Strass, imitation gems, originally applied to a compound named after the 18th-century French jeweller who developed it, subsequently to paste in general.

Strawberry dish, a name attached to almost any silver or glass dish like a small, low-sided bowl with fluted or gadrooned sides and scalloped edge, sometimes on three feet, from the late 17th century. **233**

Strawberry Hill Gothic, furniture in 18th-century Gothic Revival style, as displayed in the 'little Gothic castle' built by Horace Walpole at Twickenham, near London, in the mid 18th century. **117**

Strawberry lustre pattern, a design of strawberries in red and green lustre found on some 19th-century English porcelain.

Straw chair, a basketwork armchair; see **Beehive chair.**

Straw shank, or stem: see **Drawn stem.**

Straw work, the decoration of furniture surfaces with small slivers of straw, set at different angles and sometimes coloured, time-consuming and thus usually made by nuns, prisoners-of-war, or others with time on their hands, chiefly 17th to 19th centuries; also, any small articles made of straw.

Street sign, a trade sign, signpost, etc., conveying information pictorially rather than by words, for those who could not read, surviving examples from the 16th and 17th centuries, now coming into fashion again though for different reasons.

Stretcher, a horizontal member linking (and strengthening) the legs of chairs, tables etc., whether a simple bar or a large, ornately carved and shaped board. **163, 240**

Stretcher table, a term usually applied to a 'refectory'-type table with two end supports linked by a broad and solid longitudinal stretcher, a traditional 'country' piece very common again today; or a 16th or 17th-century table with heavy, functional stretchers at floor level; also, the frame on which a painter's canvas is stretched, a collapsible bed for casualties, a crosspiece in a rowboat, etc.

Striated, fluted, reeded or striped; strictly, referring to the narrow bands between flutes in Classical architecture, sometimes applied to the wavy lines visible in ill-worked glass vessels.

Strigil, in ancient times a bladed instrument for scraping oil or sweat off the skin during ablutions; hence, similar more recent instruments such as a scrubbing brush or backscratcher.

Strike, of clocks, where the hours, quarters, etc., are sounded on one bell only; see also **Chime.**

Strike-silent clock: see **Silent-striking clock.**

256 Faience soup tureen. Strasbourg, about 1753. (Musée des Arts Décoratifs, Paris)

257 Rouen faience plate with lambrequin decoration. About 1680. An early example of an oriental-inspired European design. (Musée des Arts Décoratifs, Paris)

258 Stand for a tea dish. Chinese, Northern Sung period (960–1125). Ju ware. The subtle glaze with its fine crackle was highly esteemed. (British Museum, London)

259 Silver sugar basket with blue glass liner and bail handle. English, 1776. (Victoria and Albert Museum, London)

260 Polyhedral sundial. By Don Stefano Bonsignori, Florence, about 1570. When (on the latitude of Florence) three gnomons indicate the same hour, the exact solar time is shown. (Morpurgo Collection, Amsterdam)

259

260

String box, a small box of any suitable material for keeping string, sometimes shaped to fit a ball of twine, otherwise usually indistinguishable from caddies.

Stringing, a very narrow strip of inlay, often a light colour offsetting dark veneer, sometimes a strip of brass, a common decorative device in furniture from the mid 18th century; also, applied ornamental threads of glass on glassware. **240**

Stripped pine, a contemporary fashion (perhaps now receding) for old deal furniture such as kitchen cabinets and dressers which were originally almost invariably painted, stripped down to the bare wood, revealing all the once carefully obscured knots.

Struck moulding, on furniture, moulding carved on the relevant member itself, i.e. not applied.

Stucco, plaster, usually containing powdered stone, used for covering ceilings, walls, and for mouldings; nowadays, usually a rough plaster on exterior walls.

Stucco lustro, imitation marble; see also **Scagliola.**

Stuck shank, or stem, in a wine glass or similar-shaped vessel, a stem made separately from the bowl (not drawn) and welded on.

Stud, a small nail with a large head, commonly brass, used where a nail was bound to show, as on a stair carpet, or for mainly or solely decorative purposes as in certain leather-upholstered chairs, chests, etc.

Student lamp, a name applied to any oil-burning lamp designed to cast a bright light on a limited area.

Stud table, a kidney- or horseshoe-shaped table, usually covered with baize, as used in professional gambling establishments, the dealer standing in the concave curve.

Stuff, the materials used in making any article, in particular textiles, especially wool.

Stuffed over, of upholstery, covering the frame so that only the cloth is visible; the term more commonly used now is 'overstuffed', though the meaning of the latter was once different (i.e. heavily padded).

Stump-end spoon, a silver spoon of the mid 17th century, with a heavy, octagonal handle widening at the end to form a finial like a flat, angular cone.

Stump foot, a term applied to a turned furniture leg which terminates in a form basically similar to the leg itself, or in no definite foot at all.

Stumpwork, a type of embroidery in which parts of the design are raised in relief, either by padding or sometimes on a carved wooden ground, decorating small boxes, mirror frames, etc., mainly a 17th-century art.

Sturzbecher, a 16th-century stoneware beaker, associated particularly with Cologne and nearby Rhineland centres, usually in the characteristic grey body with yellowish glaze.

Style cathédrale, the Neo-Gothic style in 19th-century France.

Style rayonnant, in ceramics, an abstract pattern of Baroque decoration associated with Rouen faience about 1700, apparently based on Moorish drapery, a regular leafy embroidery culminating in points directed toward the centre of a circle; see also **Lambrequins.** **257**

Sublime Harmony music box, a late 19th-century English musical box which played elaborate chords.

Subsellium: see **Misericord.**

Sucket fork, or spoon, a combined fork and spoon, a two-pronged fork at one end and a spoon bowl at the other, late 17th-century silver tableware.

Sucrier, a sugar bowl.

Sue ware, early Japanese stoneware, grey with mottled greenish glaze, probably introduced from Korea about AD 500.

Suffolk chair: see **Mendlesham chair.**

Suffolk latch, similar to a Norfolk latch but with no escutcheon plate, merely small spade-shaped (usually) ends by which the handle is attached to the door.

Sugar basin, bowl, and basket, typically silver but also porcelain, the bowl being basically circular and usually with a lid; the term basin usually applied to a later (about 1800) piece, usually oval or boat-shaped, matching a tea set; a basket is pierced, with glass liner. **241, 259**

Sugar box, a round or oval container with cover, usually footed, silver, 17th and 18th centuries. **250**

Sugar caster, or sifter: see **Caster.**

Sugar chest, a large, simple, wooden chest or bin, often with sloping lid, found chiefly in the American South, early 19th century.

Sugar crusher, cleaver, nipper etc., various metal implements, often cutters like heavy scissors with curved blade, also glass pestles, for cutting or crushing granulated sugar from the loaf in which it was usually sold, mainly 19th century.

Sugar tongs, or nippers, silver implements for lifting lumps of sugar, early examples (late 17th century) self-sprung like fire tongs, later hinged or in scissors form, the grasping ends usually shaped like small spoons, sometimes shells or claws.

Suite, of furniture, a matching set of chairs, sofas, stools, etc., formerly (16th and 17th centuries) involving a large number of pieces.

Sulky, a two-wheeled, one-horse carriage with a single seat.

Sulphides, ornaments of clay—figures, busts, scenes, etc.—embedded in glass; see also **Crystallo-ceramie.**

Sulphur tint, an aquatint in which the faintly streaked appearance is enhanced by a light dusting of sulphur on the plate.

Sultane, a couch with solid ends, cylindrical cushions or bolsters and, usually, no back, 18th century.

Summer beds, twin beds, placed fairly close together under a common canopy, a Sheraton design.

Sunburst pattern, a rayed semicircle like a stylized rising (or setting) sun, similar to a shell and often found on similar furniture, e.g. 18th-century American sideboards and cabinets, also in pressed glass; sometimes circular—the whole sun.

Sunderland pottery, purple, pink and mottled lustre, chiefly on creamware, and a variety of generally cheap earthenwares made in various Sunderland, Co. Durham, potteries from the late 18th century.

Sundial, a timepiece that shows the time (according to the sun) by the shadow cast on it by a pointer in the centre, originating in prehistoric times as a stone column set in the centre of an open place. **260**

Sunflower chest: see **Connecticut sunflower chest, Hadley chest.**

Sung dynasty, in China the period AD 960—1279, in which true porcelain was developed, divided into 'Northern' and 'Southern' Sung (from 1127). **150, 258**

Sunken, of a panel, clock dial, etc., recessed below the level of the surround.

Sunray clock, a clock having a dial in the form of a stylized sun with emanating rays usually in relief, probably first made in France in the reign of Louis XIV.

Sunstone, a feldspathic gem stone, a variable brownish-red colour, with a brightly spangled appearance resulting from haematitic inclusions.

Surbase, in stand furniture, an ornamental band or moulding on the upper part of a pedestal.

Surcoat, an overcoat, particularly one displaying a sign of rank, such as arms displayed on the coat worn over armour.

Surfeit water flute: see **Ratafia glass**.

Surtable, a centrepiece or épergne.

Surtout, 'over-all', usually applied to garments such as an overcoat or hooded cape, sometimes a coat of whitewash, also a centrepiece or épergne.

Sussex chair, a name applied to a spindle-backed chair with a rushwork seat, particularly 19th-century chairs associated with the firm of William Morris.

Sussex pig, an earthenware pig with a detachable head used as a wine cup, enabling the drinker to boast he had consumed a 'hog's-head', made at a pottery in Rye, Sussex, 19th century.

Sutherland table, the name given to a type of 19th-century gate-leg table, in which the drop-leaves represent almost the total area of the top, a narrow rectangle only three or four inches wide remaining when the table is folded; usually found as an 'occasional' table.

Swadlincote pottery, from a Derbyshire pottery, in particular Rockingham-glazed toby jugs, 19th century.

Swag, a decorative element in the form of a curve of foliage with flowers, fruit, etc., frequently employed as a moulding by Adam and in the late 18th century generally; see also **Garland**; also, a similar element in curtains. **167**

Swage, an ornamental mould for cast iron or other metal; also, the decorative pattern formed by swaging.

Swagger stick, a short cane, as carried nowadays by sergeant-majors.

Swan-neck, a descriptive term often applied to decorative elements forming a gentle S curve, suggesting a swan's or goose's neck, in particular, broken pediments in that form (usually with a central urn or vase) on cabinets, etc., late 18th century. **55**

Swansea porcelain, early 19th-century soft-paste porcelain greatly cherished by collectors, briefly produced at the Cambrian pottery, Swansea, by William Billingsley of Nantgarw in association with Lewis Dillwyn; including duck's-egg porcelain and soapstone porcelain; some fine, naturalistic floral painting by Billingsley himself and others.

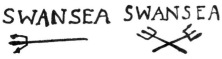

Swash turning: see **Barley-sugar twist**.

Swastika: see **Fylfot**.

Swatow ware, a rather rough type of Ming porcelain made in Fukien for the export market in the 16th and 17th centuries, with vigorous enamel painting in styles already proved popular.

Sweetmeat basket: see **Comfit basket**.

Sweetwood, a term applied to various pleasant-smelling West Indian hardwoods, from the late 16th century.

Swelling stem, in glassware, a stem with a simple knop, or one of baluster form; see also **Silesian stem**.

Swept front: see **Bow front**.

Swift, a wooden reel for winding yarn, often adjustable in size.

Swing-leg table: see **Gate table**.

Swinton ware, creamware and other earthenware from a pottery near Leeds, closely associated with Leeds in the late 18th century, owned solely by the Brameld family from soon after 1800; see also **Rockingham ware**.

Swirl, in millefiori glass, a spiral turn given to the glass canes; see also **Whorl**.

Swiss lapis, jasper stained to look like lapis lazuli.

Swivel gun, a type of heavy musket with a downward-projecting spike at the point of balance, fitting the socket of a stand so that it swivelled easily; also, a cannon similarly mounted.

Sword, any long-bladed weapon with a hilt and crossguard for cutting and/or thrusting, including sabres (cutting weapons) and rapiers (thrusting); see also **Smallsword**. **34, 222, 225, 248**

Swordstick, a walking stick or cane which is also the sheath of a thin-bladed sword.

Sycamore, a light-coloured, often slightly yellow wood with close grain, used mainly for turned members, sometimes for solid construction and veneers (particularly when stained); the name sometimes embraces plane and maple; see also **Harewood**.

Syllabub dish, for the concoction of cream and wine popular from about 1700; various vessels are so-called including a silver cup like a caudle cup and, in particular, a glass on a foot with stepped bowl providing a wide mouth.

Symphonium, a type of musical box introduced in the late 19th century in which the cylinder with projecting pins was replaced by a revolving, perforated disc.

Synagogue lamp: see **Sabbath lamp**.

Syrian carpets: see **Damascus rugs**.

Tabachi, poor-quality wool obtained with lime from the fleece of dead animals, used in some oriental carpets.

Tabard, a loose, usually sleeveless gown or tunic as worn in the Middle Ages, especially one emblazoned with coat of arms worn by a herald; also, sometimes

applied to a banner and hence a 'banner' firescreen—a piece of heavy, embroidered cloth hanging from a rail mounted centrally on a pillar.

Tabaret, an upholstery and curtain fabric with alternate stripes of satin and watered silk, the latter typically cream, contrasting with satin stripes in strong colours; see also **Tabby**.

Tabbinet, a watered silk and wool material, a more delicate variety of tabby.

Tabby, a basic weaving technique, a term applied to various kinds of (mostly) silk cloth, especially a striped or watered silk taffeta; also, a type of cement containing gravel and shells.

Tabernacle, a moveable dwelling such as a tent, in particular that serving as the dwelling-place of the Jewish God during the exile of the Israelites; hence, a shrine or niche for a holy image.

Tabernacle clock, a name given to a type of (chiefly) 16th-century spring-driven shelf clock, of generally monumental form with an elaborate openwork superstructure or tower and sometimes four dials.

Tabernacle frame, an ornamental carved frame for a recess in a wall, usually incorporating tabernacle work, fashionable in the late 18th century.

Tabernacle mirror, a looking glass of the Sheraton period with a scene painted on the upper part of the glass below a shallow, flat-topped cornice, frequently with a row of gilt balls; similar types still made in the second half of the 19th century.

Tabernacle work, a term sometimes applied to ornamental fretwork, in wood or stone, like that seen on a canopy over a shrine or tomb in a church.

Tabinet, a watered fabric similar to tabby, usually silk and wool, used for curtains and upholstery.

Table, any piece of furniture with a flat top of wood or other material, serving various purposes and made in many forms since people first started sitting on chairs (or stools) rather than the ground; also, in jewellery, the facet on top of a stone, a sheet of glass, etc.

Table bed, a 19th-century combination piece, usually in the form of a table over a cupboard containing the folded bed.

Table bench, a settle table.

261

262

261 Table clock. Late 16th century. German clock by an unknown maker. The hours are shown in Roman and Arabic numerals. (Clockmaker's Company Museum, London)

262 Lidded pewter tankard. Nuremberg, 17th century. With incised decoration of trailing plants. (Private Collection, Trieste)

263 Woman playing polo. Chinese, T'ang dynasty (618–907), pottery with polychrome glazing. (Musée Cernuschi, Paris)

264 Tabouret in gilt wood with canvas work upholstery. Early 18th century. (Victoria and Albert Museum, London)

265 Silver tankard. English, made at York, 1657–58. (Victoria and Albert Museum, London. Photo: John Webb)

Table board, a removeable table top, as found in some trestle tables, formerly a common construction.

Table chair: see **Chair table**.

Table clock, a small spring-driven clock in the shape of a drum with the dial facing upward, the earliest type of small, household clock, predecessor of the watch. **261**

Table-cut, of a gem stone, a flat quadrilateral surface bevelled at the edges.

Table desk, a term applied to a fitted writing compartment in the form of a box, placed on top of a table, perhaps the earliest type of desk.

Table dormant, a fixed table, such as was placed on a dais in a dining hall in the Middle Ages.

Table piano, a piano concealed (for some reason) in a table, not a very graceful table and perhaps not a very good piano, a mid 19th-century fashion.

Table plateau, a footed glass tray, usually circular and silver-mounted, placed under the centrepiece on the table.

Table servant, a side table.

Table supports, the frame or legs supporting a table (which generally meant a table top until the 18th century).

Tablet, an article for writing on, particularly if stone, metal or other hard material; hence, a commemorative plaque, etc.; also, a small table, a decorative panel on a mantel clock, etc.

Tablet chair, a chair (e.g. a Windsor chair) with a flat writing surface attached to the arm.

Tabouret, an upholstered stool, from the 17th century. **264**

Tabriz carpets, from the commercial capital of old Persia, the first carpets exported to Europe, including very fine silk-pile and strong wool-pile carpets, commonly with a floral design and central medallion, Ghiordes knot, various colours and (recently) variable quality.

Taffeta, or taffety, a silk material, particularly one with a shiny, watered finish, or a similar linen material, used for hangings and coverings as well as clothes, since the late Middle Ages.

Taille d'épergne, decorative linear engraving, filled with enamel colour, on small silver articles.

Talavera maiolica, the finest of all 17th-century Spanish pottery, from the long-established centre in Castile; many types of wares painted with hunting scenes, buildings, historical scenes, bullfights, etc.

Talbotype, or calotype, a picture made by a photographic process named after its inventor, who sensitized paper by treating it with silver nitrate and potassium iodide.

Talc, a soft, translucent mineral with many industrial uses; see also **Mica, Soapstone**.

Tale glass, poor quality glass, made from the metal at the top of the melting pot, the quality in 18th-century glass-works increasing from top to bottom.

Talent, a measure of silver or gold used in the ancient Near East, varying in quantity according to time and place.

Talish carpets, Caucasian carpets of a type associated with Shirvan, long pile and simple designs, sometimes a plain field.

Talisman, a small object such as a ring or brooch invested with supernatural powers, often esoterically inscribed; see also **Amulet**.

Tallboy, similar to the American highboy, a tall chest of drawers in chest-on-chest form (sometimes used less precisely), various forms from about 1700 to about 1900.

Tall-case clock: see **Long-case clock**.

Tally, a wooden stick recording the amount of a debt, which was notched at the appropriate place, and then slit lengthways, each party keeping one half as a record.

Tallyboard, a wooden board or slate on which debts were recorded, e.g. by an innkeeper.

Tambour, a shutter, sliding door, etc., made by gluing thin strips of wood to a flexible ground such as canvas, which can thus run in curved grooves, as in a roll-top desk. **97**

Tambour work, a type of crochet embroidery made on a hooped frame (like a tambourine), of oriental origin, used in dressmaking in central Europe in the 18th century.

Tam o' Shanter, a woollen bonnet like a beret but with a very wide crown and usually a pom-pom on top, named after the Burns character; also a popular 19th-century Staffordshire figure.

Tanagra figure, a Classical Greek earthenware figure of a young woman seated or standing, chiefly 3rd and 4th centuries BC, once regarded as Classical kitsch.

Tang, a spike, point, nail, etc., e.g. the point of a shoe buckle, the prong (tine) of a fork, the pin in a cotter-pin hinge, the section of a sword blade fitting into the hilt, etc.

T'ang dynasty, the 7th–9th centuries in China, something of a golden age in the arts, the period that witnessed great advances in ceramics, including the beginnings of true porcelain. **263, 271**

Tankard, a large beer mug often with lid and thumbpiece, usually straight-sided, silver, pewter, or other material, shorter and wider in diameter than a flagon, known in its familiar form since the 16th century. **262, 265**.

Tantalus, an open box-like container for decanters or bottles with a locked retaining bar over the top to prevent unauthorized tippling.

Tanzaku, Japanese verses inscribed on long, narrow printed strips for hanging on a wall.

T'ao-t'ieh, a motif in Chinese art representing a stylized lion's mask. **35**

Tap bolt, a bolt with a pointed end, like a screw.

Taper, a candle, particularly a very long one or a very thin one, sometimes coiled, used for lighting other candles; also sealing wax.

Taper box, a small box, silver or various other materials, usually cylindrical, containing a taper that could be drawn out through a hole in the top.

Taper decanter, a shape popular in the late 18th and early 19th centuries, a slender form like a wine bottle, often with vertical fluting.

Taper stand, a small metal pillar on a foot or shallow dish, usually with some type of attachment at the top for gripping the end of the taper, which was wound around the pillar; other forms also found, sometimes with extinguisher attached by a chain.

Taper stick, a small candlestick.

Tape seat, a chair seat of stout canvas tapes interwoven like rushwork.

Tapestry, originally a wall hanging in which the design is woven in variously coloured woollen weft threads on a linen warp; the technique was known in pre-Classical times, fragments surviving from Egyptian tombs; used for upholstery in the 18th century; the word is also popularly used to describe embroidered canvas work. **18, 267**

Tape twist, a white, spiralling band in the stem of a wine glass.

Tappit hen, a lidded ('tappit') pewter measure, Scottish, similar to a flagon but with a concave curve to the upper part of the body, various sizes, some very large.

Tapul, in armour, a term applied to the vertical ridge down the middle of the cuirass, with a point at the centre, first appearing in the mid 16th century, later growing more pronounced and leading to the 'peascod' or 'pigeon-breasted' cuirass; the original meaning of the term is doubtful.

Taquillon, a Spanish chest with ornamentally carved panels, from the 15th century.

Target, a small shield, particularly if round; also, an object for marksmen to fire at.

Target stopper, a type of stopper on decanters of the late 18th and 19th centuries, in the form of a disc with engraved concentric ridges.

Tari, a silver coin current in the Mediterranean area in the 16th century, with profile portrait and cross of St John, several kinds.

Tarot cards, similar to playing cards but with different characters, used for the game of tarot in Italy in the 14th century (and probably older), and for telling fortunes.

Tarsia: see Intarsia.

Tartan, a woollen material with vertical and horizontal stripes of various widths and colours, as worn by Scottish Highlanders, certain patterns identifying particular clans; popular for upholstery, and the pattern adopted for general decorative purposes in the Victorian period; also, a single-masted sailing boat.

Tass, or tassie, a wine cup or small goblet; see also **Tazza.**

Tasset, in armour, a thigh plate, or a short skirt of articulated plates serving the same purpose.

Tassie brooch, an imitation ancient cameo moulded in glass paste, also a contemporary portrait, of the type first made by James Tassie in the second half of the 18th century.

Tatami, straw mats about 6 ft by 3 ft, the standard floor covering in Japan since the Middle Ages.

Taunton chest, an 18th-century New England chest associated with the region around Taunton, Massachusetts, with carved and painted designs of somewhat stylized flowers, foliage and birds; see also **Hadley chest, Connecticut sunflower chest.**

Tavern clock, a large, simple, pendulum wall clock similar to the type known as Act of Parliament clocks, from about 1700.

Tavern table, a term usually applied to a squareish oak table of sturdy construction.

Taw, a glass or ceramic ball or large marble (Scottish); see also **Carpet bowls.**

Tazza, a shallow silver or glass bowl on a tallish stem, originally (16th century) a drinking vessel, but often applied to any vessel of this general form, sometimes with cover.

Tea board, a tea tray, usually rimmed or galleried, to be placed on a stand.

Tea caddy: see Caddy.

Tea chest, a large, square-sided, light wooden chest, metal-lined, in which tea was shipped; also, a tea caddy, especially (after about 1800), a large one with its own stand.

Teak, a very heavy, hard wood, dark brown when old, from the Far East, used mainly in building but sometimes for furniture that must tolerate rough conditions, e.g. on ships.

Tea kettle, similar to a teapot but intended for boiling the water, therefore metal (sometimes silver with stand and lamp, and perhaps salver) and with bail handle, from about 1700. **147**

Teapot, a silver or china vessel with long spout, cover and handle, made in many forms since the late 17th century. **126, 160, 209, 268.**

Teapoy, a stand on a tripod base with containers for tea and/or other ingredients, with a removeable tray top, early 19th century; also, sometimes a tea caddy on a stand, or a small side table.

Tear, or teardrop, in glass, an air bubble, as in a knop on a wine glass stem; also, a pear-shaped glass drop handle. **294**

Tea set, matching teapot, jug, basin and cups and saucers, for tea, very popular from the mid 18th century; usually in silver, excluding cups and saucers. **266**

Tea table, any small occasional table on which tea might be served in an 18th-century drawing room, some with detachable tops, some combination folding tables also for cards, some of pillar and claw construction; also a teapoy or a tea tray. **269**

Tea urn: see Urn.

Tebo figures, early English porcelain figures from several factories including Bow and Chelsea showing the influence of the French Rococo style, by a modeller of whom nothing is known save his mark.

Teco pottery, green-glazed wares in Art Nouveau style from a celebrated pottery in Terra Cotta, Illinois.

Teheran carpets, high-quality carpets from the city now capital of Iran, now rare and valuable, notable for minuteness of design, particularly of interwoven floral forms with animals scattered about; see also **Veramin carpets.**

Tê-hua porcelain: see Blanc de Chine.

Tekke carpets, woven by the nomadic Tekke peoples; see **Bokhara carpets, Turkoman carpets.**

Telamon, a male figure functioning as a column; see also **Atlantes.**

Telescope, or telescopic, applied to certain lamps, candlesticks and similar articles of cylindrical section that can be extended like a telescope.

Tempera, distemper, i.e. water-based paint combined with a binding agent; in wall painting applied to a dry surface (unlike true fresco).

Temple ware, English delftware and various later earthenwares from the pottery founded in Bristol in the late 17th century.

Tender porcelain, soft-paste porcelain.

Tendril ornament: see Acanthus.

Tenon: see Mortise-and-tenon.

Tent bed, a bed with a dome- or tent-shaped canopy, similar to a fieldbed, especially popular in the early 19th century.

Tent stitch, or petit point, a type of embroidery in which the stitches make a diagonal pattern (half a cross-stitch) on a fabric ground; see also **Berlin work, Canvas work.**

Term, a pillar or pedestal, especially one surmounted by the armless trunk and head of a Classical figure; a boundary marker, a fence post, etc.

Terraced, ascending in a series of steps, a term often applied to a dome form interrupted by steps, e.g. in the foot of a wine glass.

Terra cotta, literally 'baked earth', applied chiefly to figures and other objects modelled in natural clay and hardened by firing, sometimes painted or otherwise decorated, often left in the natural (usually reddish) colour; an ancient art known in many prehistoric societies, perhaps the finest examples in modern times found in Renaissance Florence and among 18th-century French sculpture. **271**

Terra de pipa, or terre de pipe, fine-quality earthenware similar to English creamware, late 18th century.

Terraglia, the Italian version of creamware or faience-fine.

Terra sigillata, Roman pottery dating from the 1st century BC, red-bodied, decorated with slip and impressed designs and bearing the potter's mark.

Terre de Lorraine, the fine-quality clay used at Lunéville and associated potteries.

Terret, a type of horse brass consisting of a ring within which an ornament or emblem hung, the ring being mounted

266 English silver tea set. Teapot by Humphrey Payne, 1713, sugar bowl by William Fleming, 1718, and cream jug by Starling Wilford, 1723. (Ashmolean Museum, Oxford)

267 *Wild woman with a unicorn.* Tapestry, Upper Rhine, late 15th century. (Historisches Museum, Basle)

268 Silver teapot. By Pehr Zethelius. Stockholm, 1798–9. (Nationalmuseum, Stockholm)

269 Mahogany tea table with ball and claw feet. English, about 1750. (Victoria and Albert Museum, London)

upright between the horse's ears and sometimes surmounted by a cockade of bristles.

Terre verte, a siliceous mineral providing a green pigment, used in ceramics; also, unfired earthenware.

Terry clock, strictly, a clock made by the famous Connecticut clockmaker Eli Terry (1772–1852), applied more generally to early 19th-century Connecticut clocks in his style (many made by ex-apprentices), particularly a type of mantel clock of architectural (side pillars and curved pediment) form with a painted glass panel below the dial.

Teruel ware, Hispano-Moresque pottery from the centre in Aragon, with designs in which Western and Islamic influences mingle, often painted in green and dark blue, from about about the 13th century; later, lustreware similar to Manises.

Tessellated, tiled; or, a pattern composed of squares, rectangles, etc.

Tessera, a small four-sided piece of stone, wood, glass, etc. used in a mosaic or inlay.

Tester, the canopy over a four-poster bed, flat on top.

Tête-à-tête: see **Confidante.**

Tetrachord, a particular series of four notes in music; also, a type of Ancient Greek four-stringed lyre, plucked with the fingers.

Textilograph: see **Stevengraph.**

Thaler, a large German silver coin, first issued in the early 16th century, many varieties in different European countries; the origin of the dollar.

Thaumatrope, a type of magic lantern of the late 19th century that created 'movement' by optical illusion.

Themata, applied ornamental silver or other metal strips with embossed design.

Theorbo, a type of lute with a long neck and double head, the upper part curving forward to keep the bass strings clear of the treble stops, 16th–17th centuries. 274

Therm: see **Term.**

Thetford ware, the name given to a type of Anglo-Saxon pottery, a hard, greyish, unglazed earthenware, examples of which—squat pitchers and pots—were found in the neighbourhood of Thetford, Norfolk.

T hinge, the two leaves, individually L shaped, together forming a T.

Thistle bowl, in a wine glass, a bowl tapering inwards from the rim to a pronounced waist, the bottom of the bowl being rounded (and often solid), the whole resembling the shape of a thistle flower; also found in silver standing cups, certain Scottish mugs, etc.

Thomas clock, made by Seth Thomas (1785–1859), once employed by Eli Terry, or bearing his name (still current); see also **Terry clock.**

Thonet chair, one of the bentwood chairs first made by the Austrian cabinet-maker Michael Thonet (1796–1871).

Threading, on glass particularly, applied decoration of thinly drawn threads of metal, e.g. around the neck of a pitcher; see also **Trailed decoration.**

Three boys porcelain, referring to a common motif in Hirado porcelain.

Three-mould-blown, of glass vessels blown full-size in a three-piece mould, an early 19th-century practice for cheaper wares, sometimes simulating hand-cut glass; superseded by pressed glass.

Three-piece glass, a vessel such as a wine glass in which the three main parts (bowl, stem and foot) were made separately and welded together.

Thrown, in ceramics, formed on a potter's wheel, the term deriving from a time when the lump of clay was actually 'thrown' on to the revolving wheel prior to shaping; also, turned.

Thrysma, a small gold coin of Anglo-Saxon times, based on a Roman model; see also **Tremissis.**

Thumb glass, a drinking glass with impressed niche for the thumb and sometimes fingers, German, 16th century.

Thumb moulding, on the rim of a table, chest, etc., a downward-curving quarter-circle; also a series of indentations similar to thumbprints.

Thumbpiece, the vertical projection next to the hinge on the lid of (most typically) a tankard, and used for opening it, the numerous forms often furnishing a guide to date and place of manufacture.

Thumb ring, worn on the thumb rather than the finger, chiefly in the East, said to have been worn by executioners to allow a better purchase when garrotting.

Thuyawood, from a North African tree, a much admired (and rare) wood used in 18th-century veneers, a rich brown with strong wavy lines and speckle marks.

Tiara, originally a domed headdress or crown, as worn in ancient Persia and (now) by the pope; subsequently, any ornamental headdress.

Tical, a Siamese coin current in medieval times (and later), of interest largely because of its unusual form—a piece of silver wire doubled back against itself.

Tickenhall pottery, from the Derbyshire centre; in particular, 17th-century dark-bodied slipware; see also **Cistercian ware.**

Ticking, a very strong linen or cotton cloth, usually woven in stripes, for covering mattresses, pillows, etc., or for hanging in doorways in sunny climates.

Ticking work, embroidery on a ticking ground.

Tidal-dial clock, an English clock showing the time of high tide at a particular port (most frequently London), from the 17th century; some were capable of being adjusted to show the time of high tide at any port.

Tiefschnitt, in glass or gems, a deep-cut design in intaglio, as opposed to Hochschnitt (cut in relief), a technique in German glass from about 1700.

Tiffany glass, American Art Nouveau glass by (or in the manner of) Louis Comfort Tiffany (1848–1933), notable for alluring plant-like forms and glowing colours; see also **Favrile glass.** 100, 270

Tiffany lamp, a lamp in Art Nouveau style with a coloured glass shade, frequently of mushroom form, by or based on the designs of L. C. Tiffany of New York.

Tiger-eye, a variety of quartz, brownish-yellow, which can be cut to give a stripey effect in jewel stones.

Tigerware jug, a Rhineland stoneware jug covered with a mottled glaze imported to England in the 16th century and imitated at various English potteries; see also **Malling pottery.**

Tigerwood, a name applied to several woods used in veneers, having a striped appearance, e.g. zebrawood.

Tile, a shallow slab of stone or clay used for roofs, floors, walls, stoves, etc., frequently ornamented when for indoor use, a notable article in tin-glazed earthenware particularly. 272

Till, a fitted drawer in a dressing table or desk, or a similarly fitted tray in a chest or worktable; as in a modern cash register.

Tilting chest, a name given to a Gothic chest with jousting scenes carved in relief.

Tilt-top, any folding table in which the entire surface can be raised to a horizontal position, chiefly round-topped pedestal tables, from the late 18th century.

Time lamp, any lamp combining the functions of lamp and timekeeper, usually by gradations marked on the side of the reservoir relating the falling level of oil to the passage of time.

Timepiece, a clock with no striking or chiming mechanism.

Tin, a silvery white metal, not very durable but resistant to oxidation, used chiefly in alloys and as a coating on other metal; see also **Tin-plate.**

Tinderbox, a metal box containing tinder (some easily ignited material) plus flint and steel, for making fire.

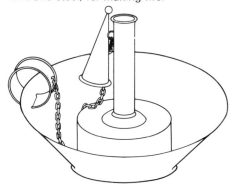

Candlestick with tinderbox in base

Tine, a prong of a fork (or stag's antler).

Tin-glaze, in earthenware, a glaze containing tin oxide, glassy and (naturally) white; the distinguishing characteristic of earthenware known variously as delftware, faience and maiolica; used in ancient times and introduced to Spain via the Muslims in the Middle Ages.

Ting ware, a type of Chinese porcelain of the Sung period, generally with a creamy white glaze (occasionally brown or black), mainly bowls and dishes, distinguished by delicate floral or animal designs in low relief or incised.

Tin-plate, tinned, or sometimes merely 'tin', when applied to a metal article, usually implying tin-plated iron or steel sheet; either permeated by the molten tin (tin-plate) or merely coated (tinned); see also **Japanned, Tinware.**

Tin safe: see **Safe.**

Tinsel, thin strips of glittering metal used for various ornamental purposes; in particular, cut out to make pictures in the 18th and 19th centuries; also, a glittering cloth, the effect achieved by interwoven metal threads; or, metaphorically, worthless frippery.

Tinware, generally cheap household articles made of tin from ancient times until the development of thin sheet iron, similar to pewter.

Tipstaff, a ceremonial staff of office having some kind of metal tip, often in the form of a crown, associated with various legal officials such as court ushers, bailiffs, etc.

Tithe pig, a popular figure in English earthenware in the 18th and 19th centuries, various versions, the pig representing tithe paid in kind to the parish priest, sometimes with anticlerical verse.

TLV decoration, a motif in Chinese art looking like the letters TLV. **122**

Toad-back, an obscure term apparently describing a type of moulding seen on the legs of late 18th-century furniture, two flattened S curves flanking a central convex semicircle.

Toad mug: see **Frog mug.**

Toasted-cheese dish, a silver dish like a rectangular frying pan with a lid, sometimes incorporating a hot-water container below, sometimes with a tray, from about 1800.

Toaster, any implement for toasting bread at a fire, e.g. an adjustable iron stand, a long wooden handle with a horseshoe-shaped piece at the end, against which the bread is held by prongs, something like a paperclip.

Toasting fork, a long-handled fork for toasting muffins at the fire, known in silver in the 16th century.

Toasting glass: see **Firing glass, Toastmaster's glass.**

Toastmaster's glass, a thick-walled drinking glass, holding less in reality than in appearance.

Toast-rack, known in many forms (sometimes perhaps for letters rather than toast) and materials since the 18th century, most typically a series of thin, arched bands on a base or frame with four feet, in silver.

Tobacco box, or jar, etc., various containers for tobacco—silver boxes, earthenware jars, etc.—since the mid 17th century, in numerous forms, sometimes not intended for this specific purpose.

Tobacco grater: see **Snuff grater.**

Tobacco pipe, made since the early 17th century in Europe, usually of clay; see also **Churchwarden, Meerschaum.**

Toby jug, an earthenware jug in the form (originally) of a man in a tricorn hat with a mug of ale, first introduced in the mid 18th century apparently by Wood of Burslem and very popular ever since, many different versions e.g. John Bull, Martha Gunn, etc.

Toddy glass, an English rummer with rudimentary stem and heavy foot, sometimes square; sometimes applied to a glass similar to a dwarf ale glass or large dram, for toddy—a hot drink of rum with sugar and fruit juice.

Toddy ladle, in particular, 19th-century Scottish punch ladles with silver bowls and whalebone handles.

Toddy lifter, a glass vessel shaped something like a bottle with a hole in the bottom; the thick end being immersed and the hole at the top stopped, a measure of toddy could be removed.

Toe, in furniture, the junction of a chair arm with the seat.

Toft ware, Staffordshire slipware of the late 17th century, especially large dishes (sometimes nearly 2 ft across), with portraits or other designs in trailed brown slip, some early examples bearing the name of Toft on the broad rim. **249**

Toga, a loose, ankle-length gown worn draped over the shoulders and leaving the right arm free, standard dress in ancient Rome.

Toile, a pattern in cloth, for dressmaking, etc.

Toile de Jouy, linen cloth printed (originally with wood blocks) in imitation of oriental technique, originally made at Jouy, near Paris, in the mid 18th century.

Toile peinte, linen or cotton cloth 'painted' (or printed) with floral patterns, scenes, etc., first imported from India in the 17th century; see also **Chintz.**

Toilet, originally a covering for a table in a bedroom; later, a dressing table.

Toilet looking glass, originally a mirror to hang on the wall or stand on a table; later a mirror fitted to a dressing table.

Toilet set, a set of tools and gadgets needed to accomplish the day's toilet, varying according to age and fashion. **273**

Toilet table, a fitted dressing table. **275**

Toiletta, a dressing table.

Toison, a Burgundian gold or silver coin issued in the late 15th century bearing the insignia of the Order of the Golden Fleece (toison d'or).

Token, an unofficial coin issued by local landlords, tradesmen, local governments, etc. in various times and places to supplement or replace the regular coinage, e.g. during the American Civil War.

Tôle, painted sheet-iron wares of various kinds, the French equivalent of Pontypool ware, from the second half of the 18th century; see also **Japanned.**

Toledo pottery, medieval Hispano-Moresque wares, especially large jars, fonts, basins, etc. as well as smaller articles and tiles, tin-glazed; later maiolica generally rather vigorous in style and inferior to Talavera.

Toledo steel, very fine-quality steel since the Renaissance, known throughout Europe as the best sword blades. **222**

Tompion clock, the work of the famous English clockmaker Thomas Tompion (1639–1713), who was responsible for several important improvements; particularly in long-case clocks.

Tonbridge ware: see **Tunbridge ware.**

Tongue-and-groove, a joint used for parallel flat boards as in floorboards, or table tops, a projecting ridge on one edge fitting a corresponding groove in the other, found on some early gateleg tables.

Toothed ornament: see **Dentate.**

Topaz, a precious stone, commonly a yellowish-brown but also various other colours and in nature most frequently colourless; until modern times, a different stone (peridot) may have been involved.

270

271

270 Art Nouveau glass vase by
L. C. Tiffany, about 1900. The vase
represents a flower from the bulb
to the petals. (Museum of Modern
Art, New York)

271 Chinese terra cotta figurines of
dancing girls. T'ang dynasty
(618–907). (William Rockhill
Nelson Gallery of Art, Kansas City)

272 Islamic glazed tile with lustreware decoration. Persian, Kashan,
about 1300. (Museo di
Capodimonte, Naples)

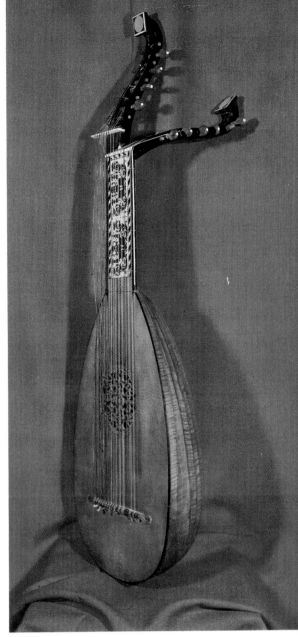

▲ 273

274

273 Part of a silver toilet set. By Paul de Lamerie, 1728. Ewer, snuffers, a tray, candlestick, circular basket and small waiter. (Ashmolean Museum, Oxford)

274 Theorbo. Made by Magnus Tieffenbrucker in 1610. (Richard-Wagner Museum, Lucerne)

275 Bow-fronted mahogany toilet table with cross-banding. English, about 1800. (Victoria and Albert Museum, London)

Torchère, a tall stand or pedestal for a candlestick or (later) a lamp.

Torelli maiolica, 19th-century earthenware imitating Renaissance styles from a factory in Florence.

Torond silhouette, the work of Francis Torond (1743–1812), perhaps the best-known of English (though born in France) artists in this field, noted particularly for 'conversation' groups of families.

Torricellian tube, a stick or cistern barometer, so named after its inventor, Evangelista Torricelli (1608–47), disciple of Galileo.

Tortoise brooch, an early medieval Scandinavian bronze or gold ornament the shape of a tortoise shell with engraved motifs in latticework panels.

Tortoise clock, a 17th-century conceit, subsequently reproduced (though rare), a table clock (horizontal dial) with concave centre filled with water in which a metal tortoise floats round following a hidden magnet moved by the mechanism, indicating the time with his nose.

Tortoiseshell, a horn-like material derived from the plates on the back of the hawk's-bill turtle, a translucent yellow, mottled with reddish brown, and capable of a high polish; used for making small articles (combs, snuffboxes, etc.), for inlay in furniture and other purposes since pre-Classical times.

Tortoiseshell ware, ceramics resembling tortoiseshell in appearance, an effect achieved by mingling coloured glazes to create a mottled effect; late 18th and early 19th centuries; see also **Whieldon ware. 277**

Torus moulding, in section a convex semicircle, as seen on monumental plinths, etc.

Touch, in pewter, a mark signifying the name of the maker and place of manufacture, a trade mark (as distinct from a hallmark), often of quite complex design; unreliable as a guide because of scanty records.

Touch pin, a small knob on the dial of a watch or clock, to aid in telling the time in the dark.

Touchstone, a stone such as flint, or other suitable material, used to scratch the surface of precious metal to test for standard.

Toulouse faience, a few surviving pieces only of early 18th-century faience from Toulouse, a pottery-making centre since Roman times.

Tourmaline, a highly translucent precious stone occurring in a great variety of colours, in jewellery usually pink or green, used for small carvings in China.

Tournai ware, faience from the 17th century and, more notably, soft-paste porcelain from the mid 18th century, from Tournai (now in Belgium), chiefly French-influenced designs, notable for white biscuit figures, later (19th century) chiefly tableware.

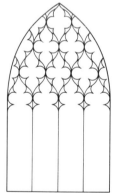

Towel horse: see **Horse furniture**.

Tower clock: see **Turret clock**.

Townsend furniture, the work of a well-known family of cabinetmakers in Newport, Rhode Island, in the 18th and early 19th centuries, notable for block-front furniture.

Toy, an article made for the amusement of children; also, formerly, a small ornamental article such as a snuffbox, cane top, bottle stopper, etc., especially in glass.

Tracery, in Gothic architecture, ornamental stonework, e.g. in windows or openwork screens; hence, similar carved ornament on wooden furniture.

Tracy chair, a Windsor chair made by the Connecticut chairmaker, Ebenezer Tracy, in the late 18th century.

Trade mark, a manufacturer's mark on any article, the mark (though not necessarily the article) being copyright since the early 19th century in most countries; see also **Mark, Touch**.

Trade money: see **Token**.

Trade sign, hung outside all shops in days when many could not read, symbolizing the service performed or goods sold, e.g. mortar and pestle for a druggist, a hat for a hatter, etc., wood or metal.

Trafalgar, a name applied to several articles after the British naval victory of 1805, especially a light and elegant Regency chair with cane seat, sabre legs and often cable moulding in top rail and uprights; also, a Sheraton chair loaded with dolphins, anchors and other nautical symbols, an extending table and other pieces from Morgan & Sanders 'Trafalgar' workshop, or china and glassware celebrating the battle.

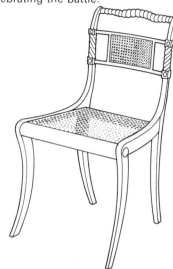

Trailed decoration, in ceramics and glass, most commonly on slipware, relief ornament applied in the form of a thread; see also **Threading. 223**

Trammel, a mechanical device for raising and lowering a hanging lamp, pot over a fire, etc.; also a type of fishing net, shackles or an instrument for drawing curves.

Transfer picture, on glass, an engraving glued to the back of the glass, most of the paper rubbed away, and the picture painted in with enamels, a technique used in the late 17th century.

Transfer-printed, an engraving printed on china, a technique invented in England in the mid 18th century, the design being transferred from an engraved plate to the surface (under- or overglaze) via paper or a 'bat'; at first mainly in underglaze blue; polychrome from the early 19th century; often the outline only printed and colours painted in by hand.

Translucent, allowing light to pass through but not (or not necessarily) transparent, the most obvious characteristic distinguishing porcelain from earthenware.

Transom, in architecture, a supporting crosspiece, hence applied to transverse members in cruciform objects, a horizontal stone bar in a Gothic window, a railway-line sleeper, etc.; also, a small window above a door.

Transylvania carpets, Turkish carpets, similar to Ushak and Bergama, found in churches in Transylvania and neighbouring regions; some dating back to the 16th century.

Trap-cut, of gems, cut in steps, or terraced, as in most emeralds.

Traveller's samples: see **Samples**.

Travelling clock, any clock designed to tolerate the motion of travelling; see **Carriage clock, Sedan clock**.

Travelling set, a set of cutlery and domestic gadgets for use in the days when it was necessary for a traveller to be self-sufficient. **276**

Traverse, a large screen to divide a room, or a curtain fulfilling the same purpose.

Tray, a flat board for carrying tableware etc., made in silver, wood and other materials, often with two handles and (usually) a galleried rim, round or rectangular, sometimes with small feet as a container for cruets, toast-racks, etc.; see also **Voider.** **151**

Tray-topped, any smallish table with a galleried and usually detachable top.

Treen, or woodware, all kinds of basins, dishes, cups, etc., including very simple peasant wares for domestic use and more finely wrought silver-mounted articles, in general use before the availability of pewter for household wares, e.g. in early colonial America.

Tree of Life, a motif common in oriental design (e.g. carpets), symbol of immortality, generally a stylized design, different types of tree being identified with different countries (cypress, fig, etc.); a similar motif, deriving from Classical design, is found in European peasant art.

Tree seat, a garden chair or bench made from roughly sawn logs.

Trefoil, or trifoil, in Gothic design, a form like a clover leaf—three lobes divided by cusps, sometimes seen as a small window.

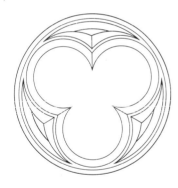

Trek, a blue or black outline, painted as a guide to the pattern, in Dutch delftware.

Trellis work: see Latticework.

Trembleuse, a small footed stand, usually silver gilt, placed on a table for a teacup, mid 18th century. **280**

Tremidos, the wave-pattern mouldings around panels characteristic of 17th-century Portuguese furniture in particular.

Tremissis, a small gold coin, one-third of a solidus, first issued by the Emperor Constantine and widely copied in Europe throughout the Middle Ages.

Tremolo: see Wrigglework.

Trenail, a wooden pin or dowel for holding joints in timber construction.

Trencher, a meat dish; originally, a wooden slab or large wooden dish, for meat, sometimes placed on top of a silver dish to preserve it from damage.

Trencher salt, a term sometimes applied to an individual silver salt cellar with flat base and glass liner; see also **Salt.**

Trenck beaker, a simple pewter beaker of the late 18th century engraved with a quotation from Baron Friedrich von der Trenck, the military adventurer imprisoned by Frederick the Great and eventually executed by Robespierre.

Trespolo, a tall three-legged table (Venetian), such as might support a candelabrum, vase, or a looking glass in a dressing room; hence **trespolo chair.** **278**

Trestle, a support or stand, particularly for a type of cheap dining table, of X-form ends linked by a heavy stretcher, common in the Middle Ages when the top was detachable.

Trestle foot, a square or rectangular block terminating trestle supports, for extra stability.

Trial piece, in ceramics, a vessel (often marred in some way) used for experiments in painted or other design.

Triangle table, a table with a three-sided top, sometimes made in fours to fit together as a large square; also, an envelope table.

Trichterkannen, Rhineland stoneware jugs, cylindrical below the rim, swelling outward towards the base.

Trick glass, a drinking glass, of fantastic form, or designed in some way to discompose the unsuspecting drinker and amuse the company, e.g. by spraying liquid into his face from concealed holes below the rim; see also **Puzzle jug, Yard-of-ale.**

Tricorn, 'three-cornered', usually referring to the hat widely worn by men in the 17th and 18th centuries.

Tricoteuse, a worktable with a recessed or galleried top for storing balls of wool etc. and, sometimes, a pull-out writing surface, late 18th century. **279**

Tridarn, or trydarn, a type of Welsh cupboard, in three stages: open shelves (or shelf) for display of plate on top, small cupboards (or drawers) below and larger cupboards at the bottom.

Trident, a three-pronged spear, as carried by Neptune, occurring (for example) as a mark on Swansea porcelain.

Triens, a Roman bronze coin bearing the head of Minerva and marked with four small discs indicating four unciae.

Trifid, or trefid, divided into three by lines or grooves, in particular, of a late 17th century silver spoon with stem flattened at the end in a three-lobed finial.

Trifle pewter, metal of intermediate quality (until the late 17th century, the best quality in England), 79 per cent tin, 15 per cent antimony and 6 per cent lead.

Trig, a wooden wedge placed under barrels laid on their sides to hold them stationary.

Triglyph, ornamentation of the frieze in the Doric order consisting of a block with three vertical grooves (glyphs) at regular intervals, alternating with metopes; see also **Doric.**

Trilateral leaf, the drop leaf (three-sided) of an octagonal table.

Trinket, a small article such as jewellery, usually of little intrinsic value; in particular, a small article belonging to a set or associated with a specific purpose.

Tripod, a three-legged stand; in particular, for a candelabrum or vase; also, a pillar and claw table. **207**

Tripoli earth, a fine, hard clay used in polishing and cutting glass and bringing up a shine on furniture, found near the North African city.

Triptych, originally an altarpiece consisting of three panels with painted scenes (e.g. of the Birth, Crucifixion and Resurrection of Christ), hence any similar construction, such as a three-piece, hinged looking glass on a dressing table.

Triskele, an emblem consisting of three human legs emanating from a common centre, as seen in the badge of the Isle of Man.

Triton, a sea-god from Classical mythology, having a fish's tail, found in various forms decorating silver candlesticks, fountains, etc., often in association with dolphins.

Trivet, strictly, a small three-footed metal stand for a pot or kettle over a fire, often applied to any type of stand for a kettle in the hearth.

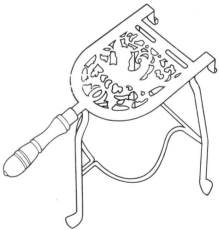

Trompe l'oeil, in fine art, painting that gives an intense impression of three-dimensional reality; in particular, panels offering a perspective view of an interior, buildings or landscape.

Trophy, an ornamental device usually in relief of a group of arms and banners, or any other group of associated objects, such as musical instruments, a popular motif in the Rococo period particularly; see also **Boiserie, Chute.** **28**

Troubadour style, decoration in 19th-century Gothic style, a term of opprobrium implying romantic medievalism run riot.

Truckle bed, or trundle bed, a low bed on wheels (truckles) that could be kept underneath an ordinary bed, for body-

276 English silver travelling set. Beaker, double spice or salt box, knife, fork, spoon with detachable handles and screw ends to hold smaller items, a toothpick, 3 napkin hooks, nutmeg grater, seal ring with a sheathed corkscrew in the handle. (Private Collection)

277 Tortoiseshell porcelain plate. Sèvres, 1792. (Musée National de Céramique, Sèvres)

278

279

278 Three-legged 'trespolo' chair with chip-carved decoration. Typical country furniture in Europe from the 15th to the 18th century. (Museo del Castello Sforzesco, Milan)

279 Tricoteuse. French, by Beurdeley & Son (active in the second half of the 19th century). Faithful copy of a Louis XVI worktable, decorated with inlay and enamel medallions, and gilt bronze. (P. Lécoules Collection, Paris)

280 Porcelain cup and *trembleuse* saucer. Sèvres, 1766. (Musée du Louvre, Paris)

guards, nurses, servants, etc., from the Renaissance period.

Trumeau, a pier mirror (or pier).

Trumpet, a term applied to various objects having the flared shape of the bell of a trumpet, including vases, lamp shades, wine glasses, etc. **1**

Trumpeter clock, similar to a cuckoo clock, a figure with trumpet replacing the cuckoo.

Trundle bed: see **Truckle bed**.

Trunk, formerly a standing chest, perhaps one hollowed from a tree trunk; since the 16th century a travelling chest, especially one with a curved top; see also **Coffer**; also, a term sometimes used in the sense of 'torso', e.g. the trunk of a long-case clock (between hood and base).

Trunk beaker, similar to a claw beaker.

Truss, a large supporting corbel or bracket.

Trussing bed, in Tudor times, a bed that could be packed up for travelling; see also **Campaign furniture**.

Trydaarn: see **Tridarn**.

Tschinke, or Teschner, a type of light, wheel-lock gun for hunting, originating in Silesia, with a concave curve in the stock behind the lock, late 16th to 17th centuries.

Tsun, a Chinese vessel for storing wine.

Ts'ung, a squared block pierced by a cylindrical hole, a burial object from the Far East, emblem of earth.

Tub chair, a chair with a rounded back and semicircular seat, found in Gothic furniture and also (upholstered) in the 19th century; see also **Barrel chair**.

Tubular furniture, mainly chairs and tables, having a frame of (usually) steel tubes, made since the mid 19th century.

Tucker porcelain, perhaps the most sought-after 19th-century American china, produced by William Ellis Tucker of Philadelphia and his successors in the 1820s and 1830s, a hard-paste porcelain similar to contemporary Sèvres, with fine enamel-painting and gilding, including portraits and scenes.

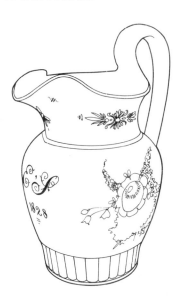

Tudor green, the name given to a class of 16th-century English pottery with a green glaze on a paleish body.

Tudor style, the English style in the 16th century, sometimes the early 16th century (before Elizabethan), the last stage of Gothic; characterized in furniture by heavy oak construction (before the days of the true cabinetmaker), architectural in derivation, with much carving; Italian influences becoming more noticeable as time advanced.

Tufft furniture, the work of the late 18th-century Philadelphia cabinetmaker, Thomas Tufft, in Chippendale style, particularly fine chests and highboys.

Tulaware, the niello work of the goldsmiths of Tula, Russia, 19th century.

Tulip chest, an early American carved and painted chest featuring a flower like a tulip, sometimes occurring in panels with the sunflower motif; see **Connecticut sunflower chest**.

Tulip motif, a common decorative device particularly in 17th-century furniture (probably originating in Holland), slipware, and in oriental decoration.

Tulip tankard, a type of 18th-century pewter tankard with sides in a gentle S curve resembling the form of a tulip.

Tulipwood, a heavy, close-grained tropical hardwood, yellowish- or reddish-brown with darker stripes, rather similar to rosewood in appearance, imported from Brazil for veneers in the second half of the 18th century particularly; also called bois de rose.

Tulle, a fine silk net, named after the French town where it originated, used for veils and in women's bonnets, etc.

Tumbler, originally, a cylindrical drinking glass with rounded base so that, if put down crookedly, it rights itself; since the late 18th century, a flat-bottomed glass, shorter than a beaker, often with straightish sides tapering in towards the base.

Tun, a large container, sometimes a chest but usually a large barrel or flask for beer or wine, in particular one with a capacity of four hogsheads (252 gallons); also, a silver beaker.

Tunbridge ware, small wooden articles decorated with a form of inlay originating in Tunbridge Wells, Kent, in which thin strips of 'matchsticks' of naturally contrasting woods were glued together in bundles to form a pattern when viewed end-on; the bundles then being sliced across to produce many identical patterns; also used to decorate furniture, from the mid 17th to late 19th century, later examples usually pictures, early ones geometric patterns.

Turchino, a dark blue glaze on Italian Renaissance maiolica.

Tureen, a large basin for serving soup, notably in silver from about 1700, when often highly decorative with elaborate finials on covers, etc.; also china; sometimes with matching salver, sometimes footed, usually with two handles. **281**

Turkestan carpets: see **Turkoman carpets**.

Turkey red, a dark orange-red found in some Turkish carpets, obtained basically from the root of the madder plant; also, a type of red linen cloth used particularly for handkerchiefs, originally imported from the Near East.

Turkey sofa: see **Ottoman**.

Turkey work, European imitation of oriental carpets, sometimes by a similar technique, sometimes stitched on a canvas ground, used for tablecloths, upholstery, etc. from the 16th century.

Turkish carpets, from the many carpet-making centres of Turkey, particularly Izmir (Smyrna) and its neighbourhood, usually Ghiordes (Turkish) knot, designs usually geometric or highly stylized, traditionally with longer pile than Persian carpets and, in general, smaller size.

Turkish knot, in carpet-making; see **Ghiordes knot**.

Turkoman carpets, woven chiefly by nomadic peoples in a vast region of the U.S.S.R. north of Iran and Afghanistan stretching from Sinkiang to the Caspian Sea, including Bokhara, Samarkand, etc. **30**

Turned, of furniture, e.g. chair legs, shaped on a lathe, decorative form being imparted with a chisel while the member revolves; also metal and other materials; a technique known to the Romans and common since the 16th century. **298**

Turner blackware, black Egyptian or 'basaltes' in imitation of Wedgwood's product produced by the Staffordshire potter, John Turner, and his sons, equally well-known for white stoneware, in the late 18th and early 19th centuries.

Turpentine, a volatile oil derived from the resinous exudation of pine trees, many uses as a solvent, particularly as a thinning agent in varnish and enamel paints.

Turquerie, furniture and decoration in 'Turkish' style, 19th century; a term similar to chinoiserie.

Turquoise, a precious stone that takes its name from Turkey (whence exported to Europe) and gives it in turn to its characteristic blue-green colour, much used since ancient times, e.g. by American Indians, seldom used today though often imitated in jewellery; also, a name given to a type of 19th-century sofa in 'Turkish' style.

Tunbridge ware

Turret clock, a large clock, sometimes with four dials, mounted in a tower; such clocks predated domestic clocks in general use, from about 1300.

Turtle-back, ornament in relief of the form described, found on some 17th-century furniture.

Tuscan order, one of the Roman orders of architecture, somewhat similar to Doric, i.e. relatively simple without decorated capitals.

Tutenag, a white-metal alloy containing copper, zinc and nickel; also a tea chest of that metal.

Twig chair, a wickerwork chair.

Twist, in the stem of a wine glass, an air twist; in furniture, cable moulding or spiral turning.

Tyg, a communal vessel like a large beaker, with two or more handles ranged round the sides, found in early Staffordshire slipware.

Tympanum, the flat-sided section of a pedestal; also, the triangular (or semicircular) space under a pediment, or over a doorway, especially when ornamented; also, a drum.

Type, in numismatics, the stamped design, usually in relief, on a coin or medal.

Typograph, a typewriter (19th century).

Überbauschrank, a type of dresser first appearing in Germany in the early Baroque period, a cupboard with an upper stage set back, often richly carved and inlaid.

Ultramarine, a blue colour, particularly a dark blue, originally obtained from lapis lazuli which came from 'beyond the sea'.

Ultra-violet light, light rays beyond the range of the visible spectrum which create a kind of fluorescence in certain substances, enabling the expert to determine whether the material concerned is what it is supposed to be, or whether an article has been restored, etc.

Umber, a reddish brown earth used as a pigment, particularly in calcined form (burnt umber), presumably originally obtained from Umbria (Italy).

Umbrella stand, a hall stand, typically a tall and narrow wooden frame or iron pillar with rings, and drip tray, for umbrellas and walking sticks, 19th century.

Unaker, china clay (kaolin) found in colonial Virginia, used (and named) by the Cherokee, imported to England and used in the earliest English porcelain at Bow as well as colonial American porcelain (of which almost none survives).

Undercut, carving basically in high relief in which parts of the design are actually separated from the surface.

Underglaze, in ceramics, colours applied to the body (biscuit) before glazing, restricted to those that will tolerate high temperatures, notably cobalt blue; see also **High-temperature colours**. 22

Undine, or Ondine, a water nymph, a popular ornamental figure in the Victorian period particularly.

Unguentarium, a small jar, earthenware or glass, for oils or ointments, as found in archaeological sites; see also **Balsamarium**.

Ungulate, hoofed, e.g. of the handle of a spoon, foot of a chair leg, etc.

Unicorn, a mythological animal in the form of a white horse with straight, pointed horn like a narwhal, sometimes appearing in Renaissance and Baroque design; said to be shy and elusive, except when approached by a virgin. 267

Union, a name applied to various American articles from the late 18th century, celebrating the union of the States.

Union glass, the name of several early 19th-century American glassworks in Pennsylvania and West Virginia, and of the Somerville, Massachusetts, makers of kewblas.

Unite, a gold coin equivalent to a sovereign, issued by James I of England, referring to the union of the crowns of Scotland and England, later issues having laurel crowned busts.

Universal, a work applied to several articles of furniture in the 19th century having some special versatility, e.g. an extending table, an adjustable easy chair, a clock dial that shows the time throughout the world, etc.

Unterweissbach figures, figures in white-glazed porcelain after sculptures by Ernest Barlach, from the Schwarzburger Werkstätten before World War I.

Upholsterer's chair, a simple type of single chair in which none of the woodwork is visible except the legs; often leather-covered, since the 17th century.

Upholstery, the covering of seat furniture and beds with soft, padded or

stuffed and (since the 19th century) often internally sprung material, a separate craft since at least the 15th century, when concerned with bed hangings, curtains, etc.; usually restricted to the modern sense since about 1700.

Upside-down chair, a chair, particularly a type of low-back Windsor, exactly the same below and above the seat, the top rail forming the base when turned upside-down and vice-versa.

Urbino maiolica, Renaissance maiolica from the great Italian centre, after Faenza a leader of fashion in the changing styles of the 16th century, particularly the istoriato (narrative) style in brilliant colours, and Raphaelesque painting. 283

ALF.
P.F.
VRBINI
1606

Urceolate, shaped like a pitcher, i.e. relatively narrow near the top with swelling body, normally applied to organic objects, e.g. shells.

Urn, a Classical form of vase, originally for the ashes of the dead, distinguished by large capacity, with wide mouth, S curved body, two handles and foot, popular as a decorative motif in the Neo-Classical period; sometimes found on a pedestal accompanying a sideboard; also, a covered metal vessel with a tap at the base, containing hot water for making tea, usually heated by a red-hot iron bar in the base, from the mid 18th century; the term is also applied to various articles shaped like an urn; see also **Krater, Pitcher**.

Urn stand, a small table for a tea urn, sometimes with a sliding shelf for the teapot.

Useful arts, a term employed, sometimes slightly euphemistically, to describe amateur crafts, embracing cooking, pottery, embroidery, flower-arranging, and do-it-yourself carpentry, etc.

Ushabti, or ushibdi, etc., human figures like dolls, often of glazed earthenware, found in Egyptian tombs in fairly large numbers; also, similar life-size figures.

Ushak carpets, similar to Sivas, since the 19th century rather loosely knotted, long-pile carpets, often with a central medallion on a plain ground; earlier Ushak carpets fine and rare.

Usk ware, japanned tinware, an offshoot of Pontypool in the second half of the 18th century.

Vademecum, an object that its owner is never without, usually referring to a reference book or manual of some kind.

Valais flagon, a type of 17th-century pewter tankard with boldly swelling body, relatively narrow neck, and heart-shaped lid, apparently originating in the Swiss canton.

Valance, a narrow piece of drapery attached lengthways over a window,

Umbrella stand

281

282

281 Small soup tureen and plate decorated by J. P. Ledoux. Soft-paste porcelain. Vincennes, 1753. Ledoux specialized in painting landscapes and birds. (Musée des Arts Décoratifs, Paris)

282 Ornate Venetian drinking glass. Late 18th century. (Museo di San Martino, Naples)

283 Urbino maiolica vase. 16th century. Made for the palace of prince Alfonso II d'Este. (Galleria Estense, Modena)

284 Louis XV veilleuse. Designed by Jean Nadel (active mid 18th century). A kind of daybed which often stood on one side of the fireplace). The wood is carved and lacquered. (Rijksmuseum, Amsterdam)

285 Octagonal Victorian walnut table. English, after a design by A. W. Pugin, made by Crace & Sons about 1847. Gothic Revival crockets decorate the legs. (Victoria and Albert Museum, London)

canopy, etc., or a similar wooden element, e.g. the horizontal boards below the surface of a table.

Valencia maiolica, early Hispano-Moresque tin-glazed lustreware from the old-established pottery centre, similar to Màlaga ware (and often classed under that description), probably the original 'maiolica'—exported to Italy via Majorca; see also **Manises ware. 132, 164**

Valenciennes lace, a type of pillow lace made since the 15th century in the French (formerly Flemish) town, characterized (apart from fine quality) by a regular diamond-shaped mesh with ornamentation (chiefly conventional floral forms) worked at the same time as the mesh.

Valentine, a greeting card or small token (glass, china, etc.) sent by one person to another on St Valentine's Day (February 14); originated in the 1830s.

Vambrace, in armour, a plate protecting the arm.

Van Vianen style, associated with a famous family of Dutch silversmiths of the 17th century (of whom Christian worked in England), suggesting strange anatomical forms; see also **Auricular decoration, Knorpelwerk.**

Vargueño, a well-known type of Spanish cabinet, made since Renaissance times, a chest on a stand (or chest) with a drop-front writing surface, in particular such a piece richly decorated with inlay, gilding etc. with trestle-type stand featuring openwork arcading which suggests the ecclesiastical origin of the piece.

Varnish, a resinous liquid containing spirit (as a solvent) applied like paint in several coats, dries into a very hard, thin, protective coating; types of varnish have been used on furniture since the 17th century; see also **French polish.**

Vasa diatreta, a name sometimes applied to Roman cage cups, actually implying cut glass vessels in general.

Vasa Murrhina: see Murrhine glass.

Vase, a hollow vessel in any suitable material the purpose of which is primarily ornamental (e.g. for a mantelpiece), usually comparatively tall and thin but may be almost any shape; see also **Urn.**

Vase-and-collar turning, as seen on the stretchers of some Windsor chairs, two horizontal vase or baluster forms divided by a central ring.

Vase-back chair, a shield-back, usually restricted to those shield-back chairs that have a vase motif in the splat but sometimes applied to any such chair.

Vase carpets, oriental carpets, in which the basic pattern is a vase of flowers, found on carpets from Teheran among other Persian centres; vases also appear in some prayer rugs.

Vaseline glass, a name given (in some desperation one would think) to a type of coloured glass in the late 19th century, a paleish green resembling the well-known pharmaceutical product.

Vaucanson mechanical toy, dating from the early 18th century, the work of Jacques Vaucanson and his successors, including a wooden faun that played a flute in an authentic way (air coming from the mouth and fingers covering the holes), a duck that pecked up corn and digested and excreted it, and other incredibly ingenious devices.

Vault, an arched ceiling, or a subterranean chamber with such a ceiling.

Vauxhall bevel, a wide, shallow bevel on plate glass.

Vauxhall glass, the product of a glassworks established in London by the duke of Buckingham in the reign of Charles II, making plate glass chiefly; hence occasionally, a term for old looking glasses in general.

Veduta, a view or landscape, especially of buildings, e.g. on 18th-century porcelain.

Veilleuse, an 18th-century cross between a daybed and armchair, with deep seat, curved backrest and upholstered arms; see also **Duchesse. 284**; also, a china food or teapot warmer, best known in delftware, basically cylindrical with an opening at the base for a lamp or candle, sometimes found in the form of a human figure.

Vellum, fine-quality parchment, particularly if made from the skin of young animals.

Velocipede, an early type of bicycle, originally one which was propelled by the feet pushing against the ground.

Velocipede horse: see Cantering horse.

Velour, velvet.

Velvet, a silk material with a very dense, upstanding pile, usually formed by weaving in loops and then cutting the loops, made in Italy since about the 13th century, used for upholstery, curtains, etc.; some varieties (especially in the Low Countries) wool.

Velveteen, a material similar to velvet in appearance, made of cotton.

Veneer, a very thin sheet of reasonably ornamental wood (1/8th of an inch or less) glued to the surface of furniture that is made of wood of less attractive appearance (such as deal), a practice adopted primarily for cheapness (imported wood being expensive), an ancient technique but rare in England before the late 17th century.

Venetian blind, thin slats hung on knotted cords against a window, their angle adjustable by pulling the cords, to restrict the admission of light, since the 18th century.

Venetian glass, the outstanding European glass from the 15th century (and presumably earlier) to the 18th, a fine, highly malleable soda glass wrought into intricate shapes, coloured glass and lace glass, imitations of precious stones, etc.; see also **Façon de Venise, Latticino. 282**

Venetian lace, the outstanding needlepoint lace that influenced all European manufacture during the late Middle Ages, several varieties including cutwork, reticella, various meshes and guipure (no ground) lace, as well as the heavy, raised point (Gros Point de Venise) very popular in the 17th century.

Venetian porcelain, overshadowed by the unsurpassed glass of Venice, early soft-paste porcelain (almost contemporary with the Meissen breakthrough); maiolica in the contemporary Italian style was also made at Venice in the 16th and 17th centuries.

Venison dish, a meat dish, particularly a large, oval, silver dish on three feet.

Venus-hair stone, a quartz stone marked with fine streaks.

Veramin carpets, from the centre south of Teheran, generally fine quality, dense pile, Sehna knot, floral decoration, sometimes ranged around a central diamond or based on a vase motif, sometimes scattered with animals, often in bright colours.

Verde antico, or verd antique, a form of impure serpentine, cut and polished like marble for tabletops in the 18th century.

Verdigris, a greenish substance naturally formed by corrosion of copper or copper alloys (including brass); made artificially as the basis of a pigment widely used in the arts.

Verdure, decoration of pastoral scenes, trees, flowers, fields, etc., particularly in tapestry.

Vermeil, gilded metal, usually silver, occasionally bronze; also, a bright red colour, hence applied to a type of garnet.

Vermicelli pattern, wriggling lines; see also **Vermiculated.**

Vermiculated, or vermicular, strictly, wormy; usually applied to ornamentation of wood or stonework resembling the sinuous wrigglings of worms, or similar decoration on porcelain (often gilt).

Verne carpets: see **Sumak carpets**.

Vernis Martin, the varnish (vernis) first perfected by the brothers Martin, French ébénistes of the mid 18th century, in imitation of oriental lacquer, typically green but also other colours.

Verre de fougère, 'fern glass', the French equivalent of the German Waldglas.

Verre de Nevers, glass from the old-established French centre, associated particularly with small articles, 'toys' and figures modelled from rods of metal, since about 1600 and no doubt earlier; the term is sometimes applied generically to such glassware made elsewhere in France and even in other European countries.

Verre églomisé: see **Églomisé**.

Verriere, a wine cooler for two glasses (one person); see also **Monteith**.

Verrière: see **Monteith**.

Verso, the left-hand page of a book, as opposed to recto.

Vertu: see **Object of Vertu**.

Verzelini glass, rare Elizabethan glass made in London by the Venetian Giacomo Verzelini, who escaped the dire penalties promised absconding craftsmen from Venice.

Vesica pattern, a characteristic cut-glass pattern seen in Irish decanters of the late 18th and early 19th centuries, a band of alternate ovals and diamonds filled with cross-hatching and 'stars', usually with fluting around the base.

Vestibule vase, the name given to a very large china jar or vase in the 19th century, intended to stand on the floor as ornaments in spacious halls.

Veuve Perrin faience, perhaps the most sought-after of Marseille faience, from the factory run for a time by the widow of Claude Perrin in the second half of the 18th century, noted for brilliant enamel colours.

Vicar and Moses, a popular Staffordshire anticlerical group of the late 18th and early 19th centuries depicting parson and clerk in their stalls, the former dozing while the latter conducts the service.

Victoria, a hooded, four-wheel carriage for two passengers plus driver, similar to a cabriolet.

Victorian, relating to the reign of Queen Victoria (1837–1901) in England, but often used of other countries in roughly the second half of the 19th century, characterized by the enthusiastic revival of numerous earlier styles (Gothic, Renaissance, Baroque, Chinese, etc., sometimes bastardized), by the advent of general mass production and the corresponding 'arts and crafts' reaction against it; of furniture the term is still sometimes employed in a derogative sense. **285**

Vignette, in Gothic architecture, an ornamental band of vines or foliage; also, ornamentation in a manuscript or book, particularly of a capital letter; a portrait miniature in which the subject shades imperceptibly into the ground, etc.

Viking style, late 19th-century Scandinavian furniture influenced by old Norse and Danish design (or what was known of them), bold stripes and fierce animal forms mingling with contemporary Art Nouveau ideas.

Vile furniture, the work of the London cabinetmaker William Vile (d. 1767), employed by George III, of which a number of outstanding pieces survive; his partner was John Cobb. **64**

Vinaigrette, a small ornamental container, often silver gilt, variable shape, pierced, to contain a small sponge impregnated with sweet-scented vinegar, mainly 18th and early 19th centuries; also, a small handcart and, nowadays, a flask for vinegar.

Vincennes porcelain, the soft-paste porcelain of Sèvres, before it moved to the latter location in the 1750s. **281**

Vinegar stick, the name given to a pierced, box-like container mounted on a stick, often silver, containing some aromatic substance that, waved about the room, purified the air, 17th century.

Vinovo porcelain, from a short-lived factory near Turin in the late 18th century.

Viol, a group of early members of the violin family of stringed instruments, roughly contemporary with the violin, softer in tone, most types played with the body on or between the knees.

Violetwood: see **Kingwood**.

Violin, a term applied descriptively to various articles resembling in shape the musical instrument, including chairbacks, 19th-century coloured-glass bottles, decanters, etc.

Violin-back, a name sometimes applied to an 18th-century chair type in which the splat is shaped like a violin, or to veneer like the back of a violin.

Virginal, a stringed, keyboard instrument of the Renaissance, the strings plucked rather than struck, a term 'widely used in England ... to cover all keyboard instruments of the plucked kind, and in some cases the clavichord, a struck instrument, as well' (Alan Kendall); see also **Spinet**.

Virginia walnut, darker and less strongly figured than English walnut, used by cabinetmakers chiefly in the first half of the 18th century.

Virgin spoon, a silver spoon similar to an Apostle spoon, with finial in the form of a figure of the Virgin Mary.

Visite, a lightweight (usually silk) woman's cloak, with or without sleeves.

Visor, or vizor, in armour, a hinged plate attached to the helmet which when lowered covered the face, from the 14th century. **10**

Visscher glass, rare early 17th-century Dutch glass engraved by one of two sisters of that name, particularly Anna who 'possessed a complete mastery of the use of the diamond on glass' (E. M. Elville).

Vitra lapis, imitation marble.

Vitrine, a glazed cabinet, for display of china, etc.

Vitro a reticelli, a more complex version of vitro di trina.

Vitro di trina, Venetian lace glass.

Vitro porcelain, glass resembling porcelain; see **Milk glass**; more particularly, a type of late 19th-century English streaky slag glass.

Vitruvian scroll, a border pattern of S shapes, rather like waves in a Japanese print, sometimes seen in bronze, on furniture especially, primarily a motif of the second half of the 18th century. **4**

Vogeldekor, a type of Baroque pattern of painted flowers and birds scattered over the surface of (in particular) the narrow-necked jugs of Hanau faience.

Voider: see **Voyder**.

Voisinlieu, French art pottery of various kinds, from the mid 19th century, made at the pottery near Beauvais.

Volcano lamp, an oil lamp with a glass shade ending in a funnel.

Volkstedt porcelain, the product of various 19th-century factories in the German centre, also some 18th-century tableware generally similar (but inferior) to Meissen.

Voltaire chair, an easy chair of the first half of the 19th century, made by Duncan Phyfe among many others, with a head-high, curving back.

Volute, a Classical scroll form, as on Ionic capitals, occurring in pairs.

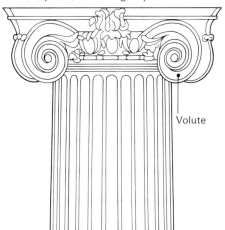

Volute

Votive, dedicated to a religious purpose, whether serving a function (as in 'votive lamp') or as an offering (e.g. 'votive jewels').

Voulge, a primitive type of halberd, the head consisting of an axe blade with a point at the top and two rings that encircle the head of the staff.

Voyder, a tray (usually metal) with two handles, or a large dish or pail, for 'voiding' a table after the meal.

286 Louis XV voyeuse. Designed by J. B. Tilliard (1685–1766). The top of the back-rest is padded so that the spectator could lean on the back and follow the game in progress without distracting the player sitting in the chair. (Musée des Arts Décoratifs, Paris)

287 Library Cross Hall, Winterthur. The walls are covered with a French wallpaper; the clock, signed Simon Willard, dates between 1790 and 1810; the chairs and small writing desk come from Boston; all are of the Federal Period. (Henry Francis du Pont Winterthur Museum, Winterthur, Delaware)

288

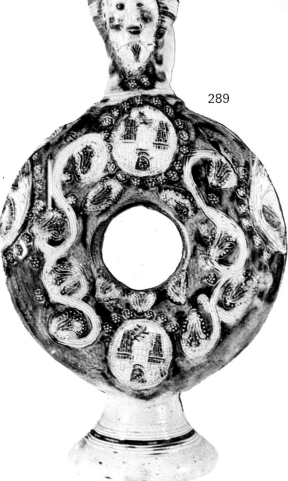

289

288 Jasperware vase with Classical decoration showing the Apotheosis of Homer. English, Wedgwood, 1768. (The Wedgwood Museum Trust, Josiah Wedgwood & Sons, Barlaston, Stoke on Trent)

289 Weight-driven clock. By A. Liechty of Winterthur, Switzerland, 1596. (Science Museum, London)

290 Vessel with high relief decoration. Westerwald salt-glazed stoneware, German, 17th century. The type is called a *Ringkrug* and stems from the 16th century. (Victoria and Albert Museum, London)

Voyeuse, a 'back-to-front' chair, sometimes called a cockfighting chair though in its usual form (French Neo-Classical) clearly intended for spectators of more genteel pastimes, i.e. card games; see also **Reading chair.** 286

Vulcanized, hardened by being subjected to heat, typically of rubber.

Vulliamy clock, late 18th- and 19th-century clocks made by Benjamin Vulliamy, father and son, in particular shelf clocks with artistic ceramic cases and turret clocks.

Wafer iron, a waffle iron; also, an instrument like a pair of tongs with patterned discs at the ends, for pressing wafers for sealing letters.

Wager cup, the English name for a standing cup with pivoted bowl and second bowl inside stem (often a female's skirt), known in silver in the 17th century; see also **Jungfrauenbecher.**

Wagon seat, a type of small, slat-back settee intended to serve as an ordinary seat or as a wagon seat in country districts.

Wagon-spring clock, a type of early 19th-century New England shelf clock, typically in a 'Gothic' case, driven by an adaptation of the ordinary leafed wagon spring, originally made by Joseph Ives in Brooklyn, New York.

Wag-on-the-wall, a popular name for any pendulum wall clock without a case so that weight and movement are visible, including some with wooden movements.

Wainscot, originally, it is said, wood (usually oak) of a quality good enough for making wagons (wains), subsequently, any good-quality oak and thus the actual wood panelling for which wainscot was used in the 16th century.

Wainscot chair, chest, etc., terms applied to furniture of panelled oak in Gothic style.

Waisted, especially of the bowl of a wine glass, tapering inward from the rim to the 'waist', then less sharply outward to form a rounded base to the bowl.

Waiter, a tray or salver, nowadays one not more than about nine inches wide.

Waldenburg jug, from a Rhineland stoneware pottery, distinguished by a characteristic zig-zag pattern around top and bottom, seldom found elsewhere.

Waldglas, 'forest glass', medieval German glass made in the Black Forest and other plentifully wooded areas providing potash, characteristically greenish (or brown or yellow).

Walker colt, a Colt revolver made in co-operation with Captain Samuel Walker about 1850, over 15 inches long, more successful than Paterson Colts, now rather rare.

Wall clock, any clock that is hung on the wall, especially early weight-driven clocks. 292

Wallendorf porcelain, made in the late 18th and again since the late 19th century in the Thuringian town, originally chiefly imitations of Meissen and wares similar to Kloster-Veilsdorf and Limbach.

Wall fountain: see **Lavabo.**

Wall light: see **Sconce.**

Wallpaper, patterned paper for covering the walls of a room; since the 18th century. 287

Wall period, the earliest period of Worcester porcelain (roughly the first thirty years), named after Dr John Wall (d. 1777), one of the original partners who for part of this period managed the enterprise.

Wall pocket, a china flower vase often in the shape of a cornucopia, with flattened back for attaching to a wall, a popular Staffordshire piece.

Walnut, a light brown wood with well-defined markings (especially near joints in the tree), the most popular cabinet-wood, in England especially, in the late 17th and early 18th centuries (the 'age of walnut'), used solid and as veneer; also, the black variety, darker and less strongly marked; see also **Butternut, Grenobles wood, Virginia walnut.** 91

Walsall brasses, horse brasses from the Staffordshire town that was a major centre of the harness trade in the 19th century.

Walsenkrug, a mug, of the standard cylindrical form.

Waltham clocks, and watches, made by a well-known Massachusetts firm founded in Boston in the late 19th century, notable especially for its watches of that period, simple, elegant and unsurpassed for quality; see also **Howard clocks.**

Walton figure, a Staffordshire figure, usually backed by bocage, modelled by John Walton of Burslem in the early 19th century, presaging the 19th-century decline in this art.

Wampum, the round beads generally made from shells and threaded on a string, used by the Algonkins as both ornament and currency.

Wanded, made of twigs; see also **Wickerwork.**

Wandering-hour watch, in which the numeral recording the hour moves along a scale of 60 minutes, usually arranged in a semicircle, and disappears on reaching the end, whereupon the next hour appears at the beginning; from the late 17th century.

Wanfried ware, German slipware from Wanfried-an-der-Werra in Hesse, 16th–17th centuries, exported to England among other places; see also **Hafner ware.**

Warburton pottery, 18th-century creamware, among other wares, including perhaps some made by Wedgwood and decorated by the Warburton family at Cobridge, Staffordshire.

Wardian case, a glass case with rounded top containing a pot for growing plants indoors, named after its early 19th-century inventor Nathaniel Ward, very popular in Victorian homes.

Wardrobe, formerly, a chamber where clothes were kept; subsequently, a large cupboard with shelves for the same purpose, virtually synonymous with press; see also **Aumbry, Armoire.** 7

Warming pan, a device for warming a bed, typically in the form of a giant copper frying pan (to be filled with coals from the fire) with hinged lid and wooden handle, known since the early 17th century.

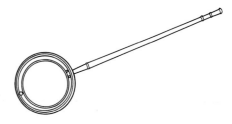

Warp and weft, the basic intersecting threads in all woven textiles, that run lengthwise (warp) and crosswise (weft); the warp threads, stretched in the loom, forming the main structural element.

Warsaw faience, chiefly 18th-century tin-glazed ware from a factory in Warsaw (which supplied the Ottoman sultan with tableware), often showing the influence of German porcelain.

Warwick carving, on 19th-century reproductions of Gothic furniture, very elaborately carved ornament, from several furniture makers in Warwick, England.

Warwick cruet, a name applied to a cruet containing three casters and two bottles (for oil and vinegar). 73

Warwick vase, a copy, on a reduced scale, of a famous Classical vase discovered in England in the late 18th century and at one time in the possession of the earl of Warwick; silver reproductions made by Storr and other silversmiths as ice pails.

Washed carpet, a modern oriental carpet subjected to a chemical wash that reduces the brightness of the colours, giving them a more traditional appearance without harming the material.

Washing dolly, a wooden implement with several projecting spokes for agitating the washing in a tub.

Washington, a name that describes a great range of American objects, from andirons to wine glasses, implying the presence of a portrait, effigy, etc. of the first American president.

Washstand, or toilet stand, a small fitted table to hold a large bowl and pitcher and sometimes other accessories, to stand in a bedroom; 19th-century types sometimes wrought iron; see also **Wig stand.**

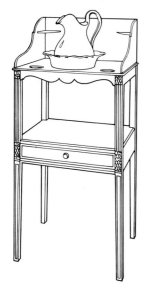

Wassail bowl, a wooden bowl, sometimes silver-mounted, said to have been for drinking wassail (a hot drink of spiced ale); see also **Mazer, Treen.**

Waster, in the pottery trade, a broken piece or vessel that has gone wrong—collapsed in the kiln, etc.—and discarded.

Watch, a small, portable clock worn first (early 16th century) on a ribbon around the neck, subsequently in a pocket or on the wrist; until the 19th century often primarily a decorative object (not being very accurate).

Watch ball: see **Witch ball.**

Watchcock, watchbridge, a metal plate that guards the balance wheel of the watch, made from the 17th to the early 19th century usually of delicately pierced gilt brass; also called a balance cock.

Watchman's clock, an early type of punched clock, which registered the time at which the watchman, on his rounds, punched a lever.

Watch paper, a round piece of paper (sometimes cloth) placed inside the case of a watch, usually as an advertisement; examples before 1800 sometimes handwritten.

Watchstand, an ornamental stand, in silver, porcelain, wood or other material, with a recess for setting a watch at a near-vertical position to serve as a clock when not being worn.

Watcombe pottery, late 19th-century terracottas, finely modelled, by a firm in Torquay, Devonshire, reaping the benefit of fine local clay.

Watteau pleats, or cloaks, etc., 18th-century women's dress supposedly influenced by the painter Watteau, in particular pleats descending from the shoulder to the waist or hemline.

Water clock, a device to measure time by water flowing out of or into a vessel, predecessor of the hour glass; see also **Clepsydra.**

Watercolours, colours applied to a surface with the aid of water, used chiefly in fine-art drawings, employed in decorating numerous articles in 19th-century handicrafts.

Watered cloth, cloth that has been given a shimmering, lustrous finish by sprinkling it with water and pressing between rollers.

Waterfall, a term sometimes applied to a crystal chandelier.

Waterford glass, from the Irish centre in the late 18th and 19th centuries, perhaps the most eagerly collected Irish glass though not always identifiable when unmarked, associated particularly with deep-cut decanters and other wares in which the metal has a greyish blue tint; also, from a New Jersey glassworks of the same name.

Water gilding, the superior method of gilding in the Middle Ages, applied to a gesso ground primed with a mordant of some kind, and moistened with water before application of the gold leaf.

Waterloo glass, from an Irish glasshouse in Cork, early 19th century; varied but short-lived production.

Waterloo leg, an alternative name, after 1815, for a sabre leg on chairs.

Watermark, a trade mark in paper, visible when held up to the light, created by impressing the pulp from which the sheets are made.

Waters pottery, in particular, gaily decorated earthenware of the type known as Welsh ware made at the Lambeth pottery of Richard Waters in the early 19th century.

Wave pattern: see **Vitruvian scroll.**

Wax jack, a taper stand, for sealing wax. ▶

Wax painting: see **Encaustic.**

Wax-polished, furniture polished with beeswax to impart a hard shine to the surface, predating varnishes but still sometimes used; hard work.

Waxwork, models in wax of fruit and flowers, portrait miniatures in relief, etc., 19th century.

Wayne furniture, in particular, the work of the Philadelphia cabinetmaker Jacob Wayne in the late 18th century.

Wear bridge jug, a view of the iron bridge over the river Wear (built at the end of the 18th century), found on (mainly) Sunderland lustreware jugs, nearly thirty different versions.

Weathered, of wood, treated by one of many methods to create an appearance of age and wear.

Weather vane, a metal (iron, copper, etc.) plate, frequently in the form of a cock or other animal, mounted on a chimney or steeple to indicate wind direction.

Webbing, interlacing bands of some strong cloth, such as canvas, as found on the underside of upholstered seats.

Webbs glass, in 19th-century English glass, either glassware designed by the architect and associate of Morris, Philip Webb, or the products of a Stourbridge firm responsible for various innovations including the English version of Burmese glass.

Web foot, in furniture, a webbed claw and ball, usually on a cabriole leg, seen in some 19th-century Irish furniture and American country furniture; see also **Duck foot.**

Wedge, in metalwork, a wedge-shaped thumbpiece on a tankard, or a small silver stepped stand for resting a dish at an angle.

Wedgewood, found as a mark on certain 19th-century china masquerading as Wedgwood; some 19th-century American 'Wedgwood' pearlware is by a Mr Wedge Wood.

Wedging, in pottery, the chopping and beating of the clay in wedge-shaped lumps before it is thrown, to drive out air bubbles.

Wedgwood, the most famous name in English ceramics, in particular the work of Josiah Wedgwood (1730–95), his successors, the firm he founded at Stoke-on-Trent, and to Josiah's numerous success-

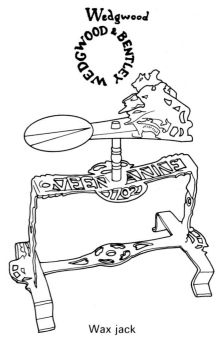

Wax jack

265

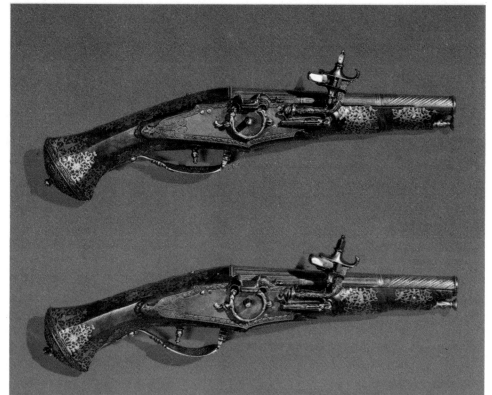

291▲

292

291 Pair of wheel-lock pistols richly decorated on the butt and barrel. Italian, second half of the 17th century, by one of the outstanding Brescian makers of the age, with the signature Giovan Battista Francino. (Wallace Collection, London)

292 Painted wall clock. Dutch, 18th century. (Morpurgo Collection, Amsterdam)

293 Wine cooler. English, made by Thomas Farrar, 1727. In the French Régence style with palm leaves and strapwork decoration on a matted ground. (S. J. Phillips Ltd, London)

295 Wig stand in Nevers faience.
Early 18th century. (Musée des
Arts Décoratifs, Paris)

294 Two English cut and engraved
glasses with tear-drop stems
and stepped feet. (London
Museum, London)

ful innovations, including creamware, basaltes (black stoneware), 'Etruscan' ware, and jasperware, also those of his son (also Josiah), including pearlware; still going strong. **288**

Wedgwood-arbeit, 'Wedgwood-work', German blue porcelain wares with relief decoration in white, in imitation of Wedgwood's jasperware, late 18th century.

Weeds, black clothes, worn by those in mourning.

Weesp porcelain, from the Dutch factory founded in the mid 18th century, employing German workers, moved after a few years to Oude Loosdrecht.

Weft: see **Warp and weft**.

Wegeli figures, porcelain figures made at Berlin for a short period (the Wegeli period) in the mid 18th century; see also **Berlin porcelain**.

Weight-driven clock, one in which the movement is driven by a weight hanging on a chain or cord. **289**

Welcome cup, a silver or gilt (sometimes other metal) communal goblet, usually of splendid form, sometimes with a set of beakers, used in guild ceremonies, often inscribed with some welcoming message; also, a glass vessel; see also **Willkomm**.

Well, in clocks, the hollow compartment of a long-case clock; also, the space within a spiral or turning staircase, a compartment within a chest or a desk, etc.

Wellenschrank, a south German Baroque cupboard with serpentine front, usually walnut.

Well-head, the covering over a well (for water).

Welsh dresser, a rather loosely used term nowadays for a popular dining room piece; a dresser (usually oak) with cupboards below, drawers above, with a recessed superstructure of shelves, a type also made outside Wales since the early 18th century.

Welsh ware, mainly rounded-rectangle meat dishes, slip-decorated and streaked with coloured glaze, late 18th and early 19th century; see also **Gaudy Welsh**.

Welt, an extra band or ridge of material along a border, usually referring to cloth or leather; see also **Lapped edge**.

Wesley figure, an enormously popular Staffordshire subject, notably a bust by Enoch Wood, of the founder of the Wesleyan (Methodist) movement; late 18th or early 19th century.

Westerwald stoneware, Rhineland stoneware from several centres, notably blue-glazed wares with incised or impressed decoration. **290**

Westmoreland glass, made by a company of that name in Grapeville, Pennsylvania, established in the late 19th century, noted for reproductions of early American glassware.

Whalebone, the horny, flexible substance obtained from the throats of shrimp-eating whales, used for a variety of purposes before the age of plastics, most notably corsets, also riding whips and other handles, even chair seats.

Whangee, a type of light yellow cane; see also **Bamboo**.

What-not, a small stand of open shelves for displaying ornaments of various kinds, sometimes with small drawers below, popular since the Regency period; see also **Etagère**.

Wheatsheaf, . the splat of an 18th-century chairback tapering in towards the centre and longitudinally pierced, suggesting a wheatsheaf.

Wheel-back chair, a single chair of the Hepplewhite period with a central disc in the back, from which spokes radiate outwards to a rounded rail; also, a wheel motif in the splat of some English Windsor chairs.

Wheel barometer, the commonest type of domestic instrument, with a circular dial, made since the first half of the 18th century, usually in a style similar to contemporary clock designs; see also **Banjo barometer**.

Wheel engraving, designs cut in glass or stone by small revolving metal wheels with an abrasive, a technique used in ancient Rome and perhaps at its height in glass in the 17th century.

Wheeling glass, mainly tableware, since the early 19th century made at the several glasshouses in Wheeling, West Virginia, a major centre of the industry.

Wheel-lock, a gun in which pressing the trigger allows a wheel to turn, striking a spark against a stone to ignite the powder in the pan; made from the early 16th century and still in use in the early 18th. **291**

Whieldon ware, the products of the notable Staffordshire potter Thomas Whieldon (1719–95), partner of Wedgwood and master of Spode, associated particularly with marbled glazes, 'cauliflower' ware and tortoiseshell ware in a fine clay body that was the predecessor of Wedgwood's creamware.

Whimsies, a term applied particularly to small glass articles of a curious character (hats, shoes, etc.) from various glassworks; see also **End-of-day glass**.

Whistle tankard, a silver tankard with a small hole in (usually) the handle to allow air to escape during manufacture but traditionally said to be for whistling for a refill.

Whitefriars glass, from an old-established London glassworks, notable in the 19th century for fine designs in tableware by the architect Philip Webb; there was a glasshouse in Whitefriars in the 17th century, possibly at first importing Venetian wares.

White metal, any alloy, usually containing nickel and/or tin, imitating silver, e.g. German silver.

Whiteware, a white body or glaze in ceramics, e.g. 16th-century maiolica; see also **Biscuit, Parian**.

Whitewood, usually spruce or some type of deal; implying (of furniture) unfinished.

White Wycombe chair, a 19th-century English chair of the Windsor type, unpainted (i.e. left 'in the white').

Whitney glass, South Jersey glass from a Glassboro, New Jersey, factory established in the late 18th century and in operation throughout the 19th century, mainly bottles and flasks including some notable historical items.

Whitney gun, from the New Haven, Connecticut, factory established by the inventor Eli Whitney at the end of the 18th century, incorporating standardized, interchangeable parts.

Whorl, the curving spiral form seen in a conch shell, hence any spiralling design especially when suggesting vigorous movement, e.g. an ornamental disc on Gothic furniture, in marbled endpapers of books; when applied to the foot of a chair leg, a scroll or French foot.

Wickerwork, basketwork employing twigs of trees, usually willow, found in 17th-century chair seats.

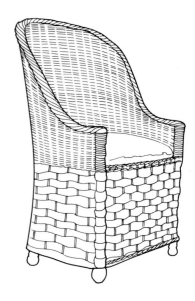

Wig-back, a name sometimes applied to 18th-century chairs having a semicircle cut out of the top rail; see **Barber's chair.**

Wig stand, the name sometimes applied to a simple type of bedroom washstand, usually on a tripod base, with a circular ring in the top for a basin; also, a rounded block of wood or ceramic on which a wig actually rested. **295**

Wilkinson & Wardle pottery: see **Denaby pottery.**

Willard clock, the work of the famous Massachusetts family of clockmakers, particularly Simon (1753–1848) and Aaron (1757–1844), the former credited with invention of the banjo clock, who made many good, wooden-cased wall and mantel clocks; a son of Aaron is associated with the lyre clock, a development of the banjo. **287**

Willemite, a rare, yellowish, translucent stone, too soft for use in jewellery.

William and Mary style, in furniture, especially in America, roughly the period of the reign of William III (1689–1702), Dutch- and French-influenced, increased restraint after the elaborate ornamentation of the Restoration period (e.g. baluster turning replacing barley-sugar twist), merging with the style of the Queen Anne period.

Williamite glass, a belated answer to Jacobite glasses, late 18th-century decanters and wine glasses with a portrait of William III, victor of the battle of the Boyne; late 18th or 19th century.

Williamsburg style, referring to the colonial town of Williamsburg, Virginia, a tourist showpiece restored to the last nail and cobblestone; usually applied to reproductions of colonial furniture.

Willkomm, a large drinking glass, similar to the Humpen, inscribed with a welcoming greeting, for visitors, from the 15th century, central Europe; see also **Welcome cup.**

Willow-pattern, a famous design on household china of a Chinese scene printed in blue, first appearing in the late 18th century and made by numerous English potteries, the scene showing slight variations, in the 19th century.

Willow wood, soft and elastic but tough, from various species of willow, yellowish in colour with greyish flecks, occasionally used for inlays, and the twigs for wickerwork.

Wilson bird prints, a set of engravings of Alexander Wilson's illustrations from his *American Ornithology,* published at the beginning of the 19th century (pre-dating Audubon).

Wilton carpets, Brussels (moquette) carpets, with the loops of the pile cut like velvet, from the Wiltshire centre established in the first half of the 18th century; knotted-pile carpets since the takeover of Axminster in the early 19th century; a generic name for the former type.

Wimple, a head-covering formed from one piece of silk or linen cloth to cover everything above the shoulders except for the space from brow to chin, now worn by nuns, more general in the 18th century.

Wincanton delftware, blue-painted, tin-glazed, 18th-century wares similar to nearby Bristol.

Winchester measure, old English measures of the bushel (and gallon) dating back to the Middle Ages, of which examples in the form of bronze bins with feet and handles survive from the late 15th century; the basis for the standard (smaller than the imperial) bushel.

Winchester rifle, the twelve-shot repeating rifle manufactured at New Haven, Connecticut, immediately after the Civil War, first made by B. Taylor Henry some years earlier.

Winchester ware, early English lead-glazed pottery, perhaps dating from the 10th century, with vigorous decoration in relief.

Windas, a mechanical device for stretching the string of a crossbow.

Windmill beaker, a silver or pewter beaker in the form of a windmill, a piece of German Baroque whimsy.

Window blind: see **Venetian blind.**

Window harp: see **Aeolian harp.**

Window seat, an upholstered seat with ends but no back, designed to be

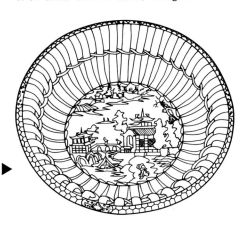

Willow-pattern

placed in a bay below a window in the Neo-Classical period; also, a built-in seat under a window, usually with a hinged top giving access to a chest, or cupboards.

Windsor bench, a long seat or settee of Windsor-chair type, i.e. turned spindles in the back, having six or eight legs.

Windsor chair, the best-known type of inexpensive chair in America and England, having turned legs, stretchers and sticks in the back, usually a saddle seat and the legs splayed, first made in England in the late 17th century but uncommon until the mid 18th; American versions similar to but more refined than English; classified in numerous divisions and subdivisions, basically by the form of the back (hoop-back, comb-back, etc.).

Windsor rocker, a stick-back rocking chair, 19th century.

Wine cooler, or cistern, a large metal bowl or a case of any suitable material (including wood) in which wine bottles were placed in ice, since the Renaissance period; many elaborate kinds in the 18th and 19th centuries; see also **Cellaret, Ice pail. 293**

Wine fountain, in particular, a type of late 19th-century decanter or urn something like a soda siphon, dispensing wine when the glass was pressed against the spout, or a tap turned.

Wine funnel, a cone with a hole in the bottom for decanting wine, silver examples known since the 17th century, usually with matching dish in which it stood.

Wine glass, a drinking glass with a bowl, a stem and a foot, an old form (in England since the 17th century) still basically the same but classified into hundreds of different types. **294**

Wine glass cooler: see **Monteith.**

Wine glass motif, a decorative pattern found in the borders of Caucasian carpets. **242**

Wine label: see **Bin label, Bottle tag.**

Wine rack, a wooden construction with compartments for bottles to lie on their sides.

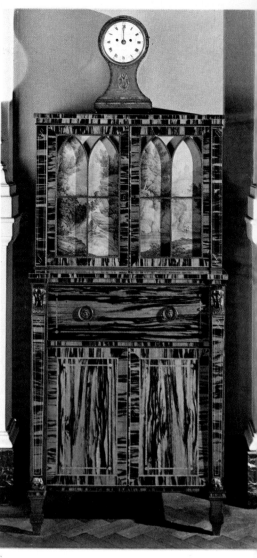

296 Porcelain plate. Worcester, about 1770. Typical of this factory is the deep blue background decoration with Rococo medallions and bouquets. (Menstrie Museum, Bath)

297 Mahogany and zebrawood cabinet. English, signed J. Baynes and dated 1808. (Victoria and Albert Museum, London)

298 ▲

299

298 Lady's worktable. By A.-L. Ringuet-Leprince (active 1851–53). With turned decoration on the supports. (Mobilier National, Paris)

299 Zoomorphic vessel. Chinese, Shang dynasty. In the shape of a stylized owl whose head forms the lid. (Freer Gallery of Art, Washington)

300 Louis XIV folding X-frame stool in gilded wood. (Musée Jacquemart-André, Paris)

Wine taster, a shallow silver or glass bowl, sometimes with a dome rising from the bottom, various other shapes since the Middle Ages, their purpose not always certain.

Wine waiter, a wooden container for up to a dozen bottles or decanters, like a stool with a compartmented tray on top, on castors.

Wing chair, an upholstered armchair with high back having two ear-shaped forward projections on either side of the occupant's head, since about 1700; see also **Easy chair.**

Winged, of a cupboard, sideboard, wardrobe, etc., having a large central section with smaller sections (wings) on each side.

Winged stem, in a wineglass, delicate ornamental mouldings as in Façon de Venise.

Wing lantern clock, a lantern clock converted to a pendulum (in the late 17th century), with recessed 'wings' at the back to guard the swinging pendulum which is often in the shape of an anchor.

Winslow chair, a panel-back oak Gothic chair of a type said to have been used by Governor Winslow of New Plymouth (Massachusetts).

Winterthur ware, early tin-glazed earthenware tiles and other wares from the Swiss town, long a centre of stove-making.

Wirework, in silver and gold, articles such as toast-racks, fruit baskets, etc., constructed of wire, made by drawing it through a series of holes of decreasing diameter, also in Sheffield plate in the late 18th and early 19th centuries, and in various base metals for many purposes.

Wishbone doll, an early American doll made of a turkey's wishbone wrapped in cloth with a wax head moulded on the flat piece beyond the joint.

Wistar glass, or Wistarburg, early New Jersey glass made (some of it anyway) by Caspar Wistar (1695–1752), a German immigrant who founded a glassworks in Salem county in 1739, mainly bottles and sheet glass, also drinking vessels and off-hand items, sometimes in coloured glass and with applied ornament.

Witch ball, a hollow glass ball variously coloured, often silvered on the inside, originally made (perhaps) to ward off evil spirits, by the 19th century chiefly for ornament (e.g. on Christmas trees in the Victorian period).

Wok, an iron cooking vessel of oriental origin, similar to a frying pan but with rounded sides and base.

Wolf's teeth, a hound's-tooth pattern, usually in cloth.

Wolverhampton ware, japanned ware of the type known as Pontypool, though of cheaper quality than true Pontypool, in the 18th and 19th centuries; the city was also the centre of the locksmithing trade from the early 17th century.

Woodcut, a print made from a design cut in a wood block, used for textiles in the early Middle Ages and on paper from the 15th century (much earlier in China and Japan); the common method of illustrating early printed books.

Wooden clock, a clock with a wooden movement (rather than—superfluously—a wooden case), made up to the early 19th century.

Wood engraving, a woodcut; in particular, an impression from hardwood cut across the grain, rather than softwood cut with the grain as in woodcuts up to the 18th century, and in which the actual design, not the ground, is cut away.

Woodenware: see Treen.

Wood pottery, various products associated with the famous family of Staffordshire potters, especially Ralph (1715–72), noted for fine figures and Toby jugs, and his nephew Enoch (1759–1840), responsible for a vast variety of wares and figures including some porcelain.

Woodward ware, Victorian imitation 'majolica' made by James Woodward at Swadlincote, Derbyshire.

Woodware: see Treen.

Woodworm, the furniture beetle whose larvae are responsible for the tiny neat holes, accompanied by fine wood dust if the insect is still active, in furniture; the symptoms sometimes dubiously regarded as a sign of the wood's age; less common in America than Europe, especially partial to walnut and fruitwoods.

Woof, in cloth, the weft; see **Warp and weft.**

Wool weights, bronze weights bearing the English royal arms, for weighing wool by the tod, sack, stone, etc., made since the late Middle Ages and supposedly destroyed on the death of the reigning monarch, therefore genuine examples rare.

Worcester, English porcelain from the factory in continuous production in the West Country city since the mid 18th century, two factories combining to form the Worcester Royal Porcelain Co. about 1850; later absorbing other competitors; originally soapstone porcelain, bone china also from about 1800, ivory biscuit from about 1850; influenced by contemporary Chinese and silver designs, later by Meissen and Sèvres; employing outside painters of great ability; figures rare before the mid 19th; unequalled porcelain ornaments (e.g. birds) since the late 19th century; see also **Chamberlain porcelain, Flight & Barr porcelain, Wall period. 296**

Worktable, a lady's sewing table, a small square or oval-topped table with hinged top containing compartments for needlework articles, sometimes with bag or pouch below; from the mid 18th century; see also **Pouch table, Sewing table, Tricoteuse. 279, 298**

Wreathing, raised spirals found on the interior of some earthenware pots, e.g. in Bristol delftware, the result of building up the thickness of the body at vulnerable parts in order to prevent collapse in the kiln.

Wrigglework, decoration of wavy lines, in particular such decoration on silver or pewter in the late 17th century, achieved by a rocking motion of the engraving tool.

Wrisbergholzen faience, from an 18th-century factory near Hanover, mainly blue-painted ware in the manner of Delft.

Wristband, a broad metal bracelet.

Wrister, the name given to a projecting ridge or collar found on what is the ankle rather than the wrist of a furniture leg in the William and Mary period, particularly in New Jersey and Pennsylvania, usually above a knurled foot.

Writhen, or wrythen, writhing, etc., twisted like rope, applied in particular to silver spoons with finial in that form, 15th–16th centuries, or similar thumb-pieces on tankards; also, an engraved or applied spiral pattern on glass.

Writing arm, a flat surface for writing, attached to the arm of a chair, usually of Windsor type.

Writing cabinet, a bureau-bookcase.

Writing desk: see Desk.

Writing screen, a shallow, fall-front desk with cupboard below, raised fairly high on arched legs so that the user may warm his feet while screening the rest of his body from the fire; late 18th century.

Writing table, a variety of different pieces, usually with pull-out writing surface; a lighter version of a pedestal desk, the drawers on either side not extending to the floor; see also **Desk, Escritoire, Library table, Pedestal desk.**

Wrockwardine glass, from an 18th-century Shropshire glassworks making 'Nailsea' glass.

Wrotham pottery, 17th-century (and perhaps earlier) slipware from Wrotham, Kent, usually trailed white decoration on the red body under a brownish lead glaze, including basins, pitchers, tygs, etc.

Wrought iron, malleable iron (as distinct from pig iron which is cast but not 'wrought'), shaped or forged into various forms by a blacksmith, seen at its most decorative in gates, railings, lamp standards, etc. **72, 149, 162**

Würzburg porcelain, from a short-lived factory in Würzburg, about 1780, of considerable interest to scholars but not (because of scarcity) to collectors.

C · G

W

Wych elm, rosy brown wood used for chair seats and construction, usually more attractive in appearance than most elm-wood.

Wycombe chair, Windsor chair; see also **White Wycombe.**

Wyvern, a mythical creature, like a winged dragon, but only two feet.

Xanthin, or xanthine, yellow.

X-form, cross-shaped, e.g. of diagonal stretchers on a chair.

X-frame, of chairs and stools, shaped like an X when looked at either from the side or the front, the upper sections extending (in the case of chairs) to the arms and back; a type of construction known in ancient Egypt, familiar in the Renaissance, and recently employed in the Barcelona chair. **15, 108, 300**

X-ray technique, used in studying normally invisible characteristics in many media, notably in fine art, also the structure of precious stones, etc.

Yard of ale, a glass drinking vessel in the form of a long tube (often less than a yard in fact) flared at the mouth with a globe at the other end, up to about two imperial pints capacity, to be drained at one draught—usually resulting in a flood of beer in the face when the decreasing level reaches the globe; known since the early 17th century.

Yastik, a small rug or a cushion (Turkish).

Year clock, a clock that goes for a year without winding.

Yellowbacks, cheaply bound Victorian books (usually novels) with paper (commonly yellow but also other colours) pasted on boards, bearing an illustration and sometimes advertisements.

Yellow metal, Muntz's metal; also, a colloquial term for gold.

Yellow ware, early Staffordshire creamware decorated with a yellow glaze; also, 19th-century ovenware with a yellowish body and clear glaze.

Yew wood, hard and durable, light brown to reddish brown wood, structurally used mainly in country furniture especially thin turned members (e.g. in Windsor chairs); when interestingly marked occasionally as veneer and in parquetry.

Yezd carpets, modern Kerman carpets made at the nearby village of Yezd.

Yi-hsing ware, Chinese unglazed red stoneware, especially teapots (often of various imaginative designs), imported in the 17th and early 18th centuries and often imitated in Europe, e.g. by Elers; see also **Boccaro ware.**

Yin-Yang, in Chinese art, the motif representing male and female. **54**

Yoke, a curved wooden beam fitting the neck and shoulders of a person to carry a pail of milk at either side (or a similar device for harnessing oxen), sometimes applied to articles of furniture of this approximate shape, e.g. a curved top rail in certain Queen Anne chairs that extends beyond the uprights of the back.

Yomud carpets, made by a nomadic people of that name in northern Iran and Turkestan, dark red or blue ground and lighter patterns (frequently diamonds), Sehna knot.

Yorkshire chair: see **Derbyshire chair**.

Yorkshire clock, a term applied to certain English long-case clocks of the late 18th and early 19th centuries (not solely from Yorkshire), of generally bulky form and somewhat grandiose appearance.

Yorkshire dresser, a name given to a dresser with a built-in clock, found chiefly in northern England.

Yorkshire grit, a type of stone used for polishing marble or copper plates before engraving.

Yorkshire pottery, in particular, lead-glazed earthenware with decoration in creamy slip, a type made at many centres in the 18th century but continuing in Yorkshire until the late 19th.

Yü, a Chinese vessel for storing sacrificial food.

Yüeh ware, green-glazed grey stoneware made throughout the period from the Han to Sung dynasties, vessels of novel form with delicate relief decoration; see also **Celadon ware**.

Yuruk carpets, from south-eastern Turkey, mainly nomadic, various geometric designs, rather loose weave, generally bright colours.

Zaandam clock, an early (late 17th century) Dutch pendulum clock.

Zaffre, or zaffer, zaffare, etc., a form of cobalt-blue pigment widely used in ceramics since the Renaissance, e.g. on English delftware; see also **Smalt**.

Zanesville glass, the product of the Ohio city in the first half of the 19th century, including Stiegel-type coloured glass.

Zebrawood, from a South American hardwood tree, marked in bands of very light and very dark brown, much desired (especially for banded edges) in the 18th century but comparatively scarce. **297**

Zechlin glass, from the 18th-century centre in Silesia, particularly glassware with applied ornament in the form of portrait medallions, usually gilded.

Zeeland chest, a low, elaborately carved two-stage cupboard on ball feet, made at various places in the Low Countries in the Renaissance period, later (Baroque) examples often with geometric mouldings suggesting Spanish influence.

Zephyr, applied to various forms of cloth, meaning very light-weight or gauze-like.

Zerbst faience, short-lived but widely varied production, under-glaze blue and enamel painted, from an 18th-century factory in the town north of Leipzig perhaps better known for its silversmiths and its beer.

Ziegler carpets, Persian carpets imported by a well-known Manchester firm with branches in the Middle East in the second half of the 19th century.

Zig-zag, decoratively, a jagged line like a representation of lightning, as in chevron mouldings, etc.

Zinc, a white metal that tarnishes only slightly, alloyed with copper to form brass, now widely used for galvanizing iron and steel.

Zircon, a brilliant, translucent stone occurring in many different colours, in white sometimes a substitute for diamond, formerly called hyacinth (especially, it seems, the red variety).

Zoëtrope, i.e. 'wheel of life', an instrument of cylindrical form with a strip of pictures showing successive stages of an action (e.g. a child playing with a ball) pasted inside, an impression of movement being created when the cylinder revolves and the pictures are viewed through slots in the cylinder; late 19th century.

Zoomorphic, in animal-like form. **9, 299**

Zoophorus, in Classical architecture, a frieze ornamented with figures of animals (usually men as well) in relief, sometimes imitated in Renaissance and Neo-Classical furniture.

Zumpe piano, the earliest make of English piano, made by Johannes Zumpe in the 1760s, a shallow box on a stand, not intended to rival the harpsichord in concert halls.

Zurich porcelain, from a factory operating during most of the second half of the 18th century, reflecting contemporary German and French styles but including richly painted Swiss scenes on tableware as well as much-admired figures; high-quality faience-fine made from the late 18th century.

Zwischengoldglas, an ancient form of decorative, double-walled glass, in recent times associated chiefly with 18th-century Bohemia, in which the outer surface of a vessel was engraved and decorated with gold leaf and the vessel then fitted inside another, slightly larger; usually on straight-sided drinking glasses, the bottom made separately; sometimes in silver (zwischensilberglas).

Published by
The Hamlyn Publishing Group Limited
London   New York   Sydney   Toronto
Astronaut House, Feltham, Middlesex, England

This edition © Copyright The Hamlyn
Publishing Group Limited, 1974
Fourth impression 1979

Colour illustrations © Copyright Fratelli Fabbri Editori,
Milan

ISBN 0 600 30154 0

Line drawings by Peter Fitzjohn and Leigh Jones

Phototypeset in England by
Filmtype Services Limited, Scarborough

Printed in Italy by Fratelli Fabbri Editori, Milan